Adopting Internet Printing Protocol for Windows

Seamlessly Transition Microsoft Printer Networks to the New Protocol

John Marion

Apress®

Adopting Internet Printing Protocol for Windows: Seamlessly Transition Microsoft Printer Networks to the New Protocol

John Marion
Sparks Glencoe, MD, USA

ISBN-13 (pbk): 979-8-8688-2009-0 ISBN-13 (electronic): 979-8-8688-2010-6
https://doi.org/10.1007/979-8-8688-2010-6

Managing Director, Apress Media LLC: Welmoed Spahr
Acquisitions Editor: Ryan Byrnes
Coordinating Editor: Gryffin Winkler

Cover designed by eStudioCalamar

Cover image by Unsplash.com

Distributed to the book trade worldwide by Springer Science+Business Media New York, 1 New York Plaza, New York, NY 10004. Phone 1-800-SPRINGER, fax (201) 348-4505, e-mail orders-ny@springer-sbm.com, or visit www.springeronline.com. Apress Media, LLC is a Delaware LLC and the sole member (owner) is Springer Science + Business Media Finance Inc (SSBM Finance Inc). SSBM Finance Inc is a **Delaware** corporation.

For information on translations, please e-mail booktranslations@springernature.com; for reprint, paperback, or audio rights, please e-mail bookpermissions@springernature.com.

Apress titles may be purchased in bulk for academic, corporate, or promotional use. eBook versions and licenses are also available for most titles. For more information, reference our Print and eBook Bulk Sales web page at http://www.apress.com/bulk-sales.

Any source code or other supplementary material referenced by the author in this book is available to readers on GitHub (https://github.com/Apress). For more detailed information, please visit https://www.apress.com/gp/services/source-code.

If disposing of this product, please recycle the paper

For my mother and father, who gave everything for us children – thank you.

For my wife, Janice, who is still the best decision I have ever made.

For what does it profit a man to gain the whole world and forfeit his soul?

Mark 8:36-38

Table of Contents

About the Author

John Marion is a seasoned developer with over 30 years of experience across multiple operating systems, including Windows, Linux, and embedded systems, with a primary focus on Windows environments. His expertise spans programming in C/C++, .NET, and Assembly, particularly in developing robust solutions for microcontrollers. Currently, John manages a large-scale network supporting over 70,000 users, where he has cultivated extensive knowledge in client-server print systems.

About the Technical Reviewer

Smith Kennedy has worked at HP Inc. (and Hewlett-Packard Company) since 1999. Smith served as PWG Chair from 2015 to 2021 and has served as PWG Vice-Chair since 2021. Smith has represented HP Inc. in the PWG since 2011 and has served as the editor of a number of recent PWG specifications and documents, including IPP Enterprise Printing Extensions v2.0, IPP Driver Replacement Extensions v2.0, IPP Finishings v3.0, IPP Implementor's Guide v2, and others. Smith has also represented HP Inc. at the Wi-Fi Alliance, Connectivity Standards Alliance, Bluetooth SIG, NFC Forum, USB Implementers Forum, and IEEE 802.11. Smith was the co-author of the USB-IF's IPP USB standard and the NFC Forum's Device Information RTD, Verb RTD, and Connection Handover v1.4 specifications.

Acknowledgments

Many thanks to everyone at Apress who worked to make this book possible. To my family, particularly my wife, Janice, who patiently waited while I made countless changes and technical edits. To my grandson TJ, who waited for Papa John to get done with the computer so we could go play.

I would also like to thank Smith Kennedy who graciously provided technical review, thus ensuring the accuracy and integrity of the book's content.

Introduction

I first became interested in the Internet Print Protocol (IPP) back in 2022. I had seen references to it infrequently since 2015, but large IT networks are generally lethargic: changes require cataclysmic events to shake them from existing conventions. Such an event occurred in the Fall of 2022 when our network was immersed in reactive mode to the infamous "Print Nightmare" fix developed by Microsoft. I got called into a meeting where management was keenly interested in why Point and Print clients could no longer download print drivers from the print server unless they had administrative privileges. Of course, this was the necessary step Microsoft had to take to protect end users from nefarious entities that wished to hijack client print systems. In the end, Microsoft would forever alter how their print subsystem interacted with printers; users would gain a much improved and scalable way to perform enterprise print.

I had also been keenly aware that mobile clients sometimes had a difficult time using printers in enterprise environments even when they were authenticated on the network. In the past, there was no single standard or protocol universally supported across all mobile and enterprise printer combinations. With the IPP protocol and Mopria/IPP Everywhere, a single solution is now realistic to implement. While searching the web, I came across various articles on Mopria technology and the idea that certain document formats could be naively processed on the printer. A while later, I came across the IPP get-printer-attributes request that would essentially provide a sort of "dynamic print driver" for the client. Putting two and two together, I decided that I needed to be more informed on the IPP protocol and how it worked. This was the beginning of a two-year renaissance in the knowledge of client-server print technology.

Thus, I went searching all the book vendors for a technical reference on the protocol and how it could fit into our environment. To my surprise, I failed to locate any books and found little published information concerning the subject other than RFCs and some vendor-based documentation. Of course, system administrators or engineers looking for informative learning material based on client-server print systems as a whole know this very well. For whatever reason, client-server print systems tend to be shortchanged when it comes to technical information and references. Thus, the impetus for this book.

For this book, I strove to provide examples that reinforced the basic concepts I believe would benefit the reader. Some of this is code exercises, which I encourage the reader to participate in - if so inclined. However, it is not necessary to be a developer as you may simply run the binaries created for each chapter. I also encourage the reader to download and learn to use Wireshark if they have not already done so. It is an invaluable tool to not only learn the IPP protocol but also to troubleshoot possible print issues in the future. Where possible, this book includes Wireshark traces to reinforce the subject matter.

The code you will find enclosed in this book was written for illustrative purposes and thus entirely unsuitable for production. It was written to reinforce some of the concepts introduced to the reader, and I encourage you to run it to fully understand select subject matter. While all attempts were made to ensure accuracy of the contents, the IT world is a fluid chasm, forever in flux. Some of the material, especially concerning graphics on existing Microsoft products, could be deprecated by the time of print.

I hope you find this book informative and helpful.

CHAPTER 1

Windows Legacy Print

The art of printing on paper what is written or drawn on the screen is truly a complex endeavor. Almost every IT technician or administrator comes to dread the request from a user to fix printout issues. Maybe that is because for the most part, the references available to understand or fix client/server print are few and far between. This book is an attempt to remedy the dearth of print system knowledge or at least cast some light on this (unpopular) subject. For the purposes of this book, I will concentrate on the Windows print system as it is by far the most popular OS in existence today. However, many of the concepts discussed here either started with or are incorporated into other systems in existence today (LPR/IPP/spooling), so a greater understanding of them should be beneficial to understanding printing on all operating systems.

Throughout this book I attempt to intersperse technical data on a given subject with real-world software code. My goal is not to make the reader into a software developer, but rather to add a new dimension that reinforces the underlying concepts. During my career in the IT industry, I have read books on technical concepts that introduce a subject area but do not provide the details necessary to provide the comprehension I would have liked. My goal is for you, the reader, to walk away with a proficient understanding of the subject matter and therefore help you in your careers. When appropriate, I will also try to involve network traces using Wireshark to further aid in understanding the subject matter.

Client/server print in Windows can be divided for the most part into two types: Direct print and Point-and-Print connections (print from a print server). Direct printers are typical in the home or small office computer world as they do not require another Windows computer to create print jobs. Microsoft typically refers to direct printers as local printers, a custom that invokes some ambiguity (as print connections from Point and Print are "local" to the machine). For this reason, I will designate these as direct (as in from the local machine to the printer without an interleaving print server) printers for the remainder of this chapter. I will intersperse Point and Print (a Microsoft product term) with print connections, so keep in mind that they refer to the same technology.

J. Marion, *Adopting Internet Printing Protocol for Windows*, https://doi.org/10.1007/979-8-8688-2010-6_1

The direct print setup is typical of what most home Windows users are accustomed to. The print driver is installed by a setup program or via the Windows "Add a printer" interface. The user will be required to furnish a print driver (whether downloaded or from a CD) and will be asked for printer connection information. Typically, the printer is connected via USB or via a TCP (wireless or wired) connection. You will be asked to name the printer and whether you want to share the printer out for others to use. Depending on the underlying connection, you might also be asked to furnish an IP address, DNS name, or URL to the targeted printer. Because this level of technical detail might be imposing on users in a corporate enterprise, Microsoft developed what is branded as "Point and Print" technology.

Point and Print (as the name alludes to) requires another computer running Windows (the server) to spool and ultimately finish the print request. Point and Print is described by Microsoft as the capability of allowing a user to create a connection to a remote printer without providing disks or other installation media. All necessary files and configuration information are automatically downloaded from the print server to the client [6]. As you might imagine, using Point and Print is a convenience that greatly aids in the use of the Windows print system for enterprise networks. Despite the classification differences, there are more similarities than differences between the two types of printers on a Windows computer, so most of the print infrastructure we will go over applies to both types.

To start off with, I should go over the main reason Point and Print has been such a popular way for businesses to employ print services in the enterprise. Simply put, it allows standard users (those without any special local or network administrative privileges) to begin printing on a network with little effort. That is, the standard user can type into Windows Explorer by the name of the print server (if known) and select one of the shared printers made available. If the user right-clicks the desired shared printer and selects **Connect**, the local computer will connect to the server and download all the necessary software and then install the printer. Alternatively, if the user decides to delete a print connection, they (in the Windows 11 Printers and Scanners dialog) can click the printer and choose **Remove**. All the necessary registry entries, driver software, and configuration information are handled automatically at the behest of the user. Of course, such convenience hides the abstraction of the underlying complexity - we will dive into this at a later point in this chapter.

We will return to more technical details on both printer types, but for now let's take a look at how the Windows OS gleans properties about print hardware, despite there being literally hundreds of products out on the market.

Printer Configuration

We should start off our discussion with an understanding of how all those print configuration property choices are made available to the user in Windows. Just how does the OS know all the particulars from the vast array of printer makes and models available? We know that today's print hardware has expanded capabilities available, and to make choices on these offerings, the user must be provided with the potential choices. The most important file for the installation of a printer (in the Windows OS) is the INF file. This is a file required by Windows to provide hardware product identification and includes subsequent driver installation information critical to printer operation.

The creation of an INF file can be a very detailed subject matter and deserves a chapter unto itself. If you are interested in just such an endeavor, you should read Walter Oney's *Windows Driver Model* book as it is very detailed on this subject. For the purposes of this book, I will only concentrate on parts of the INF file of interest to the print subsystem. You will see many references to a Globally Unique ID (GUID). This value is guaranteed to be unique (at least on the system it is created on) as it combines the date, time, second, and millisecond of creation together with the MAC address of the network interface card.

Specific to printers, the INF file should provide the following sections: Version, Manufacturer, PrinterModels, PrinterDriver, DriverCopyFiles, DestinationDirs, SourceDisksNames, SourceDisksFiles, Strings, Setup, and DriverAddReg sections. I'll go through some important entries you will find in the INF file.

Let's start with the Version section – in this section the overall purpose of the INF file is detailed. The Class property specifies a name in the device setup class for the type of device that is installed by using this INF file. This name is usually one of the system-defined class names, such as Printer or Display, the list of which you can find (within the Windows DDK) in devguid.h. In devguid you will find the definition of the printer device class:

```
DEFINE_GUID(GUID_DEVCLASS_PRINTER,0x4d36e979,0xe325,0x11ce,0xbf,0xc1,0x08,
0x00,0x2b,0xe1,0x03,0x18);
```

Thus, you would expect a printer INF file to make use of this GUID, and for my Epson WF-4734 printer, it certainly does:

```
[Version]
Signature       = "$Windows NT$"
Provider        = %EPSON%
ClassGUID       = {4D36E979-E325-11CE-BFC1-08002BE10318}
Class           = Printer
DriverVer       = 05/11/2020, 2.66.00.00
CatalogFile     = E_WF1QDE.CAT
DriverIsolation = 2
```

The Class entry allows the device (in this case printers) to be grouped together when enumerated in applications such as Device Manager, so they are easier to identify and work with.

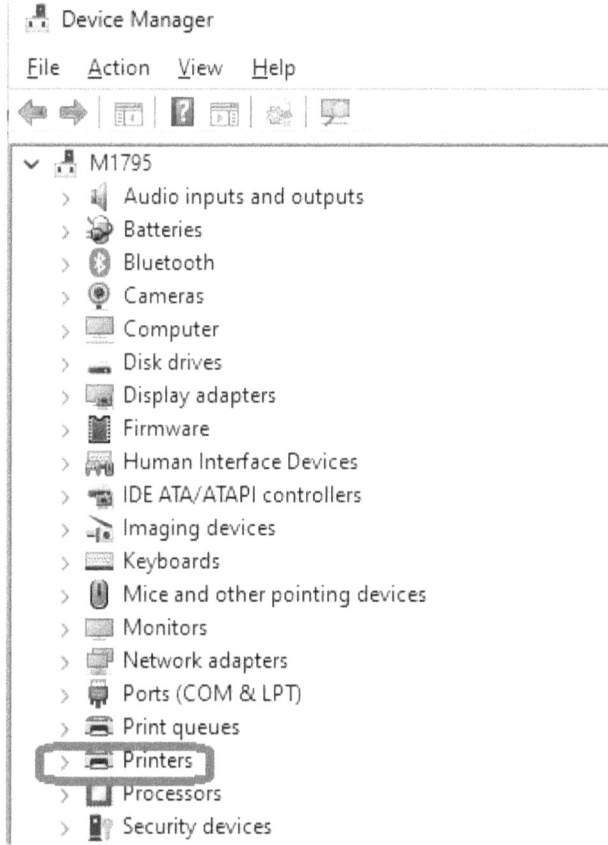

Printer Objects in Device Manager

The Printer ClassGuid also shows up in the registry, among other places, at HKLM\SYSTEM\CurrentControlSet\Control\Class\{4d36e979-e325-11ce-bfc1-08002be10318}. During installation, Windows stores similar component entries together as a class in the registry path HKLM\SYSTEM \CurrentControlSet\Control\Class, and as you may have guessed, {4d36e979-e325-11ce-bfc1-08002be10318} is the GUID reserved for all components of the printer class. Under this registry hive you will find all the installed printers (enumerated from 0000 to xxxx) along with information such as driver date, driver description, driver version, INF path, etc. - it is a treasure trove of configuration data. Most of the information contained in this hive comes from the INF file used to install the printer.

We will discuss in a later section the DriverIsolation entry. This entry is important to stabilize the user mode spooler system in the event the driver causes instability. For now, I will leave it at the fact that a 2 assigned to this entry indicates that the driver can be run isolated from the spooler service process, while 0 indicates that it cannot. We will discuss driver isolation in more detail later in this chapter as it is an important concept for the Windows spooler system. From the INF file entry, my Epson WF-4734 can run isolated from the spooler service process if necessary.

You should also notice (under the Version section) an entry for CatalogFile. Quite simply, this specifies the certified source for printer installation files. This file should contain a digital signature, the catalog version, and a date that for all purposes ensures the files being used for installation are not tampered with. All the files that comprise your print driver come from this (usually compressed) source.

To uniquely associate physical hardware (the printer) with the software used on the device, each manufacturer will assign a hardware id (coded into NVRAM or EEPROM associated with print hardware) that the INF file will specify. For my home Epson multi-function printer, the INF entry looks something like this:

```
[EPSON]
;-- Product:01 ------------------------------------------------------------
"EPSON WF-4730 Series" = EPNDRV_Mdl_01,USBPRINT\EPSONWF-4730_Series172B
"EPSON WF-4730 Series" = EPNDRV_Mdl_01,LPTENUM\EPSONWF-4730_Series172B
"EPSON WF-4730 Series" = EPNDRV_Mdl_01,WSDPRINT\EPSONWF-4730_Series172B

[EPSON.NTamd64]
;-- Product:01 ------------------------------------------------------------
"EPSON WF-4730 Series" = EPNDRV_Mdl_01,USBPRINT\EPSONWF-4730_Series172B
```

```
"EPSON WF-4730 Series" = EPNDRV_Mdl_01,LPTENUM\EPSONWF-4730_
Series172B"EPSON WF-4730 Series" = EPNDRV_Mdl_01,WSDPRINT\EPSONWF-4730_
Series172B
```

This hardware id is what "plug and play" will use to identify the printer and look for a suitable driver (if one was installed). You can view this hardware id if you look in Device Manager, right-click your printer under the Printers section (set the View tab to Devices by Type), and choose Properties. Now click the Detail tab and then choose Hardware Ids from the Properties combo box. For my Epson WF-4734 printer, I see the following:

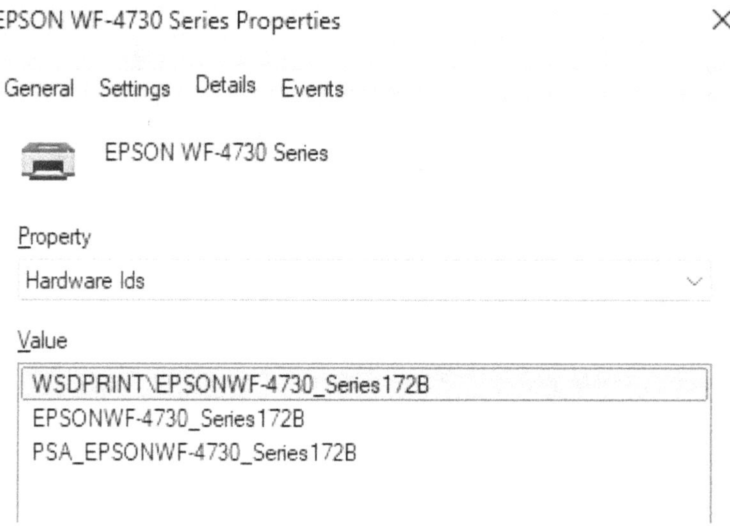

If you look in the registry, you should see **wsdprint\epsonwf-4730_series172b** as a MatchingDeviceId property (placed there by the printer INF file) during installation. The process is similar for other USB printers as well.

Older print protocols (LPR, Port 9100 RAW) used on the Windows platform provided these capabilities via configuration files such as INF files (for installation) and PPD/GPD files for general model capabilities. If the user wanted to make use of a new printer, they would require the necessary printer driver installed on their computer. Often (especially in older Windows OSs) the user would have to install the driver if it were not already on the system, and to do that, typically they would require enhanced or administrative rights to do so. If the printer that the user required existed on a network print server, another route (Point and Print) to service could be used, but for now we should explore what it takes to install a direct printer.

The Driver Store

Starting with Windows Vista, Microsoft provided a centralized location for device driver storage and streamlined installation. The driver store provided centralized management of driver resources and reduced duplication, allowing for more dependable plug-and-play operation. Since it has been designed as a secure location where administrators can copy driver software, standard users are then permitted to install (put in service) the requisite print driver.

As mentioned previously, older print protocols relied on configuration files to provide print hardware configuration options. For this purpose, Microsoft built a print driver framework in Windows that provides a universal data rendering component for both PCL (Unidrv.dll) and PostScript formats (Pscript5.dll). Along with these DLLs, Microsoft provided a user mode DLL that standardizes user print property sheets (what the user sees for print configuration) as well. What was required of the print hardware manufacturer within this framework was a text-based file that specified individual printer features and options available for the model. In other words, a file that provided for the differences between print options differentiated the different models. This framework worked well enough to allow numerous print vendors and models to exist in the Windows environment and provide a consistent user interface to boot.

I have made mention of user mode several times in this chapter, and though most readers undoubtedly are well versed with this (and the corresponding kernel mode term), for completeness I should explain. "User mode" and "kernel mode" are two distinct but complementary terms used to describe operating states of a computer OS. Processes initiated in user mode have limited privileges and cannot directly access system resources, while kernel mode processes have unrestricted access to the same. This design was developed to foster stability and reliability in the OS, as user mode processes can be terminated without affecting the integrity of the system. In the initial stages of Windows NT development, print drivers were loaded in kernel mode, but subsequent Windows versions have relocated these to user mode as stability of the OS was deemed paramount.

Because visual input helps reinforce the learning process, you should take a few minutes to view these configuration files yourself. At the very least they will provide insight on how the Windows OS communicates with the print hardware and how the printer property sheet is uniquely adapted to each printer make and model. To do this, you will need to investigate the Windows driver store, which is a place where drivers are stored (but not necessarily installed) within Windows. The driver store is in the C:\Windows\System32\DriverStore path on my Windows 11 machine, and the file repository for the driver store is in the C:\Windows\System32\DriverStore\FileRepository path. While these paths have been consistent for the past few versions of Windows, it is good practice to use system APIs to get the path on any given Windows installation.

For example, find a .PPD file (for PostScript printers) or .GPD file (Generic Printer Description File for PCL printers) and open it up using Windows Notepad for examination. To do this, you will have to sort through the folders in the driver store FileRepository folder, each of which is created as a GUID-like name to ensure uniqueness. Be aware that the FileRepository holds all driver files, not just print driver files, so you will see a confusing multitude of folders with GUID strings as names before you. The best advice I can provide is to download Driver Store Explorer, a freeware product hosted on GitHub. This is a great tool to provide information on driver store files you plan to look at. You can find this utility here: `https://github.com/lostindark/DriverStoreExplorer`.

If you have the utility installed, you can open it up (it takes a few seconds to scan the DriverStore files) and sort by Driver Class (by clicking on the column title). Once this is done, you can then scroll down to the area where the printer drivers are displayed. The utility provides a column that lists the driver version, which is extremely helpful in the event several versions of the same driver are in the driver store.

Driver Store Explorer allows you to see all the printer drivers staged (but not necessarily installed) on your system. If you want to further investigate the files grouped together to create the driver, you can right-click the INF file and choose Open Folder Location to see where (under what GUID-like folder) your driver is installed in the FileRepository folder.

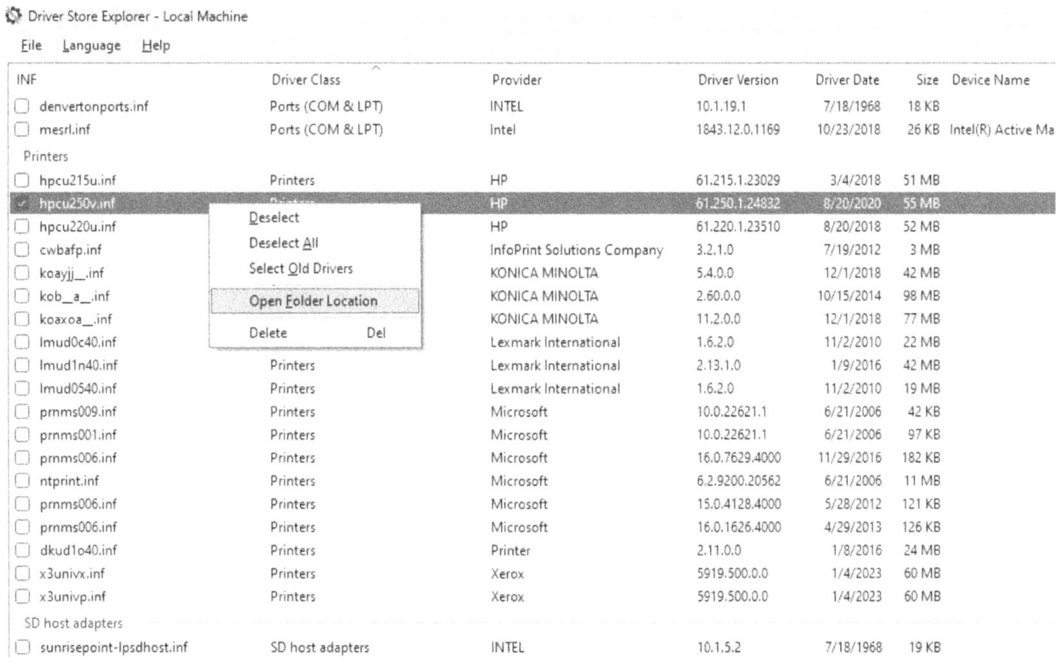

Driver Store Explorer - Local Machine

File Language Help

INF	Driver Class	Provider	Driver Version	Driver Date	Size	Device Name
denvertonports.inf	Ports (COM & LPT)	INTEL	10.1.19.1	7/18/1968	18 KB	
mesrl.inf	Ports (COM & LPT)	Intel	1843.12.0.1169	10/23/2018	26 KB	Intel(R) Active Ma
Printers						
hpcu215u.inf	Printers	HP	61.215.1.23029	3/4/2018	51 MB	
hpcu250v.inf		HP	61.250.1.24832	8/20/2020	55 MB	
hpcu220u.inf		HP	61.220.1.23510	8/20/2018	52 MB	
cwbafp.inf		InfoPrint Solutions Company	3.2.1.0	7/19/2012	3 MB	
koayjj__.inf		KONICA MINOLTA	5.4.0.0	12/1/2018	42 MB	
kob__a__.inf		KONICA MINOLTA	2.60.0.0	10/15/2014	98 MB	
koaxoa__.inf		KONICA MINOLTA	11.2.0.0	12/1/2018	77 MB	
lmud0c40.inf		Lexmark International	1.6.2.0	11/2/2010	22 MB	
lmud1n40.inf	Printers	Lexmark International	2.13.1.0	1/9/2016	42 MB	
lmud0540.inf	Printers	Lexmark International	1.6.2.0	11/2/2010	19 MB	
prnms009.inf	Printers	Microsoft	10.0.22621.1	6/21/2006	42 KB	
prnms001.inf	Printers	Microsoft	10.0.22621.1	6/21/2006	97 KB	
prnms006.inf	Printers	Microsoft	16.0.7629.4000	11/29/2016	182 KB	
ntprint.inf	Printers	Microsoft	6.2.9200.20562	6/21/2006	11 MB	
prnms006.inf	Printers	Microsoft	15.0.4128.4000	5/28/2012	121 KB	
prnms006.inf	Printers	Microsoft	16.0.1626.4000	4/29/2013	126 KB	
dkud1o40.inf	Printers	Printer	2.11.0.0	1/8/2016	24 MB	
x3univx.inf	Printers	Xerox	5919.500.0.0	1/4/2023	60 MB	
x3univp.inf	Printers	Xerox	5919.500.0.0	1/4/2023	60 MB	
SD host adapters						
sunrisepoint-lpsdhost.inf	SD host adapters	INTEL	10.1.5.2	7/18/1968	19 KB	

Deselect
Deselect All
Select Old Drivers
Open Folder Location
Delete Del

Find the Folder Where Your Driver Files Are Using Driver Store Explorer

One other thing I should mention is that the location provided by the Windows Application Programming Interface (API) GetPrinterDriverDirectory is not where the driver store files are located. Rather, the return from the GetPrinterDriverDirectory API specifies where the Windows spooler service places in-use printer drivers. You can use the SetupGetInfDriverStoreLocation API to find the location of an INF file in the driver store.

Configuration Files

If you open a PPD or GPD file, you can see how they provide (to Windows) some of the print hardware capabilities that you can see available (on a model-by-model basis). GPD files are text files describing a printer to the Windows operating system using the Unidrv (Universal Printer Driver) architecture. The idea for UniDriver architecture was for the vendor to only write device-specific data while the core functionality of the driver type (PCL/PS) was written by Microsoft [11]. Optimally, the vendor might only need to update the GPD/PPD text files to introduce their new printer.

Vendors use the GPD language to describe a printer providing distinct types of information including printer attributes, printer commands, printer features, printer options, printer font descriptions, and conditional statements [1]. GPD files take the following format:

```
* EntryName: EntryValue
{
Variable1: Value1
Variable2: Value2
.
.
}
```

EntryName follows the asterisk and is always a predefined keyword that Unidrv's GPD parser recognizes.

An example of a GPD file for an XPSDrv print driver:

```
*%
*% Copyright (c) 2004 - 2006 Microsoft Corporation
*% All Rights Reserved.
*%
*GPDFileVersion: "1.0"
*GPDSpecVersion: "1.0"
*GPDFileName:    "plugfest.gpd"
*Include:        "StdNames.gpd"
*%
*% Include XPSDrv include file
*%
*Include:        "MSXpsInc.gpd"
*ModelName:      "Microsoft XPS Passthrough Driver Sample"
*MasterUnits:    PAIR(1200, 1200)
*ResourceDLL:    "unires.dll"
*PrinterType:    PAGE
*MaxCopies:      1

*%
```

```
*% IHV Private Namespace
*%
*PrintSchemaPrivateNamespaceURI:"https://www.ihv.com/schema/2006"
*%
*% IHV Private Feature
*%
*Feature: IHVStapling {
*PrintSchemaKeywordMap: "JobStapleAllDocuments"
*Option: Enabled {
  *PrintSchemaKeywordMap: "StapleTopLeft" }
*Option: Disabled {
  *PrintSchemaKeywordMap: "None"  }
}
```

The Windows GPD file parser will load the above file and additional GPD files specified by the Include statement stipulating all subsequent files as one file [2]. For the GPD file above, the additional GPD files would be StdNames.gpd and MSXpsInc.gpd. The root GPD or PPD files are specified in the INF file as the driver's DataFile when the driver is installed [10]. The GPD/PPD file must include configuration keywords that describe the features that the printer supports. These options are provided when you open a printer property sheet to choose printer options prior to printing your document. For instance, can the printer be duplexed, and if so, what types of duplexing are available? What print quality is available and what are the maximum copies you can choose?

Sometimes a vendor will include the driver files used in the property sheet About tab – this can provide information to track down the root GPD file if you are interested.

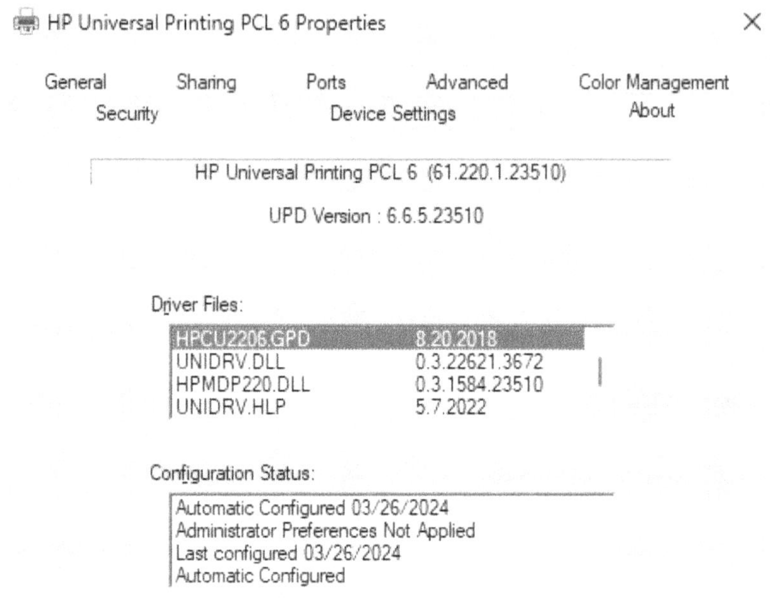

HP Print Driver About Tab

The graphic above shows the HP Universal Printing PCL 6 (61.220.1.23510) driver using the HPCU2206.GPD file, among others. Going back to Driver Store Locator, we can now open the folder to that driver version and (if you are so inclined) investigate the GPD file.

Registry Entries

Earlier in this chapter, we discovered that Windows groups like hardware (i.e., laser printers, multi-function devices, Bubble Jets, etc.) together as a "class" and enter these components into the registry in this manner. This action helps ensure features that are common to a class of hardware are accounted for in a uniform and consistent manner when installing the component or reading display properties. However, Windows also stores critical hardware and software properties of printers in other areas of the registry as well. Operation data for each printer is stored in the registry path HKLM\ SYSTEM\ CurrentControlSet\Control\Print\Printers. This hive contains configuration settings and properties for each printer installed. Details such as monitors, printer ports, drivers, and other settings specific to each printer are stored here. It manages the operational aspects of each printer.

Throughout this book you will see references to the Windows registry. This is essentially a binary store file of Windows configuration information that persists data between OS reboots. The registry has several "hives," or inverted tree search paths, to store this data. Three of the most important hives are HKEY_LOCAL_MACHINE (HKLM), which stores machine-specific data; HKEY_CURRENT_USER (HKCU), which stores information about the currently logged-on user; and HKEY_USERS (HKU), which stores data about all the users configured for the machine. The HKCU hive is a sub-hive of HKU that is loaded at logon and represents the currently logged-on user.

As Windows is a multiple-user OS, it follows that individual printer preferences should be stored for each user as a convenience. User preferences for any printer are stored in the HKCU\Printers registry hive, where HKEY_CURRENT_USER represents the currently logged-on user. User print connections (i.e., shared printers) are stored in the HKCU\Printers\Connections path. Per-printer preferences for items such as paper size and print quality are stored in the HKCU\Printers\DevModesPerUser and DevModes2 paths. The information in the DevModesPerUser and DevModes2 hives is typically in binary format, which, while efficient for storage, is difficult to read. Since the HKCU\Printers registry path is part of the overall user profile, this information can follow the user between login sessions to provide a consistent user experience, at least for printer settings.

Print Drivers

So now you understand a bit about how Windows draws the printer hardware configuration data from which a user can select their print job preferences. Of course, Windows will do this for all print drivers that are installed on the system. Installed printers are considered those print drivers whose files are placed in the print driver directory and whose registry entries are installed in the system. In my Windows 11 machine the print driver directory is in C:\Windows\System32\spool\drivers\x64 folder (since my machine is x64 architecture). Within this folder, you will find the 3 (for Type 3 driver), where most of the print driver files are copied to (from the driver store) when installed.

Microsoft classifies print drivers as either type 3 or type 4 drivers. Of the two types, type 4 is the newer one and was an attempt (beginning with Windows 8) at a universal driver that came pre-installed in the OS. These drivers have fewer features than their type 3 cousins but work across 32/64-bit architectures and do not need special files downloaded from the server. Type 3 drivers are not universal and are specific to the hardware printer but may provide more features than the type 4 versions. If you are using point and print technology in your enterprise, the big advantage afforded to type 4 drivers is that they are not affected by the Microsoft print nightmare fix. Thus, users in the post-print nightmare world that make use of type 4 drivers are not encumbered with policy restrictions that may affect those using type 3 drivers.

I had alluded earlier that one of the reasons that Point and Print has become so popular (at least in large enterprises) is the ease with which a user can add a shared printer off a print server. Essentially, the client for Windows OS will replicate the print driver setup on the server (for the requested printer) without having the client install driver files. What is more, every time the client wants to use the printer, it will compare driver files with the server and update its local files in the event they are older than the driver file on the server.

An explanation of what is going on is in order. When the Windows client attempts to print using a Point and Print connection, the client performs a Remote Procedure Call (RPC) connection to the server. At this point, the Windows client compares the local driver files associated with the shared printer to the driver files on the server from where the print connection exists. The files being compared are the drivers within the spool folder, usually in C:\Windows\System32\spool\drivers\x64\3 (for type 3 driver) on both the print client and print server. The driver package (usually a *.cab file) is where the package print driver files are drawn from will usually be in C:\Windows\System32\spool\drivers\x64\PCC on the print server. After the files in the \3 folder are compared between devices, if they do not match, the cabinet file package (shown in the figure on the next page) in the PCC folder (on the print server) is installed. This works very well in the enterprise and allows the clients to update their print driver files automatically when the server print driver (for the shared printer) is updated. Keep in mind that this process happens every time the client is started up; thus, the print driver files (at least for the shared print connections) are theoretically kept up to date.

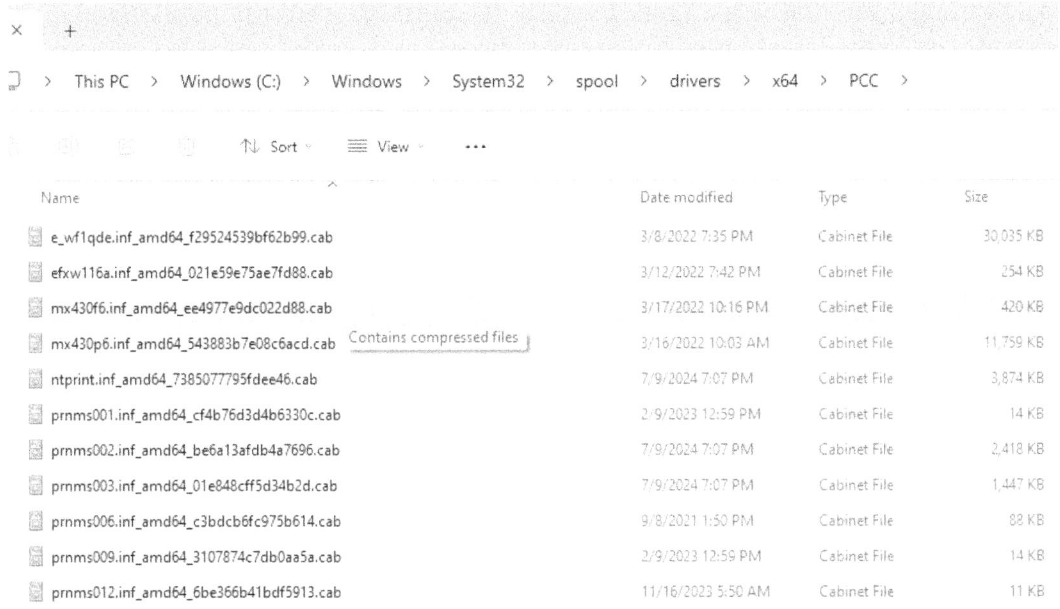

> This PC > Windows (C:) > Windows > System32 > spool > drivers > x64 > PCC >

Sort View ...

Name	Date modified	Type	Size
e_wf1qde.inf_amd64_f29524539bf62b99.cab	3/8/2022 7:35 PM	Cabinet File	30,035 KB
efxw116a.inf_amd64_021e59e75ae7fd88.cab	3/12/2022 7:42 PM	Cabinet File	254 KB
mx430f6.inf_amd64_ee4977e9dc022d88.cab	3/17/2022 10:16 PM	Cabinet File	420 KB
mx430p6.inf_amd64_543883b7e08c6acd.cab Contains compressed files	3/16/2022 10:03 AM	Cabinet File	11,759 KB
ntprint.inf_amd64_7385077795fdee46.cab	7/9/2024 7:07 PM	Cabinet File	3,874 KB
prnms001.inf_amd64_cf4b76d3d4b6330c.cab	2/9/2023 12:59 PM	Cabinet File	14 KB
prnms002.inf_amd64_be6a13afdb4a7696.cab	7/9/2024 7:07 PM	Cabinet File	2,418 KB
prnms003.inf_amd64_01e848cff5d34b2d.cab	7/9/2024 7:07 PM	Cabinet File	1,447 KB
prnms006.inf_amd64_c3bdcb6fc975b614.cab	9/8/2021 1:50 PM	Cabinet File	88 KB
prnms009.inf_amd64_3107874c7db0aa5a.cab	2/9/2023 12:59 PM	Cabinet File	14 KB
prnms012.inf_amd64_6be366b41bdf5913.cab	11/16/2023 5:50 AM	Cabinet File	11 KB

PCC Folder from Where Driver Package Files (on the Server) Are Used for Installation

Initially, this was a sound design concept – the client updates the local print driver files from packages installed on the server. In the past, this architecture worked well and provided administrators with an automated way of ensuring up-to-date print driver files (assuming the server's print drivers were kept current). It also provided convenience: you simply query the print server for shared printers any time you travel or go to a new office. No ports or drivers to install, and a standard (read non-administrative account) is allowed to install server-based printers assuming they are shared on the server. Even better, using a server print queue allows the print jobs for any printer to be enqueued/dequeued and sent to the printer. This queue operation allows for a large office to send print jobs to a printer without having to worry about overloading the remote printer's memory with multiple simultaneous print connection requests. In other words, this process serializes print job requests for printer hardware, thus managing office print more efficiently.

I should mention there are occasions when dealing with external files that call for the document to be sent directly to a printer. For instance, if the document is already formatted in a PDL that the printer can natively render, a print driver might not be needed. This can be the case where an outside OS (say, for instance, a mainframe process) has already formatted the job completely. In this case, you can direct the job to a chosen printer and eschew a print driver (pass-through) completely. This is termed "pass-through" printing; you will need the handle from the OpenPrinter API to use in a subsequent call to the WritePrinter API to accomplish this. I will present details of this arrangement later in this book.

Network Trace of Submitted Print Job

Now that we have some printers to use, we should examine a print job from a Windows 11 machine to a networked printer, in this case an HP M608 networked printer. This is a directly connected printer installed on the client as opposed to a print connection. This will be our first (but not last) use of Wireshark to provide details on what is happening behind the scenes. (See the appendix for basic Wireshark setup and usage instructions.) In this example, our networked printer accepts both LPR and Port 9100/Appsocket print protocols. On Windows 11, port 9100 is the default print protocol and thus what this example will make use of. Additionally, for this example, the workstation is configured with a printer employing the HP Universal PCL driver. This is typical of what would be configured on a Windows machine; a Linux machine would likely be using the LPR print protocol.

For my test I have created a text file and will send it to the network printer for processing. The Page Description Language (PDL) used is PCL, as we are using the HP Universal PCL driver. Below are the results of the print job submission.

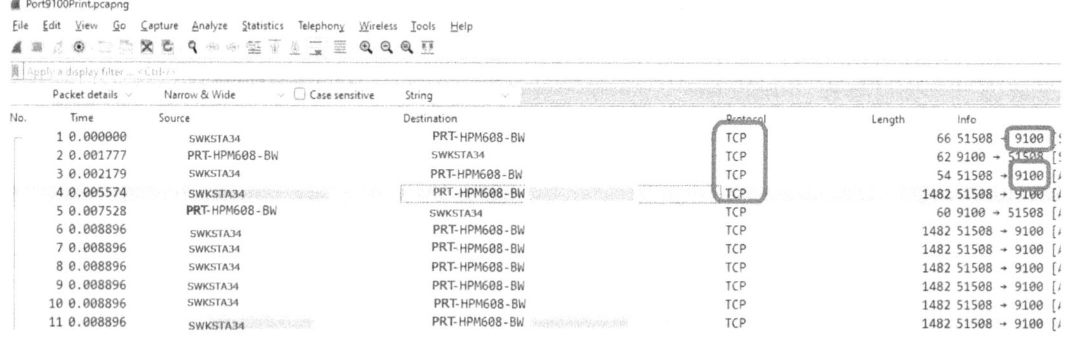

No.	Time	Source	Destination	Protocol	Length	Info
1	0.000000	SWKSTA34	PRT-HPM608-BW	TCP	66	51508 → 9100
2	0.001777	PRT-HPM608-BW	SWKSTA34	TCP	62	9100 → 51508
3	0.002179	SWKSTA34	PRT-HPM608-BW	TCP	54	51508 → 9100
4	0.005574	SWKSTA34	PRT-HPM608-BW	TCP	1482	51508 → 9100
5	0.007528	PRT-HPM608-BW	SWKSTA34	TCP	60	9100 → 51508
6	0.008896	SWKSTA34	PRT-HPM608-BW	TCP	1482	51508 → 9100
7	0.008896	SWKSTA34	PRT-HPM608-BW	TCP	1482	51508 → 9100
8	0.008896	SWKSTA34	PRT-HPM608-BW	TCP	1482	51508 → 9100
9	0.008896	SWKSTA34	PRT-HPM608-BW	TCP	1482	51508 → 9100
10	0.008896	SWKSTA34	PRT-HPM608-BW	TCP	1482	51508 → 9100
11	0.008896	SWKSTA34	PRT-HPM608-BW	TCP	1482	51508 → 9100

Several things should jump out to you looking over the next few Wireshark traces. The first is the TCP port 9100 used in the transmission, which is how the protocol got the name. The next trace component (for the same print job) shows the context of the print job itself.

I should note that it is possible to view PCL data in Wireshark, even over unencrypted TCP connections. While many of the characters in the PCL stream are ASCII and technically human-readable, deciphering them is not straightforward. This is because printable characters are typically surrounded by escape sequences and formatting commands that instruct the printer on how to render the page. For example, if we wanted to print a bold "B" and an underlined "c," the PCL stream might look like this: `<ESC>(s3B B <ESC>&d0D c <ESC>&d1D`. As you can see, this is not easy to interpret with the eyes. For larger print jobs, interpreting the full content from the raw PCL stream can be quite difficult. To translate the binary PCL back into human-readable text, you will need a utility such as **GhostPCL**, which we will use to reconstruct the original document content from the PCL stream captured in Wireshark. If you want this utility, you can find GhostPCL (32/64-bit versions and source code) here: `https://ghostscript.com/releases/gpcldnld.html`.

```
0000  74 ad 98 a0 df 0b 6c 02  e0 b1 d7 fe 08 00 45 00   t·····l· ······E·
0010  05 bc fd ae 40 00 80 06  3d 7a 0a e5 63 01 0a 1c   ····@··· =z··c···
0020  42 11 c9 34 23 8c cf 78  10 20 65 52 7b e5 50 10   B··4#··x · eR{·P·
0030  02 01 31 c5 00 00 1b 25  2d 31 32 33 34 35 58 40   ··1····% -12345X@
0040  50 4a 4c 20 53 45 54 20  53 54 52 49 4e 47 43 4f   PJL SET  STRINGCO
0050  44 45 53 45 54 3d 55 54  46 38 0a 40 50 4a 4c 20   DESET=UT F8·@PJL
0060  4a 4f 42 20 4e 41 4d 45  3d 22 54 65 73 74 2e 74   JOB NAME ="Test.t
0070  78 74 20 2d 20 4e 6f 74  65 70 61 64 22 0a 40 50   xt - Not epad"·@P
0080  4a 4c 20 43 4f 4d 4d 45  4e 54 20 22 4c 6f 63 61   JL COMME NT "Loca
0090  6c 20 48 50 20 50 6f 72  74 20 39 31 30 30 20 50   l HP Por t 9100 P
00a0  72 69 6e 74 65 72 20 28  30 2e 33 2e 31 35 38 34   rinter ( 0.3.1584
00b0  2e 32 33 35 31 30 29 3b  20 57 69 6e 64 6f 77 73   .23510);  Windows
00c0  20 31 30 20 45 6e 74 65  72 70 72 69 73 65 20 31    10 Ente rprise 1
00d0  30 2e 30 2e 32 32 36 33  31 2e 31 3b 20 55 6e 69   0.0.2263 1.1; Uni
00e0  64 72 76 20 30 2e 33 2e  32 32 36 32 31 2e 33 36   drv 0.3. 22621.36
00f0  37 32 22 0a 40 50 4a 4c  20 43 4f 4d 4d 45 4e 54   72"·@PJL  COMMENT
0100  20 22 55 73 65 72 6e 61  6d 65 3a 20 37 37 38 32    "Userna me:
0110  32 30 3b 20 41 70 70 20  46 69 6c 65 6e 61 6d 65     ; App  Filename
0120  3a 20 54 65 73 74 2e 74  78 74 20 2d 20 4e 6f 74   : Test.t xt - Not
0130  65 70 61 64 3b 20 38 2d  38 2d 32 30 32 34 22 0a   epad; 8- 8-2024"·
```

Since the print job used a Page Description Language (PDL) of PCL, we have a bit more work to do (with Wireshark) to convert the ensuing PCL data to a format we can read. To do this in Wireshark, you need to know a bit about TCP sessions, at least what marks the beginning and what marks the end of each. In TCP, every session begins with a SYN flag and ends with a FIN flag. Thus, we must tell Wireshark to capture the data in a session (specifically the one where the PCL print job was serviced by the printer). In the capture, click the initial session line (in the Wireshark trace identified as [SYN]) and then choose **Analyze** from the menu and then **Follow** and finally **TCP Stream**. The session initiation is the first line in the Wireshark trace (from our workstation source to the printer destination) that you can identify as your print job and uses the TCP protocol.

In the next illustration, you should right-click the initial print request packet identified and then choose **Follow**. From the popup menu, you should then choose TCP Stream for the next step.

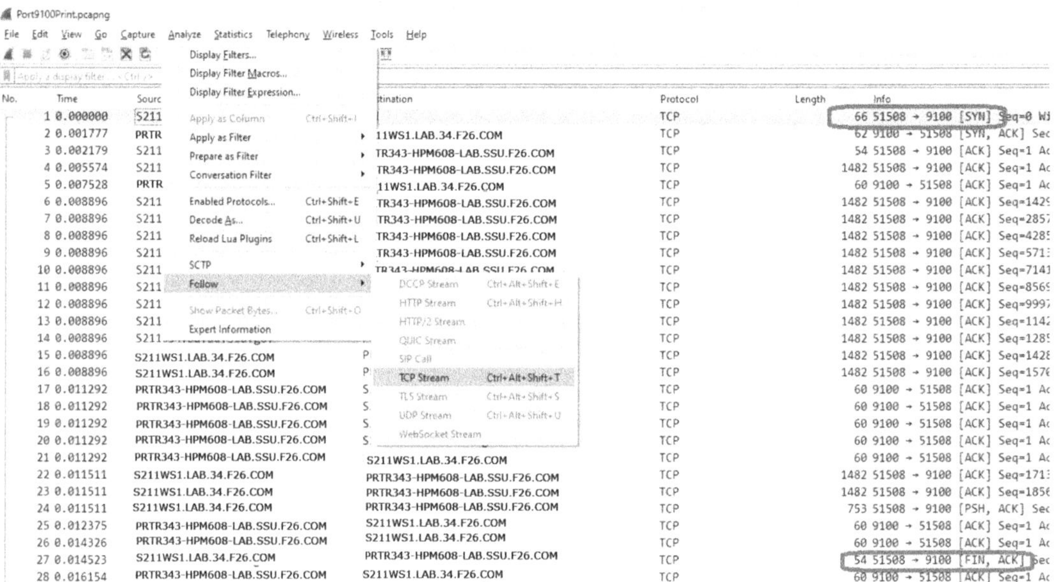

You should see the "Follow TCP Stream" dialog, which is a consolidation of all the TCP packets from sender to receiver both ways. For this example, we are only interested in decoding the PCL stream sent from the user to the printer. We want to set the direction one way (from client to printer) to reflect this. Finally, set the **Show Data As** drop-down control to **RAW**. Both actions can be seen in the next graphic, circled (near the bottom) in red. Now save the file with whatever descriptive name you desire and append a PCL extension for information reasons.

Now just to remind you: we are going through the stream capture to a file exercise to convert the clear text PCL-formatted print stream back to the original data sent by the source workstation. We hope to recover the original document data sent by the user. As mentioned earlier, PCL data is not very human readable due to formatting commands employed by the PCL specification, but the print stream itself (for port 9100 print) is clear text.

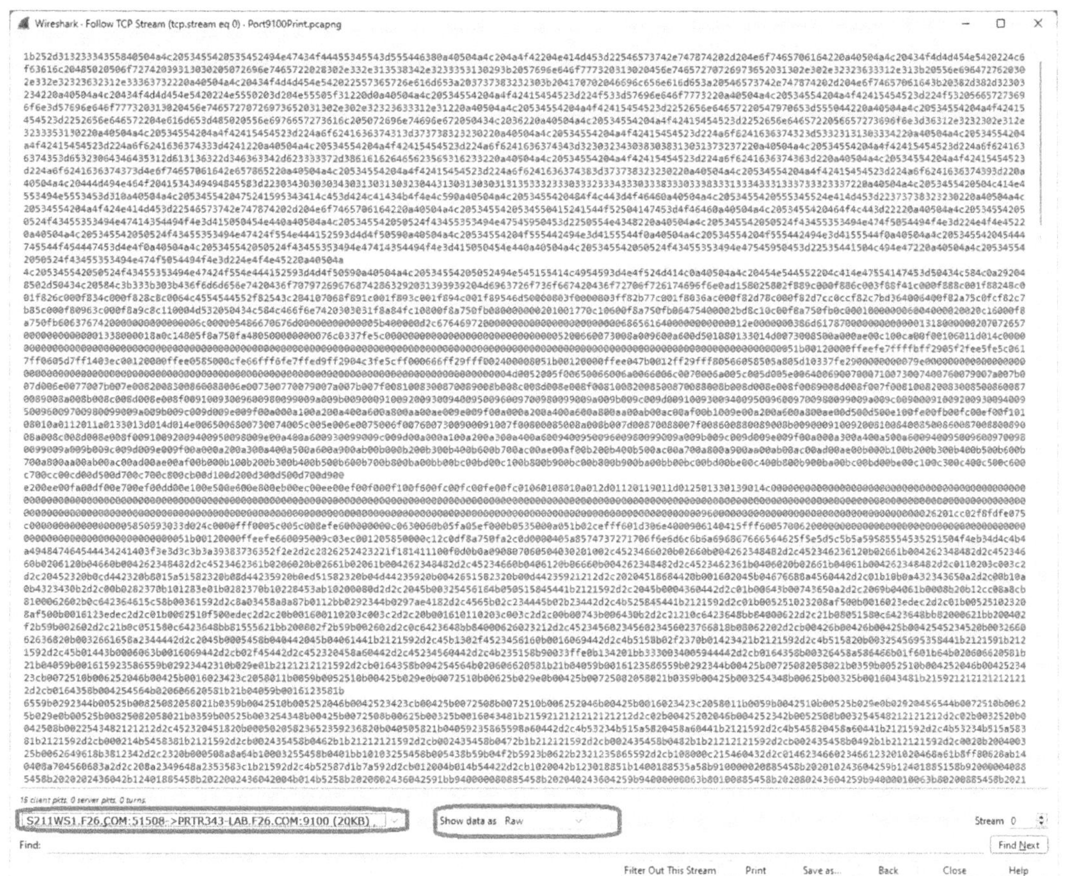

At this point, you should have an xxyyy.pcl file whose data describes a one-way session (from client to printer) with data saved in RAW format. Save this to a folder you will remember as we will use this shortly. You will need to decode the RAW PCL data in the file to a human-readable format. The best utility for this is GhostPCL, available under the GNU General Public License. This is a fantastic utility and tailor-made for what we want to do. GhostPCL can convert the RAW data to the original (pre-PCL encoded) format – the original file contents before it was printed. Use the following command line argument to accomplish this:

```
gpcl6win64 -dNOPAUSE -sDEVICE=pdfwrite -sOutputFile=<Desired pdf
file>  <RAW file>
```

```
For example: gpcl6win64 -dNOPAUSE -sDEVICE=pdfwrite -sOutputFile=C:\Temp\
Test.pdf C:\Temp\test.pcl
```

Once executed, you will find a pdf file (C:\Temp\Test.pdf in the example) that contains essentially what was in the send print document. What should jump out here is the contents - in this case the packet trace shows the contents of the print job that can be converted to human-readable text. In the event a print job is sent using port 9100 (or LPR) print protocols, the contents of the print job are visible to anyone using a packet sniffer. That is because neither Port 9100 nor LPR protocols are encrypted while they transit through the network. We will return to this later in this book, but for now just remember that anything sent using these 2 print protocols is clear text. If you have sensitive data from customer records, this could potentially be compromised if someone employed a network sniffer. The developers of IPP certainly had this in mind when the standard was developed, as we will see later.

Why Use a PDL?

At this point, I want you to get the concept of what exactly a Page Description Language does - in this specific case, PCL. To get this point across, I created a project called RawPrintStreamTest - it is located in the code section for this chapter. The purpose of this exercise is to show you how PCL functions to provide the printer with information necessary to render a complex document. Keep in mind that you can always send arbitrary text to a printer using port 9100, and it will print out. The issue is formatting the text sent and limiting the number of characters to set on a line. The RawPrintStreamTest project actually encompasses one of my passions - that of classic muscle cars. The project creates the following paragraph and sends this to the printer in unformatted (no PCL) and formatted (PCL encoded) formats. The paragraph reads:

> "I love classic cars, especially early and late 60s Mustangs and Corvettes and Chargers. To me, these represent the epitome of 60's styling."

On the surface, this is a simple set of sentences that should be easy to print out. But if you send this to a printer without PCL formatting and using port 9100, you will start to see some issues. First, the end of the second sentence is truncated and malformed. Where did the last part of the sentence go? The issue here is that the printer does not have a concept of a character limit, and without you explicitly setting one, the end of the second sentence does not print out at all. Now, let us add some complexity to this by making the car names bold. How do you tell the printer to bold the car names, and how would you tell the printer not to truncate the last sentence? Turns out that PCL is the answer to these issues (along with a host of other formatting issues) - in the case of this exercise, we format the text stream with PCL to set the character limit to 60 (\x1B&l60F) and to enable word wrap (\x1B&k2G) so we don't run off the end of the physical printout. We also ask the printer to make the car names bold (\x1B(s3B) as well. When you run the RawPrintStreamTest project, it should create two printouts using the same paragraph: one that is not formatted in PCL and one that is formatted in PCL. Although this is a simple test, it should reinforce the need for a language (PCL in this case) the printer can use to properly format complex documents.

One other point I need to bring up - how does Windows know the character limit the printer can accept without running off the paper? Obviously, in this example we set an artificial limit of 60 characters, but how would this be done in the standard Windows print dialog? The answer is a bit involved, but the Windows OS reads a DEVMODE structure (Device Mode) that contains a few properties such as:

- **dmPaperSize**: Specifies the paper size.
- **dmPaperWidth**: Specifies the width of the paper.
- **dmPaperLength**: Specifies the length of the paper.

Of course, the values used for this structure are provided when you install the print driver. The actual computation for the number of characters that can fit on a line depends on (among other metrics) the size of the font, the paper size, and the font width between characters setting. For instance, the Windows API GetTextMetrics provides a structure (TEXTMETRIC) that contains information about selected font height, max character width, leading, etc. You supply a handle to the current device context, and the information (structure) about the current font selected is returned. The computation that provides the maximum number of characters that can fit on a line is derived from information gleaned from the DEVMODE structure and the TEXTMETRIC structure. If you are interested in learning more on this, I would encourage you to read Windows Graphic Programming by Feng Yuan - it is an excellent resource to understand the graphics system on Windows.

Windows Print Components

We begin the technical dissection of the Windows print subsystem by investigating the various constituent components. We already know the print system needs a print driver. But what does the print driver do? The answer to that question depends on what Page Description Language (PDL) the print driver was created to use. Today, there are 2 common PDL types in use (at least on Windows); these are PostScript (PS) and Printer Command Language (PCL). To be sure, there are other PDLs, but to narrow the focus, we will consider only these two. The overall goal of a print driver is to convert files from application formats to a format that the printer can natively work with, in this case either PCL or PS. Both PCL 5 (and higher) and PS create vector-based files as opposed to raster files for efficiency and scalability purposes. Vector-formatted files are based on mathematical functions to create lines and curves to describe images and text. The advantage here is that the resulting file is device independent, meaning they should display the same on multiple devices. This is not true for raster-based formats that typically are device dependent. Think of the old Word Paint bitmaps you could create pixel by pixel, and then how poorly they performed when you wanted to make them larger (scale up) or smaller (scale down). If you took that same raster file to another computer, it might not display as well or with the same coloring as the newer device might have a better graphics card or resolution. So, to perform better on multiple printers, modern PDL languages are vector-based.

Windows currently has two major print paths available: the traditional GDI and the XPS path. These 2 paths provide two distinct ways that application documents may be converted to a PDL as the hardware printer requires. The legacy path uses Graphics Device Interface (GDI) calls while converting the document to a Page Description Language (PDL) like PCL or PostScript. The second path derives from an approach that does not use GDI but an XML-based standard. With .NET, application developers using Windows Presentation Foundation (WPF) have a rich set of printing and print system management APIs. The core of this functionality is the XML Paper Specification (XPS) file format and the XPS print path [4]. We will go over both paths in this book, but the GDI path in greater detail since it is still (and likely will remain) the dominant path.

The GDI path itself is influenced by the data type that the print processor defaults to. This data type can be changed by the user if desired. Traditionally, the print processor default data type was EMF, which meant the print process used an intermediate file format as a spooler file and then translated that to the final format the printer required (usually either PCL or Postscript). In recent years, the print processor's default data type can be RAW, which means sending the contents of the spooled file directly to the printer. This is because many print drivers now convert GDI calls directly to PCL without using an intermediate format such as EMF. There are advantages to converting data directly to PCL or PostScript; the print process is faster and less complex while using fewer resources. However, converting document contents to EMF as an intermediate format before converting to PCL is considered better for graphic-laden documents as they can be rendered with better quality. The next section will describe the print path using an intermediate format (EMF), but keep in mind that conversion from GDI directly to PCL or PostScript (without the EMF intermediate step) is also possible.

Before diving into specifics, I would like to provide a high-level outline of the GDI path before diving into the details of each component. You can refer to this outline to track the overall flow while taking in greater detail. For this example, I present the conversion to PCL, but keep in mind that this process can be used to convert to PostScript as well. So, without delay, I present a high-level flow for a document processed by the Windows print service:

1. The document contents are converted to EMF format, and a file is created for the contents of this EMF data and placed in the Windows print spooler.

2. The Windows print spooler service looks at the files with SPL and SHD extensions (both files are created for the same print job) and from these calls the appropriate Print Processor.

3. The Print Processor picks up the EMF file and converts it to the format the printer requires, then copies the converted files back on the spooler. The converted file format can be PCL or PostScript, but for this example we will use PCL.

4. The Spooler service calls a Language Monitor (if one is required). The Language Monitor adds job-specific commands to the existing PCL-formatted file (*.spl). The Language Monitor gets status messages back from the printer.

5. The Spooler service calls the appropriate Print Monitor that the installed printer specifies. The Print Monitor reads the metadata from the spooled file and routes the print file to the appropriate Port Monitor.

6. The Port Monitor sends the job to the appropriate printer connected to the computer the job originated on.

So that is a generic structure used in any given print job. Of course, not all components are used exactly as outlined here, as each vendor may deviate to enhance efficiency as needed. Do not worry that much of the detail of each step was missing - we will provide greater detail as we examine each component.

GDI Print Path

Let us begin our investigation with the Graphics Driver Interface (GDI) path since it is the older of the 2 print paths. For some document files, the conversion to a print-ready format such as PCL or PS might not happen in one fell swoop. Take, for example, a Word document created that consists of bolded text, graphic illustrations, and possibly some paragraphs with italics and underlines dispersed throughout for impact. How does this get converted to PCL for the printer to render? The application might typically (if specified by the print processor data type) convert the Graphics Device Interface (GDI) calls that describe the document to Enhanced Metafile (EMF) format. The EMF format is a Windows native vector graphic format that describes a document you see on the screen. For traditional applications, GDI is used to convert document content into a format that can be understood by the printing subsystem. If the print processor's default data type is EMF, the print system generates a sequence of drawing commands that are device independent.

On Windows, the Graphics Device Interface (GDI) is a collection of Win32 APIs that describe screen pixel information. For instance, if you wanted to draw a rectangle on the screen or copy the contents of the screen to a file, you would call one of the many GDI APIs. Since documents are displayed on the screen, we need to convert the screen composition of the document to a file format (text and graphics) that the printer can render. In short, we need GDI to describe the exact way to recreate what we see on the screen through a disk file. GDI calls (in the format of Win32 APIs) get recorded into an EMF file so they can be played back (eventually) to the host print driver chosen by the user. This process (conversion to EMF) is typically done to create a spooler file the Windows print subsystem can use. Remember that the EMF file is an intermediate file format created for conversion to a print description language such as PCL or Postscript. Also, keep in mind that some drivers do not use the EMF intermediate format at all.

This is how the GDI calls are translated into EMF:

1. Create the Enhanced Metafile (EMF): The GDI calls made by the application are captured into an EMF file instead of being sent directly to the printer. This is done by creating an EMF device context using **CreateEnhMetaFile**. The application then makes the same GDI calls, but they are recorded in the EMF.

   ```
   HDC hdcEMF = CreateEnhMetaFile(hdcPrinter, fileName,
   NULL, NULL);
   ```

2. Recording GDI Calls: The GDI calls, such as TextOut, Rectangle, and others, are made in the context of this EMF device context. These GDI calls describe the document created by the user – the application that created the file could be Word, WordPad, LibreOffice, etc.

```
SelectObject(hdcEMF, hFont);
CreateFont(24, 0, 0, 0, FW_NORMAL, FALSE, FALSE, FALSE,
DEFAULT_CHARSET, OUT_OUTLINE_PRECIS, CLIP_DEFAULT_PRECIS,
CLEARTYPE_QUALITY, VARIABLE_PITCH, TEXT("Arial"));
TextOut(hdcEMF, 100, 100, TEXT("Hello, World!"), 13);
Rectangle(hdcEMF, 200, 200, 400, 400);
```

3. Close the EMF: Once all GDI commands have been recorded, the EMF is finalized by calling the CloseEnhMetaFile API.

```
HENHMETAFILE hEmf = CloseEnhMetaFile(hdcEMF);
```

The resulting EMF file contains a sequence of records that represent all the GDI commands made for rendering the document. This includes font selections, color settings, text drawing commands, and image blitting commands. When this EMF file is played back (e.g., by a printer driver or a viewer), the GDI commands are executed to reproduce the document exactly as it was formatted. At this point, the Windows subsystem saves the file into the Windows spool directory, and each print file gets represented by the *.SPL and *.SHD extensions. These SPL/SHD files get a numerical file name (i.e., 00002.SPL and 00002.SHD) and are used to provide the print subsystem information it needs to process the file.

Now converting the EMF file (stored in a *.spl file) into a PCL document and sending it to the user-chosen printer involves a few more steps. The .SHD file does not actually contain any of the printed document data but rather serves as a meta file about the print job itself. For instance, the SHD file contains information on the printing preferences chosen by the user, the user's name, the document name, and other print job information. The SPL file contains the actual document data, and the Print Processor uses this file to further process the print request.

The print spooler service is required to read the SPL/SHD files and find the printer requested. The association made between the printer and the requisite print driver is one created in the registry when the printer is created (in Windows). If you are curious as to where in the registry these associations are made, take time to peruse HKLM\SYSTEM \CurrentControlSet\Control\Print\Printers and look at the entries created for each printer. The print driver responsible for rendering the data into PCL or PS is obtained from this registry path. This registry association provides a lot of information pertinent to accomplishing printing using this printer, including the model and port necessary. The SHD file will divulge the settings specified by the user (such as paper size, print quality, etc.).

At this point, the print configuration area in the registry provides the path to the print driver DLL (Dynamic Link Library) that handles the conversion of the print data. The driver could be a Unidrv-based driver for PCL, a PostScript driver, or a custom driver provided by the manufacturer. The Print Processor is now called by the spooler service to oversee the process of converting the SPL file using the chosen print driver. The converted (now Raw) file containing PDL data will then be created in the spool folder for the next step. We will stop here momentarily to introduce the second print path used by Windows: the XPS print path.

XPS Print Path

XPS (XML Paper Specification) is a format developed by Microsoft that is like PDF. It provides a way to represent fixed documents in a way that preserves their layout and appearance across different systems. WPF (Windows Presentation Foundation) was designed with built-in support for XPS, which allows for seamless document creation, viewing, and printing. In comparison with the GDI path, XPS provides:

1. A fixed layout document format that ensures consistent rendering across different devices and platforms. This is crucial for preserving the exact appearance of documents, including fonts, colors, and layout, irrespective of the printing or viewing environment. GDI, being an older graphics API, lacks this built-in guarantee of document fidelity.

2. A vector-based graphics model that supports high-quality scaling and rendering. This allows for crisp and clear output of any size. GDI primarily uses raster-based graphics, which can result in pixelation or loss of quality when scaling. XPS supports advanced features such as transparency, complex text rendering, and precise color management. GDI's capabilities in these areas are more limited.

3. A more streamlined process – the XPS print path supports creating print-ready documents that can be directly sent to printers or saved as files. This is more efficient than the GDI approach, which often requires conversion between different graphics contexts and formats.

4. Cross Platform ability - XPS documents can be used across different Windows platforms and potentially other systems, provided they have XPS support. GDI, being specific to the Windows graphics subsystem, does not offer the same level of cross-platform compatibility.

The goal was to have the XPS print driver convert WPF document layout data directly to the XML format used by XPS print. Additionally, it was hoped that manufacturers would natively rasterize XPS formats on the print hardware RIP processor. Unfortunately (for Microsoft), the vendor's adoption of the XPS standard was underwhelming, and the technology, while powerful, never really took off. The clear winner in the portable vector document standard was PDF, especially when it comes to IPP.

In practice, the Windows spooler would be required to glean information from the printer driver as to how to manage and process print jobs. If the printer supported XPS, the spooler would then handle XPS documents without conversion. If the printer did not natively support XPS, the spooler or driver would have to perform the necessary conversions (perhaps to PCL or PS) before sending it to the printer. As it stands, because many printers do not natively rasterize XPS, the spooler must convert the XPS format to a suitable PDL, which tends to undermine the efficiency of the protocol.

In summary, the XPS standard never achieved widespread popularity due to the dominance of established standards like PDF, limited printer support, lack of widespread software adoption, and the complexity of implementing XPS.

Print Subsystem Components

The next section of this chapter is built on expounding the details of the major print subsystem components referred to in the GDI path outline. We will delve into the spooler router, print providers, print processors, print monitors, language monitors, and finally port monitors in that order. Keep in mind that each of these components is supplied by Microsoft; however, vendors typically develop their own version(s) and include them in their driver package. The reason for this is typically what you would expect in a competitive environment: more features are typically associated with a more complete product. Note that the development specifications (provided by Microsoft in the DDK) for each component must be fastidiously adhered to. Thus, vendors are expected to provide required interfaces and methods so that the spooler service can successfully process the print job. The spooler service calls methods of each component and expects these to be implemented, or the process will fail.

Spooler Router

The job of the Spooler Router (spools.dll) is to deliver the print job to the appropriate print provider who will effectively process the job. To do this, the spooler router uses the OpenPrinter API, which takes as arguments the printer's name, an empty handle, and a PRINTER_DEFAULTS structure that defines what rights you want on the printer as arguments along with a DevMode that defines the printer capabilities. A successful return of OpenPrinter will also return the default data type for a printer as well as the handle to the printer for subsequent API calls. When OpenPrinter succeeds, the OS shows it recognizes the name of the printer. Thus, the spooler router can call each print provider in the system and provide the requested printer name until a provider returns a legitimate printer handle.

Print Provider

The print provider is the overall manager of the print job and directs submitted print jobs to the appropriate printer, whether locally attached (USB/LPT1) or connected to the network. The print provider manages print queues and can start, stop, or enumerate print jobs by communicating with the Windows print spooler. In effect, the print provider calls the appropriate Win32 spooler APIs to usher the job to completion and thus oversee the entire print job lifecycle, from submission to completion. The Windows OS provides a network print provider, a local print provider, and an internet (IPP) print provider, to name a few. The print provider implements the following API functions, among others:

- **OpenPrinter**: Opens a handle to a specified printer or print server.
- **SetPrinter**: Sets the data for a specified printer or print server.
- **GetPrinter**: Retrieves information about a specified printer or print server.

Print Processor

You can think of the print processor as the data conversion manager - this component is responsible for converting the GDI (or XPS) data file into a format the printer can understand. To do this, the Print Processor needs some information about the print job to perform the job. In the GDI section, I outlined that the print spooler service reads the SPL/SHD files and from this information can thus select the proper Print Processor to convert the data. One is converted by the Print Processor; the converted data is then written back to the spooler .spl file. The Print Processor has some other tasks it is assigned. Chief among these is responding to application requests to pause, cancel, or resume the print job.

Microsoft provides a default Print Processor called WinPrint, however, vendors may provide their own Print Processor if desired. If you look at the print processor for your printer, you will see the default data type created (RAW in this case) and other formats available.

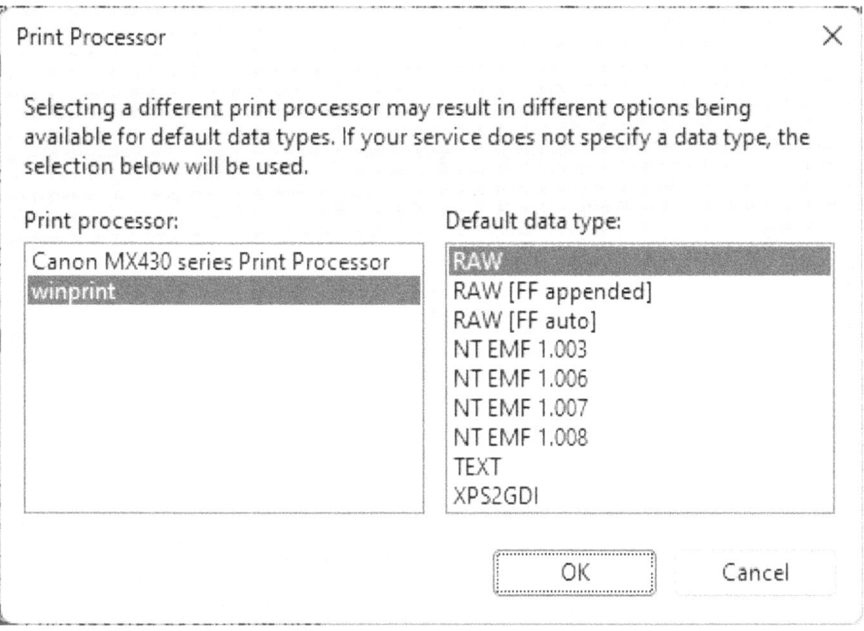

The Default Data Type Used Is Displayed for Each Print Processor

The RAW setting in the Print Processor shown above means it sends the print job data to the printer without any modification. Think of Raw as the format the printer can natively render. In this case, the data is sent to the printer in the spooled format, whether PCL, PostScript, or another format. For many modern printers, the data is often in PCL (Printer Command Language) format, but if curious, you can check the print job properties. To do this, pause the printer (in Windows) and then send a print job to that printer.

I often miss the more detailed Devices and Printers dialog when using Windows 11 Home edition. While the Printers and Scanners dialog has a more modern feel. It lacks a straightforward way to pause the print queue. To get the older Devices and Printers dialog, you can create a desktop shortcut:

1. Right-click on your desktop and select New/Shortcut.
2. Enter explorer shell:::{A8A91A66-3A7D-4424-8D24-04E18069 5C7A} as the location and click Next.
3. Name the shortcut "Devices and Printers" and click Finish. You can now access it directly from your desktop.

To pause a printer, open Devices and Printers from the shortcut created above. Right-click your target printer and choose **See What's Printing**. In the Printer menu, click Pause Printing to keep all documents from printing. Just remember to un-pause the print queue so the print flow is restored.

Looking at the documents in the print queue, click the paused document and then select Properties from the Document menu. In the case of my document, the data type was EMF, as shown below.

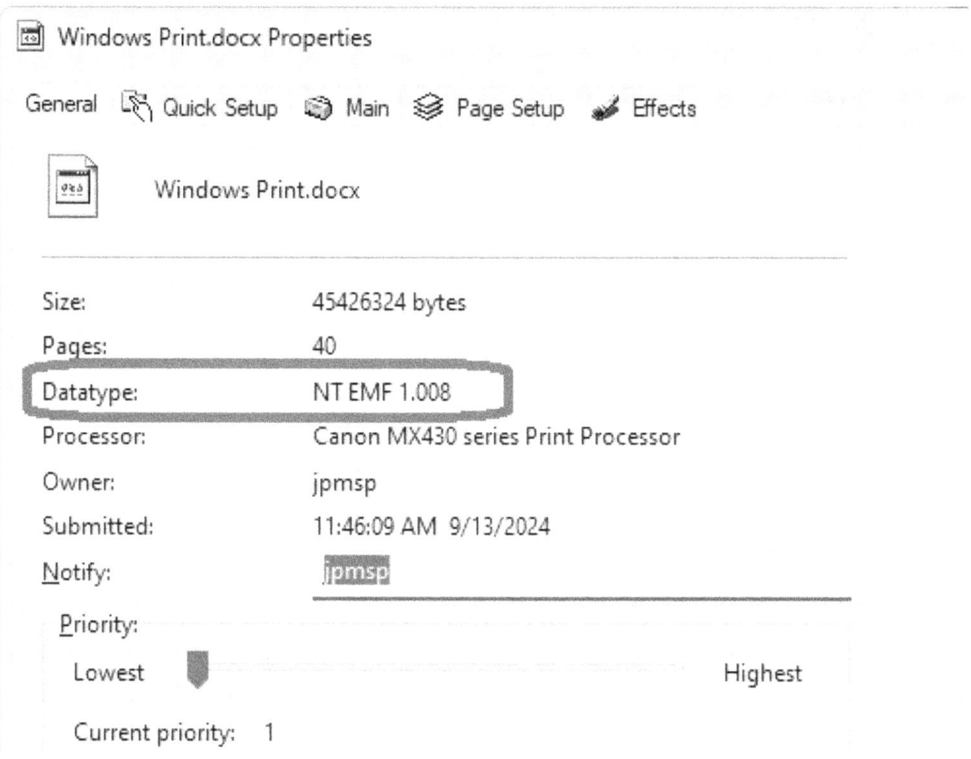

The Data Type Used Is Shown

Since my print queue was paused, the document format is in an intermediate format - the print processor has not yet converted the EMF to the proper PDL type (PCL, PostScript, etc.). Once the print processor is done, it determines if a language monitor is needed or whether the job can be passed directly to the appropriate port monitor. For this decision, the print processor relies on the printer driver's configuration to see if a language monitor is associated (or not) with the printer. If the driver specifies a language monitor, the print processor will call it to modify the data stream as needed.

Print Monitor

This is a general term that can refer to both language monitors and port monitors. It is used as an umbrella term for components that manage the data flow between the print spooler and the printer. So, when you hear "print monitor," it could mean either a language monitor, a port monitor, or both, depending on the context. They work together to ensure the data is properly formatted and delivered to the printer.

Language Monitor

At this point, we have raw data (a spooled file of PCL) that a printer can use to print out document pages. If the document was composed of one page and the font and color were consistent throughout, we might be ready to print. It would also help at this point if we were the only user to submit a print job (to the printer) during the same time. However, these are not realistic expectations, as we should assume the possibility of multiple simultaneous print jobs and a truly diverse set of fonts, graphics, and pages to comprise our document. This is where a language monitor plays a significant role in the print stream. A language monitor is a user-mode DLL that provides a full duplex communications path and overall print job enhancements to the RAW data stream [8].

A language monitor typically modifies the data within the print job. This can include print job commands, which are used for managing job control at the printer level. For instance, the language monitor can include commands to start or end a job, set up the environment (like duplex printing), or manage the interaction between various parts of the print job. A language monitor relies on specific patterns or commands in the print stream to determine where to inject the job commands. Page breaks in a PCL stream are often indicated by specific PCL commands (like ESC E for form feed), which signal the end of a page or a section within the print job. While there are several language file formats, the most predominant version is Print Job Language (PJL), developed by Hewlett Packard (HP), so we will concentrate on this language monitor from here [9]. Also note that while PJL was designed to augment PCL, it has been adopted by many PostScript printers as well.

What does augmenting or modifying a PCL file stream entail, you might ask? Some examples of PJL incursion into the PCL stream might be to add a PJL command such as

```
@PJL ENTER LANGUAGE = PCL
```

at the start of a job or insert @PJL SET commands between pages to change settings like resolution or duplex mode. In short, the language monitor complements the printer driver, which knows the specifics of the printer capabilities and the format of the print data. The print driver creates a PCL data stream while the language monitor augments it with additional PJL commands. Let's review some of the enhancements being discussed to understand the concept more fully.

Environment Configuration: PJL can set specific printer configurations for a job, such as duplex printing, resolution, or paper tray selection. These settings can be changed between pages or at the start of the job, depending on the requirements.

Dynamic Adjustments: PJL allows the printer settings to be adjusted dynamically within the job, something that PCL alone cannot do. For instance, if different pages need different paper types or print quality, PJL commands can instruct the printer to change these settings at mid-job.

Job Tracking: PJL can include job identifiers (like job names or usernames), which the printer uses to track the job. This is useful for both the user and system administrators who may need to monitor or audit print jobs.

Printer Status: PJL can request and receive status information from the printer, such as whether the printer is ready or if there are errors (e.g., out of paper). This information can be communicated back to the print server or client for better job management.

Example Workflow:

1. **Application sends print data**: The application generates print data, which is passed to GDI and then to the printer driver.
2. **Driver generates PCL stream**: The printer driver converts the GDI commands into a PCL stream, which includes print data, form feed commands, and other control data. (The RAW file is a byte-for-byte representation of what will be sent to the printer, including the PCL commands.)
3. **Language Monitor intercepts and augments**: The language monitor reads the PCL stream, detects page breaks, and injects the appropriate PJL commands.
4. **Spooling and Printing**: The augmented print job (now containing both PCL and PJL commands) is sent to the spooler, which eventually sends the completed job to the printer.

This process ensures that the print job is correctly interpreted by the printer, with all necessary commands in place to handle page breaks, job settings, and other print-specific instructions. One final job of the language monitor (predominantly PJL) is to check the print hardware status. One way to accomplish this is to embed the status check in the print job itself. To do this, the language monitor sends a PJL command to check the printer's status (e.g., @PJL INFO STATUS). If the language monitor needs immediate status information (before starting a job), it might transmit a standalone @PJL INFO STATUS command directly to the printer. The printer, upon receiving this PJL command, processes it immediately and generates a response that contains the requested status information, such as whether the printer is online, a paper jam exists, or the level of toner is low. If the printer reports errors, the language monitor or print subsystem can take corrective actions or prompt the user before the print job starts.

Now that the RAW data stream has the PCL and job commands embedded and is ready to print, it needs to be sent to hardware either attached to the printer directly (USB/Serial) or via a network connection (TCP). The job of the next monitor is to do just that.

Required Interfaces:

IPrintLanguageMonitor: The main interface for language monitors.

Some Required Methods:

StartDoc: Similar to print processors, initializes a document.

StartPage: Begins a new page.

Write: Sends the formatted data to the printer.

EndDoc: Ends the document processing.

Port Monitors

The spooler service should identify the port associated with the job that will complete job submission to the hardware printer and is responsible for calling the appropriate port monitor. When a print job is ready to be sent to the printer, the spooler service determines the correct port monitor based on the printer configuration. The transmission of the job to the actual printer is thus the domain of the port monitor. The transmission method for the print job depends on the type of port monitor required.

Typically, you might have a network port monitor (TCP based), a USB port monitor, a Serial Port monitor (although these are becoming obsolete), etc. Each of these monitor types is a special piece of software, but for illustrative purposes (for this chapter) I will go into detail on the TCP and USB port monitors as they are the most prevalent in enterprise networks.

Port monitors are DLLs that maintain a communications path between the user-mode print spooler and the kernel-mode port drivers that access I/O port hardware. This software sends the RAW stream from the spooler file to the print hardware. For Windows there are several port monitors in use - each of which allows a different virtual path or hardware port to communicate with external print hardware. As mentioned earlier, some of the Windows port monitor types are WSD port monitor, TCPMon, LocalMon, and USB port monitor. The WSD port monitor is particularly interesting as it has significance to the way Microsoft chose to implement IPP in the Windows OS. I will not go into LocalMon, which supports COM and LPT ports as their use has waned markedly in the print world in the past 10 years - that leaves us with the USB, TCP, and WSD port monitors. If you are curious as to which port monitors your local machine currently uses for printing, you can run the GetWindowsPortMonitors solution (in the code section of this chapter) to print them out.

Interestingly, port monitors use basic Win32 APIs such as CreateFile to send data to the I/O drivers in kernel mode. CreateFile is a user mode API commonly used in Windows to open a handle to I/O devices with the intent of communicating with them. You can then use the Read File and Write File APIs to send data to the port. In fact, CreateFile can be used to communicate with many devices in Windows, including but not limited to files, file streams, directories, physical disks, volumes, console buffers, tape drives, communications resources, mail slots, and named pipes [18].

USB Port Monitor

In Windows, when you connect to a USB printer, the OS creates a virtual printer port named USB00X (where X is a positive, incrementing integer). This port is then managed by the USB Port Monitor. The USB Port Monitor is responsible for handling the data transmission between the computer and the printer over the USB connection. It manages the flow of print jobs to the printer and receives status information from the printer. When a USB printer is connected, the USB Host Controller on the computer initiates the enumeration process. The printer responds by identifying itself, providing descriptors that include information about its capabilities (e.g., supported USB class, vendor ID, product ID). These printer descriptors are embedded in the printer firmware and, in the case of vendor ID (VID) and product ID (PID), are integral to the plug-and-play architecture used by Windows. The VID/PID combination is part of the printer INF file sections and points to any driver required for the device to function correctly.

USB printers contain multiple endpoints for communication with the host. The endpoints act as buffers for a particular communication request or stream, and data is sent to them as necessary. Typically, a USB printer has the following endpoints:

Control Endpoint (Endpoint 0): Primarily for printer control and configuration requests.

Bulk Out Endpoint: Used by the host (computer) to send print data to the printer. This is where the RAW print stream is delivered (to the printer) on.

Bulk In Endpoint: Used by the printer to send status or data back to the host.

Interrupt Endpoint: Used to raise hardware interrupt signals from the printer to the host.

Print jobs sent over USB involve first configuring the device when the USB printer is plugged into the host computer. In effect, the host requires details by identifying and configuring the peripheral device, implementing interfaces, and setting endpoints. A deep dive into how USB identifies and sets up a peripheral device on a host automatically is beyond the scope of this book, but you can satisfy any curiosity by reading John Hyde's "USB Design by Example" book or perusing Microsoft Learn.

The host (computer) runs initialization software, which allows devices to be added or removed at any time. Once enumerated, the device is assigned a unique id used for interaction from the host to the device during operation. There are 4 transaction types defined: Interrupt, Bulk, Isochronous, and Control - our Wireshark traces will show Control and Bulk scans for USB printers.

If you are curious, you can find the USB Vendor ID for all manufacturers here: `https://devicehunt.com/all-usb-vendors`.

Since our printer is an HP printer, we can see that the vendor ID is 0x03f0 for our product, and the idVendor returned from the device matches that. The initialization software on the host will request a Device and Configuration descriptor from the USB device to discover what has been attached to the host.

Let us begin to investigate how a USB printer interacts with the Windows operating system. Many years ago, I was in school learning French, and we were instructed to learn about how a French student attended school by memorizing "Dans La Salle de Classe," a description of a French schoolroom. If the idea were to impart fluid French on me, it failed miserably, but I did remember some of the story I was supposed to memorize and recite. Thus (to illustrate the USB process), my file to print will be entitled accordingly.

Notice The Wireshark traces taken for the USB port monitor require that you install the USBPcap filter driver for Wireshark. You can verify that USBPcap is installed by clicking *Help* in the Wireshark menu, then *About Wireshark*, then clicking the *Plugins* tab.

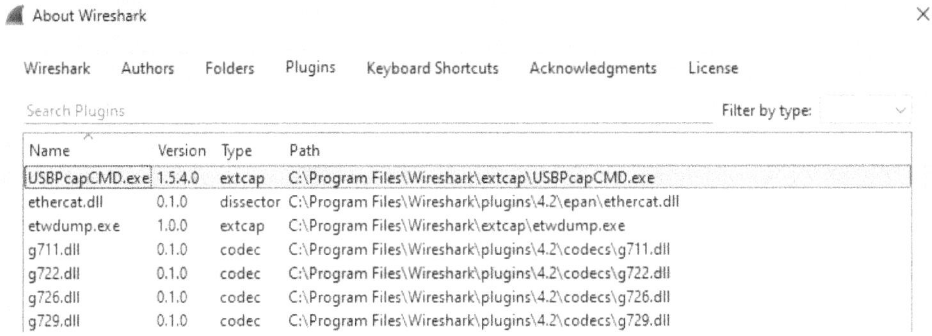

About Wireshark

Wireshark Authors Folders Plugins Keyboard Shortcuts Acknowledgments License

Search Plugins Filter by type:

Name	Version	Type	Path
USBPcapCMD.exe	1.5.4.0	extcap	C:\Program Files\Wireshark\extcap\USBPcapCMD.exe
ethercat.dll	0.1.0	dissector	C:\Program Files\Wireshark\plugins\4.2\epan\ethercat.dll
etwdump.exe	1.0.0	extcap	C:\Program Files\Wireshark\extcap\etwdump.exe
g711.dll	0.1.0	codec	C:\Program Files\Wireshark\plugins\4.2\codecs\g711.dll
g722.dll	0.1.0	codec	C:\Program Files\Wireshark\plugins\4.2\codecs\g722.dll
g726.dll	0.1.0	codec	C:\Program Files\Wireshark\plugins\4.2\codecs\g726.dll
g729.dll	0.1.0	codec	C:\Program Files\Wireshark\plugins\4.2\codecs\g729.dll

In newer Wireshark versions, the setup program will provide a dialog that allows you to install USBPcap during installation – ensure you enable this option.

Using Wireshark, you will find that it picks up all USB activity on the hosts, which is good for captures but bad for analysis since it can be difficult to find what you want (in this case a USB endpoint for a printer). One tip to find a printer endpoint is to search for **bInterfaceClass: Printer** in the Wireshark search bar. This is because any Wireshark trace will naturally include other devices such as mice, keyboards, or any HID device attached to the host. Once you search on **bInterfaceClass: Printer**, you should find the USB bus id, Device Address, and Endpoint of the printer you are investigating, and thus target this endpoint for further study.

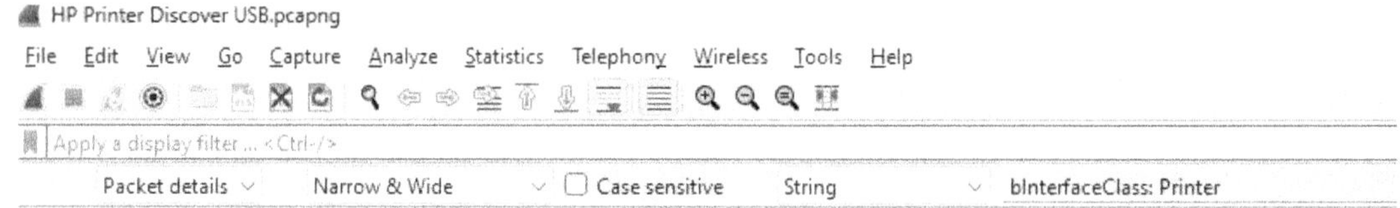

The USB device initialization for a printer involves an attempt to get configuration information from the device by Windows. The best way to visualize what is happening in this phase is to look at a Wireshark trace of the process. The host (Windows) starts by sending the endpoint (in this case, 1.20.0) a Get Status message.

	Time	Source	Destination	Protocol	Length	Info
620	4.513745	host	1.20.0	USB	36	GET STATUS Request
572	4.095649	1.20.0	host	USB	44	GET STATUS Response
574	4.095793	1.20.0	host	USB	140	GET STATUS Response
617	4.508966	1.20.0	host	USB	30	GET STATUS Response
623	4.517684	1.20.0	host	USB	30	GET STATUS Response
619	4.513676	host	1.20.0	USBPRI...	36	GET_DEVICE_ID request
627	4.526374	host	1.20.0	USBPRI...	36	GET_DEVICE_ID request
629	4.532255	host	1.20.0	USBPRI...	36	GET_DEVICE_ID request
631	4.536389	host	1.20.0	USBPRI...	36	GET_DEVICE_ID request
633	4.542506	host	1.20.0	USBPRI...	36	GET_DEVICE_ID request
621	4.516117	1.20.0	host	USBPRI...	160	GET_DEVICE_ID response
628	4.529582	1.20.0	host	USBPRI...	160	GET_DEVICE_ID response

The Get Status USB Message

560	4.085249	host	1.20.0	USB	36	SET CONFIGURATION Request
6	0.000000	1.2.0	host	USB	28	SET CONFIGURATION Response
12	0.000000	1.3.0	host	USB	28	SET CONFIGURATION Response
18	0.000000	1.10.0	host	USB	28	SET CONFIGURATION Response
24	0.000000	1.12.0	host	USB	28	SET CONFIGURATION Response
30	0.000000	1.13.0	host	USB	28	SET CONFIGURATION Response
36	0.000000	1.14.0	host	USB	28	SET CONFIGURATION Response
42	0.000000	1.11.0	host	USB	28	SET CONFIGURATION Response
48	0.000000	1.4.0	host	USB	28	SET CONFIGURATION Response
54	0.000000	1.5.0	host	USB	28	SET CONFIGURATION Response
60	0.000000	1.6.0	host	USB	28	SET CONFIGURATION Response
66	0.000000	1.7.0	host	USB	28	SET CONFIGURATION Response
72	0.000000	1.1.0	host	USB	28	SET CONFIGURATION Response
78	0.000000	1.8.0	host	USB	28	SET CONFIGURATION Response
84	0.000000	1.9.0	host	USB	28	SET CONFIGURATION Response
568	4.095174	1.20.0	host	USB	28	SET CONFIGURATION Response
609	4.493282	host	1.20.0	USB	36	SET INTERFACE Request
616	4.505952	host	1.20.0	USB	36	SET INTERFACE Request

The Set Configuration USB Message

A very brief USB setup order process for printers is described below:

1. Get_Status: The OS checks the status of the device to ensure it's ready for further communication.
2. Get_Device_Id: The OS retrieves the device descriptor to identify the printer and its capabilities.
3. Set_Configuration: The OS sets the printer to a specific configuration, which includes setting up the necessary interfaces and endpoints.
4. Set_Interface: The OS may select an alternate setting for an interface if the printer supports multiple operational modes.

One thing you will notice immediately with many USB devices and printers is that there are usually multiple endpoints for the same device. So, when you see the xx.yy.zz decimal notation in Wireshark, you should think about the USB Bus id, Device Address, and Endpoint and be aware that many devices employ multiple endpoints to handle different tasks.

A complete description of the USB process requires a book unto itself, but I will describe the purpose (for printer hardware) of the different endpoints typically required.

Control Endpoint: This is configured for standard control transfers, such as configuration and status requests.

Bulk Out Endpoint: This is used as a high-capacity print job transfer medium. For USB 2.0, full speed means the maximum packet size is 64 bytes, but High Speed sets the maximum packet size to 512 bytes. USB 3.0 improves USB 2.0 speed, as the maximum packet size is now 1024 bytes.

Bulk In Endpoint: This is used to communicate from the endpoint (printer) to the OS host. This can be used for job status information, error messages, job acknowledgement, etc. While not the same, think about how a language monitor gets printer status on a TCP-connected printer, and you have the right idea.

One final thing I wanted to convey is how the device (printer) provides the VID/PID or hardware device information to the OS via a Wireshark trace. It is this identification that allows the OS to identify and use the matching print driver necessary for operation.

A device descriptor is requested first – the host issues a GET_DEVICE_DESCRIPTOR request for this information. Below is the Wireshark trace of the reply.

```
> Frame 546: 46 bytes on wire (368 bits), 46 bytes captured (368 bits) on in
v USB URB
    [Source: 1.20.0]
    [Destination: host]
    USBPcap pseudoheader length: 28
    IRP ID: 0xffff928bf9b1e720
    IRP USBD_STATUS: USBD_STATUS_SUCCESS (0x00000000)
    URB Function: URB_FUNCTION_CONTROL_TRANSFER (0x0008)
  > IRP information: 0x01, Direction: PDO -> FDO
    URB bus id: 1
    Device address: 20
  v Endpoint: 0x80, Direction: IN
      1... .... = Direction: IN (1)
      .... 0000 = Endpoint number: 0
    URB transfer type: URB_CONTROL (0x02)
    Packet Data Length: 18
    [Request in: 545]
    [Time from request: 0.003278000 seconds]
    Control transfer stage: Complete (3)
v DEVICE DESCRIPTOR
    bLength: 18
    bDescriptorType: 0x01 (DEVICE)
    bcdUSB: 0x0200
    bDeviceClass: Device (0x00)
    bDeviceSubClass: 0
    bDeviceProtocol: 0 (Use class code info from Interface Descriptors)
    bMaxPacketSize0: 64
    idVendor: HP, Inc (0x03f0)
    idProduct: Unknown (0xd42a)
    bcdDevice: 0x0100
    iManufacturer: 1
    iProduct: 2
    iSerialNumber: 3
    bNumConfigurations: 1
```

Vendor ID and Product ID Provided

Finally, we get to the submission of the actual print job, suitably encoded in PCL for the printer to render the physical pages. In the “Dans La Salle De Classe” file print, the host computer sends the file to the destination printer identified as 1.18.1 URB bus id, Device Address, and EndPoint, respectively. The actual print job is sent as a bulk transfer, which is a series of packets (size based on USB family) sent from host to endpoint.

Does the O/S recognize the printer?

Most issues I have run across with USB-connected printers involve recognition issues – i.e., the O/S simply does not see the USB printer hardware attached. Optimally, a USB printer should show up in the Printers section of Device Manager. However, I have seen improperly configured printers show up as Unknown Devices or even under the Universal Serial Bus Controllers area. Newer USB printers use a Vendor ID/Product ID (VID/PID) to identify themselves to the O/S, which then uses the VID/PID obtained from the Get_Device_Id message query to select a print driver. Always look in the Device Manager Printers section if you have any issues with recognition. Try swapping out the USB cable, trying the printer on another computer, or rebooting the O/S if you run into problems.

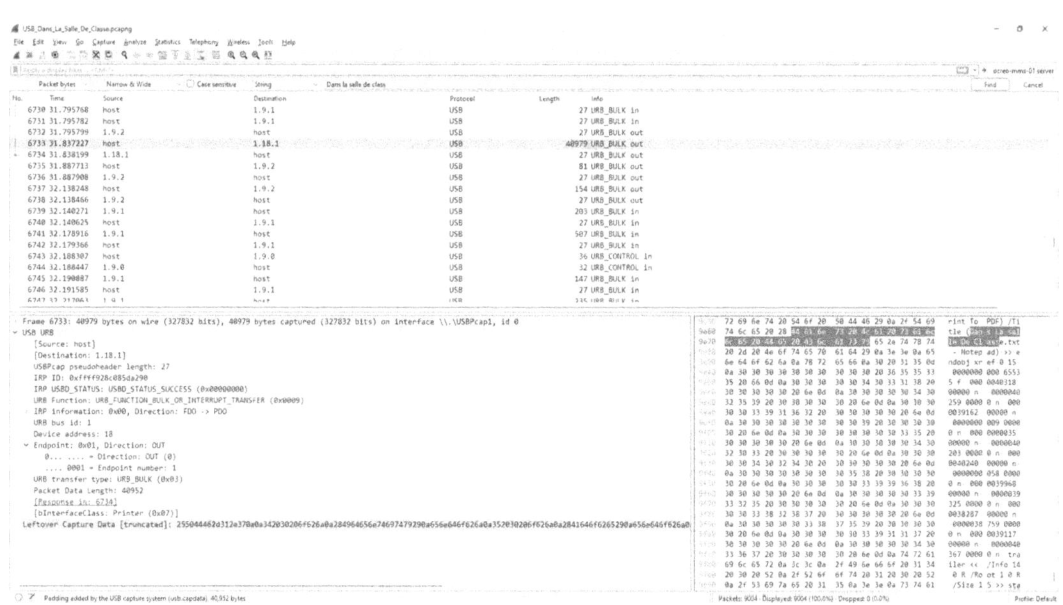

The actual message is PCL encoded, so we'd have to use the Wireshark "Follow Data Stream" trick (see the **Network Trace of Submitted Print Job** section for review) again to read the contents, but you can see the file name being sent. The USB endpoint (our HP LU Enterprise M406 printer) responds back to the URB_BULK request with a USB status message, USBD_STATUS_SUCCESS, meaning the transmission of bulk data was successful. The bottom line is that a USB print job submission is like that of a TCP print job. Both require a PDL language like PCL-encoded data for the printer to render and only significantly differ in the port monitor used to transfer the job itself.

TCP Port Monitor

Another port monitor is the TCP port monitor. It differs from the USB port monitor in that it is designed to send print data over a network connection. On Windows, port 9100 print is referred to as the Standard port monitor, and it remains the recommended choice. Older versions of Windows used LPR as well, but the standard port monitor has been the Microsoft recommendation since Windows 2000. There are significant differences between the Standard (port 9100) port monitor and the LPR port monitor. For one, the LPR port monitor complies with RFC 1179, which standardizes TCP ports to lie between ports 721 and 731, while the standard port monitor defaults to port 9100. Another difference is that the Standard port monitor uses SNMP to communicate with the printer for status and error reporting, while LPR does not. Finally, the Standard port has no timeout specified, while LPR defaults to 3 minutes [3].

Raw port 9100 printing, also referred to as JetDirect, AppSocket, or PDL-datastream, is curiously not a printing protocol by itself. Instead, all data (from the print client) is sent to the printer in a format that the printer understands and can therefore render. When a language monitor is used, the user can get print status format messages back from the printer. Raw printing is robust, efficient, and relatively reliable, but natively processing each data stream sent to the port can pose issues for the printer itself. I will outline why this is a problem later in this chapter in the section "Some Issues with Legacy Print," but for now keep in mind that the printer cannot distinguish a legitimate print data stream from a random character stream. In other words, everything that comes across the network on port 9100 for that printer IP address will result in characters printing out. For now, think of port 9100 print as a sort of highway that connects the client to the hardware printer, except it interprets every byte sent to it as print data.

WSD Port Monitor

The Web Services for Devices (WSD) is a special port monitor designed to communicate over the network using a series of SOAP (Simple Object Access Protocol) messages over UDP and HTTP(S). The WSD specification allows the client to send a discovery probe on the network to which listening devices will respond. The response from the WSD networked devices provides information that the OS can use to add/remove/modify the configuration on the client. For printers, the WSD Port Monitor is employed by Windows to communicate with devices and respond to print service events sent by the printers. The printers can send Hello and Bye messages to which the client should add or remove the printers dynamically; at least that was the intent. These messages are sent to UDP multicast port 3702, so a prerequisite on any network employing WSD devices is to ensure this port is allowed to pass through any interleaving firewall.

The WSD protocol was intended to be a dynamic device enumeration and configuration process that can be used over the network. Technically, WSD uses a multicast discovery protocol to locate device services over a network. WSD employs Simple Object Access Protocol (SOAP) as the message protocol, which is written in XML format and includes a header and body within the SOAP envelope.

As such, it was designed to be used with a host of devices, and for printers specifically you will be required (for development purposes) to include the following print namespaces:

```
http://schemas.microsoft.com/windows/2006/08/wdp/print
http://schemas.microsoft.com/windows/2006/08/wdp/print
```

in your code. Be aware that Microsoft provided the wsdapi.lib library for development, but it was primarily intended for C coders. As of this writing, I am not aware of any official .NET libraries for this technology.

The WSD discover probe can be used to automate the task of enumerating printers with a listening WSD port on a network, but there is a limitation. By default, the Time-To-Live (TTL) field on an IP packet is set to one, meaning any time the packet traverses a router, this is decremented to zero, and the packet cannot pass through another router. The bottom line is that only the printers in your locally attached segment will respond to your discovery request. In smaller networks, this might not be an issue, but in large corporate networks, this can be a significant limitation.

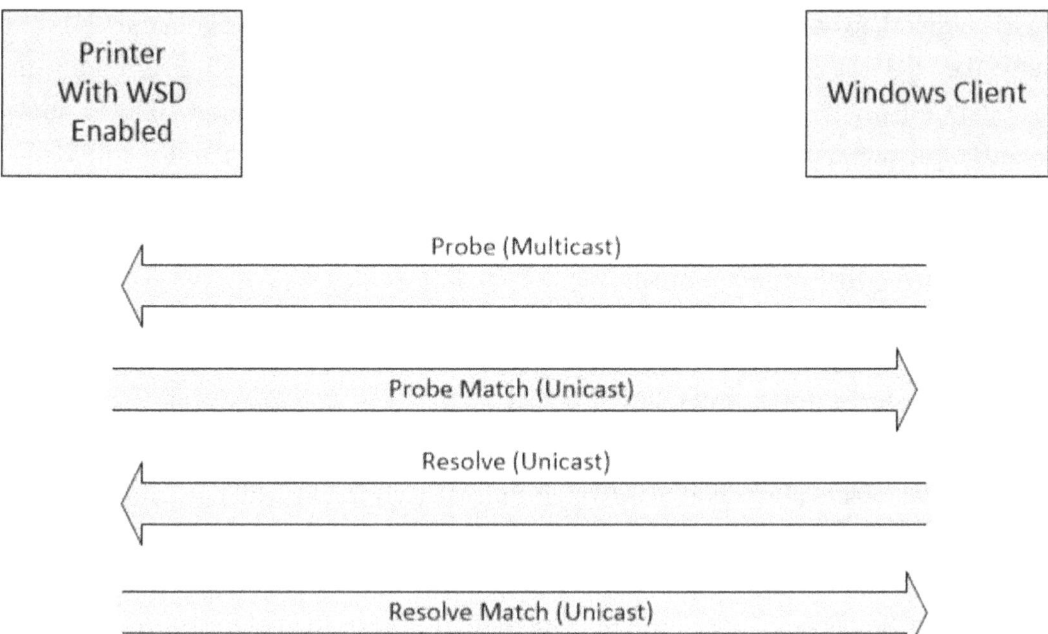

*WS-Discovery Protocol [**13**]*

In my own implementation of WSD for enterprise networks, the protocol worked well – provided all firewalls allow for the UDP multicast port 3702 exception. The one router hop limitation is an issue, as physical CAT-5/6 wiring does not always coincide with logical network layout. For instance, the printers nearest to your physical location may not be on the same IP subnet and therefore will not be discovered unless the 1 hop TTL is increased.

Overall, WSD was a decent concept and worked in practice, but never really gained traction. When introduced, the networked devices segment grew with various competing standards and technologies. Alternatives like Universal Plug and Play (UPnP) and more broadly adopted protocols had already established themselves, making it harder for WSD to gain traction. Despite this, I have included a utility in the code section of this chapter for WSD printer enumeration. The code will return the printers that respond to the WS-Discovery probe along with some basic print properties they are configured with. If you do decide to experiment with WSD, you will have to ensure that all print devices have the WSD service activated and they are within the 1 router hop limitation. For those willing to experiment, the router hop limitation can be modified (I show you how in the example code included with this chapter), but doing so increases variability in the results as network congestion and dropped packets (the multicast packet is UDP) will increase depending on the number of printers that answer the probe.

Despite the lack of adoption of the protocol by other vendors, Microsoft has employed WSD printer ports since the introduction of Windows Vista. In fact, WSD ports are an integral part of the IPP adoption plan for Windows 11. One issue I sometimes come across when troubleshooting WSD-connected printers is the abstraction created by using a GUID instead of clearly providing a URL or IP address in the property layout of the port. If you are unsure of the IP address or URL of a WSD printer port, click the "Configure Port Properties" button in the Ports tab of the printer properties page to find this information.

As I mentioned earlier, I am not aware of any official .NET libraries for WSD, but I have attempted to replicate what a probe for WSD printers might provide. You can view the WSDPrinterProbe solution yourself in the code section of this chapter, but a typical run (using 2 hops) on my computer displayed:

```
---------------------------------------------------------------------------
IP Address: 102.15.82.122
Uri: 102.15.82.122:3911/ http://[fe80::ca29:d2ff:fe2c:3839]:3911
Guid:uuid:4a504244-5a33-3635-3932-c8d9d2cc3839
wsdp:FriendlyName: HPLJ839 (HP LaserJet M402dn)
wsdp:FirmwareVersion: 20180201
wsdp:SerialNumber: JPBDZ36592
wsdp:ModelName: HP LaserJet M402dn
wsdp:ModelNumber: M402dn
wsdp:ModelUrl: http://www.hp.com/support/ljM402
wsdp:PresentationUrl: http://102.15.82.122:80/
wsdp:ManufacturerUrl: http://www.hp.com/
wsdp:ServiceId: http://www.hp.com/schemas/imaging/con/wsprint/2007/05/
hp_wsprint.wsdl
PNPX:HardwareId: VEN_03F0&DEV_M402DN&SUBSYS_01&REV_20180201 VEN_03F0&DEV_
M402DN&SUBSYS_01 VEN_03F0&DEV_M402DN
PNPX:CompatibleId: http://schemas.microsoft.com/windows/2006/08/wdp/print/
PrinterServiceType
---------------------------------------------------------------------------
```

```
IP Address: 102.229.66.118
Uri: 102.229.66.118:3911/ http://[fe80::f639:90f:fe25:f5f1]:3911
Guid:uuid:4a504244-5a33-3931-3531-f43909f5f5f1
wsdp:FriendlyName: HPLJ0Q5 (HP LaserJet M402dn)
wsdp:FirmwareVersion: 20180201
wsdp:SerialNumber: JPBDZ39151
wsdp:ModelName: HP LaserJet M402dn
wsdp:ModelNumber: M402dn
wsdp:ModelUrl: http://www.hp.com/support/ljM402
wsdp:PresentationUrl: http://102.229.66.118:80/
wsdp:ManufacturerUrl: http://www.hp.com/
wsdp:ServiceId: http://www.hp.com/schemas/imaging/con/wsprint/2007/05/
hp_wsprint.wsdl
PNPX:HardwareId: VEN_03F0&DEV_M402DN&SUBSYS_01&REV_20180201 VEN_03F0&DEV_
M402DN&SUBSYS_01 VEN_03F0&DEV_M402DN
PNPX:CompatibleId: http://schemas.microsoft.com/windows/2006/08/wdp/print/
PrinterServiceType
-------------------------------------------------------------------------
```

This can help identify the printer, the associated WSD port, and the URL employed by the print device attached to the port. As a reminder, for a printer to be discovered by the WSD probe, the Web Services protocol must be enabled on the printer. In addition, the command line argument for this utility specifies the default time to live as 2. Be cautious when testing higher limits than two since significant traffic can occur depending on the number of WSD-enabled printers on your network. In addition, any interleaving firewalls need to pass the WSD default port (3702).

Port Monitor Required Interfaces:

IPrintPortMonitor: The primary interface for port monitors.

Some Required Methods:

OpenPort: Opens a connection to the port.

ClosePort: Closes the connection.

WritePort: Sends data to the port.

ReadPort: Reads data from the port.

How Windows Enumerates Printers on the Network

When you click the "Add Device" button in the "Printers & scanners" settings on Windows 11, the system searches for available printers and scanners on the network. In large networks, you may notice printers that are not physically nearby appearing in the dialog. This happens because Windows uses network discovery protocols to locate devices. Specifically, Windows sends multicast messages, typically via mDNS (Multicast DNS) or WSD (Web Services Discovery), to which printers respond if these services are enabled. The printer replies to the multicast message with a service advertisement, sent as a unicast response to the address provided in the multicast message.

When the "Add Device" button is clicked, Windows broadcasts WSD Discovery packets over UDP port 3702. Printers on the network that support WSD respond with a unicast SOAP (XML) message containing details about the device, including its unicast address. Similarly, Windows sends mDNS multicast queries over UDP port 5353. Printers supporting mDNS respond (typically via multicast) with service information, such as support for IPP/IPPS in a non-XML format. Many printers support both mDNS and WSD and respond to both types of queries. Importantly, both WSD-Discovery and mDNS are sent with a Time-To-Live (TTL) value of 1, which means they are not forwarded beyond the local network segment by default. (The WSDPrinterProbe project lets you experiment with altering the Time to Live.) To observe the enumeration process, you can use a packet capture tool like Wireshark with the following capture filter to monitor mDNS and WSD traffic:

UDP port 5353 or UDP port 3702

Point and Print Using RPCs

At this point you know the possible port monitors used to transport the print job to a printer when using direct print. But you may be curious how a print job created on a computer using a printer shared off a server manages to get its print job placed in the target server's print spooler. Once it gets placed in the server print spooler, the path to the printer is identical to that used by the direct print process. To place the print job in the target server's print spooler, the local computer makes use of Remote Procedure Call (RPC). A little background for those who might not be familiar with what RPCs are and how they are used. Put simply, RPCs allow you to call a function that, instead of being executed on your local machine, is instead processed on a machine elsewhere on the network [7]. This allows networks to allocate computer hardware that can process RPC calls and free up local computer resources for the task. Let us look at how Point and Print uses RPC connections between the client and print server, and how the basic print process is remarkably similar to that of a local printer.

When a client attempts to use Point and Print to connect to a shared printer, it communicates with the RPC Endpoint Mapper to find the exact location of the server Print Spooler service. This is necessary because the actual port number the Print Spooler uses might vary each time the service starts. By using a consistent UUID, Windows ensures that clients running different OS versions or updates can still locate and interact with the Print Spooler service without needing adjustments or special configurations.

1. The client initiates a connection to the server's RPC Endpoint Mapper, typically on port 135, and requests the specific UUID 12345678-1234-ABCD-EF00-0123456789AB.

2. The server's RPC Endpoint Mapper checks its registry of services and their associated UUIDs. Upon finding the UUID, it identifies the associated Print Spooler service.

3. The Endpoint Mapper then returns the network endpoint (such as an IP address and port number) where the Print Spooler service is listening. If the spooler is using a dynamic port, this port will be included in the response.

4. Armed with the endpoint details, the client can now establish a direct RPC connection to the Print Spooler service on the server.

So, let us walk through the steps required for the client to submit a job on a remote print server using the RPC APIs that would be required. I want you to take notice of how careful Microsoft is on the RPC APIs to follow the function declarations of the GDI counterparts, which do a similar operation. To start off, the remote client would need to call RpcStartDocPrinter. This API notifies the print server that a document is being spooled for printing. Looking up the API on the Microsoft website, we can see the arguments required.

```
DWORD RpcStartDocPrinter([in] PRINTER_HANDLE hPrinter, [in] DOC_INFO_
CONTAINER* pDocInfoContainer, [out] DWORD* pJobId);
```

The hPrinter is a handle returned from a call to a function such as **RpcOpenPrinter**, which itself has an argument requesting the access level the client requires for this printer. **RpcStartDocPrinter** requires an unsigned integer pointer (pJobId), which will receive a print job identifier. The job will be created with an identifier that is unique to this printer. The next API to be used would be

```
DWORD RpcWritePrinter([in] PRINTER_HANDLE hPrinter,[in, size_is(cbBuf)]
BYTE* pBuf, [in] DWORD cbBuf,[out] DWORD* pcWritten);
```

This API takes the printer handle (as did **RpcStartDocPrinter**) and uses that to send the print job data (pBuf), whose buffer size must be provided by cbBuf. The out parameter (pcWritten) in turn receives the number of bytes of data that were written. Notice how similar **RpcWritePrinter** is to its GDI counterpart, the WritePrinter API, which does essentially the same operation.

```
BOOL WritePrinter([in]HANDLE hPrinter, [in]LPVOID pBuf,  [in]DWORD cbBuf,
[out] LPDWORD pcWritten );
```

Once the print job has been written to the spooler, the operation can be closed. To do this, the call **RpcEndDocPrinter** is used, which simply takes the printer handle as an argument.

```
DWORD RpcEndDocPrinter([in] PRINTER_HANDLE hPrinter);
```

Which again is very similar to the GDI version:

```
BOOL EndDocPrinter([in] HANDLE hPrinter);
```

Thus, creating and sending a print job to a directly connected printer is remarkably similar to doing so through a server print connection and only differs in using RPC calls to the server. This helps make the Windows print subsystem consistent and scalable across all OS versions. At this point we have finished investigating the process of creating and routing a print job. The next part of this chapter deals with troubleshooting the Windows print spooler service and identifying limitations of Windows workstations as print servers. We finish the chapter by analyzing some of the security concerns associated with downloading print drivers from a server.

Printing in Windows

So now that you understand some of the components of the print subsystem, you might be wondering how applications interact with the Windows API to print. For most applications, the Win32 Print Spooler APIs can be used. In fact, this is exactly what the printer common dialogs included in many integrated development environments (IDEs), such as Visual Studio, use. You can also use these APIs directly in your application if you desire more control of the process. I will not go into any of the API details as it is out of scope for this chapter; however, some of the more common Spooler APIs used to print are shown below.

> OpenPrinter - Opens a handle for the target printer.
>
> StartDocPrinter - Informs the spooler of a new document to be printed.
>
> StartPagePrinter - Informs the spooler of a new page to be printed.
>
> WritePrinter – Writes data to the spooled file.
>
> EndPagePrinter – Closing API call for StartPagePrinter.
>
> EndDocPrinter – Closing API call for StartDocPrinter.
>
> ClosePrinter – Closing API call for OpenPrinter.

You can also send a file with raw data (can be processed on the printer as is) to a printer without using the Spooler APIs. As mentioned in the section on port monitors, you can use Win32 APIs such as CreateFile to talk to I/O drivers, and we can employ the same tactic to send data directly to a printer.

I ran across this request dealing with some of our legacy mainframe applications that used active emulator sessions to print. The mainframe application has already formatted the data in PCL and only required a path to a printer. Thus, you can use the CreateFile API to open communications to the printer and then the SendFile API to send the data to the printer.

The Windows Print Spooler

Central to the efficient operation of the Windows print subsystem is the print spooler service. The spooler service is where jobs are rendered and finalized for printing, and whose efficient operation is thus critical. Though it sounds like a single component, the spooler service is composed of 2 parts: a user mode and a kernel mode component. This division was designed into the system for stability: in an intelligently designed client-server operating system, direct hardware access is not allowed. Instead, a user mode component is separated from the kernel mode component, and therefore any software bug or failure on the user mode side will not bring the entire operating system to a halt.

Conceptually, you should imagine the kernel mode component of the spooler system (win32k.sys) would deal with low-level port access and things like USB communications with various printer hardware endpoints. User mode components would deal with user interaction (dialogs, error messages) and print job rendering. Kernel mode also operates with a higher privilege level than do user mode components; this increases efficiency of operation while reducing security vulnerabilities common to software that interacts with the user.

A binary named spoolsv.exe is loaded as the user mode service that creates tasks like queuing print jobs, managing all the print queues, and interacting with print drivers to ensure jobs are ready for printing. A Windows service is usually an executable that runs with SYSTEM privilege (although this can be modified) and is designed to run continuously after system boot. The SYSTEM privilege bestowed on the spooler service allows it system access necessary to do the task but can represent a target for nefarious entities determined to wreak havoc. More on this in a bit, for now just remember that compromising the spooler service has been a high priority for hackers and a prime headache for administrators.

A key operation of the Windows print subsystem is, of course, rendering print jobs. This happens when the spooler service loads the requisite print driver. Do you remember the .spl and .shd files discussed earlier in this chapter when explaining how the GDI system works? The print processor uses the spooler service to read those SPL/SHD files and find the printer requested. As you now understand, the association made between the printer and the requisite print driver is one created in the registry when the print driver INF is installed (in Windows). It is from this association that the spooler service can now load the proper print driver into memory and process the .spl file in the queue. Of course, a print driver isn't just a single monolithic file but is composed of multiple binaries and DLLs that comprise the software libraries necessary to convert the .spl file into a format the print hardware can make use of. Think of the print driver as the container for the print processor, language monitor, print monitor, port monitor DLLs, and the INF file together with the GPD or PPD files.

Normally this operation (for well-written print drivers) is well designed and works well with the operating system - i.e., no exceptions are thrown to the processing software we call the print driver. But what if there are issues - what if the user mode print driver loaded into memory causes a software exception to be thrown? In this case, we must hope the exception is caught and does not go to the OS default exception handler. If not, the results are predictable: the process where the unhandled exception is thrown will be shut down to protect other software running on the system. If the process where the exception is thrown happens to be the spooler service (which has loaded the bad print driver to process a job), the service is shut down and printing on that machine halts.

During operation, what would cause a print driver to crash the spooler service? Typical culprits might be memory access violations (attempting to access memory not in your process), null pointer dereferences, race conditions (multiple threads trying to concurrently access a resource), egregious memory leaks, etc. Obviously, we can see the wisdom of separating the spooler system into discreet user and kernel mode components now. While Microsoft can ensure the kernel mode (and to some extent user mode) components are well vetted and tested, the ability to completely control vendors' print drivers' behavior is not realistic. To make matters worse, some poorly written print drivers that were written years ago and have not been updated take advantage of new security measures that ensure code integrity.

When the Windows print spooler system crashes, finding the culprit for the crash can be daunting. And while there are no absolute certainties when it comes to isolating the problem, there are strategies you can take to enhance your chances.

The initial place to check for issues would be in the Windows Log section of the Event Log in Windows. I start my search in the system log area as the print spooler is a system component, and error events are recorded here. To find print service issues, open Event Viewer and navigate to the Applications and Services Logs. Choose Microsoft, then Windows, and finally Print Service/Admin. As a test for log entries, I stopped the spooler service and then renamed tcpmon.dll to _tcpmon.dll. The tcpmon module is used to control printers directly connected to a TCP/IP network and thus is vital for talking to printers attached over the network. When trying to print to one of my port 9100 printers, the following entry was recorded in the event log:

> The print spooler failed to load a plug-in module tcpmon.dll, error code 0x7E. See the event user data for context information.

In this case, failure to locate an essential print service component registered as an event log entry. Unfortunately, not all print issues are this obvious and recorded in the Windows event log, so you might have to take more action to pin down the issue. Setting suspected troublesome drivers in driver isolation is an effective way to implicate or eliminate suspected drivers from your investigation. You can set suspected drivers in isolation and see if the print spooler continues to crash or if the crash goes away once the driver is put into isolation. This has the added benefit of not having to delete drivers or driver entries manually in Windows, so it can be a fast way to pin down the issue. Remember, though, that driver isolation takes up additional Windows memory and CPU resources, so this should be only a troubleshooting step, not a permanent fix.

Isolate Troublesome Drivers

Does your print driver support driver isolation? You can find this answer through the GUI or from the INF file used for installation. When looking at the INF file, locate the DriverIsolation keyword if it exists. Setting DriverIsolation=2 means the print driver supports driver isolation. If DriverIsolation=0, then the driver does not support driver isolation. If the DriverIsolation keyword does not exist in the INF file, the effect is setting DriverIsolation=0. As an example, looking at the INF file for my Epson WF-4734 printer:

```
[Version]
Signature       = "$Windows NT$"
Provider        = %EPSON%
ClassGUID       = {4D36E979-E325-11CE-BFC1-08002BE10318}
Class           = Printer
DriverVer=05/11/2020, 2.66.00.00
CatalogFile     = E_WF1QDE.CAT
DriverIsolation = 2
```

You can clearly see that it supports driver isolation in the event you want to test whether this driver is causing an issue. In terms of what settings you are allowed to use for driver isolation, Microsoft provides the following choices [15]:

Driver-isolation mode	Meaning
Shared	Run the driver in a process that is shared with other printer drivers but is separate from the spooler process.
Isolated	Run the driver in a process that is separate from the spooler process and is not shared with other printer drivers.
None	Run the driver in the spooler process.

If you cannot run your driver with the spooler service, the next best option would be to have it run in a shared environment with other drivers. In the event your driver is causing frequent spooler systems to crash, you might want to consider running it isolated. Of course, there are trade-offs to any choice, and in this case driver isolation takes up more system resources such as memory and CPU usage. This is because each isolated driver runs in its own instance of printisolationhost, so use driver isolation only if necessary. Sometimes, especially if you must use an outdated print driver, you have no choice, and it is a good option to use it in these cases.

You can set a print driver into isolation mode in all versions of Windows via the print management tool, except for the Home editions of Windows (the print management tool is not available with the Home edition). However, you can set print driver isolation in the Windows Home edition by using PowerShell:

```
Set-PrinterDriver -Name "YourPrinterDriverName" -Isolated
```

For other versions of Windows, the job is a bit easier and can be done in a GUI. For this I would recommend using the Print Management tool included in later versions of Windows. For Windows 11, you can navigate to this tool (except in the Home edition) by selecting Windows Tools from the menu and then selecting Print Management.

If this is the first time you have used Print Management, you will need to add your own computer to the utility as a Print Server. To do this, open the utility and right-click on Print Servers, then click on the Add/Remove Servers menu choice to add your computer as a print server. Once completed, you can view all the printers and print drivers that exist on your computer.

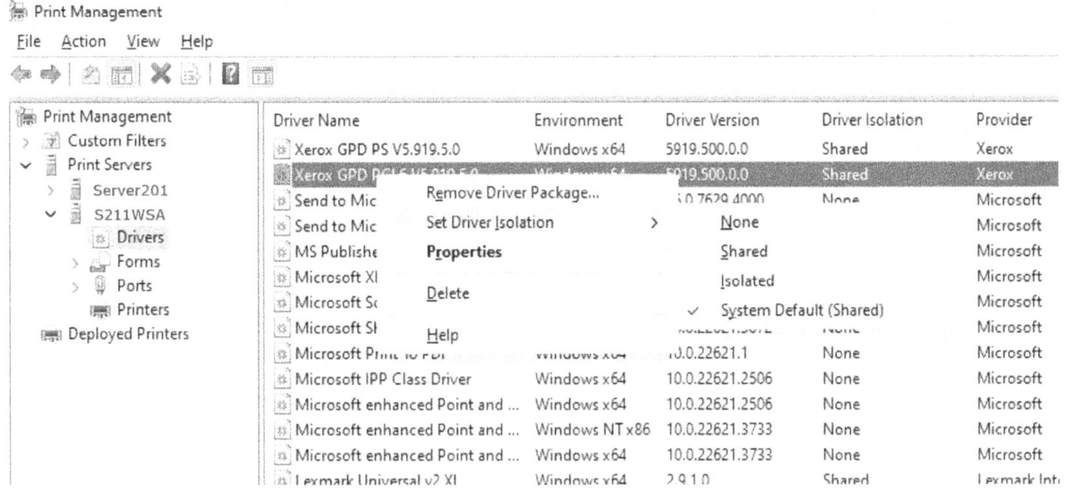

Print Management GUI

Also note that you might need to run the utility with higher privileges in the event you plan to modify the print setup. You can run as administrator by right-clicking the utility and selecting "Run As Administrator" if necessary.

To run a troubling print driver in driver isolation, expand the Drivers section under your computer (print server) and then click Drivers to review all the installed print drivers. At this point, you can right-click on a driver and choose "Set Driver Isolation" from the popup menu choice.

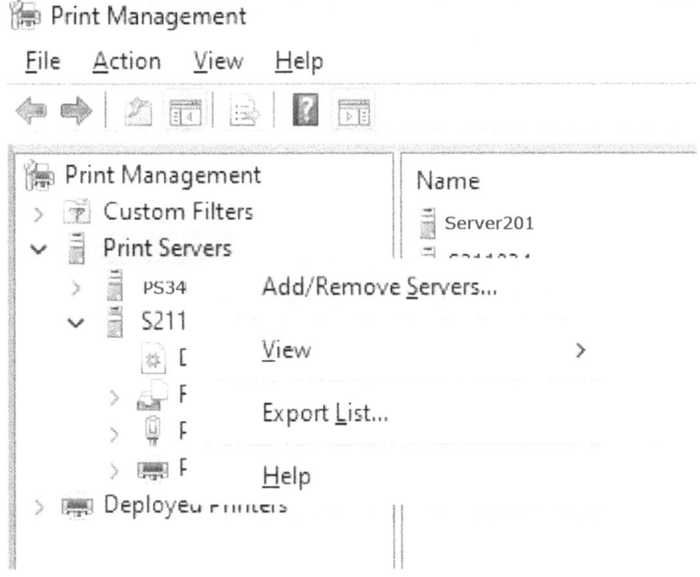

Setting a Print Driver in Isolated Mode

You can now choose to run your driver in total isolation (Isolated) or share a process with other print drivers (yet separate from the spooler process) by choosing Shared. Again, if you do choose Isolated, remember the tradeoff with resources for this step and contact the driver's manufacturer or find another driver to correct the issue. Obviously, if the print system issues with spooler crashes stop when a certain driver is isolated, this would be your clue for further investigation.

For particularly vexing issues (i.e., a spooler service that continually stops), you can employ Windows Debugging Tools to gather debug crash file information. In fact, your print driver vendor might want you to provide a crash dump file so they can more easily isolate the issue. The debugging tools are used to create a crash file that can later be analyzed to implicate the culprit.

To enable crash dumps for the spooler:

1. Open the Registry Editor (regedit).
2. Navigate to HKLM\SYSTEM\CurrentControlSet\Services\Spooler.
3. Create a new key named CrashOnCtrlBreak and set its value to 1.
4. When the spooler crashes, it will generate a dump file in %SystemRoot%\Minidump.

If you have a crash file, you can either send it to the vendor or Microsoft for analysis. If you have a copy of Visual Studio, it is easy to view the dump file if you are so inclined. To illustrate, I will walk through a print spooler crash and show you what to look for and how to use the crash dump file that was created.

The crash dump file created from my (renaming of tcpmon.dll) crashing spooler service is now in the C:\Temp\CrashDumps folder and is called Spoolsv.dmp. I had several dump files, and each subsequent dump file got an integer appended to it. Once the dump file is created, we can look at the contents in Visual Studio to get an idea of what is causing the spooler service to hiccup. To do this, start Visual Studio, click Open under the File menu, and then choose Crash Dump...

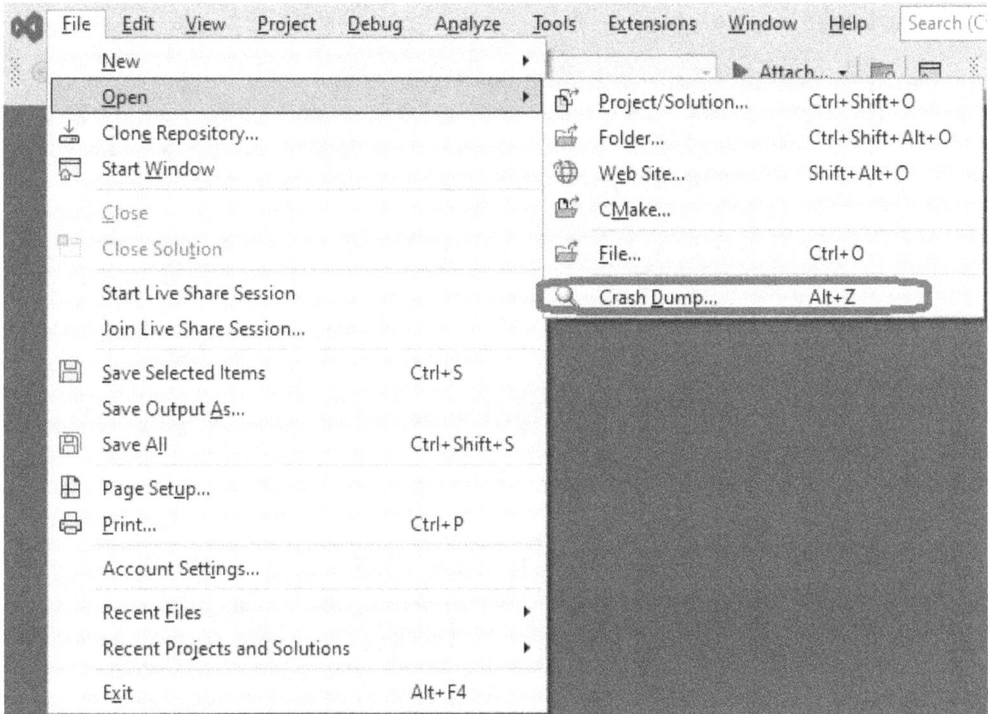

Loading a Crash Dump File in Visual Studio

Choose the crash dump file you want to open, then look in the Debugger Immediate Window. It is likely you will not have the symbol file(s) necessary to associate the hex address to module names in code, but your vendor should.

Unless you are familiar with assembly (and even then, if you do not have the symbol file(s)), the data collected will not be immediately helpful, but you can glean some valuable information if you let Visual Studio analyze the dump file. To do this, type **!analyze -v** in the text box at the bottom of the Debugger Immediate Window and then hit Enter.

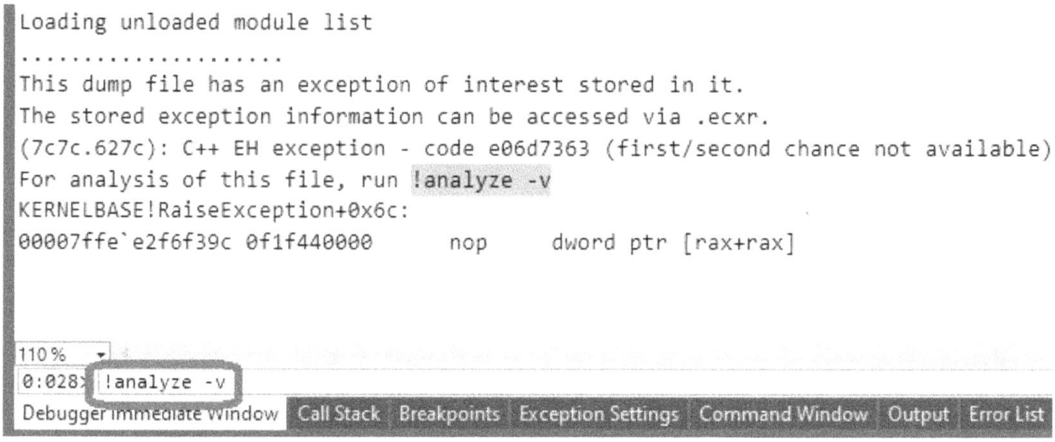

```
Loading unloaded module list
.....................
This dump file has an exception of interest stored in it.
The stored exception information can be accessed via .ecxr.
(7c7c.627c): C++ EH exception - code e06d7363 (first/second chance not available)
For analysis of this file, run !analyze -v
KERNELBASE!RaiseException+0x6c:
00007ffe`e2f6f39c 0f1f440000      nop     dword ptr [rax+rax]

110 %
0:028> !analyze -v
Debugger Immediate Window | Call Stack | Breakpoints | Exception Settings | Command Window | Output | Error List
```

Analyze the Crash Dump File in Visual Studio

For my crash file, you can see that the process running was the user mode spooler component spoolsv. You should also get an exception code and the address of the exception.

```
ExceptionAddress: 00007ffee2f6f39c (KERNELBASE!RaiseException+0
x000000000000006c)
   ExceptionCode: e06d7363 (C++ EH exception)
  ExceptionFlags: 00000081
NumberParameters: 4
   Parameter[0]: 0000000019930520
   Parameter[1]: 0000000002fdcc90
   Parameter[2]: 00007ffebfe26e80
   Parameter[3]: 00007ffebfe10000

PROCESS_NAME:  spoolsv.exe

ERROR_CODE: (NTSTATUS) 0xe06d7363 - <Unable to get error code text>
```

The analyze command added the stack frame seen at the time of the crash and the module that caused the exception to be thrown. It's important to understand that although the spooler system process was affected, the culprit could be dependent on files used by the spooler system. In my case, the analysis showed the error originated in msvcrt.dll, which is the Microsoft C runtime library. With this data in hand, you can send your vendor the .dmp file that was created for further analysis.

Print Server versus Workstation

Not well known is that your local Windows computer also runs a server service. Because of this, small offices can make use of a Windows workstation (as opposed to a Windows server) to provide print server services, just like a Windows server. Thus, for a small office, you could provide Point and Print convenience without having to buy Windows Server. However, you should know that there is a limit to the number of RPC print connections the workstation will allow. According to Microsoft documentation, the limit is 10 concurrent print connections that can be maintained on Windows 11 Enterprise computers before the print connections get rejected. How does the Windows OS know the number of concurrent print connections, you might ask? It boils down to the number of RPC connections incoming that the OS keeps track of. You can see this for yourself by using the **netstat -a command** line utility. The -q switch "Displays all connections, listening ports, and bound non listening TCP ports." If you do a netstat -q query on a computer prior to any remote print connections being established and then compare that to a netstat -q query after creating a print connection from another machine to your target machine, you can see the difference.

The number of concurrent connections is increased for every print connection made from a remote machine. In the case of an office where a computer has three print connections and another computer has four print connections, the total is counted as seven print connections even though these were made from only two Windows machines. Once you exceed the total number of allowed print connections, subsequent print connection attempts (from remote computers) will fail. Keep this in mind if you are planning to use a Windows 11 desktop as a print server.

Printer Management

Modern print hardware involves multiple discrete components to provide the seamless delivery of printed output. Processors, stepper motors, lasers, servos, and rotating assemblies, not to mention operating systems and firmware interaction, must operate at peak efficiency. Consumables, including toner, paper, and fusers, must also be managed to ensure continuous operation. In a business, decisions are best made on data collected from the printer units in production. In the IP world, the Simple Network Management Protocol (SNMP) has been the Internet standard to provide this data about managed devices. The idea was to embed a software agent on the remote device that provides information about select components that might be of interest and send this data back to a management station. IT components such as routers, terminal servers, and printers are just some of the devices managed by SNMP. The communication may be bidirectional: the manager requesting specific values from the agent, or the agent providing event status to the manager [19].

Enterprises employ SNMP to access printer availability, status, toner and paper levels, printer model, serial number, firmware level, page counts, etc. The SNMP protocol for this interaction can fetch values, set values, or provide event messages to alert the management station operator. The protocol can be intricate when the protocol's data structure and object mapping are considered. It should follow that to retrieve information from an object across the network, you need to know:

1. That the object exists and is defined.
2. Where the object is on the target.

To fulfill the above requirements, the Management Information Base (MIB) was conceived. The MIB provides an essential structure of object definitions that the remote agent manages. The object definition has a human-readable format together with an Object Identifier (OID). When the manager decides to get a value from the remotely managed agent, the human-readable format chosen is then converted to the OID value that the agent understands.

Version:	SNMPv1
Community:	public
PDU Type:	GET Request
Request ID:	123
Error Status:	0
Error Index:	0
Variable Bindings: OID: Value:	 1.3.6.1.4.1.343 Value: NULL

MIB Packet Structure

The OID has a hierarchical tree structure with each object separated by dots (.) in the tree. Each level represents a company or organization and their managed objects, arranged in a top-down format. When the remote agent gets the packet, it can then retrieve the value being sought within its own database. To ensure the protocol was fast and efficient, the developers of SNMP chose the User Datagram Protocol (UDP) over Transmission Control Protocol (TCP). Because of this, some packets or requests may be dropped, so there is no guarantee of delivery. While SNMP has been the standard for Internet management since the 90s, it does require management software and MIBs specific to the object being managed. As you might imagine, in the printer world this can sow some confusion as there are multitudes of vendor offerings available. To quell some of the criticism, the Network Working Group developed RFC 3805, which is a standard printer MIB that most print hardware manufacturers agree to support. Despite the advantages of a mutually supported printer MIB, in many cases more features, capabilities, and granular control are often found with MIBs specific to the vendor for print hardware.

If you would like to peek at what type of information can be gleaned from a printer using the RFC3805 mib, there is a solution (PrinterInfo) in the code section of this chapter. It uses the excellent SnmpSharpNet library to recover information from target printers. For this to work, you will need to know what community string is used on the target printer(s). The default SNMP version is set at 2 (in the CSnmp.cs file), which can be modified as you want.

Printer Object Security

Like many objects in Windows, a printer is secured by an Access Control List (ACL), which contains Access Control Entries (ACEs) from trustees. By providing discretionary access control entries, administrators can effectively control what actions can be performed on the printer. Windows employs access tokens to identify the user when a thread interacts with a securable object (i.e., printer). Every process has a primary token that describes the security context of the user account associated with the process. By default, the system uses the primary token when a thread of the process interacts with a securable object [20]. For printer objects, available permissions consist of Print, Manage Printer, Manage Documents, or some special combination of ACEs. You can either allow or deny these permissions to users or groups as necessary.

The permissions applied to a printer object in Windows are obviously not on the physical printer itself, but rather on the computer registry location HKLM\Software\Microsoft\Windows NT\CurrentVersion\Print\Printers\<printer_name>\Security (name/value) pair.

For the curious wanting to understand what printer permissions are available, the following list should provide a starting point. Remember that Print/Manage Documents/Manage Printers is a grouped collection of Access Control Entries (ACEs) that have a name. You can see this if you look at the PrintSecurity code I had written many years ago that provides a console utility that automates the modification of ACEs in the discretionary ACL on printers in Windows. This code is available to experiment with and is included in this chapter's code section. Look at the Ace.cpp file if you are curious how the explorer – viewable permission sets are created.

Print – This permission allows users to print, pause, resume, start, and cancel their own documents on printers. Members of the Everyone group are given this permission when a print queue is created.

Manage Documents – This permission allows users to change or modify individual print job settings for documents. Users assigned this permission can also delete, pause, and restart documents.

Manage Printers – This permission provides the user with the ability to change printer settings such as printer sharing, spooler settings, printer permissions, etc.

While Windows GUI provides the best way to adjust these permissions, in an enterprise network you might need to modify printer permissions via automation or through a scripted method. In the code section of this chapter is the PrintSecurity solution written in C/C++ that provides the ability to add/modify/view the discretionary ACL of a printer object from the command line. To modify or change the printer ACL, you will need to be a member of a group that can do so, or you will receive the Access Denied (Win32 Error 5) error. You can run the utility for permission for a single printer or for all (hardware) printers enumerated on the computer. When running this utility on my Windows 11 machine for all printers enumerated, the following is the result.

```
C:\PrintSecurity>Printsecurity /ALL /E domain\User2:FC
-64 bit PrintSecurity-
------Permissioning: Printer1------
Successfully permissioned: Printer1
------Permissioning: Printer2------
Successfully permissioned: Printer2
------Permissioning: Printer3------
Successfully permissioned: Printer3
------Permissioning: Printer4------
Successfully permissioned: Printer4
------Permissioning: Printer5------
Successfully permissioned: Printer5
```

The utility grants Full Control permission to User2 for all the printers enumerated. By default, the utility will not permission printers it feels are software-only printers, like OneNote or Print to PDF. If you are so inclined (and have some knowledge of C/C++), you can change this default behavior.

Print Job Cancellation

You might be surprised to learn that cancelling a print job in Windows does not actually remove the job from the printer itself – rather, you are requesting the print provider to remove the .spl and .shd file associated with the print job from the spooler. Depending on whether the binary print stream data has already been stored in the physical printer memory or not, deleting the job may not actually stop the physical printout on the printer. In most cases, you will need to reboot the printer to clear the binary data from printer memory in addition to removing the spooled job in Windows. This is one area where IPP provides an improved way to stop the job from completing the physical printer and/or halts any physical printout in progress.

Some Issues with Legacy Print

At this point, you should have an idea of how a print job in Windows is processed on the local machine and then sent to the target printer for printout. While this process has proven to be durable and (considerably less) scalable, it is obvious that there are a lot of discrete components required to make it happen. Think about what we have investigated: the print provider, the print processor, the language monitor, various port monitors, not to mention a host of GPD/PPD configuration files. This is the basic list when we use the universal driver framework; when we use a custom vendor-supplied print driver, it is much more extensive. These components (port monitor, print monitor, etc.) are recognized as DLLs or binaries such as *.exe files. Of course, these files are required to be installed on the client prior to submitting a print stream to the printer; on direct (Microsoft uses "local" printer terminology), this installation requires the user to pick a vendor and a legitimate download source and hold administrative rights on the Windows computer to do so. For point and print clients, this installation (or update) process happens after the server print connection is referenced by the client. You know as well that the actual print operation for direct printing and server print connections is virtually identical except for the fact that a server print connection uses RPC calls to place the rendered job on the server's print spooler. You also know that a printer shared off a server requires the requisite print driver files to be downloaded from the server in the event they are not identical to the files on the client.

In a perfect world where computer hackers and nefarious elements do not exist, this reliance on remote file sources would not pose an issue. Unfortunately, we do not live in a perfect world, and this reliance on remote file sources provides a distinct security exposure issue. At best, a hacker might alter required binaries or configuration files to print out annoying messages on corporate print hardware. Unfortunately, there exists a real possibility of remote execution schemes designed to damage or reveal corporate data, compromise security features, or just deny the usage of key computer resources to the user.

As an example of a silly trick that works on most port 9100 connected printers, type in the following on your browser address bar:

http://<printer url>:9100

For instance, if your printer's name were printer23, you would type in `http://printer23:9100` and watch as the browser tries to connect. The browser will just sit and never display any content since what is running on port 9100/TCP is not actually a web server [21]. Click the stop button on your browser, and you should see something like that shown below print out (depending on your web browser).

```
GET / HTTP/1.1
Host: hpm528:9100
Connection: keep-alive
DNT: 1
Upgrade-Insecure-Requests: 1
User-Agent: Mozilla/5.0 (Windows NT 10.0; Win64; x64) AppleWebKit/537.36 (KHTML,
Accept: text/html,application/xhtml+xml,application/xml;q=0.9,image/avif,image/w
Accept-Encoding: gzip, deflate
Accept-Language: en-US,en;q=0.9
```

This is an example of how port 9100 print can be exploited, even if the exploit was by accident. In large organizations where security probes of TCP ports are common, you will find complaints of wasted paper output from probe connection attempts. Imagine what might happen if nefarious agents could make repeated connection attempts to your corporate print fleet that operates on port 9100.

PrintNightmare

As you may recall, the convenience of Microsoft Point and Print technology allowed a user to connect to a shared printer off the server and seamlessly download any requisite driver software to the host Windows computer necessary to print. If the local computer already has the printer software resident, the cabinet file package on the server is queried to see if the files on both client and server match. If client and server files do not match, the requisite files are downloaded from the server to remedy the situation. Since the Windows print spooler service runs with elevated privileges (by default SYSTEM access), it can load and execute all the print subsystem components (print processor, language monitor, print monitor, and port monitor) necessary to manage the print system. While this allows the spooler service to process available job requests, it also provides access for nefarious entities to introduce software that can potentially compromise the client's computer.

The now famous Print Nightmare (CVE-2021-34527) revealed these vulnerabilities inherent in the Print Spooler service used on Windows. This vulnerability allowed nefarious groups to gain remote code execution (RCE) capabilities and execute malicious code on affected systems. By gaining remote code execution ability, client data could be modified or exposed, and software could be installed or removed from hapless (and unfortunately unaware) clients. Despite Cyclic Redundancy Checks (CRCs), digital certificates, hashing functions and code signing protection, attackers have found ways to gain RCE abilities using the client spooler system.

One example involves creating a driver that contains malicious code but appears legitimate. This software is designed to harm the client by introducing deliberate harmful actions such as disabling security software or creating backdoors. The attackers either trick a trusted source into signing the code or use stolen certificates to enhance legitimacy. This is particularly effective as security software on the client may trust drivers signed by reputable sources, which allows the malicious code to bypass security checks. Once a driver is installed on the client, it runs under enhanced security privileges used by the Windows spooler system and is thus free to inflict harmful actions on the client.

Another way of gaining RCE is through GDP and PPD parsing, or in this case, inserting malicious data into a GPD file to be parsed. The attacker is hoping the rogue DLL will be loaded into memory under the security context assigned to the account running the spooler system.

One of the answers to these security vulnerabilities was to require the client to only download Point and Print drivers from trusted sources such as a trusted print server. To do this, Microsoft provided a Group Policy Object (GPO) that listed print servers considered trusted by network administrators. Once the Print Nightmare fix was installed on the clients, they would not download drivers from print servers not explicitly listed in the group policy in their domain. While this can provide some protection, it is not foolproof and is clumsy in practice to employ. This fix may not address the root issue: downloading driver software will always be a point of exploitation. As it happens, a better, more secure way to print exists.

Microsoft Goes IPP

Faced with a legacy print subsystem that was proving difficult to manage and a source of security concerns, Microsoft hinted about intentions to gravitate toward IPP. In fact, Microsoft has encouraged administrators to switch to IPP when possible and encouraged industry partners to switch to IPP-based printing [16]. The article “A new, modern, and secure print experience from Windows” by Johnathan Norman was one of the first indications that Windows was adopting IPP in reaction to the print nightmare issue. Adopting IPP should mitigate some of the outstanding security concerns, especially regarding Point and Print. From the Microsoft perspective, moving away from driver-based printing offers many benefits to users and allows Microsoft to make many meaningful improvements to their print system [16]. The existing driver-based system, established decades ago, depends on many third parties and Microsoft all playing their role, which has proven to be too cumbersome for modern threats.

Taking this a step further was the introduction of Windows Protected Print (WPP) by Microsoft. According to Microsoft, WPP builds on the existing IPP print stack and further secures the print environment. WPP stipulates that only Mopria-certified printers are supported and disables the ability to load third-party drivers (read vendor V3 legacy drivers). This was intended, according to Microsoft, to make meaningful improvements to print security in Windows that otherwise would not happen [16]. One of the features of WPP was to restrict print DLLs to accepting only values that make sense in the IPP world, thus closing off another avenue of security concerns.

By July 2025, Microsoft will no longer introduce new printer drivers in Windows Update. Further, by 2027, updates to third-party printer drivers will not be allowed [17]. This means V3 and V4 print drivers are in fact being deprecated in the move to adopt the IPP print protocol. The need to understand IPP and how it works is essential to ensuring your Microsoft network maintains efficiency and reduces the vector of attack from nefarious agents.

Chapter Summary

This chapter covers a lot of ground on how the legacy Windows print subsystem works. We started by discussing direct print and shared print connections (Point and Print) and the reasons one would employ them. Point and Print is popular with users and admins alike for the sheer convenience it bestows on the user community. For many years, it also provided a terrific way to implement new and updated print driver packages without having to install them on each computer in the enterprise. We then move on to investigate how print hardware-specific data is known to the operating system, i.e., how print driver data is installed on the OS itself. Detailed are the print-specific registry hives that contain this data and how this is fleshed out by the printer INF file during installation. The reliance on configuration files, unsecure code in drivers, and GPD/PPD files by the OS underscores the concerns Microsoft had about preventing nefarious agents from achieving remote code execution. The crux of the matter is that the legacy print subsystem relied on insecure technology, and there was no real way to fix that. The chapter touched on the driver store, why it was employed, and how to view drivers (particularly print drivers) in the store. We trace a print job on the port 9100 protocol and show how to trace this with Wireshark. Most importantly, the process of saving and then converting the original job back to readable format (when captured using a network sniffer such as Wireshark) reveals the transport as clear text. The fact that your print jobs (using LPR/Port 9100 protocols) can be easily viewed in original text (using network capture techniques) is a major issue with these legacy protocols. This alone warrants a review of enterprise print technology employed.

The chapter goes into Page Description Languages (PDL), how and why they are used to foment and replicate document data. Principal Windows print paths (GDI/XPS) are reviewed, with emphasis on the GDI path and how data is translated from document format into a format the printer will understand. Examined are the principal Windows print components employed, starting with the Spooler Router, whose job entails delivering the print job to the proper Print Provider. Next up is the Print Provider, essentially the job manager, which provides user interfaces to stop/start/delete the print job. Following that is the Print Processor, the main data conversion engine, which allows the print job to render successfully (at the page level) on the target printer. We discuss the Language Monitor, essentially the "job level" manager that formats the overall job, provides status updates from the printer, and provides job tracking. Typically, the Language Monitor uses a Print Job Language (PJL) to accomplish this. Finally, we get to the principal Port Monitors, which direct how to transfer the job from the Windows computer to the intended printer. The different port monitors are discussed including USB port monitor, TCP port monitor, and WSD port monitor. To cap this off, we investigate how Remote Procedure Calls (RPCs) are employed in the Windows print process.

The chapter changes gear a bit and investigates some troubleshooting procedures for issues pertaining to the print subsystem and the spooler service. We look at using the Windows workstation (instead of Windows Server) as a print server and the possible shortfalls endemic to this approach. SNMP and its constituent components are discussed with emphasis on how it provides useful counters (managed by an agent on the printer) to a management station that uses MIBs to abstract the OID hierarchy that does the heavy lifting. Finally, we end up discussing Print Nightmare and how this event convinced Microsoft to transition the future of print on its flagship OS to IPP/IPPS.

References

1. GPD File Extension, https://fileinfo.com/extension/gpd
2. Using Multiple GPD Files in a Minidriver, https://learn.microsoft.com/en-us/windows-hardware/drivers/print/using-multiple-gpd-files-in-a-minidriver
3. The standard port monitor for TCP/IP, Microsoft, https://learn.microsoft.com/en-us/troubleshoot/windows-server/printing/standard-port-monitor-for-tcpip
4. Printing documents overview(WPF .NET), Microsoft, https://learn.microsoft.com/en-us/dotnet/desktop/wpf/documents/printing-overview?view=netdesktop-8.0
5. Port Monitors, https://learn.microsoft.com/en-us/windows-hardware/drivers/print/port-monitors, Microsoft
6. Introduction to Point and Print, https://learn.microsoft.com/en-us/windows-hardware /drivers/print/introduction-to-point-and-print, Microsoft, 01/02/2024.
7. Remote Procedure Calls, Win32 System Services page 373, Marshall Brain.
8. Language Monitors, Microsoft, https://learn.microsoft.com/en-us/windows-hardware/drivers/print/language-monitors
9. Print Job Language (PJL), Hewlett Packard, https://developers.hp.com/hp-printer-command-languages-pcl/doc/print-job-language-pjl
10. Configuration Modules Based on GPD or PPD Files, Microsoft, https://learn.microsoft.com/en-us/windows-hardware/drivers/print/configuration-modules-based-on-gpd-or-ppd-files
11. Unidrv, Microsoft, https://en.wikipedia.org/wiki/Unidrv
12. About Web Services on Devices, Microsoft, https://learn.microsoft.com/en-us/windows/win32/wsdapi/about-web-services-for-devices
13. Figure 7, Research Gate, WS-Discovery Message Sequence | Download Scientific Diagram (researchgate.net)
14. Device Identification Strings, Microsoft, https://learn.microsoft.com/en-us/windows-hardware/drivers/install/device-identification-strings
15. Print Driver Isolation. Microsoft, https://learn.microsoft.com/en-us/windows-hardware /drivers/print/printer-driver-isolation
16. A new, modern, and secure print experience from Windows, A new, modern, and secure print experience from Windows - Microsoft Community Hub, Johnathan Norman/Microsoft

17. End of servicing plan for third-party printer drivers on Windows, End of Servicing Plan for Third-Party Printer Drivers on Windows - Windows drivers | Microsoft Learn, barrygolden, mhopkins-msft, Mikebell-msft
18. CreateFileW function, CreateFileW function (fileapi.h) - Win32 apps | Microsoft Learn, Microsoft Learn.
19. TCP/IP Illustrated Volume 1, page 359, W. Richard Stevens
20. Access Tokens, `https://learn.microsoft.com/en-us/windows/win32/secauthz/access-tokens`, Microsoft Learn Challenge, 1/7/2021
21. Stupid Printer Tricks, `https://www.irongeek.com/i.php?page=security/networkprinterhacking`, Adrian “Irongeek” Crenshaw.

CHAPTER 2

Printer Talk

This chapter intends to explain the basics of how IPP printers let the OS know what attributes they provide. Contrary to how this was done in legacy print, in the IPP world this information is delivered dynamically each time the printer is queried rather than relying on configuration files. Because the printer supplies this information rather than the client relying on a driver, the client can request that information every time the printer is used. If you are just interested in learning some of the concepts without delving too deeply into the implementation of the protocol, this chapter should fit the bill. If you like to tinker around with example code to pursue a more thorough insight into IPP, this chapter can help there as well.

Before we begin, we should review the way the Windows subsystem works. For any given printer, the unique features and attributes of the printer are provided to Windows by installing the print driver specified by the manufacturer. Up until Windows 2000, each printer required a unique driver written for it, which could take up a lot of disk space and proved to be cumbersome to manage. A few years back, many vendors started issuing "universal drivers" intended to quell the criticism they received for this less-than-optimal arrangement. However welcome the new universal drivers proved to be, some of the underlying issues remained. For direct print scenarios, users were encouraged to update the universal driver when newer versions of the driver were introduced, and users were still required to have administrative access to their machines to do so. Yes, system administrators could pre-stage drivers in the driver store (users can install local printers in Windows if the driver is resident in the driver store), but what happens when a vendor introduces new print hardware that requires a driver update? For Point and Print scenarios, the print server was the staging point for driver software, and updates to the server print driver would conveniently flow to the client upon connection. For those companies that did not use Point and Print, the print driver upgrade process was cumbersome if it happened at all.

J. Marion, *Adopting Internet Printing Protocol for Windows*, https://doi.org/10.1007/979-8-8688-2010-6_2

Getting Information About the Printer

Ideally, for the printer to properly replicate (in hard page output) what the user envisioned, all the features the printer might provide should be available (to the user) before the page is sent to the printer. In other words, the client-side process needs to know all the available characteristics of the hardware printer. In legacy print systems, this required information about the printer that was provided by a host of DLLs and configuration files - in other words, the print driver provided this information source. For shared print connections off a print server, these drivers were downloaded from the print server. As you might have gleaned from Chapter 1, "Windows Legacy Print," downloading print drivers presented an opportunity for malicious intent. Unfortunately, the integrity of this process (downloading print drivers from the server) was found wanting as nefarious agents often employed malware to gain remote code execution ability on the client. Truly, a better solution was required.

Ideally, the printer itself could provide the source of information about its capabilities. Clients could connect to the printer and dynamically (versus static configuration files) create a print request based on what printer capabilities were available. This way, no static print driver would be required to formulate print requests, and the client could form a "dynamic print driver" to use. Moreover, the capabilities and attributes of any given printer would always be current even after hardware or firmware updates. This also works in the mobile world; the client requires no special software to connect to and print document files. The Internet Print Protocol (IPP) provides an operation Get-Printer-Attributes, which provides exactly what clients would need to understand the capabilities of the printer. By executing this operation, an IPP client learns the target printer's attributes and capabilities. This chapter will concentrate on the Get-Printer-Attributes operation and provide some detail as to how it works.

A brief history of IPP should be in order here. Development of the IPP project started back in 1996 as a proposal by Novell and Xerox Corporations. About the same time IBM proposed the Hypertext Printing Protocol (HTPP) while HP and Microsoft commenced work on new print services for Windows 2000. These companies proposed a common standard leading to the IETF Printing Protocol group, which concluded in 2005. This work continues in the IPP Workgroup of the ISTO Printer Working Group (PWG), which consists of 23 candidate standards with 1 new and 3 updated IETF RFCs defining the protocol, which is now an Internet Standard.[1] Successive IPP versions 1.0, 1.1, and 2.0,

[1] IPP/1.1 is now Internet Standard 92 (https://www.rfc-editor.org/info/std92)

as well as several extension specifications, continue technological development by adding new attributes and features to the original standard [9].

In Windows 11, Microsoft introduces **Modern Print**, a concept to upgrade the legacy print platform for the OS [1]. According to Microsoft Learn, Modern Print is the preferred way for clients to communicate with print hardware. Modern print implemented IPP and Mopria technology on Windows 10 and has expanded that support for Windows 11 [4]. Upgrades for Windows 11 include support for IPP over USB (`https://www.usb.org/document-library/ipp-protocol-10`), allowing driverless print over USB connections. Mopria, IPP Everywhere, and AirPrint are competing technologies that allow for print without the need to install print drivers. The main differences between them are the PDLs supported: IPP Everywhere supports PWG Raster, JPEG, and PDF, while Mopria supports PCLm, PWG Raster, and PDF [5]. Additionally, IPP Everywhere is a completely open standard, while Mopria was developed more for mobile technology. The goal is to secure and streamline the printing system compared to traditional print architectures. Microsoft acknowledged the proliferation of print driver software made verifying the integrity of the drivers themselves almost impossible. Additionally, having the attributes of the printer disseminated to the clients dynamically as required keeps configuration headaches down as compared to the legacy method of installing drivers to provide this information.

An important aspect of enhanced print system stability and security is Windows Protected Print (WPP) Mode, an attempt by Microsoft to reduce the security concerns attached to the legacy Windows print subsystem. As mentioned in Chapter 1, "Windows Legacy Print," the lack of standards amongst print manufacturers required Windows to support multitudes of Page Description Languages (PDLs), which allowed inherent security flaws to creep in. When you consider the fact that the Windows spooler service runs with elevated privileges, the attraction for malicious intent is readily apparent. To run in WPP mode, only Mopria-certified print hardware and IPP-attached printers will be allowed. Since Mopria supports only a limited PDL set, a simpler and less vulnerable print process can be realized. Additionally, Microsoft plans to reduce the supported API set for the spooler process when WPP is activated. For instance, APIs that load external libraries, like AddPrintProvider, will not be supported, and thus, potentially malicious outside modules will not have the potential to cause havoc. Finally, Point and Print (under WPP mode) will be prevented from loading third-party print drivers, thus reducing another attack vector. Below outlines Microsoft's aggressive plan to phase out updates of third-party drivers on the Windows platform.

Timeline	Plan
September 2023	Announced legacy third-party printer driver for Windows end of servicing plan.
07/01/2025	No new printer drivers will be published in Windows Update. Existing printer drivers on Windows Update can still be updated but are approved on a case-by-case basis.
07/01/2026	The printer driver ranking order is modified to always prefer the Windows IPP inbox class driver.
07/01/2027	Except for security-related fixes, third-party printer driver updates will no longer be allowed.

For those readers working in corporate or enterprise networks, enabling WPP should be a priority, if only for the reduction in security concerns. Microsoft reports that print bugs played a role in 9% of all Windows cases reported [7].

In this chapter, we will delve into the Get-Printer-Attributes request from a high-level vantage point, and in the next chapter, we will drill down into the details of how the protocol works. Thus, if your mission is to just understand the basics of the protocol on Windows and you do not have a need to fully understand the details, you might elect to read just this chapter and skip parts of the next. I will provide code examples for this chapter based on WinRT's Devices. The printer's namespace abstracts away the details and lets the reader get the concept without undue clutter. I should first provide information on the development libraries currently (as of the writing of this book) available to the developer and the advantages or disadvantages to their selection. If you plan to develop or employ production IPP code in your Windows enterprise, or you know a developer who is tasked with doing so, the choices boil down to

1. The Microsoft IPP Class Driver and WinRT library
2. The OpenPrinting IPP port to Windows

To be sure, there are other libraries or frameworks available. Looking around on the internet, you may find a few others that can also do the job. I recommend these two primarily because of active support, the former by Microsoft and the latter by the Linux Foundation's OpenPrinting group. I have used both, and your choice of which to use on the Windows platform really depends on your project's intentions.

1. Microsoft uses their WinRT library to retrieve printer attributes (of the target printer) for integration into the print subsystem. It also provides the print hardware attributes and properties previously obtained (using non-IPP printers) by the print driver configuration and installation files. Once the IPP printer is installed in the system, the print chores are handled by the Microsoft IPP Class driver. The MS IPP class driver seamlessly integrates IPP into the legacy print subsystem and the spooling process. Because this provides IPP services to the legacy print subsystem, leveraging this architecture would be the logical choice for projects whose integration with the OS is important. Support for issues should be good as Microsoft bases adoption of Windows Protected Print (WPP) on this same architecture. There are some issues with the implementation of the IPP standard that I have found. One issue is authentication: when a username and password are set on the printer, no callback mechanism is currently provided to request user credentials. As a result, when credentials are set on the printer and a print operation is requested, it will fail and provide an error rather than request credentials from the requester. This issue may be fixed by Microsoft later, but as of this writing it is still outstanding. Another issue I found disappointing was the lack of helpful information about any printing request errors that may arise: the information provided is generic in nature. For instance, when a print job fails, opening the print queue will reveal the failed job, but no helpful information (or error codes) about the failure is provided to the client to track down the cause of the issue. Despite this, integration into the existing print subsystem appears seamless to the user. The IPP protocol on Windows may also leverage Web Services Devices (WSD) ports to allow for automatic discovery if the printer is on the same subnet as the computer.

2. The OpenPrinting CUPS IPP port should be considered when implementation of the IPP standard is a primary issue, and integration into the Windows subsystem is secondary. I used this library as a basis for an "emergency printer" or even a print

solution for users who travel frequently and do not have an established base office. Since this is a C++ CUPS port, it is not integrated into the Windows OS as the WinRT library is. One drawback to this is the fact that there is no native integration with shared printers used for the Point and Print system so popular in Windows. You could deploy Linux-based print server(s) that would allow for shared printer support, but your organization may not allow for this. Thus, in a Windows environment, the OpenPrinting IPP port library is realistically limited to direct print scenarios. Another issue arising from lack of integration is that applications will not be able to natively use this library from the Windows common print dialog employed by Visual Studio. There are positives to this, namely that the OpenPrinting IPP port library does not need the Windows spooler system to function, and creation of WSD ports is not necessary. In fact, you can create a working print utility that only requires the URL of the printer – the Windows spooler service does not even need to be running! This makes the OpenPrinting IPP port option ideal for centralized print management utilities, where installation of monitored client printer instances (on the monitoring station) would prove cumbersome at best. Chapter 3, "Deep Dive into the Protocol," will detail scenarios for use of the OpenPrinting CUPS port on Windows.

Weighing the advantages and disadvantages of both libraries, one would assume most implementations use the MS IPP Class Driver and WinRT, if only because of the greater integration within the Windows OS. The choice you select should be based on the requirements of your network, the convenience for the users, and the application scope and purpose.

IPP Operations

The IPP standards, as laid out in a series of RFCs, define multiple operations a printer can provide. Each operation defined in the standard consists of a request and a response. Operations have defined attributes that affect their characteristics (for instance, the target) and are called "operation attributes." For comparison, IPP also maintains the concept of object attributes such as Printer or Job attributes.

RFC 8011 defines the following possible operations available for IPP printer objects and the section of RFC 8011 that defines them:

Printer Operations

Print-Job (Section 4.2.1)

Validate-Job (Section 4.2.3)

Create-Job (Section 4.2.4)

Get-Printer-Attributes (Section 4.2.5)

Get-Jobs (Section 4.2.6)

Pause-Printer (Section 4.2.7)

Resume-Printer (Section 4.2.8)

Purge-Jobs (Section 4.2.9)

Job Operations

Send-Document (Section 4.3.1)

Cancel-Job (Section 4.3.3)

Get-Job-Attributes (Section 4.3.4)

Hold-Job (Section 4.3.5)

Release-Job (Section 4.3.6)

Restart-Job (Section 4.3.7)

In this chapter, we will concentrate primarily on Get-Printer-Attributes printer operation. To be sure, later in the book we will cover additional operations, but the Get-Printer-Attributes operations need to be understood for you to understand why the IPP protocol has gained such acceptance and undergirds Microsoft's Modern Print technology. You should be aware that not all the operations are supported on every vendor's print hardware. For instance, the Create-Job operation is recommended for vendor implementation, but the Get-Printer-Attributes operation is required.[2] You can

[2] This is perhaps not the best example because Create-Job is required by AirPrint, IPP Everywhere, and Mopria, and also required by IPP/2.1, which is for Enterprise printers.

read the RFC for each operation to find the status of implementation, but it so happens that operations supported by the Printer object are listed by the Printer's "operations-supported" Printer Description attribute, which can be queried using the Get-Printer-Attributes operation. It is always a clever idea to check the values listed by this attribute before using other operations to ensure any operation you intend to implement is, in fact, supported on the printer object. For instance, on my home HP LaserJet Enterprise Flow MFP M528 printer, I get the following supported operations returned:

operations-supported (RFC 8011 Section 4.1.2)

```
Enum Value: 2    (Print-Job)
Enum Value: 3    (Print-Uri)
Enum Value: 4    (Validate-Job)
Enum Value: 5    (Create-Job)
Enum Value: 6    (Send-Document)
Enum Value: 7    (Send-Uri)
Enum Value: 60   (Identify-Printer)
Enum Value: 8    (Cancel-Job)
Enum Value: 9    (Get-Job-Attributes)
Enum Value: 10   (Get-Jobs)
Enum Value: 11   (Get-Printer-Attributes)
Enum Value: 57   (Cancel-My-Jobs)
Enum Value: 59   (Close-Job)
```

Thus, a developer or system admin could implement these operations in a script or code and expect them to be supported on the print device.

To better understand some of the terminology used in the Get-Printer-Attributes request, you should consult Section 4.2.5 of RFC 8011. The IPP specification describes some components of the protocol as either required or recommended for the printer vendor to support. The Get-Printer-Attributes operation is in the former category, meaning it will always be supported on printers that support IPP. You will also need the KB5044380 cumulative update for Windows 11 23H2 or higher to properly run some of the WinRT code included in this chapter. This update fixes some issues with IPP on the platform and will ensure the samples work as they should.

Operation	Section of RFC 8011	Conformance
Print-Job	4.2.1	REQUIRED
Print-URI	4.2.2	OPTIONAL
Validate-Job	4.2.3	REQUIRED
Create-Job	4.2.4	RECOMMENDED
Get-Printer-Attributes	4.2.5	REQUIRED
Get-Jobs	4.2.6	REQUIRED
Pause-Printer	4.2.7	OPTIONAL
Resume-Printer	4.2.8	OPTIONAL
Purge-Jobs	4.2.9	SHOULD NOT

Within Section 4.2.5.1 of RFC 8011 is the description of the "requested-attributes" operation attribute, which may be included in a Get-Printer-Attributes request. With this, a client may specify the IPP attributes the Printer includes in its response. If the Client does not include the "requested-attributes" attribute in a Get-Printer-Attributes request, or it does and sets the value of "requested-attributes" to "all," the Printer is supposed to return all attributes.[3] These include the version of IPP the printer supports, the status code for the request, and the request id. The request id is a 32-bit integer you supply that uniquely identifies the request - this id is then returned to you in reply. RFC 8011 specifies operations that IPP-compliant hardware may respond to. Not all operations are available on IPP-compliant printers - you should consult Section 6.2.2 of RFC 8011 to see what operations are required and which ones are optional or just recommended. As you can see, an IPP printer is required to respond to the Get-Printer-Attributes request.

In the IPP world, attributes are properties of the printer that can be read or set. As in all IPP operations, you should consult with the standard to see which attributes are required for conformance, which are recommended, and which are optional. Below is a table from RFC 8011, which lists some of the common attributes you can request, the type of attribute value, and finally what type of conformance to the standard the printer

[3] Except two: "media-col-database" and "finishings-col-database" (which both specify in their definition that the Printer MUST NOT return them in a Get-Printer-Attributes response unless they are explicitly requested).

vendor must adhere to. As of this writing, there are almost 1500 standard IPP attributes defined by either the IETF or the PWG and registered in the IANA IPP Registry (See section on IANA).

`https://www.iana.org/assignments/ipp-registrations/ipp-registrations.xml`

List of Some Supported Attributes

Attribute	Type	Conformance
charset-configured	charset	REQUIRED
charset-supported	setOf charset	REQUIRED
color-supported	boolean	RECOMMENDED
compression-supported	1setOf type2 keyword	
document-format-default	mimeMediaType	REQUIRED
document-format-supported	1setOf mimeMediaType	REQUIRED
generated-natural-language-supported	1setOf naturalLanguage	REQUIRED
Ipp-features-supported	1setOf type2 keyword	
ipp-versions-supported	1setOf type2 keyword	
job-impressions-supported	rangeOfInteger(0:MAX)	RECOMMENDED
job-k-octets-supported	rangeOfInteger(0:MAX)	
job-media-sheets-supported	rangeOfInteger(1:MAX)	
multiple-document-jobs-supported	boolean	RECOMMENDED
multiple-operation-time-out	integer(1:MAX)	RECOMMENDED
natural-language-configured	naturalLanguage	REQUIRED
operations-supported	1setOf enum	REQUIRED
pages-per-minute	integer(0:MAX)	RECOMMENDED
pages-per-minute-color	integer(0:MAX)	RECOMMENDED
pdl-override-supported	keyword	REQUIRED
printer-current-time	dateTime | unknown	RECOMMENDED

(*continued*)

Attribute	Type	Conformance
printer-info	text (127)	RECOMMENDED
printer-is-accepting-jobs	boolean	REQUIRED
printer-kind		
printer-location	text (127)	RECOMMENDED
printer-make-and-model	text (127)	RECOMMENDED
printer-message-from-operator	text (127)	
printer-more-info	uri	RECOMMENDED
printer-more-info-manufacturer	uri	
printer-name	name (127)	REQUIRED
printer-state	enum	REQUIRED
printer-state-message	text (MAX)	RECOMMENDED
printer-state-reasons	1setOf type2 keyword	REQUIRED
printer-up-time	integer(1:MAX)	REQUIRED
printer-uri-supported	1setOf uri	REQUIRED
printer-uuid	uri	
queued-job-count	integer(0:MAX)	REQUIRED
uri-authentication-supported	1setOf type2 keyword	
uri-security-supported	1setOf type2 keyword	

The idea is for you to specify the attributes ("requested-attributes") you are interested in before you make the Get-Printer-Attributes call, and the printer will return the values of the attribute set. The purpose of "requested-attributes" is to limit the request to just those the client is interested in and reduce the size of the response. I direct your attention to the conformance column as it specifies what the printer is required to return, what the committee recommends that the printer vendor return, and what the vendor is free to implement as they see fit. For instance, if you look at the pdl-override-supported attribute, you can see that a vendor is required to implement it. On the other hand, the vendor recommended implementing printer-more-info (and does) but is not required to. [4]

IANA[5]

The Internet Assigned Numbers Authority (IANA) is where IPP registrations for various enumeration values and other protocol parameters are recorded. For example, IANA records registrations for

- Enumeration values used in IPP attributes (such as job states, printer states, and operation codes).
- Attribute names and their associated values to ensure consistency across different implementations.
- Attribute names and syntaxes (name, charset, text, etc.)
- Protocol Operations, both name and reference associated with the operation.
- Status Codes used and string description thereof.
- Other protocol-specific parameters require standardized values.

Thus, if you need to look up an enumeration or operational value, IANA is a great resource to leverage. The URL for IANA is

`https://www.iana.org/protocols`

Preparing Your Printer

It should not be surprising that the printer must be actively listening for IPP requests on the well-known ports for service requests. For IPP and IPPS, this means listening to the well-known TCP port 631. Of course, the procedures for enabling IPP or IPPS on your printer depend on your vendor: each is obviously quite different. I have even run into some older Lexmark printers that had IPP enabled, but no obvious menu to enable or

[4] In Chapter 7, I will attempt to make the case that you should be relying on certification programs (Mopria, IPP Everywhere) when determining what attributes are supported rather than using IPP version(s).

[5] `https://www.iana.org/assignments/ipp-registrations/ipp-registrations`.

disable the service (in this case, ports 631 and 443 could be enabled or disabled). I have included the network services selection area for my HP printer below:

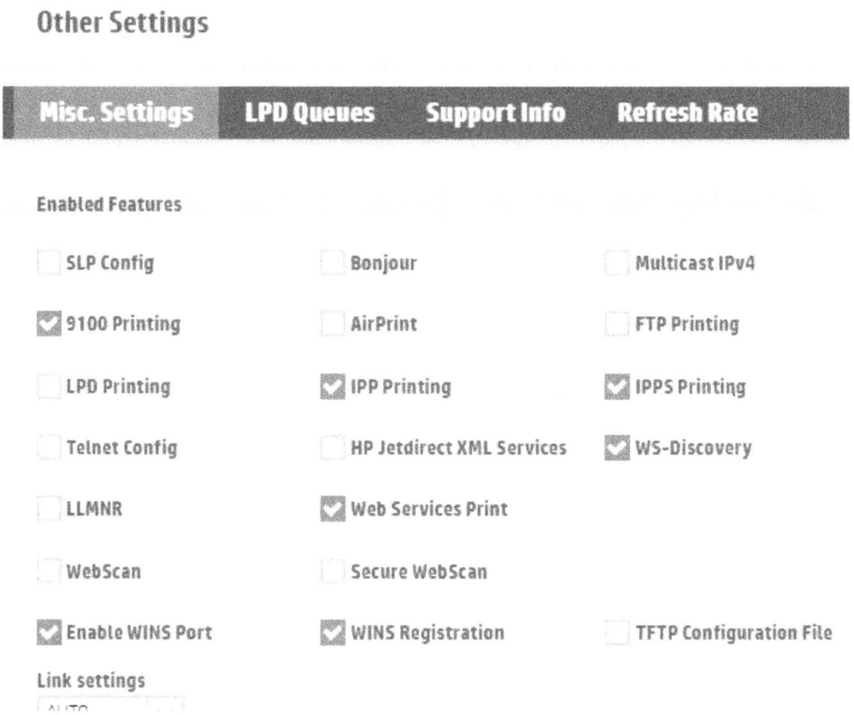

Other Settings

Misc. Settings | LPD Queues | Support Info | Refresh Rate

Enabled Features

SLP Config | Bonjour | Multicast IPv4
9100 Printing | AirPrint | FTP Printing
LPD Printing | IPP Printing | IPPS Printing
Telnet Config | HP Jetdirect XML Services | WS-Discovery
LLMNR | Web Services Print
WebScan | Secure WebScan
Enable WINS Port | WINS Registration | TFTP Configuration File

Link settings

Turning IPP/IPPS Service On/Off on HP Laser Jet Enterprise Flow MFP M528 Printer

Of course, this assumes your printer supports the IPP/IPPS protocol – most modern printers do. If you are uncertain of any models, you can get an idea of which printer models support IPP by going to the following link:

`https://www.pwg.org/printers/`

Or via Apple AirPrint Certification:

`https://support.apple.com/en-us/HT201311`

The best suggestion would be for you to contact your vendor about any printer model you want to use as a test for IPP conformity. Most printer models within the past 15 years offer some support for IPP; however, you might have to upgrade firmware to get it up to IPP version 2.0 or greater standards.

Curl Up

If you do not have the administrator password for your printer or are uncertain whether a printer is listening for IPP/IPP service on port 631 (or sometimes for IPPS, 443), you can test for this using Curl. Curl is included with Windows 10 after version 1803, offering system admins a great tool to see what ports network devices (such as IPP printers) are listening on. To use curl, open a command line and type the following for a quick check to see if the port is available:

```
curl -v <your_printer_name>:631
```

What you want to see is the line below indicating that Curl was able to connect to the printer using port 631. This indicates that port 631 is open and listening to the network.

```
* Host Printer57:631 was resolved.
* IPv6: (none)
* IPv4: 40.23.66.17
*   Trying 40.23.66.17:631...
* Connected to Printer57 (40.23.66.17) port 631 <= (What you want to see)
* using HTTP/1.x
> GET / HTTP/1.1
> Host: Printer57:631
> User-Agent: curl/8.13.0
> Accept: */*
```

If printer port 631 is not open and listening, you will see something like that shown below (port 632 used for illustrative purposes):

```
* Host Printer57:632 was resolved.
* IPv6: (none)
* IPv4: 40.23.66.17
*   Trying 40.23.66.17:632...
* connect to 40.23.66.17 port 632 from 0.0.0.0 port 51714 failed:
Connection refused
* Failed to connect to Printer57 port 632 after 2056 ms: Could not connect
to server
```

```
* Closing connection #0
curl: (7) Failed to connect to Printer57 port 632 after 2056 ms: Could not
connect to server
```

Of course, curl is capable of much more than simply testing the listening state of network ports; use the –help option to investigate all its features.

Check Your Network

If the printer has IPP/IPPS enabled but the curl test fails, something could be blocking access. You should ensure that there are no firewalls or router filters blocking IPP/IPPS between your machine and the printer. On Windows 11, you can open Firewall & Network Protection and click the Advanced link – this will open the Windows Defender and Advanced Security window. Check the Inbound and Outbound rules to ensure IPP/IPPS is free to pass. By default, Windows 11 does not block IPP or IPPS, so this should not be an issue unless someone has implemented custom firewall rules on your network.

Creating a Direct IPP Printer

Before we jump into using the code sample called WinRtIppTest, you should know a few things about how Microsoft uses this library. The IppPrintDevice object within the WinRT APIs is an abstraction for the IPP print object installed on your computer. In fact, you cannot use the IppPrintDevice object without the IPP printer it represents having already been installed on your computer. This chapter includes code examples to learn more about the Get-Printer-Attributes request that IPP provides. The WinRT APIs used in this chapter provide a high-level abstraction from the implementation specifics of the protocol and thus allow for the reader to digest important concepts easier. You will need to have an IPP printer instance installed on your Windows 11 machine to run the code examples, so I would suggest you install an IPP printer if you have not done so already. The following procedures navigate the printer installation wizard in Windows 11. You may also use an IPP print connection off a print server; the installation (on the server) is almost identical to that of the workstation.

1. Open Settings, and on the left-hand side, choose **Bluetooth and Devices**.

2. Choose **Printers and Scanners** from the listbox choices.

3. At the top of **Printers and Scanners**, click the **Add device** button.

Bluetooth & devices › Printers & scanners

Add a printer or scanner

Add device

4. Once the **Add device** button is clicked, the OS will try to search for printers on the network. When this happens, the **Add manually** link will appear - click on it.

5. The Add Printer dialog should now appear. To add an IPP printer, you should ensure **Add a printer using an IP address** or hostname is selected.

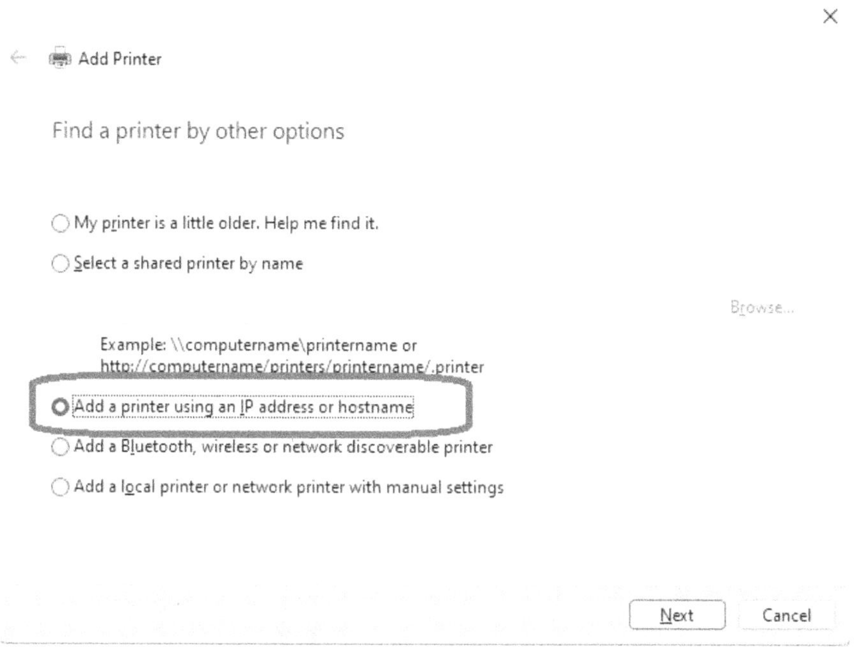

Add Printer

Find a printer by other options

My printer is a little older. Help me find it.

Select a shared printer by name

Browse...

Example: \\computername\printername or
http://computername/printers/printername/.printer

Add a printer using an IP address or hostname

Add a Bluetooth, wireless or network discoverable printer

Add a local printer or network printer with manual settings

Next Cancel

Click **Next**.

6. The Add Printer wizard will now require the IP address or hostname of your printer. Enter this information in the Hostname or IP address text box.

Add Printer

Type a printer hostname or IP address

Device type: IPP Device

Hostname or IP address: HPM528

Autodetect detects WSD and TCP/IP printers.
To search for an IPP printer, IPP must be selected from the drop down menu.

Next Cancel

Click **Next**.

7. Windows will now send a Get-Printer-Attributes IPP request to the printer address you entered in the previous step. The results of this request will be automatically placed in the newly created printer object and in the registry.

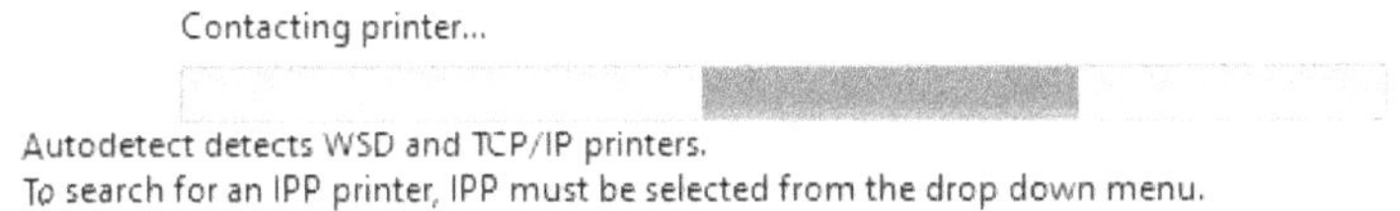

8. If successful, the IPP printer should now be created – congratulations. We will use this printer throughout the remainder of this book for all code examples. You should notice that the printer is already named for you – this (the name of the printer) is an attribute gleaned from the Get-Printer-Attributes request. Of course, you are free to change this name as you see fit.

One thing you might notice when an IPP/IPPS printer is created on Windows is that it does not use a TCP port. Instead, it uses an IPP port that employs a GUID to identify itself. Despite the

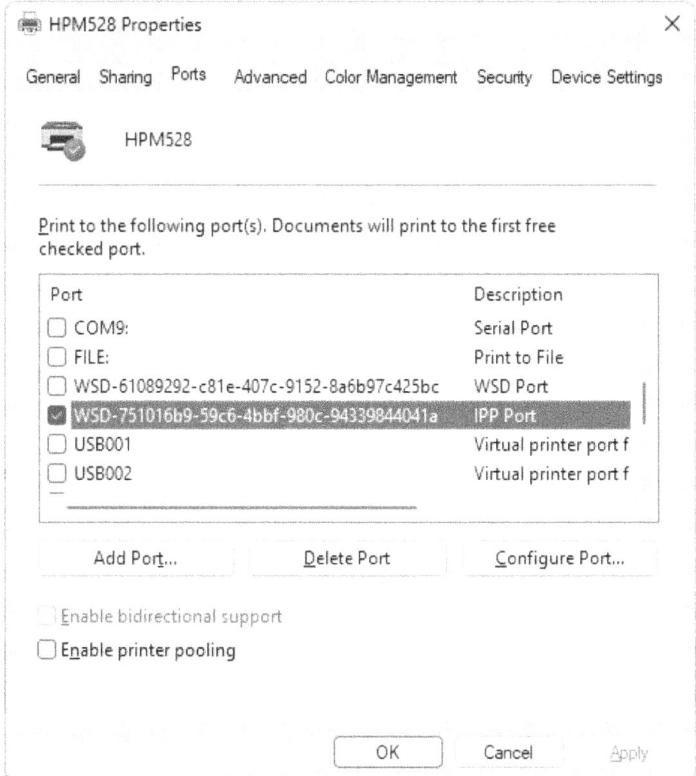

similarities with WSD ports, the IPP port created has some distinct properties that set it apart from its WSD cousins. Below is a comparison of WSD ports and IPP/IPPS ports that displays the differences.

Feature	WSD Port	IPP/IPPS Port
Protocol	Web Services for Devices (SOAP over HTTP)	Internet Printing Protocol (HTTP/IPP/IPPS)
Port(s) Used	UDP port 3702 (discovery), TCP port 5357 (communication)	TCP port 631
Discovery	Automatic discovery via WSD/UPnP/SSDP	mDNS

(*Continued*)

Feature	WSD Port	IPP/IPPS Port
Use Case	Device discovery and management in home/small office networks	Network printing (with advanced features like job management)
Supported Features	Automatic installation, basic print capabilities	Advanced print job management, status updates, job cancellation, etc.
Best for	Simple, plug-and-play network printer setup	Complex, feature-rich network printing services

While at first it is a bit confusing why Microsoft might use a WSD GUID, in practice the concept makes sense. WSD is a protocol whose primary purpose is device discovery; IPP is a protocol whose primary purpose is printing operations. Thus, the printer could potentially be discovered via WSD while print services are handled by IPP. If both WSD and IPP/IPPS services are enabled on a printer, that printer could then be discovered and then installed on the local computer using the IPP port. If you are looking for the URL or IP address used for the port, that can be found by clicking the **Configure Port** button, which will display a dialog with the information.

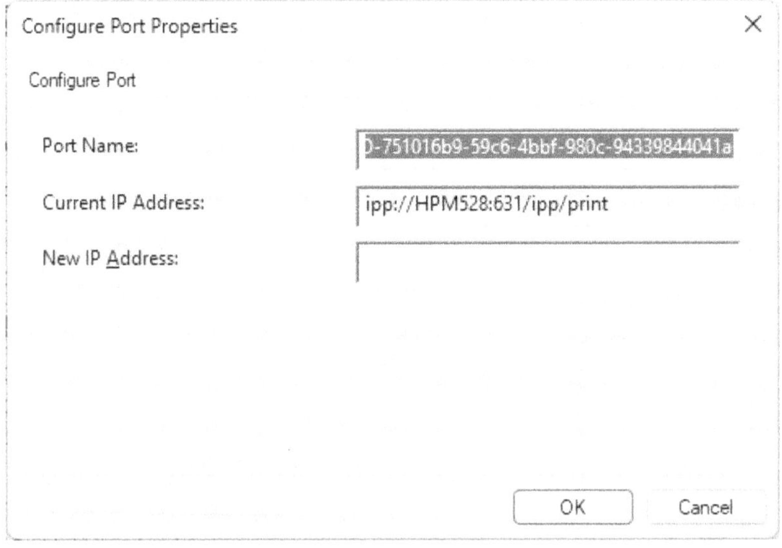

IPP URLs

What is in a URL? If that URL turns out to describe IPP printers on a Windows OS, it turns out plenty. When you use the UI or even PowerShell to add an IPP printer to Windows, you may notice that either of the following URL formats appears to work:

```
ipp://<printer-hostname>:631/ipp/print
ipp://<printer-hostname>/ipp/print
```

How can this be? Turns out, RFC 2910 and RFC 7472 specify the well-known port for the IPP/IPPS protocol is port 631: IPP is registered to port 631 by IANA. Thus, Windows assumes that a URL without a port specified is (by default) going to be using port 631. So, Windows assumes the following is true:

You provide	Windows Uses
ipps://printer/ipp/print	ipps://printer:631/ipp/print
ipp://printer/ipp/print	ipp://printer:631/ipp/print

You might also be surprised to find out that port 443, typically associated with IPPS, is ***not*** part of the RFC 8010 specification and is ***not*** a registered port for IPPS. The question then becomes, why is port 443 used? The answer lies in network firewalls, and by default they are configured to block (or pass). As you know, port 443 is associated with HTTPS and thus is not blocked on many firewalls. Because IPPS is HTTP over TLS (like HTTPS), many printers expose IPPS over port 443, allowing IPPS to work through firewalls as long as the correct URL is specified:

```
ipps://<printer-hostname>:443/ipp/print
```

It turns out that IPPS on port 443 is a practical resolution, just ***not*** a standard.

Adding an IPP/IPPS Printer via PowerShell

You can also add an IPP/IPPS printer via Windows PowerShell using the **Add-Printer** cmdlet if you prefer. To do this, you will need to start the PowerShell script running with administrative privileges on the target machine. You will also need to supply the URL of the IPP printer (IppURL argument) and the name of the printer. For instance, to install an HP printer (named HPM528) on my Windows 11 machine, I would use the following syntax:

```
Add-Printer -Name HPM528 -IppURL "ipp://hpm528/ipp/print"
```

Which installs an IPP printer on my Windows 11 machine. To install an IPPS printer, use the following syntax:

```
Add-Printer -Name HPM528 -IppURL "ipps://hpm528/ipp/print"
```

AddIppPrinter

Where I work, there is a large base of network printers, which must be converted from port 9100 print to IPP/IPPS. Converting existing Point and Print connections may not prove a difficult endeavor, but converting potentially thousands of direct printers to clients across the enterprise is another matter entirely. Doing this via a GUI is not reasonable, and the enterprise security folks will insist on using IPPS for secure transmission. The AddIppPrinter solution was created to address this issue as you can specify the port type required and convert printers to IPPS on the Windows client via a list of IP addresses (or host names). You can find this utility in the code section of this chapter. Just remember that your target printers must have IPPS enabled to use IPPS from the client.

INFORMATION ON IPPS CONNECTION ESTABLISHMENT

When an IPP printer is created, Windows will query the target printer to see if it has IPP or IPPS (or both) enabled. Based on the printer URL specified and on what protocol is enabled on the printer, the following table represents what protocol your Windows IPP/IPPS printer might employ.

Printer URL	IPP and IPPS Enabled	Protocol
ipp://printer1:631/ipp/print	Port 631	IPP
ipps://printer1:631/ipp/print	Port 631	IPPS

IPPS over port 631 on Windows uses implicit TLS – i.e., the client connects directly to port 631 and uses TLS from the start. The TLS handshake happens shortly after the TCP connection is established, without sending any data (except the TCP handshake) in an unencrypted state. In Wireshark, this TLS handshake is manifested by the TLSv1.x ClientHello packet, which sends to the printer the cipher suite and the TLS versions supported. The printer uses this information and selects the cipher suite and highest TLS version mutually supported by the client via the ServerHello message. Included in the ServerHello message is the digital certificate along with the identity of the issuing authority that (hopefully) the client Windows machine trusts. Once received, the client can now validate the certificate provided by the printer.

The next few messages consist of

Client Key Exchange: Sent by the client and contains key material (e.g., a pre-master secret encrypted with the server's public key) needed to establish the shared session key.

ChangeCipherSpec: Also sent by the client, indicating that subsequent messages will be encrypted.

Finished: The client sends a Finished message encrypted with the negotiated keys, proving that the handshake messages were received and processed correctly.

Printer **ChangeCipherSpec** and **Finished**: The printer (server) responds with its own ChangeCipherSpec and Finished messages. If all goes well, the connection is now encrypted between the client machine and the printer both ways.

It is important to know the IPP protocol itself does not mandate encryption – by default, traffic is unencrypted (IPP) unless IPPS is specified.

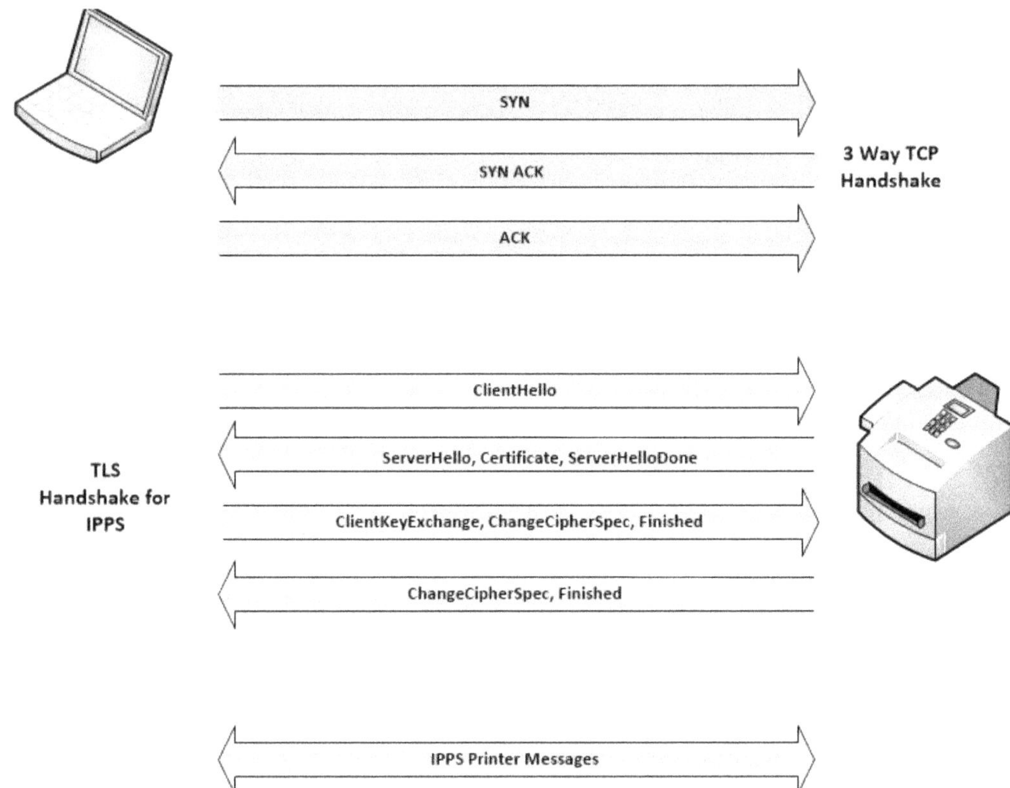

TLS Setup Diagram

Troubleshooting TLS Issues

While TLS session setup is certainly robust, it helps to know where to find information in the event of failure. If your IPPS print session repeatedly fails, you can employ Wireshark to troubleshoot potential errors, including TLS session setup issues. Below is a standardized list of TLS alert messages defined in the TLS protocol specifications (RFCs) [10] [11]. Each alert has a numeric code and a corresponding description. If you see an Encryption Alert in the Wireshark trace, you will need to recover the alert's error numeric value, which, in the case of the trace below, is 21.

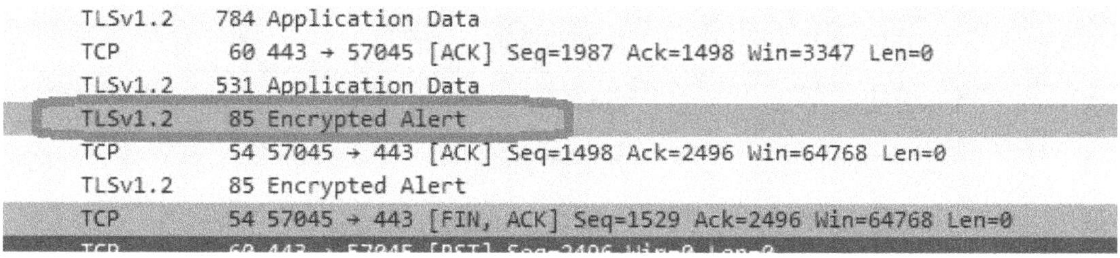

```
TLSv1.2   784 Application Data
TCP        60 443 → 57045 [ACK] Seq=1987 Ack=1498 Win=3347 Len=0
TLSv1.2   531 Application Data
TLSv1.2    85 Encrypted Alert
TCP        54 57045 → 443 [ACK] Seq=1498 Ack=2496 Win=64768 Len=0
TLSv1.2    85 Encrypted Alert
TCP        54 57045 → 443 [FIN, ACK] Seq=1529 Ack=2496 Win=64768 Len=0
```

Wireshark Display of Encryption Alerts Issues

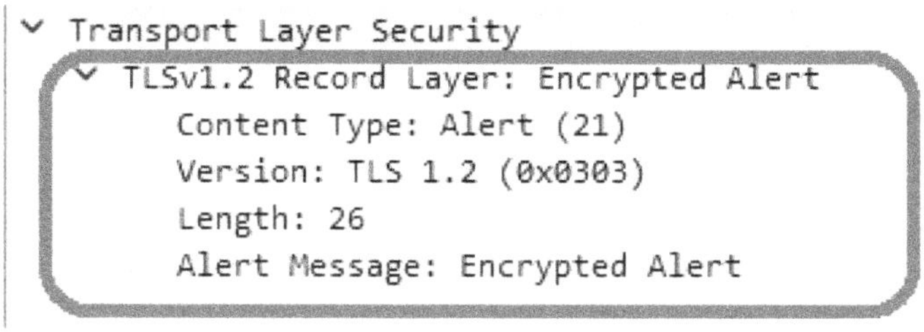

```
˅ Transport Layer Security
  ˅ TLSv1.2 Record Layer: Encrypted Alert
      Content Type: Alert (21)
      Version: TLS 1.2 (0x0303)
      Length: 26
      Alert Message: Encrypted Alert
```

Drilling Down into This Packet Provides the TLS Error Value

Enum Value	Alert Message	Description
0	close_notify	Notification that the connection is being closed
10	unexpected_message	An inappropriate message was received
20	bad_record_mac	Message authentication code failed
21	decrypt_error	Decryption failed (e.g., bad key or corrupted data)
22	record_overflow	Record length is too long
30	decompression_failure	Decompression failure
40	handshake_failure	The handshake process failed
42	bad_certificate	The certificate was bad
43	unsupported_certificate	Certificate type not supported
44	certificate_revoked	The certificate was revoked
45	certificate_expired	Certificate expired
46	certificate_unknown	Certificate unknown
47	illegal_parameter	Illegal parameter in handshake

(Continued)

Enum Value	Alert Message	Description
48	unknown_ca	Unknown certificate authority
49	access_denied	Access denied
50	decode_error	Decoding error
51	decrypt_error	Decryption error (same as 21 in some contexts)
60	export_restriction	Export restriction
70	protocol_version	Protocol version not supported
71	insufficient_security	Insufficient security
80	internal_error	Internal error
90	user_canceled	The user canceled the operation
100	no_renegotiation	No renegotiation allowed
110	unsupported_extension	Unsupported extension

This issue was the result of a printer (on Windows 11) created as an IPPS printer, while the printer itself had the IPPS service turned off. As a result, when the Windows machine tried to establish a secure TLS connection to the printer, the printer responded with a TLS alert indicating a decryption error (alert 21), because it could not correctly process or decrypt the incoming encrypted data.

Creating an IPP Printer Connection from a Print Server

One of the rewards of having IPP integrated into the Windows print system is being able to leverage printers shared off a server in the form of print connections. This can make integrating IPP into your corporate environment almost seamless as the use of print connections is very convenient. It is easy to understand why: users just need to right-click on the desired printer and select Connect from the context menu to make use of the printer. The astute reader might ask if this could potentially compromise the connecting computer: after all, this is exactly the concern the print nightmare patch addressed. The good news is that the Microsoft IPP class driver, used in Windows 10 and Windows 11, is a type 4 driver; there are no files to download, and therefore there are minimal security risks with the process.

By default, Internet Printing Protocol is not enabled on Server 2022 and requires the Print and Document Services to be installed. Once this service is added to Server 2022, adding a printer to the server is identical to adding one to a workstation. To create (and then share out) an IPP printer on Windows Server 2022, you would follow the exact same steps as outlined in the section "Creating a Direct IPP Printer" above. The only difference is that you will need to share the printer at the end of the installation wizard so that users can connect to it. From the client, you can connect to the new (shared) printer on the print server

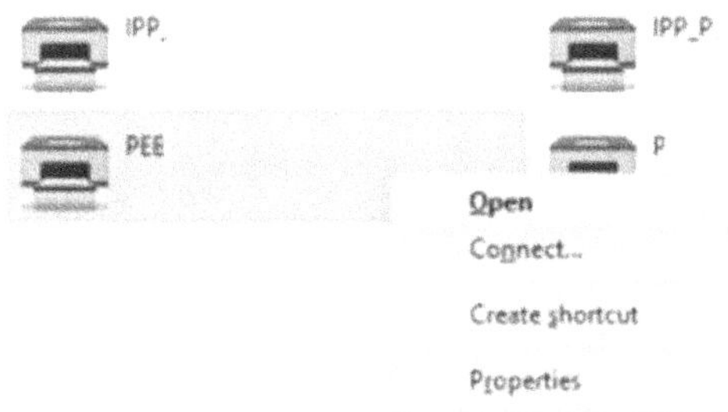

Connecting to an IPP Printer Shared Off the Server

by opening Windows Explorer, entering the server's name in the URL locator bar, and checking to see that your new printer appears. You can then right-click the printer and choose **Connect** from the context menu to add it to the local machine as a print connection. This book will cover enterprise IPP print client scenarios in more detail in a later chapter. However, since this chapter's focus is primarily understanding the Get-Printer-Attributes request, its balance will employ examples used on directly connected printers.

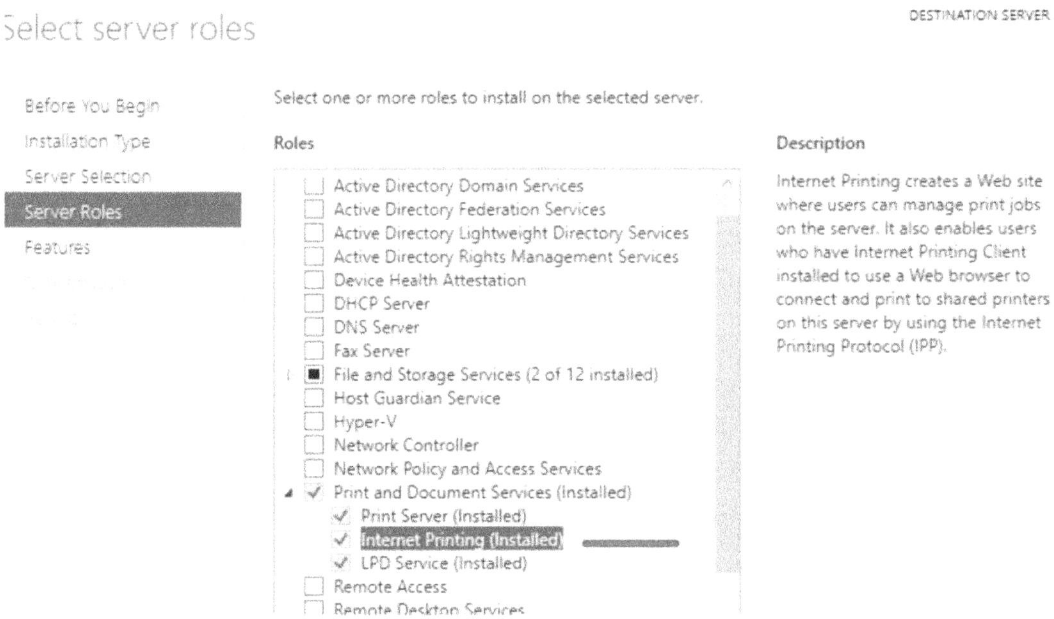

Adding the Print and Document Services to Server 2022

Installing the WinRtIppTest Code Example

This chapter started off by declaring the intention of demonstrating the WinRT library (for IPP) on Windows. This is because WinRT is a .NET library that provides a level of abstraction, which should ease the IPP learning process. What was not provided was the fact that WinRT is not natively part of the .NET desktop framework or for any of the .NET or C++ languages. With that in mind, start by creating a new project in Visual Studio. Choose Console App (.NET Framework) as the template and then click Next.

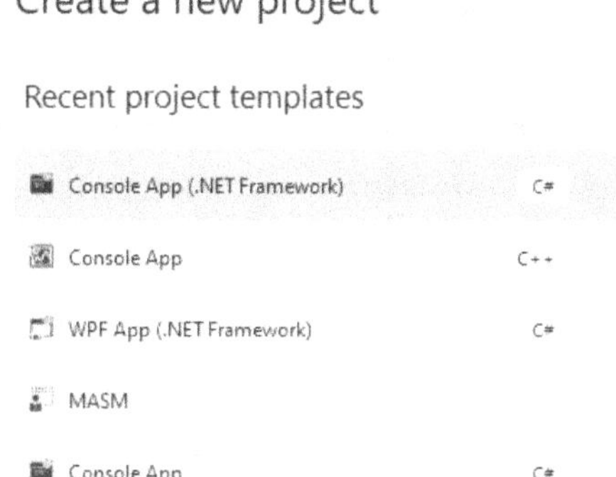

Just so we all are working from the same page, name your project WinRtIppTest as well. You can copy the code into the provided Program.cs file as this project is supposed to provide a no-frills, uncluttered look into the IPP protocol.

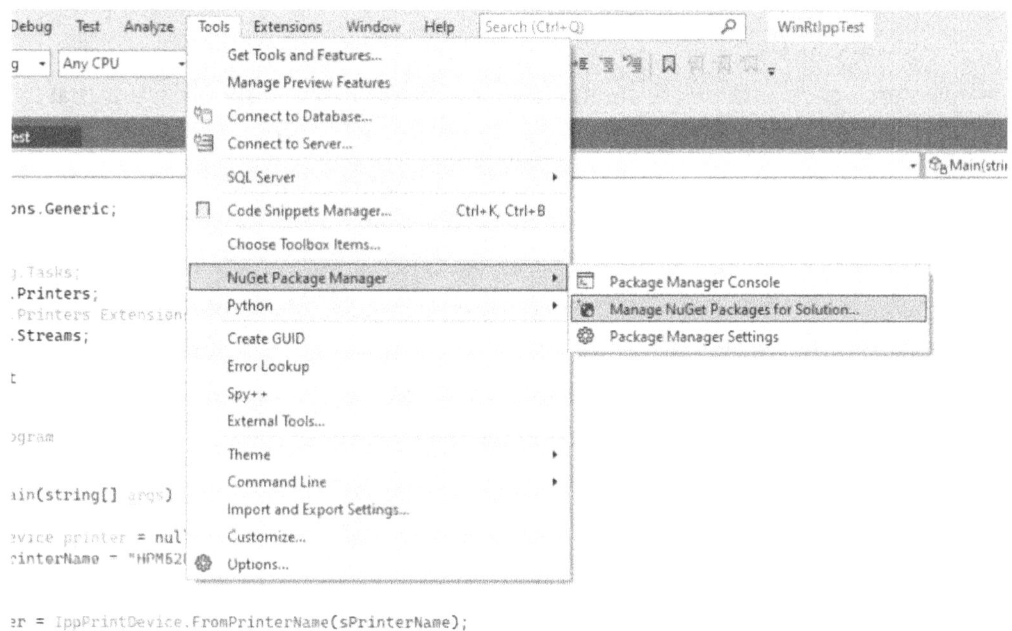

If you are developing your own WinRT code to develop IPP print applications, you will need to import a NuGet package that will provide the WinRT libraries required to build and run your project. To do this in Visual Studio, go to Tools, then NuGet Package

Manager, and from the context menu choose Manage NuGet Packages for Solution. This should open a dialog like the one below where you can browse for available packages.

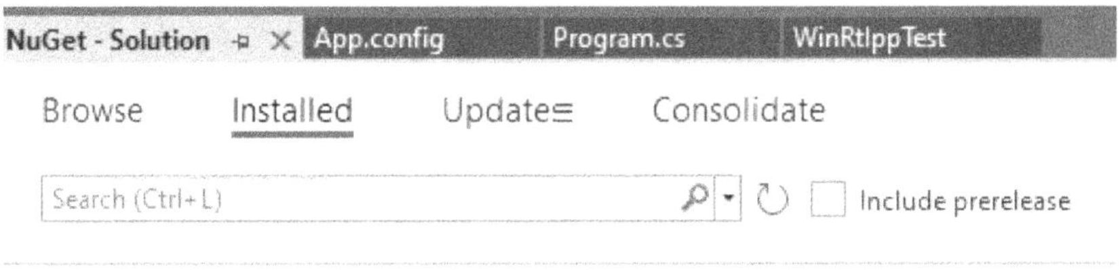

Choose Browse, then in the Search box enter ***Microsoft.Windows.SDK.Contracts*** and hit enter. The package description proclaims the Windows WinRT API Pack enables you to add the latest Windows Runtime APIs support to your .NET Framework 4.6+ and .NET Core 3.0+ libraries and apps.

If you have no interest in creating your own solution and just want to follow along with existing code, you can simply open the source code provided for this chapter and load the WinRtIppTest solution. This solution has the necessary NuGet packages already installed. Much of the interactions with IPP in this project (and in any project you might create yourself) will come from the Windows.Devices.Printers namespace. While this namespace and library are included in the project, you should know that to leverage print task configuration and print notifications, the Windows.Devices.Printers. Extensions namespace must be added as well [2]. If all goes well, you should be able to build your new project, as all the required namespaces are in the Project.cs file. The next step should involve choosing the target (networked) printer to run the request against.

The attributes requested of an IPP printer can be individual attributes as described in the list of supported attributes several pages back or groupings of attributes. Attributes can be classified as either job attributes (attributes that describe available job properties) or printer attributes (attributes that describe the printer itself) [3]. A particularly informative read for an understanding of what is available is the document "How to Use the Internet Printing Protocol," available on the Printer Working Group website. The complete set of attributes can be found in RFC8011; I would recommend you look at them.

To get you started, here are some useful attributes you can request from your printer:

ipp-features-supported:	A list of IPP features that are supported, for example, 'ipp-everywhere' and 'icc-color-matching'.
ipp-versions-supported:	A list of IPP versions that are supported, for example, '1.1' and '2.0'.
operations-supported:	A list of IPP operations that are supported, for example, Print-Job, Create-Job, Send-Document, Cancel-Job, Get-Jobs, Get-Job-Attributes, and Get-Printer-Attributes.
charset-supported:	A list of character sets that are supported ('utf-8' is required).
document-format-supported:	A list of file formats that can be printed, for example, 'application/pdf' 'image/pwg-raster'.
media-col-database:	A list of paper sizes and types that are supported, for example, 'na_letter_8.5x11in' and 'iso_a4_210x297mm'.
copies-supported:	The maximum number of copies that can be produced, for example, '99'.
sides-supported:	A list of supported one- and two-sided printing modes, for example, 'one-sided', 'two-sided-long-edge', and 'two-sided-short-edge'.
print-quality-supported:	A list of supported print qualities, for example, '3' (draft), '4' (normal), and '5' (high).
print-color-mode-supported:	A list of supported color printing modes, for example, 'bi-level', 'monochrome', and 'color'.
print-scaling-supported:	A list of supported scaling modes, for example, 'auto', 'fill', and 'fit'.
printer-resolution-supported:	A list of supported print resolutions, for example, '300 dpi' and '600 dpi'.
printer-uri-supported:	Contains at least one URI the printer supports.
uri-authentication-supported:	Identifies the authentication mechanisms that have been configured for the various Printer URIs (e.g., 'digest', 'none', etc.).

(*Continued*)

uri-security-supported:	Identifies the communication channel security protocols that have been configured for the various Printer URIs (e.g., 'tls' or 'none').
printer-info:	This (Recommended) Printer attribute provides descriptive information about the Printer.
printer-more-info:	This (Recommended) Printer attribute contains a URI used to obtain more information about this specific Printer.
printer-location:	This (Recommended) attribute should be filled out by the printer administrator about the location of the printer.
printer-uuid:	This (Recommended) attribute provides a unique, unchangeable identifier for the Printer distinct from "printer-name," etc.

To begin with, let us use the printer-up-time attribute from the RFC 8011 list of attributes table we saw earlier. Compile the WinRtIppTest example code if you have not done so already and open a command line window in the Bin folder. On my machine, this would be *D:\BACKUP\IPP Book\Chap3\Code\WinRtIppTest\WinRtIppTest\bin\Debug*; however, on your own machine, it depends on where you installed the code examples. The utility requires 2 command line arguments: the first (using the /p switch) is the target printer. The second argument uses the /r switch and requires a comma-delimited attributes list. Typing in WinRtIppTest /p=HPM528 /r=printer-up-time on the command line, I see the following return:

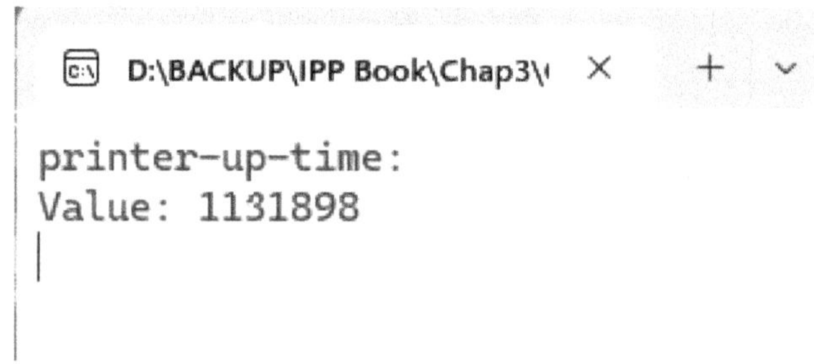

Which is about what I would expect. Now let's try the printer-message-from-operator attribute and see what that brings us:

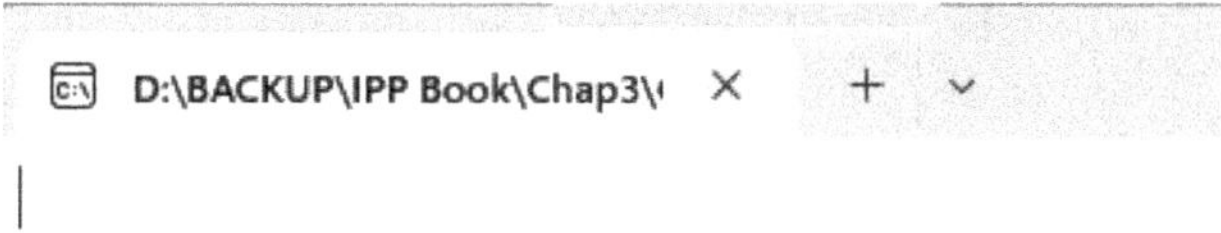

Well, it looks like no message from the printer-message-from-operator attribute came back – what is going on here? Looking again at the RFC list of attributes, the reason becomes apparent. The conformance column for printer-message-from-operator does not list this as required; in fact, there is no conformance listing at all. Keep this in mind – not all attributes are supported on all printers; only the required ones are guaranteed to be supported.

If you want a truly complete list of printer attributes from your target printer, you will enter on the command line *WinRtIppTest /p=HPM528 /r=printer-description,job-template,media-col-database* which on my machine supplied over 600 attributes from my HP M528 printer. The printer-description attribute group provides a comprehensive list of printer attributes the print hardware supports. This attribute (printer-description) is an effective way to return pertinent information about the printer hardware.

So, let's take a look at the WinRtIppTest code used in this chapter. As I alluded to earlier, using the Microsoft WinRT APIs allows us to build a Get-Printer-Attributes request with just a few lines of code. The abstraction provides a chance for those new to IPP to get familiar with some of the basics about the protocol without getting bogged down in implementation details. While integration into the Windows OS is a distinct advantage for using the WinRT APIs within .NET, there are other advantages this decision confers. To begin with, the collection of attributes returned from the printer from an IPP Get-Printer-Attributes request is formatted in a byte stream. This byte stream requires the parser to observe specific processing formats that can intimidate even seasoned developers. The WinRT APIs do much of this for you, which is a distinct advantage for those interested in developing their own code to take advantage of all that IPP offers. We will delve into the parsing process details in the next chapter, but for now try to concern yourself with all the information these attributes can provide.

Below is the result when I request the "operations-supported" and "print-scaling-supported" attributes:

```
D:\BACKUP\IPP Book\Chap3\

operations-supported:
Enum Value: 2
Enum Value: 3
Enum Value: 4
Enum Value: 5
Enum Value: 6
Enum Value: 7
Enum Value: 60
Enum Value: 8
Enum Value: 9
Enum Value: 10
Enum Value: 11
Enum Value: 57
Enum Value: 59
print-scaling-supported:
Keyword Value: auto
Keyword Value: auto-fit
Keyword Value: fill
Keyword Value: fit
Keyword Value: none
```

Looking at the reply from the Get-Printer-Attributes request above, you can see the operations-supported attribute returns an enumerated value. Looking at the code, you will see that when we print out the enumeration, we get a string value for the number of enumerated values.

```
case IppAttributeValueKind.Enum:
   var enumValues = attribute.Value.GetEnumArray();
   foreach (var enumValue in enumValues)
   {
       Console.WriteLine($"Enum Value: {enumValue}");
   }
```

While this works, it sure does not convey the most human-readable format. Further, if the user does not happen to have RFC 8011 in front of them, they are left wondering what the value of 8, 9, or any other number returned represents relative to operations supported. We can fix this by creating a mapping of enumerations. Of course, this requires that the developer dig into RFC 8011, particularly Section 5.4.15, as a guide. I have started what you might use for enumeration mapping of RFC values to make this more human readable below.

```
public static Dictionary<string, Dictionary<int, string>> enumMappings =
new Dictionary<string, Dictionary<int, string>>
        {
            { "print-quality", new Dictionary<int, string>
                {
                    { 3, "Draft" },
                    { 4, "Normal" },
                    { 5, "High" }
                }
            },
            { "media-type", new Dictionary<int, string>
                {
                    { 0, "Auto" },
                    { 1, "Plain" },
                    { 2, "Photo" }
                }
            },
            //RFC 8011, 5.4.15. operations-supported
            { "operations-supported", new Dictionary<int, string>
                {
                    { 0, "Reserved" },
                    { 1, "Reserved" },
                    { 2, "Print-Job" },
                    { 3, "Print-URI" },
                    { 4, "Validate-Job" },
                    { 5, "Create-Job" },
                    { 6, "Send-Document" },
                    { 7, "Send-URI" },
                    { 8, "Cancel-Job" },
                    { 9, "Get-Job-Attributes" },
                    { 10, "Get-Jobs" },
```

```
                    { 11, "Get-Printer-Attributes" },
                    { 12, "Hold-Jobs" },
                    { 13, "Release-Job" },
                    { 14, "Restart-Job" },
                    { 15, "Reserved" },
                    { 16, "Pause-Printer" },
                    { 17, "Resume-Printer" },
                    { 18, "Purge-Jobs" }
                }
            }
        };
```

Whether you provide a more human-readable result for your users or not, it is imperative that you pay attention to the operations your printer model supports. This can save you some frustration searching your code for a reason your operation request fails only to find it is not supported in the first place.

By recovering a host of attributes about the printer and print jobs, you can provide the user with a list of properties about the printer that they can use to customize their print request. While we learned in chapter one that these properties were previously provided by installation of the print driver on the client, we now can recover these same properties dynamically from the printer itself. This allows the OS to provide a near driverless environment that was not possible prior to the introduction of IPP. This also reduces some of the issues with the integrity of the print cycle as we are not relying on compromised software by installing or downloading the print driver for each printer model.

Default Values

The values returned, especially in a 1setOf, provide the developer a way to display the available supported attribute values to the user. This allows the user to customize their print request based on the availability of certain options. For a given "xxx" printing feature attribute, there will be a corresponding "xxx-supported" attribute indicating support for that feature. In the event the "xxx-supported" attribute has multiple values (i.e., 1setOf), an "xxx-default" attribute may exist to indicate the default value. This allows the developer to preset the value in a combo box where multiple values exist. For instance, look at the attributes returned below from a Get-Printer-Attributes request:

```
Keyword Value: text-and-graphics
Keyword Value: auto
print-quality-default:
Enum Value: 4
print-quality-supported:
Enum Value: 4
Enum Value: 3
Enum Value: 5
print-rendering-intent-default:
Keyword Value: auto
print-rendering-intent-supported:
Keyword Value: auto
Keyword Value: perceptual
Keyword Value: relative
Keyword Value: relative-bpc
print-scaling-default:
Keyword Value: auto
print-scaling-supported:
Keyword Value: auto
Keyword Value: auto-fit
Keyword Value: fill
Keyword Value: fit
Keyword Value: none
printer-config-change-date-time:
DateTime Value: 11/7/2024 6:55:44 AM -05:00
printer-config-change-time:
Value: 0
printer-current-time:
DateTime Value: 11/7/2024 8:37:20 PM -05:00
printer-device-id:
```

If you look at the attribute print-scaling, you will notice (circled above) the attribute name value of **print-scaling-default** with the value of **auto**. Further, you will notice the attribute name of **print-scaling-supported** along with several keyword values related to this attribute. Thus, when writing a utility or application to support or make use of IPP print, using these postfixed keywords will allow you to customize the user environment to the printer chosen. For instance, if we were to provide the supported print scaling capabilities of printer xyz to the user, we might provide a combo box with a collection containing auto, auto-fit, fill, fit, or none while setting auto as the default value. The same could be done for the print quality available for printer xyz. In this case, we might provide the user with a combo box with the collection of draft (3), normal (4), or high (5) as choices, with normal as the default selection.

Document Format Supported

If you look at some of the useful attributes you can request from the Printer (displayed earlier in the chapter), you will find the **document-format-supported** attribute. This attribute is required according to RFC8011, so I used that as the sole requested attribute for a run with WinRtIppTest. The results, at least for my HP M528 printer, are shown below:

```
D:\BACKUP\IPP Book\Chap2\    Settings

document-format-supported:
MimeMediaType Value: text/plain
MimeMediaType Value: application/octet-stream
MimeMediaType Value: image/jpeg
MimeMediaType Value: application/vnd.hp-PCL
MimeMediaType Value: application/vnd.hp-PCLXL
MimeMediaType Value: application/postscript
MimeMediaType Value: application/pdf
MimeMediaType Value: image/urf
MimeMediaType Value: image/pwg-raster
MimeMediaType Value: image/tiff
MimeMediaType Value: application/PCLm
```

I mention this since in later chapters the supported document formats will play a more significant role. More specifically, these formats are what the printer can successfully render to printed output. I will have more to say on this in later chapters, but just remember that printers can only render a limited number of formats. There is also a **document-format-default** attribute, which, as it implies, is the format the printer prefers - in the case of my HP LaserJet Enterprise Flow MFP M528, this was application/pdf.[6]

[6] "document-format-supported" is also important because the Client can do a Get-Printer-Attributes with "requested-attributes" = 'document-format-supported', and then choose the one it prefers, and follow up with another Get-Printer-Attributes request with "document-format" = the chosen document format ("image-pwg-raster" for instance), and the printer will reply with a filtered set of attributes and values that are supported for that specific document format.

Consumables and Supplies

Depending on the attributes requested, the get-printer-attribute request will return the levels of consumables such as toner on the printer. For instance, when using WinRtIppTest project, setting an argument /r=printer-description will return values for the "printer-supply" attribute. In the case of my HP M528 B&W laser printer, this consists of the toner cartridge maximum capacity (maxcapacity) and the current level of the unit. In this case, the current level reads 97 out of a maximum of 100, so the printer toner cartridge level appears sufficient.

```
D:\BACKUP\IPP Book\Chap2\
printer-supply:
Value: type=toner-cartridge;maxcapacity=100;index=1;level=97;colorantname=Black Cartridge
;coloranttonality:128;class:3;unit:19
printer-supply-description:
Value: Black Cartridge toner-cartridge S/N:16848229
printer-supply-info-uri:
Uri Value: http://10.0.0.215:631/hp/device/mSupplyStatus
printer-up-time:
Value: 2238618
printer-uri-supported:
Uri Value: ipp://10.0.0.215:631/ipp/print
```

Printer-supply values

Additionally, some printers will return the printer-supply-info-uri attribute, which you can also use to view the levels of consumables on the printer. For my printer, this attribute was a URI whose value is shown below:

> printer-supply-info-uri: URI Value: `http://10.0.0.215:631/hp/device/mSupplyStatus`

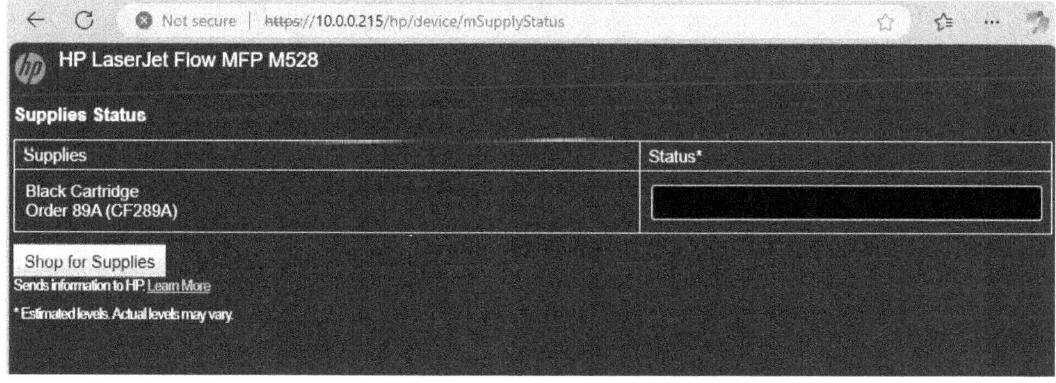

Reading the supply status from the printer-supply-uri-level attribute

If you want to track the levels of paper in each of the printer input bins, you will have to specify the "printer-input-tray" attribute. When specified, the maximum capacity of each bin (maxcapacity), the current level, and the status of each tray will be returned via the printer-input-tray attribute returned from the printer. A WPF-based utility that displays toner supply for any IPP printer is described in Chapter 3, "Deep Dive into the Protocol," based on the printer-supply attribute.

Tracking Printer Configuration Changes

If your printer supports it, the printer-config-change-date-time attribute will display the last time the printer firmware or configuration was modified or changed. This can help admins to keep track of changes to the printer network configuration or modifications to the printer's default settings. There is also a printer-state-change-date-time, which tracks when the printer last changed state, for example, from printing to error state or from idle to printing. Both attributes, if supported, can help to maintain or troubleshoot the printer in the event of a failure or error.

Check Operations-Supported

As mentioned in several places in this chapter, while most modern printers support some version of IPP (1.0, 1.1, 2.0, etc.), checking the operations-supported attribute from your printer is imperative. This is especially true in the event you want to provide printing services for your application or assume your printer can cancel a print job. According to RFC 8011, Print-Job is a required operation (all implementations must support it), whereas Create-Job is a recommended operation, and hence, some implementations might not support it [8]. Thus, you might be surprised to learn that some IPP printer models may not allow you to cancel a print job as expected. Always check the operations-supported attribute set to ensure your intended request is supported. You should also check any new printers purchased to ensure their implementation of IPP meets your enterprise requirements: more on this later.

Get-Printer-Attributes Request Versus SNMP

The astute reader might compare the counters or values returned from an SNMP request (from Chapter 1, "Windows Legacy Print") to the attributes returned from the Get-Printer-Attributes request. While they serve differing purposes, setting up the right attribute groups for the Get-Printer-Attributes request can indeed return remarkably similar information. If your maintenance or monitoring requirements can swap SNMP for IPP Get-Printer-Attributes requests, consider doing so. One of the great advantages of IPP attributes over SNMP counters is that IPP, being a standardized protocol, ensures compatibility and consistency across different printer models and manufacturers without having to locate specific MIBs for the same purpose. Additionally, ease of implementation and use as compared to SNMP (which can be complex and require more configuration) is also a benefit. Finally, IPP is more efficient to use and takes fewer network resources than does SNMP, especially for large datasets. The biggest advantage might be the cost savings realized by consolidating the information gleaned from SNMP queries with the operation of IPP in your enterprise.

PowerShell Equivalent

The popularity of Windows PowerShell, especially among the multitudes of Windows administrators and scripters, is undeniable. PowerShell eases administrative tasks by providing access to Active Directory, the file system, device, and process information, etc. It only follows that the Windows IPP community would want to use this tool for scripting purposes as well. For instance, administrators could query the printer for information such as the printer firmware version, IPP features supported, the preferred document format, the current IPP version supported, and many other attributes the printer supports. Unfortunately, at the time of this writing, WinRT is not well integrated in PowerShell. A good bet is that Microsoft will rectify this in the future, but for now PowerShell scripters have several options:

1. Create a CUPS-based IPP cmdlet in PowerShell to use.
2. Create a CUPS-based PowerShell script using HttpClient and parse the returned binary stream.

3. Call a .NET binary from PowerShell and pass arguments. Since C# can host WinRT APIs (see the WinRtIppTest project), the inclusion of WinRT is no longer a showstopper.

4. Create a cmdlet (using .NET) that contains WinRT calls and import that into your PowerShell script.

As this chapter deals primarily with integration within Windows, I opted to use the WinRT library. The next chapter will provide a PWG CUPS port approach to the issue. After contemplating the problem, I decided that using WinRT within a cmdlet might be the cleanest approach to the problem. The cmdlet is remarkably like the WinRtIppTest project with the inclusion of System.Management. Automation features are necessary to create a PowerShell cmdlet. At any rate, it makes recovering attributes from installed IPP printers in Windows a bit easier. One word of caution: you will need to use NuGet for a few assemblies not normally included in C# console projects. The issue here is that the assemblies required for PowerShell are version specific - in my case I had to specify the assembly specifically designed for version 5. If you are not familiar with using NuGet in Visual Studio, you should use Tools/NuGet Package Manager/Manage NuGet Packages Solution to open the NuGet browser.

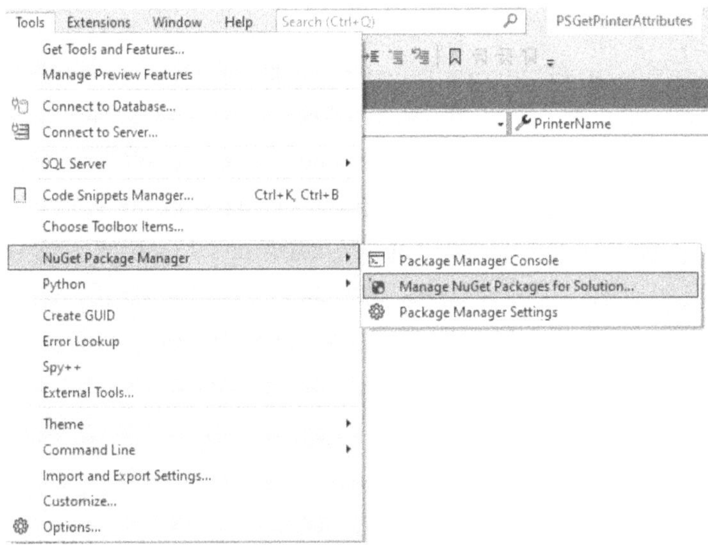

The two assemblies required to create the Cmdlet are Microsoft.Windows.SDK. Contracts (for the WinRT assemblies) and Microsoft.PowerShell.5.ReferenceAssemblies (for the Cmdlet).

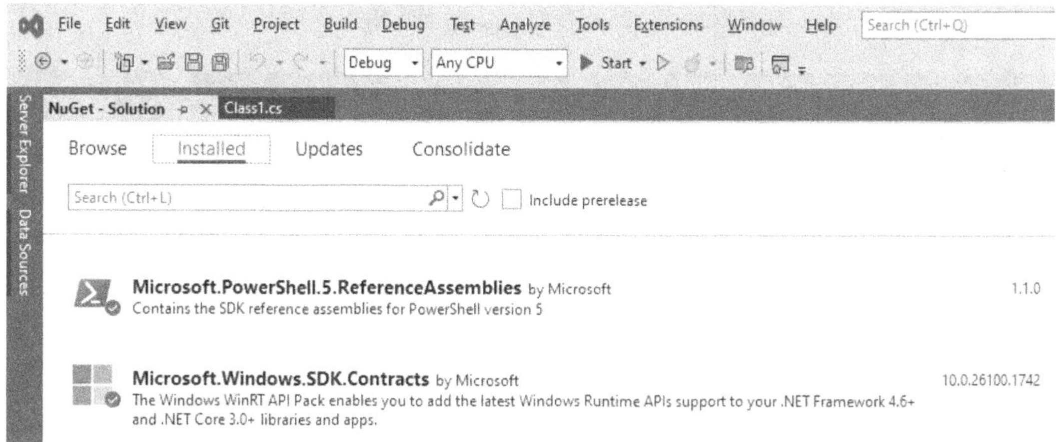

As a reminder, PowerShell version 5 was selected from NuGet since that is the targeted version; you might require a different version for your environment.

To use the cmdlet, open a Windows PowerShell ISE window. This is a good interface to design and debug PowerShell script issues before using them in a production environment. Because the cmdlet we just created is not included in PowerShell by default, you will have to load it into memory before calling it. This can be done by setting a variable to the cmdlet DLL path and then using the Import-Module command to load it into memory, as shown below.

```
$cmdletPath = "path\to\GetPrinterAttributesCmdlet.dll"
Import-Module $cmdletPath
```

Once the cmdlet is loaded into PowerShell, you can then use it – the graphic below shows how you use this cmdlet. Remember to ensure PowerShell can find your cmdlet by providing the exact path to the DLL.

Windows PowerShell ISE

File Edit View Tools Debug Add-ons Help

Untitled1.ps1*

```
# Define the path to the compiled cmdlet DLL
$cmdletPath = "D:\BACKUP\IPP Book\Chap2\Code\powershell\Cmdlet\PSGetPrinterAttributes.dll"
# Load the cmdlet
Import-Module $cmdletPath
# Use the cmdlet
Get-PrinterAttributes -PrinterName "HPM528" -AttributesRequired "printer-name,printer-state,printer-location"
```

The results of the Get-Printer-Attributes request are shown below:

```
PS C:\Users\jpmsp> # Define the path to the compiled cmdlet DLL
$cmdletPath = "D:\BACKUP\IPP Book\Chap2\Code\powershell\Cmdlet\PSGetPrinterAttributes.dll"
# Load the cmdlet
Import-Module $cmdletPath
# Use the cmdlet
Get-PrinterAttributes -PrinterName "HPM528" -AttributesRequired "printer-name,printer-state,printer-location"


Name             Value
----             -----
printer-location PEB-2J5
printer-name     Unknown
printer-state    3


PS C:\Users\jpmsp> |
```

If you want a more comprehensive attributes collection, use the following command for the cmdlet:

```
Get-PrinterAttributes -PrinterName "HPM528" -AttributesRequired "printer-description"
```

Below is the output from using the “printer-description” attributes requested by the group.

```
PS C:\Users\jpmsp> # Define the path to the compiled cmdlet DLL
$cmdletPath = "D:\BACKUP\IPP Book\Chap2\Code\powershell\Cmdlet\PSGetPrinterAttributes.dll"
# Load the cmdlet
Import-Module $cmdletPath
# Use the cmdlet
Get-PrinterAttributes -PrinterName "HPM528" -AttributesRequired "printer-description"


Name                                       Value
----                                       -----
charset-configured                         us-ascii
charset-supported                          utf-8
color-supported                            False
compression-supported                      none
document-format-default                    application/pdf
document-format-preferred                  application/pdf
document-format-supported                  application/PCLm
document-password-supported                0
epcl-version-supported                     epcl1.05
generated-natural-language-supported       en
hp-color-working-spaces-supported          hprgb-v1
hp-default-duplex-standard                 True
hp-easycolor-default                       ec-auto
hp-edge-to-edge-support                    True
hp-enhanced-mixed-orientation-supported    False
hp-image-enhancement-support               advance-image-control
hp-outputbins-supported                    System.__ComObject
hp-pc-version-major                        0
hp-pc-version-minor                        72
hp-pcl-version-supported                   Version 5.00
hp-pclxl-version-supported                 Version 3.0
hp-postscript-version-supported            Version 3010.107
hp-print-quality-supported                 System.__ComObject
hp-save-job-encryption-supported           rsakey
hp-save-job-password-max-length            32
hp-save-job-password-min-length            4
hp-save-job-password-type                  alphanumeric
hp-save-job-storage-available              True
hp-save-job-storage-supported              volatile
hp-tabbed-printing-supported               False
ipp-features-supported                     ipp-everywhere
ipp-versions-supported                     2.0
job-creation-attributes-supported          print-color-mode
job-ids-supported                          True
job-pages-per-set-supported                True
job-password-encryption-supported          sha2-256
job-password-length-supported              Unknown
job-password-repertoire-configured         iana_us-ascii_any
job-password-repertoire-supported          iana_us-ascii_any
job-password-supported                     32
jpeg-features-supported                    deep
jpeg-k-octets-supported                    Unknown
jpeg-x-dimension-supported                 Unknown
jpeg-y-dimension-supported                 Unknown
landscape-orientation-requested-preferred  4
marker-colors                              Unknown
```

Of course, since we use the WinRT library to create the cmdlet, the limitation is that it can only provide attributes from printers currently installed in Windows. We will correct this in the next chapter.

Chapter Summary

The chapter begins by contrasting how the Windows legacy print subsystem received information about printer capabilities (i.e., static files) versus how IPP can provide similar functionality dynamically. We examined Modern Print, how it implements IPP and Mopria technology on Windows 10, and expanded that support for Windows 11. While IPP provides a standardized method of communicating with the printer, it does not specify how driverless print is provided. Driverless print depends on standards such as Mopria and IPP Everywhere, which allow for print without the need to install print drivers. The term Windows Protected Print (WPP) is introduced, and the reason that your enterprise should consider adopting it is revealed. The aggressive timeline from Microsoft for IPP implementation and deprecation of third-party drivers should provide incentive to prepare for IPP introduction.

The various libraries available for IPP development are introduced, and the relative advantages and disadvantages of their use are discussed. The implementation of the WinRT APIs on Windows is also discussed, as is the requirement for installed printers for the library to target. The chapter provides instructions to install an IPP printer on Windows, both as a workstation and a server. How to test printers to ensure target printers have IPP or IPPS enabled, and installation issues are discussed as well. As a precaution, network admins are advised to use IPPS in the event the target printer supports IPPS, as encryption of the data stream is preferred. Recall that Windows uses implicit TLS – i.e., the client connects directly to port 631 and uses TLS almost from the start. When using the GUI to create an IPP/IPPS printer, the OS will take the most secure (IPPS) connection the printer will accept. Assuming your printer can negotiate TLS and process an IPPS connection, Windows should create an IPPS printer when configuring through the **Add a Printer or Scanner** wizard in Windows.

The Get-Printer-Attributes IPP request is introduced, and the advantages over legacy print systems are discussed. Various printer attributes and their usage are provided, while the need to consult the conformance columns of the RFC for any attribute is addressed. Conformance checks are especially important prior to using any of the IPP operations as not all of them are supported on all printer models. Finally, the WinRtIppTest solution is presented so the user can test out various print attributes on their own print hardware. A PowerShell version of the same utility is provided that has the same limitations (the printer must be installed on the client machine) of the WinRT APIs that are examined.

References

1. Modern print platform and Windows protected print mode, Modern print platform - Windows drivers | Microsoft Learn, Microsoft, 10/1/2024
2. Windows.Devices.Printers.Extensions Namespace, Windows.Devices.Printers.Extensions Namespace - Windows apps | Microsoft Learn, Microsoft App Development
3. How to Use the Internet Printing Protocol, The Printer Working Group, Michael R Sweet, Peter Zeher, version v2019.0117
4. Printing From Windows 11, `https://blog.mopria.org/2021/11/13/printing-from-windows-11/`, Mopria Alliance Blog, Nov, 2021.
5. Driverless Printing Standards And their PDLS, `https://openprinting.github.io/driverless/01-standards-and-their-pdls/`, OpenPrinting, 2024
6. More information on Windows protected print mode for enterprises, `https://learn.microsoft.com/en-us/windows-hardware/drivers/print/more-information-on-windows-protected-print-mode-for-enterprises`, Microsoft Learn Challenge, 10/01/2024
7. End of servicing plan for third-party printer drivers on Windows, `https://learn.microsoft.com/en-us/windows-hardware/drivers/print/end-of-servicing-plan-for-third-party-printer-drivers-on-windows`, Microsoft Learn Challenge, Jan 10, 2025
8. IPP/1.1: Model and Semantics RFC 8011, page 49, Internet Engineering Task Force (IETF) (Sweet and McDonald), January 2017.
9. Internet Printing Protocol, Wikipedia, `https://en.wikipedia.org/wiki/Internet_Printing_Protocol`
10. RFC 5246 (TLS 1.2), datatracker.ietf.org, `https://tools.ietf.org/html/rfc5246#section-7.2`
11. RFC 8446 (TLS 1.3), datatracker.ietf.org, `https://tools.ietf.org/html/rfc8446#section-6.2`

CHAPTER 3

Deep Dive into the Protocol

The last chapter provided a high-level overview of one of the central tenets of IPP: the Get-Printer-Attributes request. Because that chapter provided code created with WinRT APIs, the lower-level workings of the protocol were abstracted away. In this chapter, we take a deeper dive into the Get-Printer-Attributes request and, more specifically, the protocol workings in general. Looking into the lower-level workings is not for everyone; however, if you genuinely want to understand how IPP works and how to troubleshoot issues that arise, I encourage you to at least give this chapter a once-over.

I will try to explain the byte-stream processing in a logical format, and I will provide some stripped-down C# code that will allow you to step through the reply from the printer in a debugger. Ultimately, using a debugger and stepping through code is one of the best ways to understand how a byte stream is processed in IPP. I would also encourage you to make use of Wireshark when practical: it can save the byte stream reply of the printer so you can walk through the processing of attributes.

The IPP specification is laid out in a series of Request-For-Comments (RFC) documents. We will use RFC 8010 and RFC 8011 to design code that creates a Get-Printer-Attributes request and response. The code we develop will not be ready for production code; the main purpose is to illustrate how the request (and response) is formulated and therefore provides a terrific opportunity to learn the intricate workings of the protocol. Alongside the development process, Wireshark is employed to ensure the requests are correct and to look at the response on the network. Ideally, this reinforces the learning process and helps to firmly grasp the subject material. The IPP protocol process is easy to grasp as a concept; however, the actual workings are a bit more complex. It relies heavily on binary streams to and from the printer, and creating those streams or interpreting them can be a challenge. We will take this in from the highest level and hopefully ease the learning process.

J. Marion, *Adopting Internet Printing Protocol for Windows*, https://doi.org/10.1007/979-8-8688-2010-6_3

The IPP protocol was built on top of the HTTP protocol and uses HTTP as its transport mechanism. These (IPP) requests and responses are thus encapsulated within HTTP messages or conversations. The infrastructure for IPP to communicate over LAN (or WAN) networks is also provided by HTTP. Operations performed by IPP (printing or receiving printer attributes) are performed by HTTP POST requests, with the IPP data embedded in the HTTP request body. Responses in IPP are similar, with data sent back to the HTTP response body. IPP also makes use of Uniform Resource Locators (URLs) to address printers and print services the printers expose. HTTP is also used as the transport protocol for IPP, while IPPS makes use of HTTPS. IPP requests are sent over HTTP unencrypted, while IPPS requests are sent over HTTPS, providing an additional layer of security through encryption.

The data within an HTTP POST message may be in various formats, like text (XML and JSON) or binary (for files or images). The Content-Type header specifies the format of the data included in the HTTP request. The designers of IPP favored the binary approach, likely for efficiency - binary data can prove more compact than text, which reduces the size of data that needs to be transmitted. Binary data can also express value better as text base numbers such as floating point might lose precision during conversion. The downside to using binary data is obviously readability, but the designers of IPP correctly assumed that efficiency of transport was paramount to the success of the protocol.

Conceptually, you might think of this binary IPP/IPPS Request Body being within the HTTP/HTTPS envelope like the following:

```
IPP Request Packet (HTTP)
POST /ipp/print HTTP/1.1
Content-Type: application/ipp

Host: printer.example.com
Content-Length: [length]
[IPP Request Body]
```

Or graphically as

HTTP Request Line	POST /ipp/print HTTP/1.1\r\n
Content-Type	Content-Type: Application/ipp\r\n
Host	HPM528 \r\n
Content-Length	n-bytes Ex: 155 \r\n
IPP Request Body	0x01 0x01 0x00 0x0B 0x00 0x00 0x00 0x01...

Version Number	0x01, 0x01
Operation ID	0x01, 0x0B
Request ID	0x00, 0x00, 0x00, 0x01
Operation Attributes Tag	0x01
Attribute Name	Byte Equivilent Of "Attributes Charset"
Attribute Value	Byte Equivilent of "utf-8"
Attribute Name	Byte Equivilent of "attributes-natural-language"
Attribute Value	Byte Equivilent of "en-us"
Attribute Name	Byte Equivilent of "printer uri"
Attribute Value	Byte Equivilent of "http://printername/ipp/print"
End Of Attributes	0x03

If you are looking at a Wireshark capture, you can clearly see how the IPP packet is wrapped in the HTTP packet:

```
> [2 Reassembled TCP Segments (295 bytes): #6(140), #8(155)]
v Hypertext Transfer Protocol
  > POST /ipp/print HTTP/1.1\r\n
    Content-Type: application/ipp\r\n
    Host: hpm528\r\n
  > Content-Length: 155\r\n
    Expect: 100-continue\r\n
    Connection: Keep-Alive\r\n
    \r\n
    [Full request URI: http://hpm528/ipp/print]
    [HTTP request 2/2]
    [Response in frame: 20]
    File Data: 155 bytes
v Internet Printing Protocol
    [Response In: 20]
    version: 2.2
    operation-id: Get-Printer-Attributes (0x000b)
    request-id: 1
  > operation-attributes-tag
    end-of-attributes-tag
```

IPP Attribute Syntaxes

IPP makes use of attribute syntaxes – terms used to describe encoded values sent and received between the client and the printer. While many of these attributes are intuitive to anyone who has worked in IT for any length of time (Integer, Boolean, etc.), providing a quick description might provide additional clarity. In the next few chapters, you will see these attribute types in various contexts, so you should be familiar with what they are and how they are used.

Attribute Syntax	Description
Integer	A 32-bit signed integer used to represent numbers such as copies, etc.
Octet String	A byte sequence with no specific encoding – may or may not be interpreted as characters.
TextWithLanguage	Used in internationalization where text must be associated with a specific language. Includes the text and language tag associated with the text.

(*Conitnued*)

Attribute Syntax	Description
NameWithLanguage	Used for names associated with language. Like TextWithoutLanguage, but specifically used for names to ensure correct interpretation. Includes the name and language tag associated with the name.
MimeMediaType	Represents the standardized identifiers used to indicate the nature and format of a file. They are essential for ensuring that the printer correctly interprets and processes the document.
TextWithoutLanguage	Used for text that does not need to be associated with a specific language.
NameWithoutLanguage	Used for names that do not need to be associated with a specific language.
Keyword	A defined string that represents a value or option. Standardizes specific values or options.
Charset	Used to specify a particular charset (UTF-8, ASCII, etc.) to ensure text is displayed in each language as intended. Important in environments with multiple languages and character sets.
Boolean	Used to represent true (0x01) or false (0x00) states.
Uri	A string of characters used to identify a resource on the Internet. In IPP, URIs are used to identify printers, jobs, and other resources.
DateTime	A format to specify the date and time, including seconds and milliseconds.
UriScheme	Specifies the protocol used to access the resource identified by the URI. In the IPP world, UriSchemes use IPP and IPPS to specify the protocol.
Enum	An enumerated integer value that is in the range from 1 to 2**31 - 1 (MAX). Each value has an associated 'keyword' name.
rangeOfInteger	An ordered pair of integers that defines an inclusive range of integer values.
resolution	Specifies a two-dimensional resolution in the indicated units. It consists of three values: a cross-feed direction resolution (positive integer value), a feed direction resolution (positive integer value), and a unit value.

Range and Resolution

Two attributes that bear additional explanation are Range and Resolution.

Resolution is defined as a measure of the definition or legibility of the printed output. It is typically defined using two integer values: horizontal resolution, vertical resolution, and a byte value indicating the unit of measurement (dots per inch or dots per centimeter). According to the RFC, all three values must be present even if the first two values (i.e., 300,300 or 600,600) are the same. The third value specifies a unit value: i.e., '3' represents dots per inch, while '4' represents dots per centimeter. Improved resolution allows for sharper images and improved detail, essential for producing quality prints and graphics. Of course, there are trade-offs to consider: memory and processing requirements (on the printer) increase substantially when higher resolutions are requested.

Range is defined as the pairing of integers ordered to represent the pages to be printed. For example, for a 25-page report, a range of 3,14 would provide printing from pages 3 through 14. The left integer represents the lower bound, while the right integer represents the upper bound of the page ranges to be printed. This attribute is crucial to preventing wastage associated with printing out whole documents when a subsection is all that is needed.

Tags and Request Structure

It should prove helpful for you to know the organization of the return operation (from Get-Printer-Attributes) and how it is structured. To start off, there are 2 types of "tags" that signal discrete sections within the return of a request. One of the tags is the *delimiter tag*, which indicates major sections of the return stream. Of these delimiter tags, the operations-attribute-tag signals attributes that deal with the request operation (for instance, the charset used, the language used, etc.). The printer-attributes-tag delimiter signals that the next cluster of attributes deals with printer properties. The job-attributes-tag, as the name alludes to, signals that the attributes that follow deal with job properties. The very last delimiter tag must be the end-of-attributes tag as this signals the end of the operation. Inclusion of an end-of-attributes delimiter tag is mandatory for conforming IPP printers.

Delimiter Tag Value	Meaning
0x00	Reserved
0x01	operations-attribute-tag
0x02	job-attributes-tag
0x03	end-of-attributes-tag
0x04	printer-attributes-tag
0x05	unsupported-attributes-tag

The second type of tag is a value tag, which is the first octet of an attribute. This tag indicates the type of value (integer, DateTime, Boolean, etc.) in the attribute. We will encounter many types of value tags in the Get-Printer-Attributes return operation.

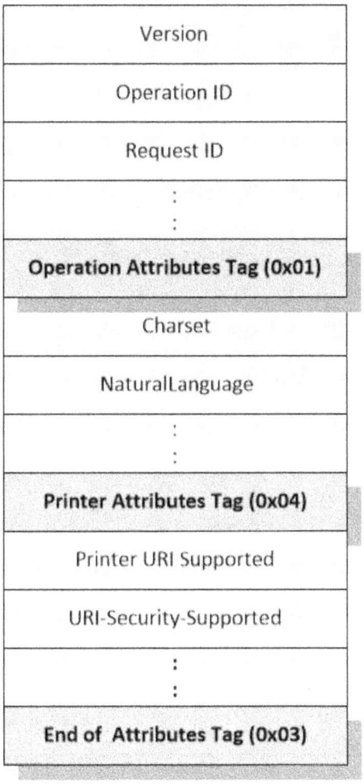

Version
Operation ID
Request ID
:
:
Operation Attributes Tag (0x01)
Charset
NaturalLanguage
:
:
Printer Attributes Tag (0x04)
Printer URI Supported
URI-Security-Supported
:
:
End of Attributes Tag (0x03)

The diagram above is the basic layout for the Get-Printer-Attributes operation. This will include the requisite version and operation id along with the request id. The Operation Attributes Tag (0x01) starts the section for operational attributes, while the

Printer Attributes Tag (0x04) starts the section for printer-specific attributes. As always, the end-of-attributes tag (0x03) signifies the end of the attributes returned.

Now that you have a basic understanding of how the Get-Printer-Attributes operation is structured, you should understand how attributes are encoded. First up will be the single-value attributes and single-value attributes with additional values. Single-value attributes are straightforward and are represented by the first (top) block in the illustration below.

Value Tag i.e. 0x44, 0x21, etc.	1 Byte
Name-length i.e. # of bytes	2 Bytes
Name i.e. "sides-supported"	x Bytes
Value-length i.e. 9 bytes for "one-sided"	2 Bytes
Value i.e. "one-sided"	y Bytes

First additional value

Value Tag i.e. 0x44 for keyword	1 Byte
Name-length 0x0000 to signal additional-value	2 Bytes
Value-length i.e. 9 for one-sided	2 Bytes
Value i.e. "one-sided"	x Bytes

Second additional value

Value Tag i.e. 0x44 for keyword	1 Byte
Name-length 0x0000 to signal additional-value	2 Bytes
Value-length i.e. 9 for two-sided	2 Bytes
Value i.e. "two-sided"	x Bytes

An example of this might be "copies," which logically has only one value associated with it. There are also times when an attribute may be multi-valued – for example, "sides-supported" would have several values (one-sided, two-sided, etc.). In this case, the attribute would be encoded with additional values as illustrated above. Notice the name-length of the additional values is always 0 bytes long – this is because the name has already been provided.

The collection attribute is a bit more complex and is illustrated below:

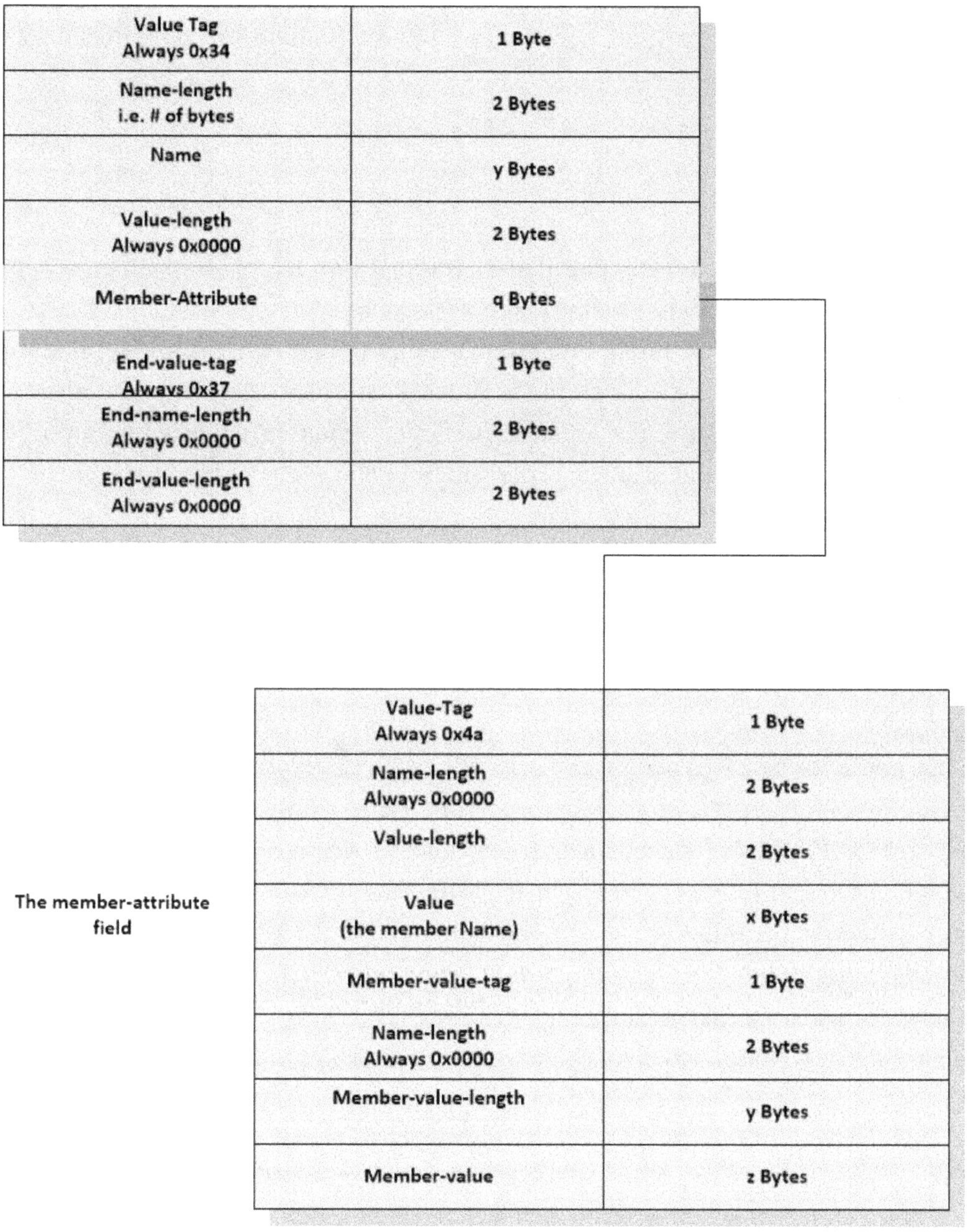

Value Tag Always 0x34	1 Byte
Name-length i.e. # of bytes	2 Bytes
Name	y Bytes
Value-length Always 0x0000	2 Bytes
Member-Attribute	q Bytes
End-value-tag Always 0x37	1 Byte
End-name-length Always 0x0000	2 Bytes
End-value-length Always 0x0000	2 Bytes

The member-attribute field

Value-Tag Always 0x4a	1 Byte
Name-length Always 0x0000	2 Bytes
Value-length	2 Bytes
Value (the member Name)	x Bytes
Member-value-tag	1 Byte
Name-length Always 0x0000	2 Bytes
Member-value-length	y Bytes
Member-value	z Bytes

The collection attribute, as the name implies, hosts a collection of related data. Think of a folder that contains documents, where each document holds a piece of information related to the folder itself. A collection attribute might be useful when you need to represent complex data structures that involve multiple pieces of information. The member attribute structures are the individual pieces of data within the named collection. Each member attribute has its own name and value and, combined, forms a detailed description of the collection.

Byte Streams

Because the IPP request packet is based on encoding bytes, the concepts in this chapter require understanding of byte streams and how they are created. We should start the process by going over some basics so that you are equipped to understand what is going on. As you might know, a byte can store 8 bits, 0-255, or 256 possible discrete values. In binary talk, there are only 2 values, and a bit is "set" when the value is 1 as opposed to 0. The decimal equivalent of a byte is derived from counting the binary weight of each place where a 1 is set, and the value is 2^i, where i is the bit index from 1 to 8. For example, a byte with bits set as 10000111 would have (from left to right) the value of 128 + 0 + 0 + 0 + 0 + 4 + 2 + 1 = 135 in decimal. You might see how cumbersome this could get for 64-bit machines with 8 bytes, so developers usually denote byte values in hex. Windows 10 and 11 provide the Calculator utility, which has a handy programmer setting. When in a programmer setting, it is easy to convert from binary to hex or decimal and vice versa – you will make use of this often. Knowing the decimal value of a hex number is important, as Wireshark, one of the best troubleshooting tools you will encounter for IPP, displays each byte in hex by default. As examples, 255 would be 0xFF, 19 would be 0x13, and 68 would be 0x44 in a Wireshark trace. It is important to get these concepts down as IPP relies on byte stream formatting to work successfully. If this is unfamiliar to you, open the Calculator application and click the pie control in the upper left-hand corner to change the format type to Programmer. You can now type numbers in decimals, and Calculator will display their equivalent values in Hex, Octal, and Binary.

If you have difficulty converting the Hex values in the next few chapters, do not hesitate to employ the Calculator utility until you get the hang of it.

Of particular importance for understanding byte streams on a Windows machine for IPP is byte order. Computers store bytes in memory in an order that preserves their value. For Unix machines, this means that the Most Significant Byte (MSB) is stored in the lower memory address relative to the Least Significant Byte (LSB). Unfortunately, Windows does directly the opposite. It makes use of little-endian byte order, where the MSB is stored in the higher (relatively) address compared to the LSB. What this means is that for these types of machines (Unix, Windows) to talk, the byte order should be translated into an agreed-upon order. This order is typically Network byte order, which is understood to be big-endian in format. If it helps, you might view big-endian as the format you typically write numbers in – the left-hand digit would be the MSB, and the rightmost digit would be the LSB. When we are talking about the most or least significant byte, this is relative to the bitness of the machine. For example, on a 16-bit machine, each memory address is 16 bits or 2 bytes in length. For a 32-bit machine, this would be 4 bytes (32 bits), and for modern machines, we have 64 bits using 8 bytes.

As an example, assume we have a variable integer stored as 23 7F in memory on our Windows machine. On a big-endian machine, this number would be stored as 7F 23 in memory. Going further, a long variable (4 bytes) on a Windows machine stored in memory as 2a 3b 4c 5d would be stored as 5d 4c 3b 2a on a big-endian machine. The number values are identical; they are just stored in memory in reverse order relative to each other. For a single byte, the byte order is obviously not an issue.

The IPP protocol assumes Network byte order when receiving or transmitting byte streams. Since your Windows machine is little-endian, this means the developer must convert any multi-byte values to big-endian format. Single bytes (since endianness is based on byte order) do not require conversion, but short values (2 bytes) or 32-bit integers (4 bytes) will require a conversion to Network byte order and vice versa. I should inject here that byte ordering is for memory storage on the host computer. Because Windows machines store (and process) data in little-endian formats, if those variable values (little-endian format) were not converted to big-endian format before transmission, the big-endian machines would process those values improperly. It is up to the developer of the IPP request to ensure proper byte order for success. The fact that bits are not shifted, but bytes may be (assuming a multi-byte value), might sow some confusion. The rule to remember is that *bits are never shifted within a byte, but a byte may be shifted within multi-byte values.*

Bit and Byte Shifting

I suspect many readers are familiar with bit-shifting operations native to most development languages. However, for those who are not, I should discuss how these operations work before we proceed. For this book's purposes, you should be familiar with the left and right shift operations. The left shift operation (<<) shifts its left-hand operand leftward by the number of bits defined by its right-hand operand. Conversely, the right shift operation (>>) shifts its left-hand operand rightward by the number of bits defined by its right-hand operand. Why would you need to employ these operands, you might ask? The simple reason is efficiency and speed, especially when dealing with Network byte order transformations.

In computer science, we deal with bit-shifting, especially when developing code for microcontrollers. As a simple example: assuming we have a variable named *num*, which is a byte whose value is 10001010 (138). Further, assume we shift *num* to the right by one place. Thus, x = num >>1 would entail moving each bit one place to the right, giving us 01000101 (69) as a value. Bit shifting left one place multiplies the value by 2, while bit shifting right divides the value by 2. This is a more efficient process than using the ALU to multiply or divide by 2. When right shifting or left shifting, the last bit position vacated by the shift is filled by a 0. For this book's purposes, we will shift values by bytes (8 bits) at a time, not bits. The purpose of this shift is to convert values from Network byte order (big-endian) to the Windows format of little-endian and vice versa.

Keep in mind that the basic idea is to switch the order you place bytes on the stream when you are going from little-endian to big-endian (make a request), and to do the same (switch the bytes order) when you take bytes from the byte stream on an IPP response (i.e., going from big-endian to little-endian). In practice, you only write code to switch the byte order once for each variable type. To make matters easier for the reader, we present the basic byte order switching code seen below:

```
public static class ByteOrder
    {
        //Switch Order of Short type
        public static short Flip(short num)
        {
            return (short)Flip((ushort)num);
        }

        //Switch Order of Unsigned Short type
        //i.e. ab becomes ba
        public static ushort Flip(ushort num)
        {
            return (ushort)(((num & 0xFF00) >> 8) | ((num & 0x00FF) << 8));
        }

        //Switch Order of Integer (32 bit) type
        public static int Flip(int num)
        {
            return (int)Flip((uint)num);
        }

        //Switch Order of Unsigned Int32 (32 bit) type
        // i.e. abcd becomes dcba
        public static uint Flip(uint num)
        {
            return ((num & 0xff000000) >> 24) | ((num & 0x00ff0000) >> 8) |
            ((num & 0x0000ff00) << 8) | ((num & 0x000000ff) << 24);
        }
```

```
        //Switch Order of Integer 64 (Int64) type
        public static long Flip(long num)
        {
            return (long)Flip((ulong)num);
        }

        //Switch Order of Unsigned Integer 64 (64 bit) type
        //i.e. abcdefgh becomes hgfedcba
        public static ulong Flip(ulong num)
        {
            return ((num & 0xFF00000000000000) >> 56) | ((num &
0x00FF000000000000) >> 40) |
                   ((num & 0x0000FF0000000000) >> 24) | ((num &
0x000000FF00000000) >> 8) |
                   ((num & 0x00000000FF000000) << 8) | ((num &
0x0000000000FF0000) << 24) |
                   ((num & 0x000000000000FF00) << 40) | ((num &
0x00000000000000FF) << 56);
        }
    }
}
```

As an example, take the Flip function for ushort variable values in the class ByteOrder.

```
return (ushort)(((num & 0xFF00) >> 8) | ((num & 0x00FF) << 8));
```

Take the ushort variable *num* in the previous example – assumed to be 2 bytes long. Further, assume that byte A forms the left (upper) half of the 2 bytes and byte B forms the right (lower) half of the unsigned short (ushort) value. We know the combination of byte A and byte B forms the total value. Starting from the left, we do a logical AND operation on this value (AB) with a 2-byte (0xFF00) masking value. As a reminder, when you do a logical AND operation on two numbers, only when the bit positions of both numbers are 1 will the final value bit position be 1. This can be seen from the truth table shown where X and Y values only result in a Z value of 1 when both X and Y are 1.

Truth table for AND operation

X	Y	Z
0	0	0
1	0	0
0	1	0
1	1	1

The ultimate result of using the mask of 0xFF00 is to get the upper byte of the AB ushort (in this case the original value of A). B is ANDed with 00 and thus masked away. Looking at the operation again:

```
((num & 0xFF00) >> 8)
```

The idea is to mask AB, get the upper byte (A), and then shift it 8 positions to the right. Conversely, the operation ((num & 0x00FF) << 8)) does the opposite: it masks away A with 00 and shifts the lower byte (B) 8 positions to the left. The result of this series of operations is to reverse (or flip) the bytes of the unsigned short variable.

Thus, the ByteOrder class takes whatever variable value type and switches the order of the bytes - exactly what we want. To write an IPP request, we will be concerned with ushorts, shorts, uint32, int32s, longs, and ulongs - all of these will require byte translation from little- to big-endian formatting and vice versa.

Building a Request

Armed with the basics of how the Get-Printer-Attributes operation is structured and aware of proper Network byte order, it should be instructive to employ this knowledge into a basic C# utility that performs this operation. Our first attempt at getting printer attributes from a printer will be for a specific attribute - in this case, the version(s) of IPP the printer supports. Before we code the actual request, you need to be familiar with the structure of an IPP request, both to submit the request and then to translate the return byte stream. The best resource for discovering this information is RFC 8010, which specifies the order expected by the printer for a request and provided by the printer as a reply.

Specifically, Section 3.1.1 starts the Request and Response section, which spells out the required components of a request we want to make. Below is the basic format the IPP request byte stream will be composed of and is a quick start guide for creating requests.

Field	Size	Required
version-number	2 bytes	Yes
operational-id or status-code	2 bytes	Yes
request-id	4 bytes	Yes
attribute-group	n bytes	
end-of-attributes-tag	1 byte	Yes
data	q bytes	No

The IPP request is an HTTP POST method, with the URI formatted as *ipp://<printer_uri> /ipp/print*, where <printer_uri> is the DNS name of the target printer. We then create a binary payload for the POST request that will include the components required by RFC 8010 Section 3.1.1, which are (in C#) created as a binary stream. The code snippet below creates the first 4 fields required, i.e., version-number, operational-id, request-id, and attribute-group.

```
var ippVersionAndOperationId = new byte[] { 0x01, 0x01, 0x00, 0x0B
};      //version and op id
var requestId = new byte[] { 0x00, 0x00, 0x00, 0x01 }; // Request ID
var operationAttributesTag = new byte[] { 0x01 }; // Operation attributes
```

I should make a comment here on the version bytes required for this operation. These 2 bytes represent what version of IPP you want to converse with the printer in. Assuming the printer can accommodate your request, it should reply to you in the same version. This is like a "chicken and the egg" order as you do not initially know what IPP versions the printer can support until you get the reply from the printer. The initial version of IPP was 1.0, so this would be the default version to try in this case; you can always change the version requested when you recover what the printer can support via the **ipp-versions-supported** attribute.

```
var ippVersionAndOperationId = new byte[] { 0x01, 0x00, 0x00, 0x0B };
//version and op id
```

As an experiment, I sent an unsupported IPP version (I purposely used an invalid version 3.5) to my HP LaserJet Enterprise Flow MFP M528 printer, which claims support for versions 1.0, 1.1, and 2.0 of IPP. Debugging the IppPrintQuery project (in the code section of this chapter), error 1283 was sent back from the printer, which translates to an IPP_STATUS_ERROR_VERSION_NOT_SUPPORTED IPP error message. The point is this: the server (in this case the printer) will let you know if the version you select is not one it supports.

Once the required fields have been created, we can then concentrate on what we want the printer to provide to us in reply. As you might expect, there are essentially 2 attribute types for our Get-Printer-Attributes request: required attributes and requested attributes. To do this, we need to create attributes that the printer will understand. These attributes are created to form a byte buffer that gets appended to the existing request byte stream and forms part of the POST payload we require. Start with operational attributes that are required for the request: attributes-charset, attributes-natural-language, and printer-uri. You can find the required operational attributes specified for the Get-Printer-Attributes request via RFC 8011, Section 4.2.5.1. The operation attributes required are described by the RFC as follows:

> **"attributes-charset"** and "**attributes-natural-language**"
>
> **"printer-uri"**
>
> **"requesting-user-name"** (should be supplied by the Client)

For the following analysis, please open or load the IppPrinterQuery project, which is located in the code section of this chapter. We create these operational attributes in C# by using the CreatePrinterAttribute method of the RequestHelpers static class in the RequestHelpers.cs file. Notice the CreatePrinterAttribute method takes care of byte order formatting for us by arranging (for conversion of little-endian to Network byte order formatting) the most significant byte in the lower indexed position of the byte buffer (think leftmost position) automatically. The method also encodes any UTF-8 characters in their byte equivalents. Notice the first argument to this method takes a hex value, which represents the tag we are required to provide. You can find these values defined on page 22 of RFC 8010.

Handling Requested Attributes

Projects GetPrinterAttributesRequest and IppPrinterQuery, both in the code section of this chapter, illustrate ideas on how to handle encoding the operation's requested attributes. For IppPrinterQuery, the solution is straightforward since the example uses only "printer-description" as the only requested attribute. Thus, this example can get away with using the CreatePrinterAttribute method in the RequestHelper.cs file of that project.

```
byteList.AddRange(RequestHelpers.CreatePrinterAttribute(0x44, "requested-
attributes", "printer-description"));
```

The question is then obvious: how to handle the GetPrinterAttribute request when several requested attributes are specified? For this case, the GetPrinterAttributes project uses a slightly modified version that requires the caller to specify whether the requested attribute is the first attribute in the One Value Attribute with Additional Values type. As you recall, the first value will have a Name length, but subsequent values will not (since they share the same Name). This is handled by sending each value from the array of values (separated by ';' on the command line via the /r switch) into the CreateAttribute function of RequestHelpers.cs file as shown below:

```
for(int i = 0; i< requested_attributes.Length; i++)
{
    if (i == 0)
        byteList.AddRange(RequestHelpers.CreateAttribute(0x44, "requested-
        attributes", requested_attributes[i], true));
    else
        byteList.AddRange(RequestHelpers.CreateAttribute(0x44, "requested-
        attributes", requested_attributes[i], false));
}
```

The Boolean variable bFirstOf dictates how the Name length is encoded into the bytes stream. As shown for all the values after the first value, this means the Name length is 0.

```
public static byte[] CreateAttribute(byte tag, string name, string value,
bool bFirstOf)
 {
```

```
    var nameBytes = Encoding.UTF8.GetBytes(name);
    var valueBytes = Encoding.UTF8.GetBytes(value);

    // Convert nameBytes Integer16 length to 2 bytes, placing the MSB on
       the left (first) while the LSB on the right (second) for big-endian
       formatting,
    // then add these 2 bytes to the byte array. Concat the nameBytes
       UTF-8 formatted bytes to the byte array as well. Repeat again for
       valueBytes argument.

    if (bFirstOf)
    {
        return new byte[] { tag } // Attribute tag
            .Concat(new byte[] { (byte)(nameBytes.Length >> 8 & 0xFF),
            (byte)(nameBytes.Length & 0xFF) }) // Name length
            .Concat(nameBytes) // Name
            .Concat(new byte[] { (byte)(valueBytes.Length >> 8 & 0xFF),
            (byte)(valueBytes.Length & 0xFF) }) // Value length
            .Concat(valueBytes) // Value
            .ToArray();
    }
    else //If this is the (2nd or more) of a 1stOf list, then set the Name
    length to 0x00 and 0x00 in the byte stream
    {
        return new byte[] { tag } // Attribute tag
            .Concat(new byte[] { (byte)(0x00), (byte)(0x00) })
            .Concat(new byte[] { (byte)(valueBytes.Length >> 8 & 0xFF),
            (byte)(valueBytes.Length & 0xFF) }) // Value length
            .Concat(valueBytes) // Value
            .ToArray();
    }
}
```

The GetPrinterAttribute example uses the following attributes in the project Debug setting to illustrate this point:

```
output-mode-default
print-quality-supported
color-supported
printer-make-and-model
```

Depending on your printer vendor and model, you may have to modify this list (of course depending on what your printer supports). Let's dig a bit deeper into the CreateAttribute helper class to hopefully clarify more. The initial 2 lines of code concatenate the name and value of strings to byte arrays. The bFirstOf variable exists to ensure collections (such as the requested attributes collection) are properly formatted. Look at the Wireshark trace shown below, and in particular the requested-attributes collection that our code creates (in the example below, the requested attributes were printer-description, job-template, and media-col-database):

```
⌄ Internet Printing Protocol
    [Response In: 62]
    version: 1.1
    operation-id: Get-Printer-Attributes (0x000b)
    request-id: 1
  ⌄ operation-attributes-tag
    > attributes-charset (charset): 'utf-8'
    > attributes-natural-language (naturalLanguage): 'en'
    > printer-uri (uri): 'http://PEB-2J5-HPM608-BW/ipp/print'
    ⌄ requested-attributes (1setOf keyword): 'printer-description','job-template','media-col-database'
        name: requested-attributes
        keyword value: printer-description
        keyword value: job-template
        keyword value: media-col-database
    end-of-attributes-tag
```

This collection is a 1setOf keyword tag – essentially a data type that represents a set of values.

The name of this 1setOf keyword values is "requested-attributes", and all values (printer-description, job-template, and media-col-database in this example) follow but have no name value themselves. This type of attribute is a one-value attribute with additional values. This is covered in RFC 8010 sections 3.1.5: additional values have a Name length of 0x00. In the CreateAttribute function, when the bFirstOf value is set to false, the Name length is set to

```
.Concat(new byte[] { (byte)(0x00), (byte)(0x00) }) //The Name length is 0
```

while no Name value bytes are appended. Also notice that in all cases the Name length and Value length byte orders are reversed, or flipped, to ensure we convert to the big-endian format that is required, as shown below:

```
.Concat(new byte[] { (byte)(valueBytes.Length >> 8 & 0xFF), (byte)
(valueBytes.Length & 0xFF)
```

Processing the Response

When first approaching the byte stream response from the Get-Printer-Attributes request, it might prove intimidating to some. One way to alleviate the initial consternation might be to take a byte-by-byte approach to processing the return byte stream. You can do this on the provided C# code by stepping (byte by byte) through the response byte stream the printer provides. On any response, there are delimiter-tag values and value-tag values; these are defined in sections 3.5.1 and 3.5.2 of RFC 8010. The RFC specifies two types of response tags:

- **Delimiter-tag values**: These are used to mark the beginning of a new attribute group. They help the printer understand that an entire group of attributes is being defined. Delimiter-tag values range from 0x00 to 0x0F.

  *Each Delimiter-tag value section of attributes must be closed by an "end-of-attributes-tag" per RFC 8010.

- **Value-tag values**: These are used to specify the type of value that follows. They indicate the data type of the attribute value, such as Integer, Boolean, or Text. Value tag values range from 0x10 to 0xFF.

For the Get-Printer-Attributes request, the return from my HP M528 printer contains an "operations-attributes-tag" along with a host of attributes, each with their own value-tag. The "end-of-attributes" tag then follows to close the delimiter tag.

Of the value-tag values, there are 2 major types of attributes: the one-value attribute field and the collection attribute field. The one value attribute can have additional values, which are described as "additional-value" fields. The collection attribute contains one or more "member-attribute" fields.

These are described in Sections 3.1.4-3.1.7 in RFC 8010.

Attribute with One Value Fields

Described in Section 3.1.4 of RFC 8010, this is the easiest of the attribute fields to deal with. This is a field with a one-to-one relationship between the name and values assigned to a field; i.e., there is only one attribute value assigned to an attribute name. A high-level processing overview of this attribute on a byte-by-byte basis is described below.

1. Decipher the value tag byte to one of the supported types from Section 3.5.2 of RFC 8010. Those value tag type(s) will tell us what type of value (string, byte, integer, datetime, etc.) we should expect.

2. We will read the next 2 bytes in the stream into an integer value. This integer 16 value will be the length we need for the name of the attribute. For instance, 0x1b hex converts to 27 decimal, which is our length; thus, we should expect 27 octets (cast as UTF-8 chars) to comprise the name. You should notice that variable-length decoding does not need to be flipped for this lab exercise: big-endian format (which this stream is in) is already the format humans derive the value from (MSB in the leftmost place). Only if we were to store this multi-byte number as a value in a variable on the Windows machine would the bytes need to be flipped.

3. Once we have the length, we read the next n bytes (in step 2, for example, that would be 27 bytes) from the byte stream into a name variable.

4. After the last byte is processed from step 3, the next 2 bytes in the byte stream are processed as the length of the attribute value. As with the Name field, we must convert from hex to decimal to get the correct size. Thus, for instance, if we have a NameWithLanguage (0x36) tag (from step 1) and then process the value length bytes to discover a length of 25, we should expect 25 octet bytes to comprise the value.

5. We copy n bytes (in the example for step 4, 25 bytes) to a value variable.

6. We are finished with this attribute field; the next byte from the byte field will be another value tag byte (or possibly the end of the attributes tag). Repeat step 1 again.

As you can see, the one value field attribute is basic in approach. To cement this in your mind, let us take a simple stream of bytes comprising an Attribute with one-value field and walk through it. Suppose you were tasked with converting the following byte stream into a one-value field attribute. Using the steps above, this can be broken down as shown below:

```
48 00 1b 61 74 74 72 69 62 75 74 65 73 2d 6e 61 74 75 72 61 6c 2d 6c 61 6e
67 75 61 67 65 00 02 65     6e
```

Start the process by working left to right on the byte stream beginning at the value tag (0x48).

48 00 1b 61 74 74 72 69 62 75 74 65 73 2d 6e 61 74 75 72 61 6c 2d 6c 61 6e
67 75 61 67 65 00 02 65   6e

1. The value tag is 0x48, which from table 6 of RFC 8010 is a natural language type.

   48 **00 1b** 61 74 74 72 69 62 75 74 65 73 2d 6e 61 74 75 72
   61 6c 2d 6c 61 6e 67 75 61 67 65 00 02 65   6e

2. Read the next 2 bytes: 0x00 and 0x1b - this tells us the Name length is 27 bytes (decimal). We can then create the proper size buffer and copy 27 bytes from the 0x1b byte into this buffer in the next step.

   48 00 1b **61 74 74 72 69 62 75 74 65 73 2d 6e 61 74 75 72**
   61 6c 2d 6c 61 6e 67 75 61 67 65 00 02 65   6e

3. The 27 bytes that represent the name value - this number of bytes was determined by the bytes 0x00, 0x1b in the last step. You can look them up in a UTF-8 chart as the following:

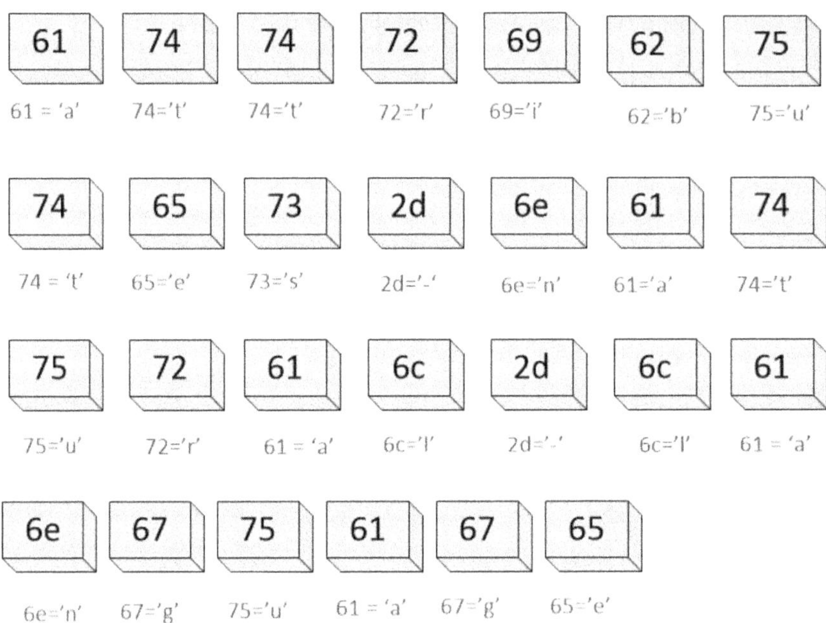

Name (27 bytes) is 'attributes-natural-language'

48 00 1b 61 74 74 72 69 62 75 74 65 73 2d 6e 61 74 75 72
61 6c 2d 6c 61 6e 67 75 61 67 65 **00 02** 65 6e

4. After the Name value, we read the next 2 bytes as the length of the value, 0x00 0x02, which translates to 2 (decimal).

48 00 1b 61 74 74 72 69 62 75 74 65 73 2d 6e 61 74 75 72
61 6c 2d 6c 61 6e 67 75 61 67 65 00 02 **65 6e**

5. We create the proper size buffer from the value (2 bytes) obtained in step 4. Since we know the tag is a natural language tag, we process the byte buffer as UTF-8 chars. From the UTF-8 chart, we see that bytes 65 and 62 convert to 'en'.

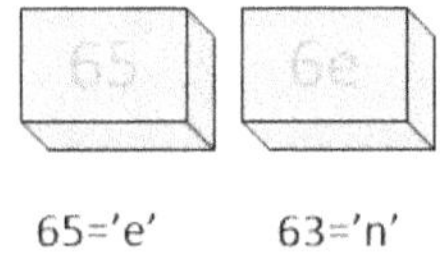

Value is 'en'

Thus, we have a name value of "attributes-natural-language" and a value of "en". Congratulations - you have successfully processed an Attribute with One-Value fields!

For simplicity in this demonstration, I processed each character assuming the US ASCII character set, which uses single-byte encoding and aligns with ASCII for easy lookup. However, IPP RFC 8011, Section 5.14.18, mandates that all text strings in IPP responses are encoded in UTF-8. Given that the code may run in diverse environments and printers may return strings in various cultural character sets, all string processing (in .NET) should use the System.Text.Encoding.UTF8.GetString method to ensure proper UTF-8 decoding. Please see the Character Encoding Addendum for more information.

One Value Attribute with Additional Values

As described in Section 3.1.5 of RFC 8010, one value attribute with additional values is only slightly more complex to handle than one with a single value. The first value is processed identically to that of the single-value attribute; the difference lies in processing the subsequent values of the collection. In the subsequent values, the name-length field (which is identical for all values since it is shared by them) has a size of 0x0000 to signify that it is an "additional-value". Thus, when you process an attribute with a collection of values, you should expect a name-length field of 0x0000 for the subsequent value-values. With this in mind, we will outline how to process these fields.

1. Decipher the value tag byte to one of the supported types from Section 3.5.2 of RFC 8010. Those value tag type(s) will tell us what type of value (string, byte, integer, datetime, etc.) we should expect.

2. We will read the next 2 bytes in the stream into an integer value - we can read the value into an integer16 variable. This interger16 value provides the length (or size) for the attribute name. So, for instance, if the length is 20, we should expect 20 ASCII octets (cast as ASCII chars) to comprise the name. This is similar to what is required for a single value attribute, but there is a twist: once the first name-length is read, subsequent name-lengths associated

with the collection will have a size of 0x0000. If you think about it, that would be a logical choice because the original name-value is naturally the same for all the subsequent value-values in the collection. Thus, there is no need to specify the same name values for each entry in the collection.

3. Once we have the length, we read (for the first element of the collection) the next n bytes (in the step 2 example that would be 20) from the byte stream into a name variable. This name-value will be shared by all the following value-values in the attribute. Of course, if the name-length from step 2 is 0x0000, we do not copy a name value as there is no need to do so.

4. After the last byte is processed from step 3, the next 2 bytes in the byte stream are processed as the length of the attribute value. As with the Name field, we must flip the byte order to get the correct size.

5. We copy n bytes to a value variable.

6. Repeat steps 1-5. After each set of steps, you will process a new attribute tag.

Again, let us look at a binary stream recovered on a recent Get-Printer-Attributes request, this time investigating additional values.

```
44 00 16 69 70 70 2d 76 65 72 73 69 6f 6e 73 2d 73 75 70 70 6f 72 74 65 64
00 03 31 2e 30 44 00 00 00 03 31 2e 31 44 00 00 00 03 32 2e 30
```

Starting at the first byte, we will progress through the byte stream according to the outline above.

44 00 16 69 70 70 2d 76 65 72 73 69 6f 6e 73 2d 73 75 70 70 6f 72 74 65 64
00 03 31 2e 30 44 00 00 00 03 31 2e 31 44 00 00 00 03 32 2e 30

1. The first byte is a value tag of 0x44, which from table 6 of RFC 8010, is a keyword type.

   44 **00 16** 69 70 70 2d 76 65 72 73 69 6f 6e 73 2d 73 75 70
   70 6f 72 74 65 64 00 03 31 2e 30 44 00 00 00 03 31 2e 31
   44 00 00 00 03 32 2e 30

2. The bytes 0x00 0x16 comprise an integer16 representing a name-length of 22 decimal.

   44 00 16 **69 70 70 2d 76 65 72 73 69 6f 6e 73 2d 73 75 70 70 6f 72 74 65 64** 00 03 31 2e 30 44 00 00 00 03 31 2e 31 44 00 00 00 03 32 2e 30

3. The octets 0x69 – 0x64 represent a name value of 22 bytes spelling out "ipp-versions-supported" when referenced in the UTF-8 chart, as shown below.

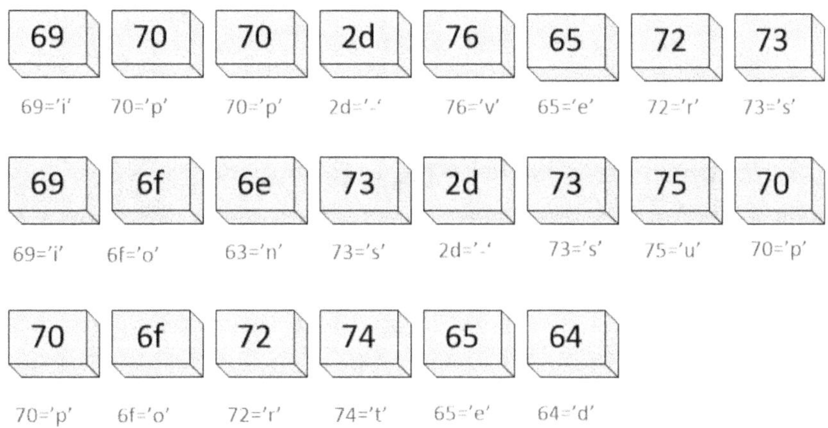

   44 00 16 69 70 70 2d 76 65 72 73 69 6f 6e 73 2d 73 75 70 70 6f 72 74 65 64 **00 03** 31 2e 30 44 00 00 00 03 31 2e 31 44 00 00 00 03 32 2e 30

4. The 0x00 0x03 bytes represent the value length, in this case 3 (decimal) bytes. This will be the length of the next value (in step 5).

   44 00 16 69 70 70 2d 76 65 72 73 69 6f 6e 73 2d 73 75 70 70 6f 72 74 65 64 00 03 **31 2e 30** 44 00 00 00 03 31 2e 31 44 00 00 00 03 32 2e 30

5. The 0x31 0x2e 0x30 bytes represent the first value in the collection, in this case "1.0" in the UTF-8 chart.

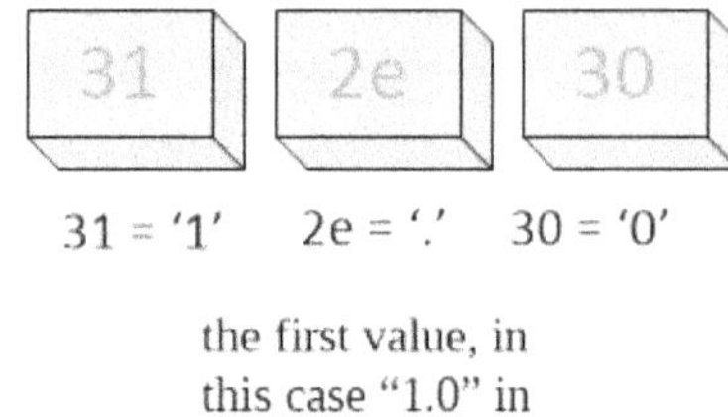

44 00 16 69 70 70 2d 76 65 72 73 69 6f 6e 73 2d 73 75 70 70 6f 72 74 65 64 00 03 31 2e 30 **44** 00 00 00 03 31 2e 31 44 00 00 00 03 32 2e 30

6. The 0x44 byte represents a value tag, which from table 6 of RFC 8010 is a keyword type.

44 00 16 69 70 70 2d 76 65 72 73 69 6f 6e 73 2d 73 75 70 70 6f 72 74 65 64 00 03 31 2e 30 44 **00 00** 00 03 31 2e 31 44 00 00 00 03 32 2e 30

7. The 00 00 bolded bytes represent the name length of 0. As a name length of 0 tells us this is an additional value, we know this value is associated with the name value of step 3.

44 00 16 69 70 70 2d 76 65 72 73 69 6f 6e 73 2d 73 75 70 70 6f 72 74 65 64 00 03 31 2e 30 44 00 00 **00 03** 31 2e 31 44 00 00 00 03 32 2e 30

8. The 00 03 bolded bytes are a value length associated with the collection. This tells us the value should be 0x03 or 3 decimal bytes long.

44 00 16 69 70 70 2d 76 65 72 73 69 6f 6e 73 2d 73 75 70 70 6f 72 74 65 64 00 03 31 2e 30 44 00 00 00 03 **31 2e 31** 44 00 00 00 03 32 2e 30

9. The next 0x31 0x2e 0x31 bytes are a value associated with the name value of step 3, in this case "1.1" from the UTF-8 table.

```
44 00 16 69 70 70 2d 76 65 72 73 69 6f 6e 73 2d 73 75 70
70 6f 72 74 65 64 00 03 31 2e 30 44 00 00 00 03 31 2e 31
44 00 00 00 03 32 2e 30
```

10. The next byte (0x44) represents a value tag, which from table 6 of RFC 8010 is a keyword type.

```
44 00 16 69 70 70 2d 76 65 72 73 69 6f 6e 73 2d 73 75 70
70 6f 72 74 65 64 00 03 31 2e 30 44 00 00 00 03 31 2e 31
44 00 00 00 03 32 2e 30
```

11. The 00 00 bolded bytes represent the name length of 0. As a name length of 0 tells us this is an additional value, we know this value is associated with the name value of step 3.

```
44 00 16 69 70 70 2d 76 65 72 73 69 6f 6e 73 2d 73 75 70
70 6f 72 74 65 64 00 03 31 2e 30 44 00 00 00 03 31 2e 31
44 00 00 00 03 32 2e 30
```

12. The 00 03 bytes are a value length associated with the additional value. This tells us the value should be 0x03 or 3 decimal bytes long.

```
44 00 16 69 70 70 2d 76 65 72 73 69 6f 6e 73 2d 73 75 70
70 6f 72 74 65 64 00 03 31 2e 30 44 00 00 00 03 31 2e 31
44 00 00 00 03 32 2e 30
```

13. Finally, the 32 2e 30 bytes are values associated with the name value of step 3, in this case, "2.0" from the UTF-8 table.
    Thus, we have finished processing additional attribute values from the byte stream. The result looks like this:

```
ipp-versions-supported
1.0
1.1
2.0
```

Collection Attribute

Described in Sections 3.1.6–3.1.7 of RFC 8010 is the collection attribute. This attribute creates a named group that holds comparable properties or related members. To be examined are the collection of media-size-supported members pulled from an actual Wireshark trace performed on an HP M608 network printer. To start with, the collection attribute should have a value-tag of 0x34 hex. The collection ends when an end-value-tag (0x37) is encountered in the byte stream. After the end-value-tag (0x37), there is an end-name-length field (2 bytes) and, following that, an end-value-length field (2 bytes), both of which are set to 0x0000. Thus, the basic format of a collection attribute consists of:

```
0x34      (value-tag)
:
:         member attributes
:
0x37      (end-value-tag)
0x0000    (end-name-length)
0x0000    (end-value-length)
```

An overall sequence of processing the byte stream could be summarized as:

1. A collection attribute always starts with a byte value of 0x34.
2. A 2-byte name-length value follows the value tag.
3. A x-number of bytes Name string is next; x corresponds to the value of the 2-byte name-length value obtained in step 2.
4. A 2-byte value-length follows step 3 and is set to 0x0000.

   ---------------------Member Attributes-----------------------

   1. Each member attribute starts with a 0x4a value tag.
   2. The name-length value (2 bytes) is set to 0x0000.
   3. The value-length of w bytes determines the size of the value in step 4.
   4. The value
   5. A member value tag now follows the value - the member tag is one of the tag values specified in Tables 4–6 in RFC 8010. For

instance, if this value is 0x21, this corresponds to an integer value (from table 4).

6. A name-length value (2 bytes) is next and is set to 0x0000.

7. A member-value-length field (2 bytes) is next and is y bytes. This length determines the length of the member-value that follows.

8. The member-value whose size is set in step 7 is set here.

-------------------------Member Attributes-----------------------------

5. The end-value-tag (0x37) follows the member attributes.

6. The (2-byte) end-name-length, which has a set value of 0x0000.

7. The (2-byte) end-value-length, which has a set value of 0x0000.

An example binary stream is a useful source to help cement the processing concepts down for collection attributes. The binary stream below (80 bytes total) was recovered from the HP M608 printer via a Wireshark trace. We will process this byte by byte following the sequence of processing summarized above.

```
34 00 14 6d 65 64 69 61 2d 73 69 7a 65 2d 73 75 70 70 6f 72 74 65 64 00 00
4a 00 00 00 0b 78 2d 64
69 6d 65 6e 73 69 6f 6e 21 00 00 00 04 00 00 54 56 4a 00 00 00 0b 79 2d 64
69 6d 65 6e 73 69 6f 6e
21 00 00 00 04 00 00 6d 24 37 00 00 00 00
```

34 00 14 6d 65 64 69 61 2d 73 69 7a 65 2d 73 75 70 70 6f 72 74 65 64 00 00
4a 00 00 00 0b 78 2d 64
69 6d 65 6e 73 69 6f 6e 21 00 00 00 04 00 00 54 56 4a 00 00 00 0b 79 2d 64
69 6d 65 6e 73 69 6f 6e
21 00 00 00 04 00 00 6d 24 37 00 00 00 00

1. The value tag is 0x34, and the name-length bytes (0x00, 0x14) equate to 20 bytes for the length.

34 00 14 **6d 65 64 69 61 2d 73 69 7a 65 2d 73 75 70 70 6f**
72 74 65 64 00 00 4a 00 00 00 0b 78 2d 64
69 6d 65 6e 73 69 6f 6e 21 00 00 00 04 00 00 54 56 4a 00
00 00 0b 79 2d 64 69 6d 65 6e 73 69 6f 6e
21 00 00 00 04 00 00 6d 24 37 00 00 00 00

2. The 0x6d, 0x65, 0x64, 0x69, 0x61, 0x2d, 0x73, 0x69, 0x7a, 0x65, 0x2d, 0x73, 0x75, 0x70, 0x70, 0x6f, 0x72, 0x74, 0x65, 0x64 bytes form an ASCII string composed of 0x14 or 20 bytes. This string spells out "**media-size-supported**".

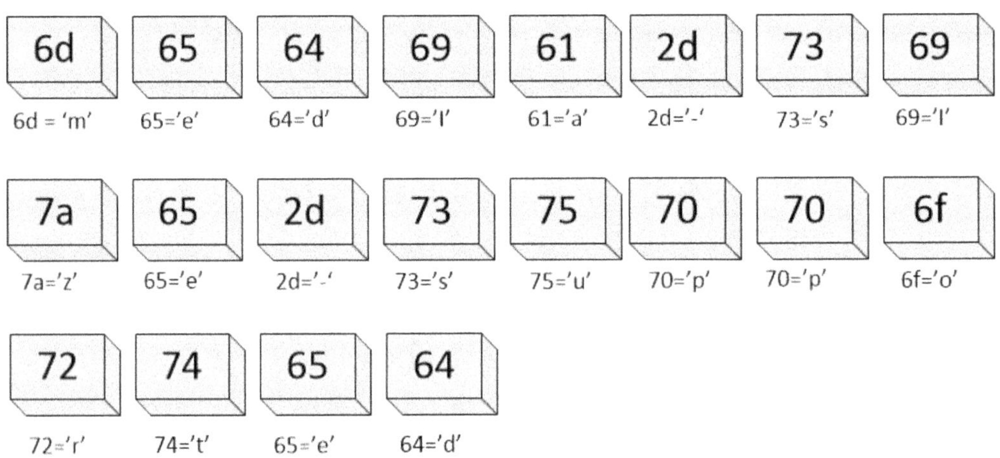

34 00 14 6d 65 64 69 61 2d 73 69 7a 65 2d 73 75 70 70 6f
72 74 65 64 **00 00 4a** 00 00 00 0b 78 2d 64
69 6d 65 6e 73 69 6f 6e 21 00 00 00 04 00 00 54 56 4a 00
00 00 0b 79 2d 64 69 6d 65 6e 73 69 6f 6e
21 00 00 00 04 00 00 6d 24 37 00 00 00 00

3. The value length is 0x00, 0x00. We start a member attribute (of the collection); the value-tag for this member is 0x4a.

34 00 14 6d 65 64 69 61 2d 73 69 7a 65 2d 73 75 70 70 6f
72 74 65 64 00 00 4a **00 00 00 0b** 78 2d 64
69 6d 65 6e 73 69 6f 6e 21 00 00 00 04 00 00 54 56 4a 00
00 00 0b 79 2d 64 69 6d 65 6e 73 69 6f 6e
21 00 00 00 04 00 00 6d 24 37 00 00 00 00

4. The member attribute name length (always set to 0x00, 0x00) and value length. In this case the value length is 0x00, 0x0b, which equates to 11 (decimal) bytes.

34 00 14 6d 65 64 69 61 2d 73 69 7a 65 2d 73 75 70 70 6f
72 74 65 64 00 00 4a 00 00 00 0b **78 2d 64**
69 6d 65 6e 73 69 6f 6e 21 00 00 00 04 00 00 54 56 4a 00
00 00 0b 79 2d 64 69 6d 65 6e 73 69 6f 6e
21 00 00 00 04 00 00 6d 24 37 00 00 00 00

5. The member-attribute Name value forms "***x-dimension***" and is 11 bytes long as provided in step 4.

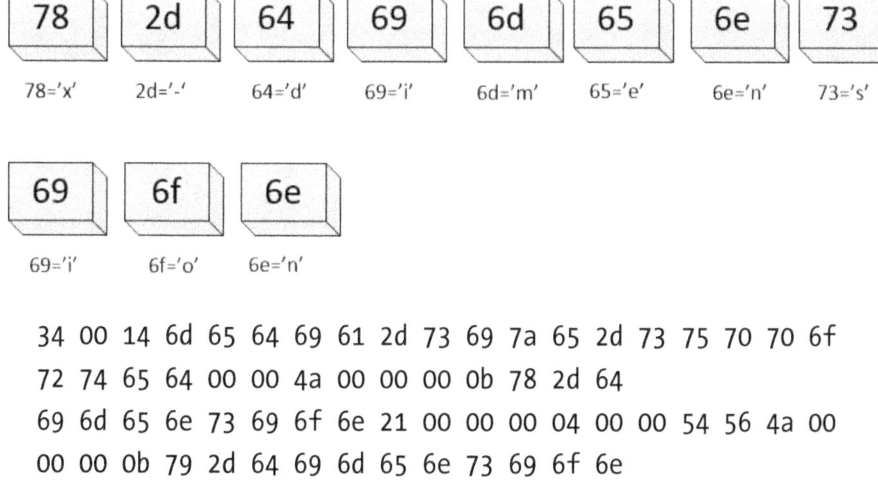

34 00 14 6d 65 64 69 61 2d 73 69 7a 65 2d 73 75 70 70 6f
72 74 65 64 00 00 4a 00 00 00 0b 78 2d 64
69 6d 65 6e 73 69 6f 6e 21 00 00 00 04 00 00 54 56 4a 00
00 00 0b 79 2d 64 69 6d 65 6e 73 69 6f 6e
21 00 00 00 04 00 00 6d 24 37 00 00 00 00

6. The 5 bytes that follow the Name value in step 5 comprise the member value tag. The byte value (0x21) equates to an Integer type when looking at Section 3.5.2, Table 4 of RFC 8010. The Name length is 2 bytes at 0x00, 0x00, which is constant. The next 2 bytes are 0x00 and 0x04, which sets the length of the value to 4 bytes.

34 00 14 6d 65 64 69 61 2d 73 69 7a 65 2d 73 75 70 70 6f
72 74 65 64 00 00 4a 00 00 00 0b 78 2d 64

```
69 6d 65 6e 73 69 6f 6e 21 00 00 00 04 00 00 54 56 4a 00
00 00 0b 79 2d 64 69 6d 65 6e 73 69 6f 6e
21 00 00 00 04 00 00 6d 24 37 00 00 00 00
```

7. The next 4 bytes (specified by the value-length size above) should be interpreted as an integer.
   The value is 27,940 in decimal. (0x6d, 0x24 = 27940, check using the Calculator program)

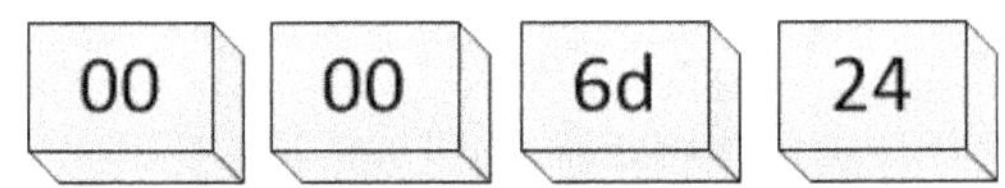

The Integer value is 4 bytes long.
The decimal value is 27,940

```
34 00 14 6d 65 64 69 61 2d 73 69 7a 65 2d 73 75 70 70 6f
72 74 65 64 00 00 4a 00 00 00 0b 78 2d 64
69 6d 65 6e 73 69 6f 6e 21 00 00 00 04 00 00 54 56 4a 00
00 00 0b 79 2d 64 69 6d 65 6e 73 69 6f 6e
21 00 00 00 04 00 00 6d 24 37 00 00 00 00
```

8. The next byte processed is the end-of-collection value tag set at 0x37 in Section 3.1.6 of RC 8010. This signifies the end of the collection.

```
34 00 14 6d 65 64 69 61 2d 73 69 7a 65 2d 73 75 70 70 6f
72 74 65 64 00 00 4a 00 00 00 0b 78 2d 64
69 6d 65 6e 73 69 6f 6e 21 00 00 00 04 00 00 54 56 4a 00
00 00 0b 79 2d 64 69 6d 65 6e 73 69 6f 6e
21 00 00 00 04 00 00 6d 24 37 00 00 00 00
```

9. The member attributes end-name-length (always set to 0x00, 0x00) and end-value-length are next. The end-value length is also constant at 0x00, 0x00 per Section 3.1.6 of RFC 8010.

Now that you have a concept of how to process the attributes you are likely to encounter in the Get-Printer-Attributes response, it might be good to look at how to process the response conceptually. We will back this up by introducing some C# code to reinforce the concept, but for now a high-level look at processing the response would be:

1. Get the IPP version.
2. Get the status code - only move ahead if the status is 0.
3. Get a delimiter-tag value.
4. Process all value-tags until.
5. You get an end-of-attributes tag.

Creating a Get-Printer-Attributes utility

To put the above in a concrete example, open the VS project GetPrinterAttributesRequest, which is a C# solution in the code section of this chapter. The solution is not intended as production code; it was created for learning purposes only. The code is virtually littered with descriptive printouts that clutter the output. While this may aid in learning how the byte stream is processed, it is hardly efficient or fast. There are several good IPP libraries out there, including, of course, the CUPS port to Windows in C. I would encourage you to use these libraries if you plan to design code for your enterprise; they are all particularly good. However, in many instances their efficient design tends to abstract away the menial or lower-layer operations, which of course makes these libraries ideal for development work. Unfortunately, this also makes it difficult for those curious to learn all the inner workings to easily follow or trace what is happening. For this purpose (to debug and trace), I present the GetPrinterAttributesRequest solution, which does not abstract any of the protocol working away and should make it easy to step through a response in the debugger.

A bit on the actual program - you will notice I make little or no effort to abstract details the purpose is to provide understanding rather than elegance or efficiency. In Program.cs, I make judicious use of LINQ's Concat method to combine arrays as this allows you to see how the byte stream is built and in what order this is accomplished. For instance, in Program.cs you should see the

```
var requestPayload = ippVersionAndOperationId
              .Concat(requestId)
```

```
            .Concat(operationAttributesTag)
            // Add the attributes
            .Concat(attributesCharset)
            .Concat(attributesNaturalLanguage)
            .Concat(printerUriAttribute)
            //Add the requested-attributes
            .Concat (concatenatedArray)
            .Concat(endOfAttributesTag)
            .ToArray();
```

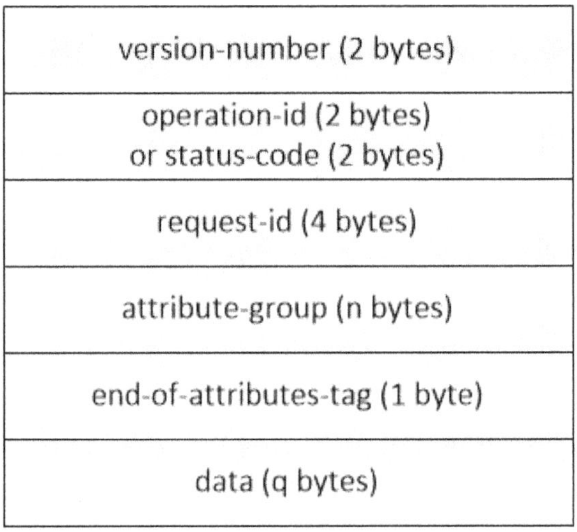

version-number (2 bytes)
operation-id (2 bytes) or status-code (2 bytes)
request-id (4 bytes)
attribute-group (n bytes)
end-of-attributes-tag (1 byte)
data (q bytes)

IPP Message Format

Byte array requestPayload is constructed according to Section 3.1.1 of RFC 8010. The HttpClient object receives a timeout of 30 seconds, and we cancel the task after this time so we can determine a TCP timeout and react accordingly with the exception catch statement.

```
using (var client = new HttpClient { Timeout = TimeSpan.FromSeconds(30) })
using (var cts = new CancellationTokenSource(TimeSpan.FromSeconds(30)))
```

As it is, this example just prints an error to the console, but you could alert the user with more informative statements if you wanted. The next few lines of code make the actual request to the printer and get a response. I created these asynchronously, which in this context does little since we are running a console application. However, if this code was in a GUI utility using WPF or WinForms, then running asynchronously would then yield to the dispatcher (WPF GUI thread) while waiting for the printer and make the program appear more responsive to the user.

```
var response = await client.PostAsync(printerUri, content, cts.Token);
await GetIppResponse(response);
```

Build the solution in Visual Studio, and you can then make some test runs using your own networked printer as the target. Ensure your printer is reachable (ping the printer) and make sure your printer has the IPP service turned on. The solution is specifically developed to use IPP over IPPS because IPPS makes use of TLS encryption. For debugging or learning purposes, it is helpful to use IPP (vice IPPS) as this will allow you to view the resultant session through the IPP dissector that Wireshark employs. If you do not have a networked printer to use, you can simulate one via the IppServer utility - see Chapter 9, "IPP Tools," for details.

If you are still a bit cloudy on IPP byte stream processing (particularly for the Get-Printer-Attributes request), you could set a breakpoint at various locations in the ResponseHelpers.cs file to walk through the process. For instance, maybe you want a breakpoint at the printer attribute tag (in the GetIppAttributes method) and then walk through the byte sequencing from there.

```
case DelimiterTag.PrinterAttributesTag:
    Console.WriteLine("This is a printer attribute tag");
break;
```

Alternatively, you might want to walk through the byte sequencing of a particular value tag. For instance, in the GetValueTagString method inside the ResponseHelpers.cs file, if you place a Breakpoint at the line:

```
case ValueTag.Uri:
return "Value Tag: Uri";
```

You would be able to walk through the byte sequencing of a Uri step by step prior to the 0x45 byte value tag in the byte stream being processed.

Writing a Simple IPP Printer Inventory Utility

I suspect you are about done with byte stream processing for a while and are ready to take a look at some practical applications for using the Get-Printer-Attributes request using the .NET HttpClient object. Despite the limitations of the GetPrinterAttributesRequest code written in C#, there are some practical variations of the code that can be useful. Because it does not use the WinRT APIs and instead uses the .NET HttpClient, it can send a Get-Printer-Attributes request to any IPP printer listening. This is exactly what you would want for a simple printer inventory utility that could query 10, 50, or hundreds of IPP printers within an enterprise. You certainly would not want to install all these printers on your Windows machine to get their attributes, and using the HttpClient object to send formatted IPP requests (aligned with PWG IPP standards) does not require you to do that.

As mentioned earlier, for production code you might want to use the OpenPrinting CUPS IPP port (C/C++) for long-term support and stability. Since we are providing examples and ideas of how to use the Get-Printer-Attributes request, I have provided some C# code that can query any number of IPP printers on your network and return information about them that might prove useful. For instance, are all your printers up-to-date with the firmware they are running? Do you know what versions of IPP your printers support and what version of Mopria? Do you know their operational and color support status? As this code follows the PWG IPP protocol design and is not built on WinRTs, it is tailor-made to centrally query IPP printer objects without having to install the printers on your Windows machine. Interestingly, since this code was built on the HttpClient object and not on WinRTs, the Windows spooler service can be stopped, and it will not affect the operation at all. To learn how this works, the next part of this chapter will revolve around the IppPrinterQuery solution in the code section of this chapter.

The IppPrinterQuery solution is intended to be a lightweight method of gathering IPP printer attributes on your network. The command line to use this is simplistic: you provide a list of printers that you want to test and an XML file of attributes you want to monitor. If you compile the solution and were to run this from the command line, you would supply a command line like the following:

```
IppPrinterQuery /p=C:\Temp\PrinterList.txt /f=C:\Temp\MyAttributes.xml
```

Where C:\Temp\PrinterList.txt would be the list of printers to test – these are placed in the text file, one printer per line. The next argument to supply bears some explanation. This is essentially a list of attributes returned from the **printer-description** attribute group that might be of some interest. Feel free to add additional requested attribute groups to expand the pool of attributes available to monitor. I kept this solution as simple as possible, but you can expand it to fit your requirements rather easily. Just keep in mind that the attributes returned are limited to the attributes contained within any attribute-request groups for components returned by the printer.

The Program.cs file in the solution starts by ensuring the command line arguments are valid, and that both the printer list text file and attributes XML files are properly processed. The **LoadXmlFile** function simply gets the attributes listed under the "SingleAttributes" node (of the attributes file) and copies them to a generic list of strings called SingleAttributes. The solution also has a folder named Collections that contains three files: IppAttributeObject, IppPrinter, and IppPrinters (.cs). The IppPrinters file is a collection of IppPrinter objects, which itself contains a list of IppAttributeObjects.

The IppAttributeObject is the representation of an IPP attribute: it contains a name (of the attribute), a list of values, and a value tag (a hex value of the attribute provided by RFC 8010).

Leveraging the OpenPrinting CUPS IPP Port to Windows

While using the C# HttpClient class can be instrumental in gaining an understanding of how the IPP protocol works, for any production code you should seriously consider using the OpenPrinting group CUPS port to Windows. The website defines this development effort as

> "The CUPS library (Libcups) provides a common C API for HTTP/HTTPS and IPP communications on Unix®-like operating systems and Microsoft Windows®" [1].

This port is maintained by the OpenPrinting group and should thus have support for the long term. While there are other libraries floating on the internet that provide IPP/IPPS developer support, the long-term support issue might be a concern. For these reasons I would recommend basing production code on the OpenPrinting IPP port.

You can find the download site here:

> GitHub - OpenPrinting/libcups: OpenPrinting CUPS Library Sources

The OpenPrinting IPP CUPS port for Windows is developed using C/C++ and is relatively straightforward to use. The LibCups solution in this chapter's code folder contains 2 projects built from this OpenPrinting LibCups download. To save time, I have included a project (WinIpp) that wraps the OpenPrinting CUPS port APIs. For the two projects in the solution, one is built using C/C++ (WinIppTest), while the other (CH_GPA_CH3) is built using C#. Both projects provide a Get-Printer-Attributes request based on the LibCups library. I should also mention that, while using the OpenPrinting LibCups download, I removed extraneous projects included in the download for clarity.

First up is the WinIppTest C/C++ project. You might need to compile the solution before you start working with any of the projects. Once you have compiled the solution, you should right-click the WinIppTest project in the solution and then select **Set as Startup Project**, as seen below.

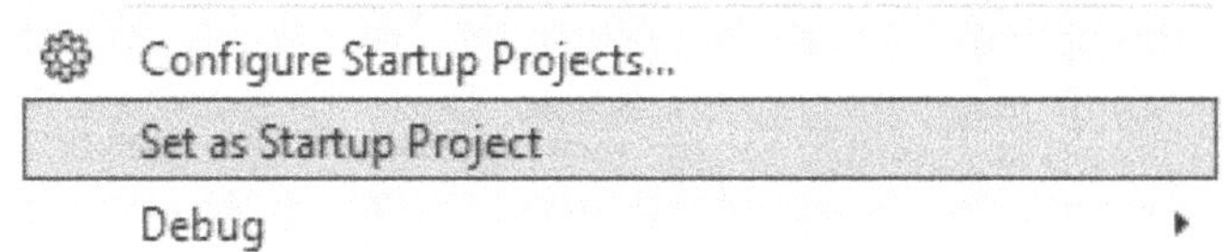

The WinIppTest project allows you to print jobs, validate jobs, cancel jobs, identify your printer, and get the attributes your printer supports. We can use this project for later chapters in this book, but for now I would direct your attention to retrieving the printer attributes as other code in this chapter has accomplished. To perform a Get-Printer-Attributes request with WinIppTest, you need to enter the DNS printer name and the /a argument, as in ***WinIppTest /p=<printer-name> /a***. WinIppTest in turn calls the WinIpp wrapper function WrGetPrinterAttributes. If you open the WinIpp project file WinIpp.dll, you can see how this function works. While much of this function is straightforward, I should comment on a few lines of code.

```
If ((encryption == HTTP_ENCRYPTION_ALWAYS) || (encryption == HTTP_
ENCRYPTION_REQUIRED))
{
      sprintf_s(szUriTag, "%s%s%s", "ipps://", hostname, "/ipp/print");
      iPort = 443;
}
else
{
      sprintf_s(szUriTag, "%s%s%s", "ipp://", hostname, "/ipp/print");
```

```
    iPort = 631;
}
```

Up to now, the discussion has not centered on IPP or IPPS as most of the code and examples are written using IPP and port 631. This code ensures that when the user calls for encryption, the underlying HTTP request uses TLS. Thus, when the caller requests encryption, the URI will use "ipps" and the port will be 443. Otherwise, if encryption is not specified, we use "ipp" and port 631. Of course, to use IPPS (port 443), your printer needs to have IPPS enabled.

```
static const char* const requested_attributes[] =
{
    "printer-description",
    "job-template",
    "media-col-database"
};
```

The wrapper locks the requested attributes to those listed above, designed to provide a more extensive set of attributes. You can change this setting as you wish for more specific applications.

```
http = httpConnect(hostname, iPort, NULL, AF_UNSPEC, (http_encryption_t)
encryption, 1, timeout, NULL);
if (http == NULL)
{
    ipp_status_t status = IPP_STATUS_ERROR_SERVICE_UNAVAILABLE;
    *retCode = status;
    NULL;
}
```

The httpConnect API is called with the proper port number 443/631 and encryption request. The TCP timeout is set to 3000 by the default argument value (set in the header file). If the connection fails for any reason, the retCode pointer value is set, and the return value of the function itself is set to NULL. This is because the function, if successful, returns a pointer to an array of attributes. A failure returning NULL should signal to the caller (in addition to the retCode pointer value) that the returned pointer should not be used.

```
request = ippNewRequest(IPP_OP_GET_PRINTER_ATTRIBUTES);
ippAddString(request, IPP_TAG_OPERATION, IPP_TAG_URI, "printer-uri", NULL,
szUriTag);
ippAddString(request, IPP_TAG_OPERATION, IPP_TAG_NAME, "requesting-user-
name", NULL, userName);
ippAddString(request, IPP_TAG_OPERATION, IPP_TAG_MIMETYPE, "document-
format", NULL, "image/pwg-raster");
```

The next thing the wrapper does is set the IPP Request code, this being set to the IPP_OP_GET _PRINTER_ATTRIBUTES constant defined in the ipp.h header file in libcups3 library.

```

typedef enum ipp_op_e            // IPP operations
{
  IPP_OP_CUPS_INVALID = -1,      // Invalid operation name for @link ippOpValue@
  IPP_OP_CUPS_NONE = 0,          // No operation @private@
  IPP_OP_PRINT_JOB = 0x0002,         // Print-Job: Print a single file
  IPP_OP_PRINT_URI,            // Print-URI: Print a single URL @exclude all@
  IPP_OP_VALIDATE_JOB,           // Validate-Job: Validate job values prior to submission
  IPP_OP_CREATE_JOB,             // Create-Job: Create an empty print job
  IPP_OP_SEND_DOCUMENT,          // Send-Document: Add a file to a job
  IPP_OP_SEND_URI,             // Send-URI: Add a URL to a job @exclude all@
  IPP_OP_CANCEL_JOB,             // Cancel-Job: Cancel a job
  IPP_OP_GET_JOB_ATTRIBUTES,         // Get-Job-Attribute: Get information about a job
  IPP_OP_GET_JOBS,             // Get-Jobs: Get a list of jobs
  IPP_OP_GET_PRINTER_ATTRIBUTES,     // Get-Printer-Attributes: Get information about a printer
  IPP_OP_HOLD_JOB,             // Hold-Job: Hold a job for printing
  IPP_OP_RELEASE_JOB,            // Release-Job: Release a job for printing
```

The ippNewRequest API returns an IPP request/response data structure (request) that will be used to hold data like the operation attributes. The ippAddString API is used to add the various operational tags to the request.

```
ippAddString(request, IPP_TAG_OPERATION, IPP_TAG_URI, "printer-uri", NULL,
szUriTag);
```

The next lines of code perform the actual request to the printer and get the response code back. Notice this is a blocking (synchronous) call as you will see if you walk through the code with a debugger.

```
response = cupsDoRequest(http, request, "/ipp/print");
status = ippGetStatusCode(response);
```

The code now uses the ippGetFirstAttribute API to count the number of return strings from the response. This is important as we must allocate a buffer with enough space to hold all this data.

```
for (attrptr = ippGetFirstAttribute(response); attrptr; attrptr =
ippGetNextAttribute(response))
{
        name = ippGetName(attrptr);
        if (name)
        {
                ippAttributeString(attrptr, value, sizeof(value));
                numStrings++;
```

As the number of strings from the function return is known, the next few steps allocate an array of char pointers.

```
*num = numStrings;
//Allocate array of char pointers...
gpArray = new char* [numStrings];
```

The code now gets each attribute (attrptr) as a pointer returned by the ippGetFirstAttribute and ippGetNextAttribute APIs and retrieves the name and value from the pointer. A proper-size char pointer is calculated from the size of the name and value of character pointers. The code places a '|' character in between the name and value so the caller can differentiate the two. The code then places this new character pointer into the previously allocated array of character pointers.

```
for (attrptr = ippGetFirstAttribute(response); attrptr; attrptr =
ippGetNextAttribute(response))
{
        name = ippGetNamc(attrptr);
        if (name)
        {
                nameSize = strlen(name) + 2; //for the preceding ':' and //
                (eventually) the null
                ippAttributeString(attrptr, value, sizeof(value));
                size = strlen(value);
                bufSize = sizeof(char) * (size + nameSize);
                gpArray[i] = (char*) new char*[size + nameSize];
```

```
            strcpy_s(gpArray[i], bufSize, name);
            strcat_s(gpArray[i], bufSize, "|");
            strcat_s(gpArray[i], bufSize, value);
            i++;
      }
}
```

Incidentally, ipp-private.h in the libcups3 solution defines attrptr (_ipp_attribute_s structure) as:

```
struct _ipp_attribute_s                      // IPP attribute
{
      ipp_attribute_t *next;                   Next attribute in list
      ipp_tag_tgroup_tag, value_tag;
      char *name;                             // Name of attribute
       size_t num_values;                     // Number of values
      _ipp_value_t values[1];                 // Values
};
```

You should notice that the allocated array of character pointers will eventually need to be freed, and it is the responsibility of the caller to do just that. The freePrinterAttributesArrayMemory function, exported by the WinIpp wrapper, provides the caller a convenient way to free the allocated memory. If you look at the caller, in this case the WinIppTest.cpp file in the WinIppTest project, you can see the code is simplistic - it simply spits out the contents of the allocated array of character pointers returned from the wrapper. Of course, we free the memory when we are finished.

The astute might point out that writing a C/C++ wrapper around the C APIs of the OpenPrinting IPP port might be duplicative in that the caller could just use the IPP port directly when developing in C. This may be true, but it also discounts the convenience (and code reduction) of such a wrapper. Also, the wrapper serves a much larger purpose when using platform invoke, an issue we will shortly address when we use the wrapper functionality in C#.

Using C# with the OpenPrinting IPP Port Wrapper

Within the same LibCups solution that housed the WinIppTest project is the CS_GPA_CH3 project. This project (CS_GPA_CH3) is written in C# but uses the wrapper via p/Invoke. This provides the ease of C# with the support of the C library written by the OpenPrinting group. The advantage here is that only a few wrapper functions need to be p/Invoked rather than the host of OpenPrinting IPP APIs that would otherwise be required. Below is a p/Invoke statement in the WinIppPinvokeMethods static class that provides access to the wrapper WrGetPrinterAttributes functionality used in the previous C/C++ code example:

```
[DllImport("WinIpp.dll", EntryPoint = "WrGetPrinterAttributes",
SetLastError = true, CallingConvention = CallingConvention.Cdecl)]

private static extern IntPtr GetPrinterAttributes([MarshalAs
(UnmanagedType.LPStr)] StringBuilder hostname, [MarshalAs (UnmanagedType.
LPStr)] StringBuilder userName, ref int num, ref int retCode, uint
encryption, uint timeout = 3000, uint ip_family = Defines.AF_UNSPEC, uint
chunking = (uint)Defines.TRANSFER_METHOD. IPPTOOL_TRANSFER_CHUNKED);
```

The output is like that of the previous C++ code example (WinIppTest), except the FormatOutput function makes it a bit easier to read.

```
D:\BACKUP\IPP Book\Chap3\
attributes-charset:
        utf-8
attributes-natural-language:
        en
printer-uri-supported:
        ipp://HPM528:631/ipp/print
        ipps://HPM528:631/ipp/print
uri-security-supported:
        none
        tls
uri-authentication-supported:
        requesting-user-name
        requesting-user-name
printer-name:
        HPM528
printer-dns-sd-name:
        HP LaserJet Flow MFP M528 \[84AF0F]
printer-geo-location:
        unknown
printer-location:
        PEB-2J5
printer-info:
        HP LaserJet Flow MFP M528 \[84AF0F]
printer-state:
        idle
printer-state-reasons:
        none
ipp-versions-supported:
        1.0
        1.1
```

This book will continue to build on leveraging the OpenPrinting IPP port for Windows for other IPP features such as printing, getting jobs on the printer, and other features. For now, though, I present a more graphical way to use IPP in this project (CS_GPA_CH3_WPF), which provides the consumables level of a target printer. The consumable counters are provided by an IPP Get-Printer-Attributes request and is a relatively simple utility. It does, however, present the concept of centrally managing IPP printers via the Get-Printer-Attributes request. Within the same LibCups solution that housed the WinIppTest and CS_GPA_CH3 project(s), you should find the CS_Multi_Check project. This project (CS_Multi_Check) is also written in C# and provides a way to check multiple IPP printers in your network. Because this utility was designed to check multiple printers asynchronously, the pInvoke method was modified to provide an 'awaiter' for the C# caller.

Uses for this utility could be to scan your network IPP printers and return attributes about those printers. While the console readout is trivial, you could modify it to create a comma-delimited file format and import certain attributes (firmware version, consumables level, IPP version, etc.) into an Excel spreadsheet or a database.

Within the same LibCups solution that housed the WinIppTest and CS_GPA_CH3 project(s), you should find the CS_GPA_CH3_WPF project. This project (CS_GPA_CH3_WPF) is also written in C# and leverages the wrapper via p/Invoke as well.

This Windows Presentation Foundation (WPF) project uses the same platform invoke methods used in the first console program:

```
[DllImport("WinIpp.dll", EntryPoint = "WrGetPrinterAttributes",
SetLastError = true, CallingConvention = CallingConvention.Cdecl)]

private static extern IntPtr GetPrinterAttributes([MarshalAs
(UnmanagedType.LPStr)] StringBuilder hostname, [MarshalAs (UnmanagedType.
LPStr)] StringBuilder userName, ref int num, ref int retCode, uint
encryption, uint timeout = 3000, uint ip_family = Defines.AF_UNSPEC, uint
chunking = (uint)Defines.TRANSFER_METHOD. IPPTOOL_TRANSFER_CHUNKED);
```

While I wanted to avoid any GUI-based code in this book, I made an exception here as an example of what IPP can provide for monitoring purposes. Using the OpenPrinting IPP port wrapper as a base, the example provides the current levels of consumables, printer firmware, printer graphics, etc.

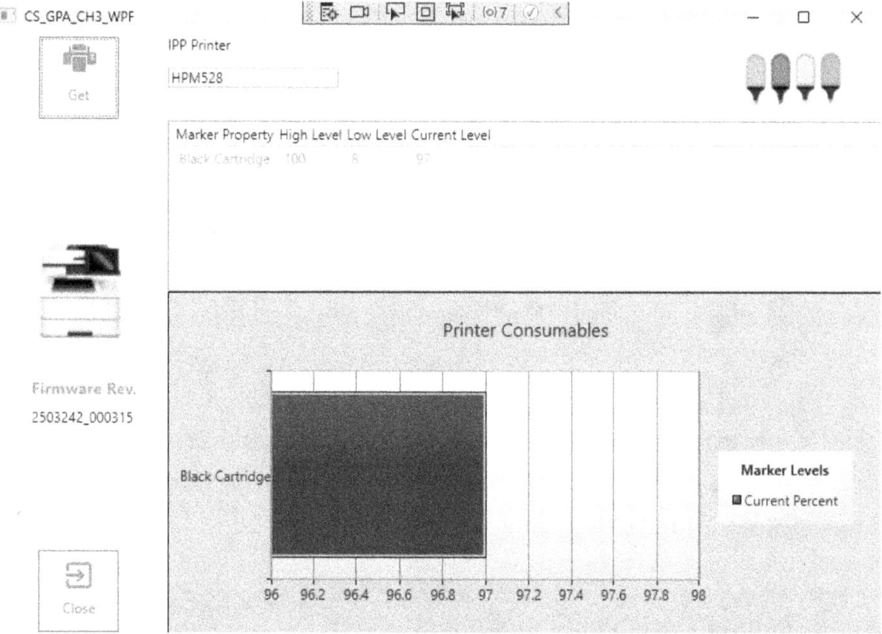

CA_GPA_CH3_WPF display

You might also include paper tray levels, IPP and Mopria versions, printer state, etc. The example uses the excellent DotNetProjects.WpfToolkit.DataVisualization project available in Visual Studio via Tools/NuGet Package Manager. On the WPF side, the example makes use of the MicroMvvm library and AutoBindEvents, which serves to effectively decouple the View from the ViewModel in MVVM.

PowerShell

As with Chapter 2, "Printer Talk," we next go into creating a PowerShell cmdlet - only this time we can query all IPP printers, not just ones installed locally on Windows. I used the PowerShellStandard.Library from NuGet for this cmdlet, which contains the reference assemblies for PowerShell Standard 5.

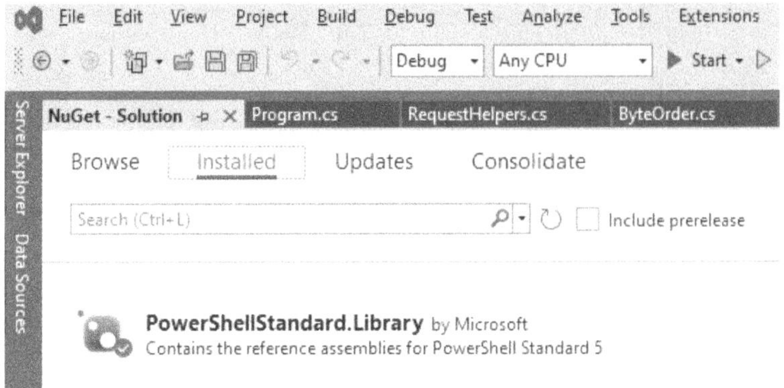

To create a PowerShell cmdlet in Visual Studio, you should first create a new .NET Class Library from the project templates available. You will also have to include the System.Management.Automation using a statement.

A boilerplate setup for a PowerShell Cmdlet:

1. *Choose a .NET Class Library Project*: Create a new .NET class library project in Visual Studio.

2. *Add a PowerShellStandard.Library Reference:* Add a **PowerShellStandard.Library** NuGet reference package. This package provides the necessary assemblies for building PowerShell cmdlets.

3. *Inherit from the Cmdlet Class*: The new class should inherit from the `Cmdlet` base class. This class will represent your cmdlet.

4. *Use the Cmdlet Attribute:* The new class should be decorated with the [Cmdlet] attribute to specify the verb and noun for the cmdlet. For example:

```
[Cmdlet(VerbsCommon.Get, "DoSomething")]
public class GetSomethingCmdlet : Cmdlet
{
    // Define parameters and methods here
}
```

5. *Define the Parameters*: Add properties to the class to define the parameters for the cmdlet. Use the [Parameter] attribute to specify parameter attributes. For example:

```
[Parameter(Position = 0, Mandatory = true)]
public string Parameter{ get; set; }
```

6. *Override the ProcessRecord Method:* Override the ProcessRecord method to implement the cmdlet's functionality. Call base.ProcessRecord within this method.

You can open the PsGpaRequest for an example of how to create a cmdlet in C#. The crucial point is that this cmdlet, unlike the one in Chapter 2, "Printer Talk," can query all IPP printers since it was written using the HttpClient object. To run the cmdlet, click the Windows Tools from the start menu, and then navigate to the Windows PowerShell ISE menu choices. Since my computer is Windows 11 64-bit and I have no backwards 32-bit dependencies in code, I selected the 64-bit (Windows PowerShell ISE) option. As in Chapter 2, "Printer Talk," since the cmdlet is not native to the installed PowerShell base, you will have to tell the Integrated Scripting Environment (ISE) where to find the DLL of the cmdlet you want to use. You will then have to use the Import-Module cmdlet to load this DLL into memory for later use. Once this is accomplished, you are ready to call the cmdlet and provide the target printer name and the requested attributes required. Looking at the following graphic, you can see I used my HPM528 printer name and "printer-description" as the attribute group. The reply from the printer is shown in the bottom half of the split screen.

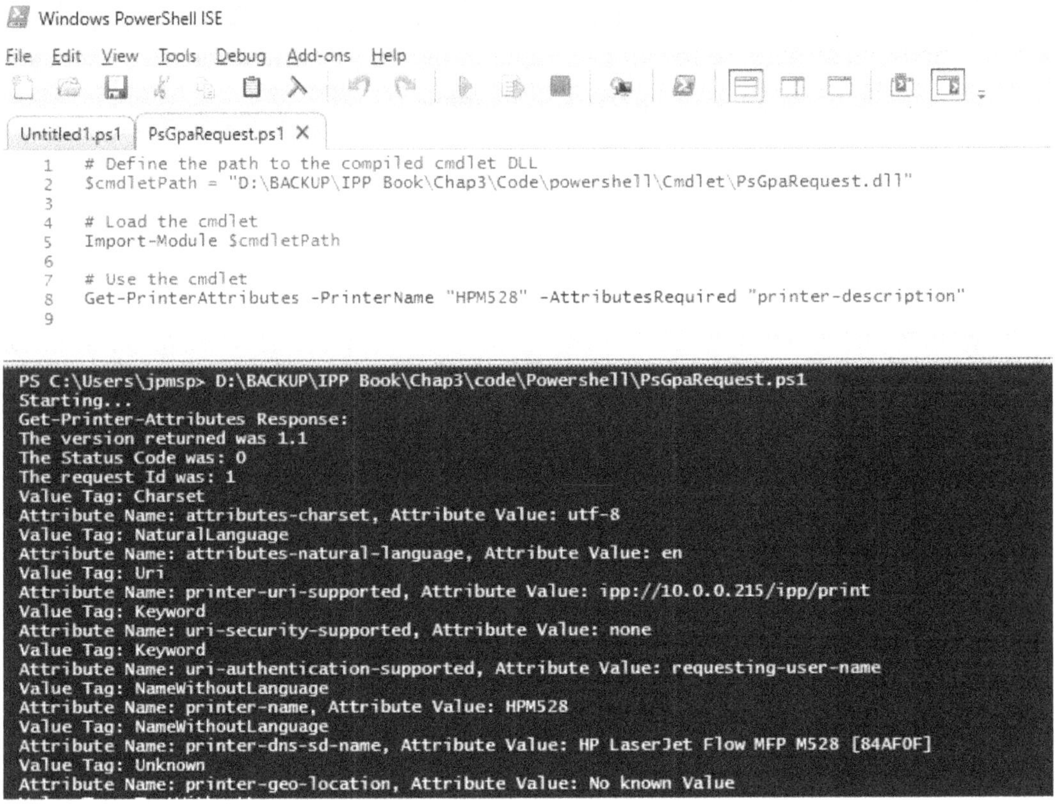

Windows PowerShell ISE

File Edit View Tools Debug Add-ons Help

Untitled1.ps1 PsGpaRequest.ps1

```
# Define the path to the compiled cmdlet DLL
$cmdletPath = "D:\BACKUP\IPP Book\Chap3\Code\powershell\Cmdlet\PsGpaRequest.dll"

# Load the cmdlet
Import-Module $cmdletPath

# Use the cmdlet
Get-PrinterAttributes -PrinterName "HPM528" -AttributesRequired "printer-description"

```

```
PS C:\Users\jpmsp> D:\BACKUP\IPP Book\Chap3\code\Powershell\PsGpaRequest.ps1
Starting...
Get-Printer-Attributes Response:
The version returned was 1.1
The Status Code was: 0
The request Id was: 1
Value Tag: Charset
Attribute Name: attributes-charset, Attribute Value: utf-8
Value Tag: NaturalLanguage
Attribute Name: attributes-natural-language, Attribute Value: en
Value Tag: Uri
Attribute Name: printer-uri-supported, Attribute Value: ipp://10.0.0.215/ipp/print
Value Tag: Keyword
Attribute Name: uri-security-supported, Attribute Value: none
Value Tag: Keyword
Attribute Name: uri-authentication-supported, Attribute Value: requesting-user-name
Value Tag: NameWithoutLanguage
Attribute Name: printer-name, Attribute Value: HPM528
Value Tag: NameWithoutLanguage
Attribute Name: printer-dns-sd-name, Attribute Value: HP LaserJet Flow MFP M528 [84AF0F]
Value Tag: Unknown
Attribute Name: printer-geo-location, Attribute Value: No known Value
```

Using the PsGpaRequest cmdlet

This form of cmdlet might serve as a base for many possibilities in the printer monitoring arena. Used as a tool to periodically monitor the IPP printers in your enterprise, for example, the results could be written to an SQL database for executive dashboards.

Chapter Summary

As with the first chapter, this chapter covers a lot of ground. The stark truth is there is no simple path to understanding the fundamentals of IPP requests without an essential understanding of the request structure and how the byte stream is processed. While not necessary for basic IPP concepts, understanding the process will elevate your troubleshooting skills and value as an engineer or developer. Along the way, a simple Get-Printer-Attributes request is built that, while not elegant (or even efficient), allows you to step through the code easily and gain knowledge and so reinforce what you learn.

The chapter commences by looking into how the IPP/IPPS protocol leverages HTTP/HTTPS and the advantages this design choice provides. IPP/IPPS was built on the architecture of HTTP/HTTPS, and much of its versatility, robustness, and efficiency is inherited from this platform. The essential IPP attribute types used in the protocol are described next. A general understanding of how they are used is helpful to understanding how the protocol operates. The basic attributes used are explained, and the overall Get-Printer-Attributes request is investigated. To round out the request composition, the constituent pieces of each attribute field are then examined.

Despite the tedious nature, you may not fully understand (or learn how to troubleshoot) IPP requests without some knowledge or understanding of how the request byte buffer is physically created. The byte buffer is composed of some values arranged in network byte order, so the concept of byte-shifting necessary for communication between a Windows machine and a Unix OS is required. Fortunately, a byte order library is provided that does the heavy lifting for both requests and responses.

The chapter then goes through the steps of building a basic IPP/IPPS request, starting with the version number, operational IDs, request numbers, and status codes. This information provides the basic building blocks for any IPP/IPPS request. The creation of each constituent byte buffer representing individual attributes is shown, and thus the composite byte buffer for the request is created. A Wireshark trace displaying a working Get-Printer-Attributes request (IPP) and how it is arranged is shown. The next steps involve how to process the response to the Get-Printer-Attributes request. The decoding steps for a one-value attribute, one-value with additional attributes, and finally a collection attribute is examined, and an example of each is provided.

A basic working project for the Get-Printer-Attributes request is provided in the code section of this chapter entitled GetPrinterAtributesRequest. While simplistic, chatty, and inelegant, it can be used to walk through the request and learn how to process the request. A similar project (IppPrinterQuery) is also provided that allows for processing multiple IPP printers in the enterprise. The latter project might be a good basis for an IPP printer inventory tool. After covering the C# development alternatives, the C code leveraging the OpenPrinting IPP port to Windows is introduced. For reasons of stability and future support, this might be the development path to follow. We follow this by covering example .NET Interop routines used to leverage the OpenPrinting IPP port wrapper for C# developers. Finally, the basics of wrapping code to form a PowerShell cmdlet are covered.

References

1. OpenPrinting/LibCups, `https://github.com/OpenPrinting/libcups`,
2. Platform Invoke, `https://learn.microsoft.com/en-us/dotnet/standard/native-interop/pinvoke`, Microsoft Learn Challenge, Nov 23, 2024.
3. Endianness: Big and Little Endian Byte Order, Endianness: Big and Little Endian Byte Order (yolinux.com)

CHAPTER 4

The MS IPP Class Driver

This chapter is an important chapter for learning the basics of sending a print job to an IPP/IPPS printer using the built-in Windows 11 IPP Class driver. Complementing this is an investigation into how Microsoft has integrated IPP/IPPS into the Windows subsystem. We will look deeper into how driverless print standards operate and how they employ IPP/IPPS as a consistent channel to submit print jobs. We will delve into the various IPP requests used to reliably print documents and how each of the requests is employed. This chapter also touches on the competing driverless print standards and why they have evolved as they have. Included in this chapter are methods to allow the curious to view Windows IPP print requests on Wireshark and see the protocol in the IPP dissector. The Windows pipeline used to translate file formats to one that is natively rendered on the host printer is discussed. Finally, we provide compelling reasons to leverage the Windows print subsystem methods and reasons you might not do so.

When printing to an IPP printer, there are two distinct ways to submit your job: the Print-Job operation and the combination of Create-Job and Send-Document operations [1]. The Print-Job request is the most compact operation, allowing you to print the job using one request. This operation sends the actual print job along with any document data at the same time. Of course, with any IPP operation, you should receive an IPP request response that verifies whether the operation was successful or not. The actual document to be printed is converted to a byte stream for efficiency and sent to the printer for processing. Because byte streams are ubiquitous, the printer needs to know what type of (hopefully supported) formats the byte stream is composed of. This information is conveyed by sending the MIME type to the printer. The downside of this one-step convenience is that you cannot realistically cancel the job once it has started. In other words, many times the entire document will be printed before you can send the Cancel-Job request. As you might expect, this could lead to waste on larger documents, especially those embedded with complex graphics. For more control of the print process, you should consider using the Validate-Job, Create-Job, and Send-Document requests.

J. Marion, *Adopting Internet Printing Protocol for Windows*, https://doi.org/10.1007/979-8-8688-2010-6_4

The Validate-Job, Create-Job, and finally Send-Document IPP requests are fully documented in RFC8010, Encoding and Transport. While I could direct you to consult these for details on the requests, I think visual confirmation of their data through Wireshark traces may provide a better understanding of what is going on. Therefore, each request description will include a Wireshark trace to provide a more visual reference to back up the information you learn.

IPP via Wireshark

I would highly recommend that technicians, developers, or network engineers get familiar with using Wireshark as it provides a visual picture of how the IPP protocol works. Newer versions of Wireshark include an IPP dissector that does an excellent job of displaying the IPP structure in the HTTP POST binary buffer. In the following graphic, you can clearly see the trace of a "Hello World" Word document rendered by the Windows IPP class driver. Notice that each IPP request is followed by an IPP response from the printer, with the status-code of each request checked for success (int value 0) prior to the next request attempt. The request type is in the far-right column, and we shall investigate what each request does in the next few pages.

No.	Time	Source	Destination	Protocol	Length	Info
2	0.103649	HewlettPacka_8...	Broadcast	ARP	60	Who has 10.0.0.50? Tell 10.0.0.214
4	0.103666	ASUSTekCOMPU_e...	HewlettPacka_8...	ARP	42	10.0.0.50 is at 04:42:1a:e6:21:bb
11	0.429898	10.0.0.50	10.0.0.214	IPP	774	IPP Request (Get-Printer-Attributes)
18	0.609690	10.0.0.214	10.0.0.50	IPP	60	IPP Response (successful-ok)
31	1.042602	10.0.0.50	10.0.0.214	IPP	235	IPP Request (Get-Printer-Attributes)
34	1.050943	10.0.0.214	10.0.0.50	IPP	196	IPP Response (successful-ok)
45	1.698806	10.0.0.50	10.0.0.214	IPP	680	IPP Request (Validate-Job)
48	1.706685	10.0.0.214	10.0.0.50	IPP	143	IPP Response (successful-ok)
60	2.145573	10.0.0.50	10.0.0.214	IPP	645	IPP Request (Create-Job)
63	2.163517	10.0.0.214	10.0.0.50	IPP	310	IPP Response (successful-ok)
...	2.664276	10.0.0.50	10.0.0.214	IPP	59	IPP Request (Send-Document)
...	3.026856	10.0.0.214	10.0.0.50	IPP	60	IPP Response (successful-ok)
...	3.505956	10.0.0.50	10.0.0.214	IPP	278	IPP Request (Get-Job-Attributes)
...	3.513813	10.0.0.214	10.0.0.50	IPP	188	IPP Response (successful-ok)
...	5.097723	10.0.0.50	10.0.0.214	IPP	278	IPP Request (Get-Job-Attributes)
...	5.225759	10.0.0.214	10.0.0.50	IPP	60	IPP Response (successful-ok)
...	6.660170	10.0.0.50	10.0.0.214	IPP	278	IPP Request (Get-Job-Attributes)
...	6.667926	10.0.0.214	10.0.0.50	IPP	188	IPP Response (successful-ok)
...	8.171758	10.0.0.50	10.0.0.214	IPP	278	IPP Request (Get-Job-Attributes)
...	8.697377	10.0.0.214	10.0.0.50	IPP	60	IPP Response (successful-ok)
...	14.183945	10.0.0.50	10.0.0.214	IPP	235	IPP Request (Get-Printer-Attributes)
...	14.192082	10.0.0.214	10.0.0.50	IPP	196	IPP Response (successful-ok)

IPP Request and Responses as viewed in Wireshark (filtered for IPP protocol)

As seen above, when processing a document (i.e., Word and Excel) through the IPP Class driver, Windows typically:

1. Sends a **Get-Printer-Attributes** request for printer information, often multiple times.
2. Validates the job using **Validate-Job** to ensure the printer can create a job with the chosen job attributes.
3. Uses **Create-Job** to set aside memory on the printer allocated for the job information and to return a job id.
4. Uses **Send-Document** to actually print the job.
5. Queries the printer in a polling fashion with **Get-Job-Attributes** to get the status of the job sent to the printer.

Get-Printer-Attributes

By now you should be familiar with the Get-Printer-Attributes request and why the client uses it. When you select the IPP printer in Windows to use (via the print dialog), the OS sends out several Get-Printer-Attribute requests to get the latest attribute values available. The first Get-Printer-Attributes request from the IPP Class driver when interacting with my HP printer was (as seen in the graphic) for the document-format-preferred, the document-format-default, and the document-format-supported attributes.

```
⌄ Internet Printing Protocol
    [Response In: 10]
    version: 2.0
    operation-id: Get-Printer-Attributes (0x000b)
    request-id: 4
  ⌄ operation-attributes-tag
    ⌄ attributes-charset (charset): 'utf-8'
        name: attributes-charset
        charset value: utf-8
    ⌄ attributes-natural-language (naturalLanguage): 'en'
        name: attributes-natural-language
        naturalLanguage value: en
    ⌄ printer-uri (uri): 'ipp://peb-2k5-hpm608-bw:631/ipp/print'
        name: printer-uri
        uri value: ipp://peb-2k5-hpm608-bw:631/ipp/print
    ⌄ requested-attributes (1setOf keyword): 'document-format-preferred','document
        name: requested-attributes
        keyword value: document-format-preferred
        keyword value: document-format-default
        keyword value: document-format-supported
```

The reply from the printer naturally provided these attributes – you can see the supported format (in red) along with the preferred document format (in blue) from the printer.

```
[Response Time: 0.149204000 seconds]
version: 2.0
status-code: Successful (successful-ok)
request-id: 4
⌄ operation-attributes-tag
  › attributes-charset (charset): 'utf-8'
  › attributes-natural-language (naturalLanguage): 'en'
⌄ printer-attributes-tag
  ⌄ document-format-default (mimeMediaType): 'application/pdf'
      name: document-format-default
      mimeMediaType value: application/pdf
  ⌄  [...]document-format-supported (1setOf mimeMediaType): 'text/plain','application/
      name: document-format-supported
      mimeMediaType value: text/plain
      mimeMediaType value: application/octet-stream
      mimeMediaType value: image/jpeg
      mimeMediaType value: application/vnd.hp-PCL
      mimeMediaType value: application/vnd.hp-PCLXL
      mimeMediaType value: application/postscript
      mimeMediaType value: application/pdf
      mimeMediaType value: image/urf
      mimeMediaType value: image/pwg-raster
      mimeMediaType value: image/tiff
      mimeMediaType value: application/PCLm
  ⌄ document-format-preferred (mimeMediaType): 'application/pdf'
      name: document-format-preferred
      mimeMediaType value: application/pdf
end-of-attributes-tag
```

Having obtained these attributes, the IPP Class driver on Windows next requests other attributes from the printer, such as the printer-output-tray, the number of copies supported, the number of copies set by default, the printer color mode, etc. The point being that the IPP Class driver may call the Get-Printer-Attributes request several times for each print request to ensure it fully knows the capabilities of the printer. This can clearly be seen in the original Wireshark trace, and you would expect the printer to reply to these requests as they are executed. The next graphic shows the requested attributes on the ensuing Get-Printer-Attributes request.

```
⌄ document-format (mimeMediaType): 'application/pdf'
    name: document-format
    mimeMediaType value: application/pdf
⌄  […]requested-attributes (1setOf keyword): 'document-format-
    name: requested-attributes
    keyword value: document-format-preferred
    keyword value: document-format-default
    keyword value: document-format-supported
    keyword value: printer-is-accepting-jobs
    keyword value: operations-supported
    keyword value: media-type-supported
    keyword value: media-supported
    keyword value: media-col-supported
    keyword value: document-format-details-supported
    keyword value: job-pages-per-set-supported
    keyword value: job-impressions-supported
    keyword value: job-password-encryption-supported
    keyword value: multiple-document-handling-supported
    keyword value: orientation-requested-supported
    keyword value: copies-default
    keyword value: copies-supported
    keyword value: media-source-default
    keyword value: media-source-supported
    keyword value: output-bin-default
    keyword value: output-bin-supported
    keyword value: printer-output-tray
    keyword value: orientation-requested-default
    keyword value: print-color-mode-default
    keyword value: print-color-mode-supported
```

Once Windows is satisfied that it has collected the attributes necessary to create the print job, it sends a Validate-Job request to that same printer to ensure the printer can create the necessary job.

Validate-Job

The Validate-Job request is required to be supported and used to validate the capabilities of the target IPP printer without creating a job. Since it only involves validating the attributes and does not create or manage a job, it uses fewer resources on the target printer. It is not necessary to provide the file to print as this request only affirms the printer's ability to support the requested attributes. If the Validate-Job request fails, a status code will be returned indicating the problem with the request. For instance, if a job attribute is not supported, the status code error value will typically be client-error-attributes-or-values-not-supported (0x040B).

In the following Wireshark trace of the Validate-Job request, all the job attributes specified for the print job are sent to the printer so the printer can validate that the attributes are indeed supported on that printer. Notice that the request-id in this trace is 2; this should be incremented in the next few requests.

```
v Internet Printing Protocol
    [Response In: 88]
    version: 2.0
    operation-id: Validate-Job (0x0004)
    request-id: 2
  v operation-attributes-tag
    > attributes-charset (charset): 'utf-8'
    > attributes-natural-language (naturalLanguage): 'en'
    > printer-uri (uri): 'ipp://hpm528:631/ipp/print'
    > job-name (nameWithoutLanguage): 'Microsoft Word - CreateJobSendDocumentAndPrinterMemoryAllocationPart2.docx'
    > requesting-user-name (nameWithoutLanguage): 'M1795\jpmsp'
    > document-format (mimeMediaType): 'application/pdf'
  v job-attributes-tag
    > copies (integer): 1
    > media-col (collection): {media-size{x-dimension,y-dimension},media-type}
    > output-bin (keyword): 'face-down'
    > print-color-mode (keyword): 'monochrome'
    > print-quality (enum): normal
    > multiple-document-handling (keyword): 'separate-documents-collated-copies'
    > sides (keyword): 'two-sided-long-edge'
    > orientation-requested (enum): portrait
    > printer-resolution (resolution): 600x600dpi
    end-of-attributes-tag
```

Validate-Job Wireshark Trace

The reply (from the printer) to the Validate-Job request is shown in the next graphic. Notice that the request-id numbers match, and the status-code was successful. As the printer validated that it could support the attributes we require of our job, the IPP Class driver now moves onto the next request (Create-Job).

```
> Frame 111: 143 bytes on wire (1144 bits), 143 bytes captured (1144 bits) on
> Ethernet II, Src: Cisco_a0:df:0b (74:ad:98:a0:df:0b), Dst: HP_ee:94:de (38:2
> Internet Protocol Version 4, Src: 10.28.66.60, Dst: 10.229.98.5
> Transmission Control Protocol, Src Port: 631, Dst Port: 59832, Seq: 473, Ack
> [2 Reassembled TCP Segments (561 bytes): #110(472), #111(89)]
> Hypertext Transfer Protocol, has 2 chunks (including last chunk)
v Internet Printing Protocol
    [Request In: 108]
    [Response Time: 0.009724000 seconds]
    version: 2.0
    status-code: Successful (successful-ok)
    request-id: 2
  v operation-attributes-tag
    v attributes-charset (charset): 'utf-8'
        name: attributes-charset
        charset value: utf-8
    v attributes-natural-language (naturalLanguage): 'en'
        name: attributes-natural-language
        naturalLanguage value: en
    end-of-attributes-tag
```

Create-Job

The Create-Job request creates (but does not print) the requested job on the printer.[1] You are supposed to provide the size of the file you want printed and the attributes requested, although the actual file byte stream is not sent to the printer yet (that will be done in Send-Document). As with the Print-Job request, the printer needs to know what format the byte stream sent is, so a MIME type must be provided so the printer can know how to process the byte stream (when sent). If successful, Create-Job will allocate resources to create and manage the job, and provide a job id. This job id can be used for further job management, such as sending documents, querying job status, or canceling the job. As in the case of Validate-Job, Create-Job will return a status code to the caller.

[1] Create-Job creates the Job object, but that's it; a Send-Document is needed to attach a Document to the Job so that there is something to process.

```
⌄ Internet Printing Protocol
    [Response In: 99]
    version: 2.0
    operation-id: Create-Job (0x0005)
    request-id: 3
  ⌄ operation-attributes-tag
    › attributes-charset (charset): 'utf-8'
    › attributes-natural-language (naturalLanguage): 'en'
    › printer-uri (uri): 'ipp://hpm528:631/ipp/print'
    › job-name (nameWithoutLanguage): 'Microsoft Word - CreateJobSendDocumentAndPrinterMemoryAllocationPart2.docx'
    › requesting-user-name (nameWithoutLanguage): 'M1795\jpmsp'
  ⌄ job-attributes-tag
    › copies (integer): 1
    › media-col (collection): {media-size{x-dimension,y-dimension},media-type}
    › output-bin (keyword): 'face-down'
    › print-color-mode (keyword): 'monochrome'
    › print-quality (enum): normal
    › multiple-document-handling (keyword): 'separate-documents-collated-copies'
    › sides (keyword): 'two-sided-long-edge'
    › orientation-requested (enum): portrait
    › printer-resolution (resolution): 600x600dpi
    end-of-attributes-tag
```

Create-Job trace on Wireshark

The Wireshark analysis of Create-Job request shows the primary purpose of the request is to create a job in memory (on the printer) which contains all the job attributes requested for print. In some implementations, the Create-Job request is supposed to contain the size of the file to be printed so the printer can allocate enough memory, but clearly the Microsoft IPP driver does not include file size in the request. If successful, a job-id is returned with the request, so the caller can either print the job or cancel it at a later time.

When considering operations that a printer supports, you might need to go further than just consulting the IPP RFCs. If a printer is certified as either Mopria or IPP Everywhere compliant, there may be additional operations they may require supported. For instance, RFC 8011 listed Create-Job as recommended status. However, both Mopria and IPP Everywhere standards require Create-Job certification. Since Windows requires Mopria compliant printers, it follows that IPP printers that work with Windows 11 support the Create-Job operation. Recall that while IPP is the print protocol, IPP Everywhere and Mopria are standards or certification programs that ride IPP to facilitate ubiquitous, driverless, and user-friendly printing solutions.

Send-Document

When Send-Document is called, it takes as an argument the job id provided back to the caller from Create-Job and prints out the document assigned to that id. There can be multiple jobs created on the printer that are not necessarily printed out immediately. Of course, each job submission (created by Create-Job) does take memory resources from the printer, so it is a clever idea to remove jobs you no longer want stored. The Send Document request provides a status code back to the caller upon completion. If you look at a Send-Document trace on Wireshark, you can see how the request works. Below, you can see the job-id that is sent with the actual document data, so the printer can identify which job (created already on the printer) attributes should be used with the file data sent over.

```
Internet Printing Protocol
  [Response In: 178]
  version: 2.0
  operation-id: Send-Document (0x0006)
  request-id: 4
⌄ operation-attributes-tag
  › attributes-charset (charset): 'utf-8'
  › attributes-natural-language (naturalLanguage): 'en'
  › printer-uri (uri): 'ipp://hpm528:631/ipp/print'
  › job-id (integer): 15
  › requesting-user-name (nameWithoutLanguage): 'M1795\jpmsp'
  › document-format (mimeMediaType): 'application/pdf'
  › last-document (boolean): true
  end-of-attributes-tag
⌄ Data (1012395 bytes)
    Data [truncated]: 255044462d312e370a0a342030206f626a0a284964656e74697479290a656e646f626a0a352030206f6
    [Length: 1012395]
```

Send-Document trace on Wireshark

The actual document data is transferred to the printer in the HTTP POST message in a series of bytes. In the job above, you can see that this document was over 1 million bytes in size, and the file format for this byte stream is application/pdf type. Looking at the IPP operation section, we can see that Send-Document (0x00, 0x06) is the request; the IPP version is 2.0, and the request-id is 4.

The reply to the Send-Document request is shown in the next graphic. The status code from the printer tells us the request was successful, and the job-id is returned as 5. Notice the request-id matches that of the Send-Document request (4) and the printer provides a job-state as "processing" – which means the job has still not been completed on the printer.

```
> Hypertext Transfer Protocol, has 2 chunks (including last chunk)
v Internet Printing Protocol
    [Request In: 196]
    [Response Time: 0.054573000 seconds]
    version: 2.0
    status-code: Successful (successful-ok)
    request-id: 4
  v operation-attributes-tag
    > attributes-charset (charset): 'utf-8'
    > attributes-natural-language (naturalLanguage): 'en'
  v job-attributes-tag
    > job-uri (uri): 'ipp://10.28.66.60/ipp/port1/job-0005'
    > job-id (integer): 5
    > job-state (enum): processing
    > job-state-reasons (keyword): 'none'
    end-of-attributes-tag
```

Note The IPP standard in RFC 8011 stipulates that if a printer supports the Create-Job and Send-Document operations, it must support the "multiple-operation-time-out" attribute. This attribute is essentially the minimum number of seconds the printer will wait between operation requests like Create-Job and Send-Document before it initiates some form of recovery action. More on this in Chapter 5, "IPP Standards Print."

Cancel-Job

If you change your mind about a job created on a printer, you can remove that job from the list of available jobs by using the Cancel-Job request. For those familiar with attempting to cancel a job on a Windows print queue, the Cancel-Job request provides immediate results. Even if the job is being printed, the Cancel-Job request will stop further processing on the printer. We will cover the Cancel-Job request in more detail within Chapter 5, "IPP Standards Print," of this book.

IPP Print Job Lifecycle

If you were to track the progression of a print request through an IPP print device, a key pattern of job processing organization would be apparent. Based on IPP operations and printer responses, a print job will move through a structured state machine whose transitions depend on the accompanying job state. These lifecycle phases include job creation, queuing, processing, completion, and then either retention or deletion. RFC 8011 describes the defined job states as shown below:

Value	Job State	Description
3	pending	Job is accepted, awaiting processing.
4	pending-held	Job is held and not yet ready to process.
5	processing	Job is currently being processed (e.g., printing).
6	processing-stopped	Job processing was paused or stopped.
7	canceled	Job was canceled by user or operator.
8	aborted	Job was aborted due to an error or system intervention.
9	completed	Job finished successfully.

Defined Job States (Section 5.3.7 RFC 8011)

You may query the state of a job (provided you have the job-id) using the Get-Job-Attributes request, which will be introduced later. These 7 states are described in the job-state attribute present in IPP implementations. A simplistic lifecycle flow diagram might look like the following:

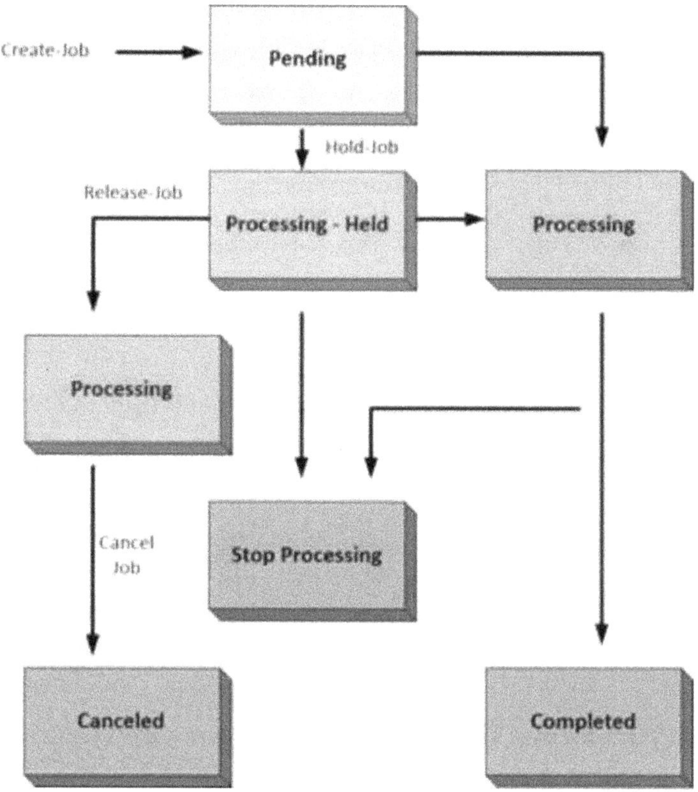

Simple IPP print job lifecycle diagram

Some Background on the MS IPP Class Driver

Overall, Microsoft did a commendable job integrating IPP into the legacy print subsystem. While the System.Drawing.Printing namespace has the IppPrintDevice object to gather printer capabilities (using the Get-Printer-Attributes request); the IPP class driver is the mechanism used to do the actual print chores. If you remember back in Chapter 1, "Windows Legacy Print," the print driver's main purpose was described as converting documents to a format the printer can natively process. In the case of PCL, this was adding tags and control characters into the print stream to instruct the printer what to do and how to process the stream. The IPP class driver performs a similar function, but the resulting stream is quite different from that of a PCL/PS stream.

For example, suppose you create a Word document and want to print this to an IPP printer installed on your Windows 11 machine. The handling of this print job and the generation of IPP requests like validate-job, create-job, and print-document are managed by the Print Spooler and the IPP class V4 printer driver model in Windows 11. A simplified flow of control might look something like this:

1. Application (Word): Sends the print job to the Print Spooler.
2. Print Spooler: Queues the job and processes it using the V4 printer driver.
3. V4 IPP Class Printer Driver: Formats the job according to the IPP protocol and sends the validate-job, create-job, and print-document requests to the printer.
4. Printer: Receives the IPP requests and processes the print job accordingly.

Diving deeper into the IPP class driver, it obviously does not create a PCL or PS stream as legacy drivers did. Instead, it constructs IPP requests in a binary format as specified by the IPP protocol. These requests include various attributes and values that define the print job and its parameters. Recall back several chapters on the construction of attributes into a byte stream prior to usage in the Get-Printer-Attributes example code. The byte stream construction (according to IPP standards) is just one of the jobs the IPP class driver must do. The driver must also format the document into a MIME format the printer can natively process. We will dive a bit deeper into this (document formatting) shortly. For now, just be aware that the IPP class driver does the heavy lifting when interfacing a user with a print request to the target IPP printer.

I should mention here that IPP/IPPS itself does not provide driverless print. IPP provides the protocol and delivery mechanism, but there needs to be a standard to dictate how driverless printing works. There are several competing standards to accomplish this, but for brevity I will compare the IPP Everywhere and Mopria standards. Both standards specify more than just what Printer Definition Languages (PDLs) to use: automatic print discovery and print job submission are just some of the functionalities described. Both standards also implement certification processes for print hardware for guaranteed compliance. Mopria and IPP Everywhere both use mDNS (Multicast DNS) in addition to DNS-SD (DNS Service Discovery) for service discovery and hostname resolution. Mopria was originally created to improve Android's less than stellar print support, while IPP Everywhere was co-created by Microsoft, Apple, and HP (among others). While theoretically Mopria or IPP Everywhere could be used on any client, the main divergence was eventual adoption: Mopria was adopted for Android and iOS mobile devices, whereas IPP Everywhere was adopted to work with Linux. The crucial point is that driverless printing standards work in part by requiring a specific document format to be supported by clients and printers along with a core set of IPP attributes and values.

Standard	Print Description Language
IPP Everywhere	PWG Raster JPG PDF
Mopria	PCLm PWG Raster PDF

Comparison of PDLs Used by Driverless Printing Standards [4]

Given the emphasis on mobile printing, it might be a surprise to find out that Windows employs Mopria technology for driverless printing. However, when you consider the large base of supported print hardware using Mopria, it is more understandable. Irrespective of the standard employed, driverless printing is made practical by narrowing down the employed PDLs and standardizing print hardware to process them. Broadly speaking about Windows, IPP provides the means for Mopria to gather information about a print device and a standardized way to send the job.

I should also mention that the PCLm print definition language in the chart above is not some derivative of PCL as the name would suggest. Rather, PCLm is a raster-only subset of PDF and is one of two raster formats defined in the Wi-Fi Direct Services Print peer-to-peer printing specification [5]. As Mopria provides support for Wi-Fi Direct, the inclusion of PCLm in supported PDLs is logical. PWG Raster (shown in the chart above) is another PDL type and was developed by the Printer Working Group (PWG). It does not require printer-specific driver methods for printing operations and is defined by PWG Candidate Standard 5102.4-2012. The main claim for PWG Raster is that it provides a consistent and predictable output that is necessary for high-quality print and provides efficiency via GZIP compression.

Using the Built-in Windows Print Framework for IPP

If you are developing a GUI application for Windows and need to print, you should use the built-in Print dialog. This dialog will use the print subsystem to spool the print and (if you are using the IPP class print driver) ensure the print is sent to the printer using IPP properly. This is important if you need to leverage the existing Windows print subsystem for management of the overall process. This will also provide the capabilities of the installed IPP printer (via Get-Printer-Attributes request) so your users can customize their print. By leveraging the IPP class Driver capabilities, print requests are translated into the necessary Validate-Job, Create-Job and Send-Document requests required by the IPP printer.

In the case where you need to send a print job via a console program or other utility where using the print dialog is impractical, you can still send the print using the Windows print subsystem. The code snippet below leverages the PrintDocument object to send a job with a few custom settings through the print subsystem to the printer.

```
using System;
using System.Drawing;
using System.Drawing.Printing;
using System.Printing;

namespace BasicIppPrint
{
    internal class Program
    {
        static void Main(string[] args)
        {

            string printerName = "HPM528";

            // Create a PrintDocument object
            PrintDocument printDocument = new PrintDocument();

            // Set the printer name
            printDocument.PrinterSettings.PrinterName = printerName;

            // Attach the PrintPage event handler
            printDocument.PrintPage += new PrintPageEventHandler(P
            rintPage);
```

```
        PrintTicket printTicket = new PrintTicket();
        printTicket.PageResolution = new PageResolution(600, 600);
        printTicket.InputBin = InputBin.AutoSelect;
        printTicket.PageMediaType = PageMediaType.Plain;
        printTicket.Duplexing = Duplexing.TwoSidedLongEdge;

        // Assign the PrintTicket to the print queue
        LocalPrintServer localPrintServer = new LocalPrintServer();
        PrintQueue printQueue = localPrintServer.
        GetPrintQueue(printerName);
        printQueue.UserPrintTicket = printTicket;

        // Print the document
        printDocument.Print();
        Console.WriteLine("fini");

    }

    private static void PrintPage(object sender, PrintPageEventArgs e)
    {
        // Define the content to print
        string text = "This is a test print page.";

        // Set the font and brush
        Font font = new Font("Arial", 12);
        Brush brush = Brushes.Black;

        // Define the rectangle to print within
        RectangleF rect = new RectangleF(50, 50, e.PageBounds.Width -
        100, e.PageBounds.Height - 100);

        // Draw the text
        e.Graphics.DrawString(text, font, brush, rect);
    }
  }
}
```

This can be replicated in C++ if you want a lower-level approach that uses the Win32 APIs. In the code section of this chapter is the Hello solution. The Hello solution uses Win32s to replicate the higher-level approach shown above. The StartDoc, StartPage, TextOut, EndPage, and EndDoc APIs are used in the given order to create a print job. The IPP Class Driver converts the GDI drawing commands into a print data format, then encapsulates that data within IPP protocol operations to submit the print job to the IPP printer.

Tracing It Out

From the Wireshark trace, we can see the basic steps used by Windows for IPP print include the following requests:

Get-Printer-Attributes

Validate-Job

Create-Job

Send-Document

The BasicIppPrint Wireshark trace reveals how Windows handles IPP print requests when using the IPP class driver. As you might suspect, the first thing Windows will do is send a Get-Printer-Attributes request to the printer to process attributes of the printer. You learned back in Chapter 2, "Printer Talk," (WinRtIppTest) that the IppPrintDevice object can get these attributes using the WinRT's GetPrinterAttributes method as shown below:

```
var attributes = printer.GetPrinterAttributes(requested_attributes);
```

No.	Time	Source	Destination	Protocol	Lengtl	Info
2	0.103649	HewlettPacka_8...	Broadcast	ARP	60	Who has 10.0.0.50? Tell 10.0.0.214
4	0.103666	ASUSTekCOMPU_e...	HewlettPacka_8...	ARP	42	10.0.0.50 is at 04:42:1a:e6:21:bb
11	0.429898	10.0.0.50	10.0.0.214	IPP	74	IPP Request (Get-Printer-Attributes)
18	0.609690	10.0.0.214	10.0.0.50	IPP	60	IPP Response (successful-ok)
31	1.042602	10.0.0.50	10.0.0.214	IPP	235	IPP Request (Get-Printer-Attributes)
34	1.050943	10.0.0.214	10.0.0.50	IPP	196	IPP Response (successful-ok)
45	1.698806	10.0.0.50	10.0.0.214	IPP	680	IPP Request (Validate-Job)
48	1.706685	10.0.0.214	10.0.0.50	IPP	143	IPP Response (successful-ok)
60	2.145573	10.0.0.50	10.0.0.214	IPP	545	IPP Request (Create-Job)
63	2.163517	10.0.0.214	10.0.0.50	IPP	310	IPP Response (successful-ok)
...	2.664276	10.0.0.50	10.0.0.214	IPP	59	IPP Request (Send-Document)
...	3.026856	10.0.0.214	10.0.0.50	IPP	60	IPP Response (successful-ok)
...	3.505956	10.0.0.50	10.0.0.214	IPP	278	IPP Request (Get-Job-Attributes)
...	3.513813	10.0.0.214	10.0.0.50	IPP	188	IPP Response (successful-ok)
...	5.097723	10.0.0.50	10.0.0.214	IPP	278	IPP Request (Get-Job-Attributes)
...	5.225759	10.0.0.214	10.0.0.50	IPP	60	IPP Response (successful-ok)
...	6.660170	10.0.0.50	10.0.0.214	IPP	278	IPP Request (Get-Job-Attributes)
...	6.667926	10.0.0.214	10.0.0.50	IPP	188	IPP Response (successful-ok)
...	8.171758	10.0.0.50	10.0.0.214	IPP	278	IPP Request (Get-Job-Attributes)
...	8.697377	10.0.0.214	10.0.0.50	IPP	60	IPP Response (successful-ok)
...	14.183945	10.0.0.50	10.0.0.214	IPP	235	IPP Request (Get-Printer-Attributes)
...	14.192082	10.0.0.214	10.0.0.50	IPP	196	IPP Response (successful-ok)

Wireshark trace on document rendered by Windows IPP Class Driver

Once the printer abilities are determined, the next major step before sending a print job to the target printer is to validate it via the Validate Job request. Using the Validate Job request is a recommended step (per RFC 3196) before sending a large print job to a printer to ensure the IPP printer will accept the job.

In the code snippet, you might have noticed the PrintTicket class being used to convey the requested print job attributes. If this PrintTicket had not been created, Windows 11 would have used a default PrintTicket for the print job. The default PrintTicket is generated based on the printer's default settings and capabilities.

In other words, if you do not provide a custom PrintTicket, the print system will rely on the printer's default configuration settings to determine the print job attributes, such as resolution, paper size, media type, and duplex settings. This ensures the print job is processed with reasonable default settings suitable for most standard printing tasks.

As you learned in Chapter 1, “Windows Legacy Print,” the registry path HKEY_CURRENT_USER\Printers\ DevModesPerUser contains default settings (visible in the Common Print Dialog) that the user has previously chosen or created by default. The other registry name/value setting in this hive, DevModes2, is used for default shared printer settings across all users.

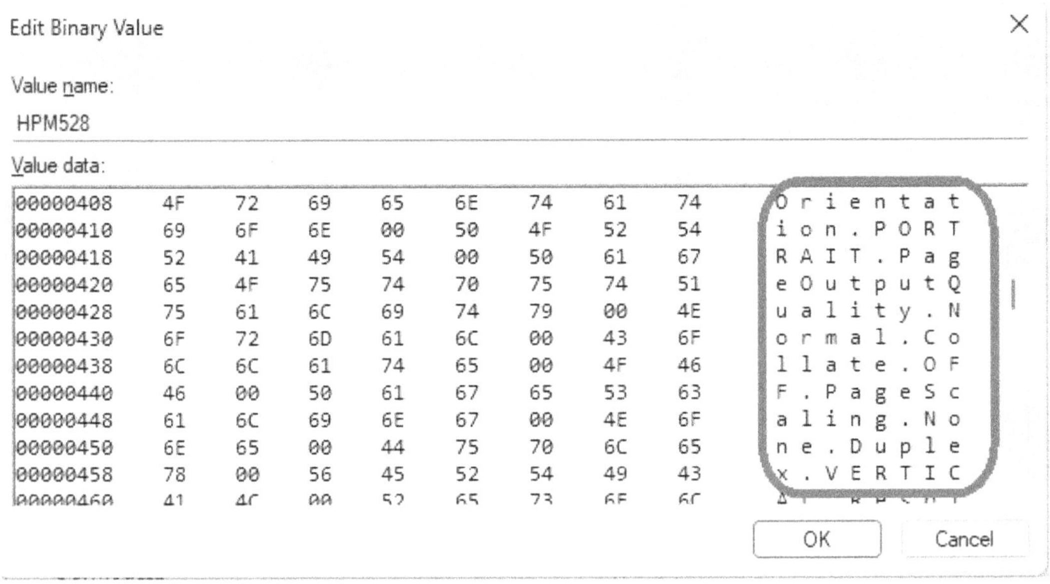

Edit Binary Value

Value name:

HPM528

Value data:

00000408	4F	72	69	65	6E	74	61	74	O r i e n t a t
00000410	69	6F	6E	00	50	4F	52	54	i o n . P O R T
00000418	52	41	49	54	00	50	61	67	R A I T . P a g
00000420	65	4F	75	74	70	75	74	51	e O u t p u t Q
00000428	75	61	6C	69	74	79	00	4E	u a l i t y . N
00000430	6F	72	6D	61	6C	00	43	6F	o r m a l . C o
00000438	6C	6C	61	74	65	00	4F	46	l l a t e . O F
00000440	46	00	50	61	67	65	53	63	F . P a g e S c
00000448	61	6C	69	6E	67	00	4E	6F	a l i n g . N o
00000450	6E	65	00	44	75	70	6C	65	n e . D u p l e
00000458	78	00	56	45	52	54	49	43	x . V E R T I C

OK Cancel

Since these registry name/value settings are binary, they are not as easy to display as string values, but you can still get an idea of what they contain by right-clicking the Name and choosing Modify. As shown above, the binary buffer is full of basic settings for standard print output. These settings can be changed if you open the Common Print Dialog and choose Preferences.

I brought this up to reinforce where Windows gets default print job settings from. When these are set in the default PrintTicket, they must be translated to appropriate IPP print job attributes the printer understands. The IPP print driver knows how to do this since these settings are described in the RFC IPP standards, and IPP printers must comply with them. While these attributes can be processed (since they are RFC standard attributes), what happens if a vendor introduces a printer feature that is not annotated in the RFC standards? As we will see several chapters later, this required Windows to introduce Printer Support Apps (PSA) to effectively handle this scenario.

As mentioned earlier, if you are writing applications on Windows, you are likely better off leveraging the built-in print APIs, which leverage the IPP Class driver, rather than using external IPP frameworks. Besides support from the Windows subsystem for queuing, there is also the document format issue. If you recall back in Chapter 2, "Printer Talk," we touched on what formats the printer will successfully render printed output. These formats are converted for you natively in the print subsystem via the IPP Class driver. For instance, you have likely written a Word document or an Excel document and printed the results. If you look at the supported-document-format attribute for your printer, the .doc/.docx/.xls document formats are not natively supported. In other words, some process must convert these formats to a MIME type the printer understands. If you are not using the built-in processes for Windows that allow for IPP printing (i.e., you are using the CUPS port), you will be responsible for the conversion rather than the native print subsystem.

This is not to suggest you should always use the built-in Windows IPP print framework; indeed, there may be cases where this would be cumbersome. For example, suppose you were tasked with providing status information of hundreds of IPP printers in your enterprise. This type of update status information is tailor-made for the Get-Printer-Attributes request. You might start out writing something like the code in Chapter 2, "Printer Talk," (WinRtIppTest), which leverages the WinRT APIs. But this code relies on installed printers - i.e., IPP printers - to function properly. In other words, you would have to install the printers on your machine first, which (for 100s of printers) would certainly not be ideal. In this case, use of the CUPS port would make sense; you would have no need for spooling or document conversion, and you could query the printers using the Get-Printer-Attributes request and simply format the results into some GUI view or simply print them out to the console. The point is you should consider the application scope and intent before deciding what IPP framework to use.

As an example, I created the familiar "Hello World" document and saved it on my local drive as a .docx file, which is the native Word format. I then started Wireshark and set a capture filter to record anything going to the IP address of my HPM528 printer. You can see the familiar pattern shown earlier in this chapter: the Get-Printer-Attributes request, which recovers, among other attributes, the document-formats-supported attribute and the default-document-format attribute. In the case of my HP528, the default format supported is application\pdf format.

File Edit View Go Capture Analyze Statistics Telephony Wireless Tools Help

Apply a display filter ... <Ctrl-/>

No.	Time	Source	Destination	Protocol	Length	Info
6	0.585160	10.0.0.50	10.0.0.215	IPP	650	IPP Request (Get-Printer-Attributes)
13	0.916504	10.0.0.215	10.0.0.50	IPP	60	IPP Response (successful-ok)
22	8.956468	10.0.0.50	10.0.0.215	IPP	232	IPP Request (Get-Printer-Attributes)
25	8.966542	10.0.0.215	10.0.0.50	IPP	196	IPP Response (successful-ok)
35	17.397348	10.0.0.50	10.0.0.215	IPP	651	IPP Request (Validate-Job)
38	17.406544	10.0.0.215	10.0.0.50	IPP	143	IPP Response (successful-ok)

Wireshark Trace Showing the Get-Printer-Attributes Request When Using Windows Print

If we expand the Validate-Job request within Wireshark, you can then drill down the operation-attributes-tag. You can see the document-format encoded is application/pdf, not docx.

Wireshark · Packet 41 · Ethernet (host 10.0.0.215)

```
> Hypertext Transfer Protocol
v Internet Printing Protocol
    [Response In: 44]
    version: 2.0
    operation-id: Validate-Job (0x0004)
    request-id: 2
  v operation-attributes-tag
    > attributes-charset (charset): 'utf-8'
    > attributes-natural-language (naturalLanguage): 'en'
    > printer-uri (uri): 'ipp://hpm528:631/ipp/print'
    > job-name (nameWithoutLanguage): 'Microsoft Word - Document2'
    > requesting-user-name (nameWithoutLanguage): 'M1795\jpmsp'
    > document-format (mimeMediaType): 'application/pdf'
  > job-attributes-tag
    end-of-attributes-tag
```

IPP dissector displaying operations-attribute-tag for Windows print

USING WIRESHARK WITH IPP/IPPS ON WINDOWS

As an aside, I should provide some tips on using Wireshark on Windows to track IPP/IPPS requests. The truth is, tracking IPPS requests is a bit more difficult to do simply because the conversation between the client and the printer is encrypted using TLS. The Wireshark dissector needs the traffic to be decrypted to work properly. The dissector is the component on Wireshark that decodes the protocol – it is a protocol parser that makes traces easier to interpret [3]. If you want to know how to decrypt traffic using the server certificate, the following link may help: `https://www.golinuxcloud.com/wireshark-decrypt-ssl-tls-tutorial/`. I have found it much easier to just turn off IPPS on the printer and recreate the printer in Windows when I am done.

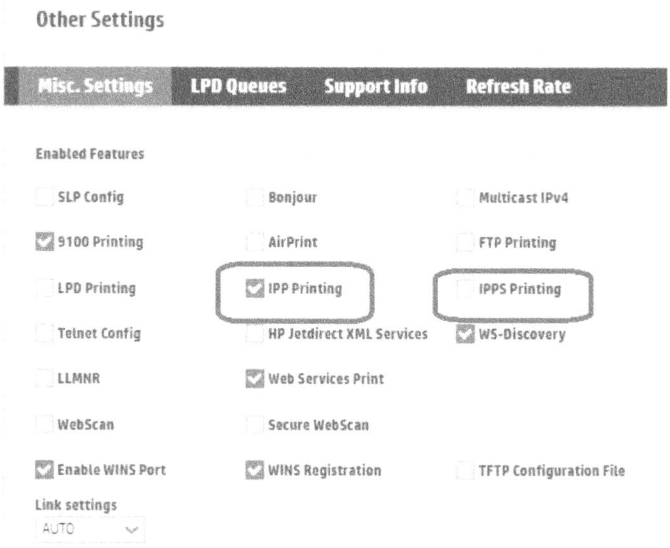

Enabling IPP/IPPS on the HP M528 Printer Using Imbedded Web Server

For those just wanting to learn the protocol and see how it is structured, you can set up your test printer as IPP, let Windows install it as an IPP printer, and then monitor those traces. Windows will always choose to use IPPS if it is available (Windows determines IPP/IPPS from the get-printer-uri-supported attribute), so you need to coax Windows into using port 631 (IPP). Since you are using IPP rather than IPPS, the dissector will work as it should, and you can look at how requests are composed. Once you are finished, delete the Windows IPP printer instance, enable IPPS on the printer, and then reinstall the printer.

Thus, the IPP class driver knew the printer could not process a docx file natively and converted the document to a pdf file. If you were using the OpenPrinting CUPS port for this print operation, it would be incumbent on you to make that conversion from docx to pdf. As you know, one of the attributes returned from the Get-Printer-Attributes request was the document-format-default attribute. This attribute tells the caller what document format the target printer prefers. For my HP M528 printer, this happens to be in application/pdf format, although the printer will support application/postscript and text/plain, among other formats. Thus, the MS IPP Class driver will try to convert the docx format into pdf so it can be natively processed on the printer.

Print Job Status

Assuming the Send-Document or Print-Job request has been processed by the printer, the client still needs information as to the job status. While every IPP operation has a status code returned that corresponds to the success of the individual operation (the first 2 bytes of the reply stream are the Major/Minor IPP version, and the next 2 bytes returned are the IPP request status code for that request), we should also expect a status of the print operation itself. For instance, is the job still being processed on the printer or has the job completed printing out? To identify the processing state of any document or print job, IPP provides the Get-Job-Attributes request.

The Get-Job-Attributes request takes as parameters the print job id for which you would want processing state information from and, of course, the printer URL where the job was processed. You can also provide additional requested attributes that identify the job, such as job-name, job-originating-user-name, job-printer-uri, job-state, etc. The list of available requested attributes for the Get-Job-Attributes request can be found in Section 4.2.6.1 of RFC 8011.

For our simple "Hello World" print job processed by the IPP class driver in Windows, the Get-Job-Attributes request may be called multiple times after the print job has been sent. For instance, look at the Wireshark trace based on the "HelloWorld" print job previously mentioned. You should notice several instances where the Get-Job-Attributes request is called, each with a corresponding IPP response.

Apply a display filter ... <Ctrl-/>

No.	Time	Source	Destination	Protocol	Length	Info
240	7.923435	10.0.0.5	10.0.0.60	TCP	54	59838 → 631 [ACK] Seq=1 Ack=1 Win=131328 Len=0
241	7.923831	10.0.0.5	10.0.0.60	TCP	241	59838 → 631 [PSH, ACK] Seq=1 Ack=1 Win=131328 Len=187 [TCP PDU
242	7.924067	10.0.0.5	10.0.0.60	IPP	284	IPP Request (Get-Job-Attributes)
243	7.927392	10.0.0.60	10.0.0.5	TCP	60	631 → 59838 [ACK] Seq=1 Ack=418 Win=4284 Len=0
244	7.928319	10.0.0.60	10.0.0.5	TCP	526	631 → 59838 [PSH, ACK] Seq=1 Ack=418 Win=64240 Len=472 [TCP PDU
245	7.933279	10.0.0.60	10.0.0.5	IPP	188	IPP Response (successful-ok)
246	7.933545	10.0.0.5	10.0.0.60	TCP	54	59838 → 631 [ACK] Seq=418 Ack=608 Win=130560 Len=0
247	7.933727	10.0.0.5	10.0.0.60	TCP	54	59838 → 631 [FIN, ACK] Seq=418 Ack=608 Win=130560 Len=0
248	7.934939	10.0.0.60	10.0.0.5	TCP	60	631 → 59838 [ACK] Seq=608 Ack=419 Win=64239 Len=0
249	8.946200	10.0.0.5	10.0.0.60	TCP	66	59839 → 631 [SYN] Seq=0 Win=64260 Len=0 MSS=1428 WS=256 SACK_PE
250	8.947400	10.0.0.60	10.0.0.5	TCP	62	631 → 59839 [SYN, ACK] Seq=0 Ack=1 Win=2920 Len=0 MSS=1460 WS=1
251	8.947634	10.0.0.5	10.0.0.60	TCP	54	59839 → 631 [ACK] Seq=1 Ack=1 Win=131328 Len=0
252	8.947848	10.0.0.5	10.0.0.60	TCP	241	59839 → 631 [PSH, ACK] Seq=1 Ack=1 Win=131328 Len=187 [TCP PDU
253	8.947976	10.0.0.5	10.0.0.60	IPP	284	IPP Request (Get-Job-Attributes)
254	8.951460	10.0.0.60	10.0.0.5	TCP	60	631 → 59839 [ACK] Seq=1 Ack=418 Win=4284 Len=0
255	8.952808	10.0.0.60	10.0.0.5	TCP	526	631 → 59839 [PSH, ACK] Seq=1 Ack=418 Win=64240 Len=472 [TCP PDU
256	8.958379	10.0.0.60	10.0.0.5	IPP	188	IPP Response (successful-ok)
257	8.958511	10.0.0.5	10.0.0.60	TCP	54	59839 → 631 [ACK] Seq=418 Ack=608 Win=130560 Len=0
258	8.958642	10.0.0.5	10.0.0.60	TCP	54	59839 → 631 [FIN, ACK] Seq=418 Ack=608 Win=130560 Len=0
259	8.959719	10.0.0.60	10.0.0.5	TCP	60	631 → 59839 [ACK] Seq=608 Ack=419 Win=64239 Len=0
260	9.995306	10.0.0.5	10.0.0.60	TCP	66	59842 → 631 [SYN] Seq=0 Win=64260 Len=0 MSS=1428 WS=256 SACK_PE
261	9.996735	10.0.0.60	10.0.0.5	TCP	62	631 → 59842 [SYN, ACK] Seq=0 Ack=1 Win=2920 Len=0 MSS=1460 WS=1
262	9.996985	10.0.0.5	10.0.0.60	TCP	54	59842 → 631 [ACK] Seq=1 Ack=1 Win=131328 Len=0
263	9.997398	10.0.0.5	10.0.0.60	TCP	241	59842 → 631 [PSH, ACK] Seq=1 Ack=1 Win=131328 Len=187 [TCP PDU
264	9.997660	10.0.0.5	10.0.0.60	IPP	284	IPP Request (Get-Job-Attributes)
265	10.045163	10.0.0.60	10.0.0.5	TCP	60	631 → 59842 [ACK] Seq=1 Ack=418 Win=4284 Len=0
266	10.046161	10.0.0.60	10.0.0.5	TCP	526	631 → 59842 [PSH, ACK] Seq=1 Ack=418 Win=64240 Len=472 [TCP PDU

Get-Job-Attributes requests

While this repetition might seem wasteful, it does serve the purpose of alerting the client to a state in the print job as processed on the printer. Below is the printer response to the

```
> Frame 245: 188 bytes on wire (1504 bits), 188 bytes captured (1!
> Ethernet II, Src: Cisco_a0:df:0b (74:ad:98:a0:df:0b), Dst: HP_e
> Internet Protocol Version 4, Src: 10.28.66.60, Dst: 10.229.98.5
> Transmission Control Protocol, Src Port: 631, Dst Port: 59838, !
> [2 Reassembled TCP Segments (606 bytes): #244(472), #245(134)]
> Hypertext Transfer Protocol, has 2 chunks (including last chunk
v Internet Printing Protocol
    [Request In: 242]
    [Response Time: 0.009212000 seconds]
    version: 2.0
    status-code: Successful (successful-ok)
    request-id: 5
  v operation-attributes-tag
    > attributes-charset (charset): 'utf-8'
    > attributes-natural-language (naturalLanguage): 'en'
  v job-attributes-tag
    > job-state (enum): processing
    > job-state-reasons (keyword): 'none'
    end-of-attributes-tag
```

Get-Job-Attributes request, and you can see that the job-state is being conveyed as "processing." We can be assured that the print job has been successfully executed and a printout (maybe) is available for pickup if the "completed" job-state is provided as shown in the graphic below.

```
˅ Internet Printing Protocol
    [Request In: 264]
    [Response Time: 0.465822000 seconds]
    version: 2.0
    status-code: Successful (successful-ok)
    request-id: 7
  ˅ operation-attributes-tag
    › attributes-charset (charset): 'utf-8'
    › attributes-natural-language (naturalLanguage): 'en'
  ˅ job-attributes-tag
    › job-state (enum): completed
    › job-state-reasons (keyword): 'job-completed-successfully'
    end-of-attributes-tag
```

RFC 8011 Section 4.2.6.1 allows for the following states:

Completed: Any job whose state is complete, canceled, or aborted.

Not completed: Any job whose state is pending, processing, processing-stopped, or pending-held.

To get the job state information, the client can either poll the printer - i.e., send out requests intermittently and process the replies until the desired job state is found - or create a subscription for job events from the printer and receive those event updates as they happen. For those familiar with microcontrollers, the choices are like the use of polling or interrupts for device events. While subscriptions would likely be the clear favorite of developers, the reality is that subscription events are currently not well supported by vendors. As in the case of all requests, you can set as requested information the attributes that correspond to information you want returned in Get-Printer-Attributes - in this case information about print subscriptions.

notify-events-supported: Lists the events that the printer supports for notifications.

notify-attributes-supported: Lists the attributes that the printer supports for notifications.

notify-pull-method-supported: Indicates the pull methods supported by the printer for retrieving notifications.

notify-push-method-supported: Indicates the push methods supported by the printer for delivering notifications.

notify-max-events-supported: Specifies the maximum number of events that can be subscribed to simultaneously.

For a push method, the printer actively sends notifications to the requestor when the desired event occurs. The requestor or client must provide a URL or address where the printer can send the notifications. Once the subscription is established, the printer will send POST requests to the registered endpoint (i.e., /my_printer/my_notification) whenever the requested event occurs. In the pull method, the client periodically polls the printer to check for any new notifications. The printer stores the notifications until the client retrieves them.

As previously stated, support for these requests from print vendors is tepid - from the Wireshark trace I obtained on the "Hello World" print job, Microsoft uses polling to obtain the print job status. RFC 3995 details provide the following information about support:

> This IPP notification specification is an OPTIONAL extension to Internet Printing Protocol/1.1: Model and Semantics [RFC2911, RFC2910] [8].

My HP LaserJet Enterprise Flow MFP M528 printer does not support subscriptions, so clients must poll to obtain the results. Chapter 6, "Additional Operations," will detail the Get-Job-Attributes request and how it can be created and used in C#, but for now it is important to understand why it is used in the first place.

Print Processing Pipeline

The IPP print processing pipeline in Windows is more nuanced than you might first assume. IPP was integrated into an existing Windows print subsystem to work seamlessly with existing type 3 and type 4 drivers. To do this, some configuration files are needed for the system to know how to work within the existing confines and processes of the Windows print subsystem. In the C:\Windows\System32\DriverStore\FileRepository\ prnms012.inf_amd64_ 6be366b41bdf5913\ folder of Windows 11 are three files that are particularly important to the overall configuration of IPP on the system. These three files are

> **msipp-manifest.ini**: This file is part of the overall V4 driver package and includes specific installation directives. It has a DriverConfig section that specifies the Datafile(s) and required files for the driver to work. Most interesting is the DriverRender section, as this implies that the data format (for the IPP Class driver) is fixed at application/pdf rather than being a product of the dynamic Get-Printer-Attributes request as the IPP was designed to do. I suspect this must do more with Mopria support, as pdf is the default file type for this standard.
>
> **msipp-pipelineconfig.xml**: This file specifies the filter pipeline for the IPP print process. It specifies the name of the default rendering filter (PDFRenderFilter.dll) and the input and output interfaces of the filter.
>
> **msipp.xml**: This file specifies the IPP print system's global configuration that determines how the print process works. This would include parameters like default page resolution, color, orientation, and optional media sizes.

How exactly does the IPP class driver convert a docx file into the proposed default document format, in this case application/pdf? It turns out Windows has several rendering filter libraries that can do the job; the one used (via the msipp-manifest.ini file) is the PdfRenderFilter library. If you need to find out what files or registry entries are employed by a process, using the SysInternal group Process Monitor (ProcMon) tool is a useful resource. Whether you use this for performance issues or for troubleshooting help, this utility is good for spying on how a process (in this case the spooler process) works. As described by the SysInternal website:

> "Process Monitor is an advanced monitoring tool for Windows that shows real-time file system, Registry and process/thread activity" [2].

The appendix of this book has a quick start tutorial on how to use the tool, and you can find out much more about it online. In this case, I filtered on the PdfRenderFilter.dll file as shown below to reduce the captured events and make analysis much easier.

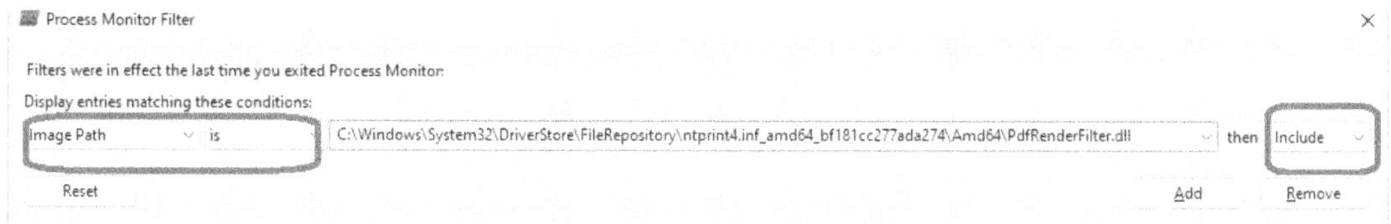

Setting Up Filtering on ProcMon to Reduce Events

If you start ProcMon and then print your docx file (in my case the "Hello World" document), you can see that the printfilterpipeline process loads this (PdfRenderFilter) library to make the conversion to the format (application/pdf) Mopria prefers.

41	12:00:...	printfilterpipeline...	22644	QueryOpen	C:\Windows\System32\DriverStore\FileRepository\ntprint4.inf_amd64_bf181cc277ada274\Amd64\PDFRenderFilter.dll	FAST IO DISALL(
42	12:00:...	printfilterpipeline...	22644	CreateFile	C:\Windows\System32\DriverStore\FileRepository\ntprint4.inf_amd64_bf181cc277ada274\Amd64\PDFRenderFilter.dll	SUCCESS
43	12:00:...	printfilterpipeline...	22644	QueryBasicInformationFile	C:\Windows\System32\DriverStore\FileRepository\ntprint4.inf_amd64_bf181cc277ada274\Amd64\PDFRenderFilter.dll	SUCCESS
44	12:00:...	printfilterpipeline...	22644	CloseFile	C:\Windows\System32\DriverStore\FileRepository\ntprint4.inf_amd64_bf181cc277ada274\Amd64\PDFRenderFilter.dll	SUCCESS
45	12:00:...	printfilterpipeline...	22644	CreateFile	C:\Windows\System32\DriverStore\FileRepository\ntprint4.inf_amd64_bf181cc277ada274\Amd64\PDFRenderFilter.dll	SUCCESS
46	12:00:...	printfilterpipeline...	22644	CreateFileMapping	C:\Windows\System32\DriverStore\FileRepository\ntprint4.inf_amd64_bf181cc277ada274\Amd64\PDFRenderFilter.dll	FILE LOCKED W
47	12:00:...	printfilterpipeline...	22644	CreateFileMapping	C:\Windows\System32\DriverStore\FileRepository\ntprint4.inf_amd64_bf181cc277ada274\Amd64\PDFRenderFilter.dll	SUCCESS
48	12:00:...	printfilterpipeline...	22644	DeviceIoControl	C:\Windows\System32\DriverStore\FileRepository\ntprint4.inf_amd64_bf181cc277ada274\Amd64\PDFRenderFilter.dll	SUCCESS
49	12:00:...	printfilterpipeline...	22644	DeviceIoControl	C:\Windows\System32\DriverStore\FileRepository\ntprint4.inf_amd64_bf181cc277ada274\Amd64\PDFRenderFilter.dll	SUCCESS
50	12:00:...	printfilterpipeline...	22644	DeviceIoControl	C:\Windows\System32\DriverStore\FileRepository\ntprint4.inf_amd64_bf181cc277ada274\Amd64\PDFRenderFilter.dll	NOT FOUND
51	12:00:...	printfilterpipeline...	22644	DeviceIoControl	C:\Windows\System32\DriverStore\FileRepository\ntprint4.inf_amd64_bf181cc277ada274\Amd64\PDFRenderFilter.dll	0x60030002
52	12:00:...	printfilterpipeline...	22644	Load Image	C:\Windows\System32\DriverStore\FileRepository\ntprint4.inf_amd64_bf181cc277ada274\Amd64\PDFRenderFilter.dll	SUCCESS
53	12:00:...	printfilterpipeline...	22644	QueryNameInformationFile	C:\Windows\System32\DriverStore\FileRepository\ntprint4.inf_amd64_bf181cc277ada274\Amd64\PDFRenderFilter.dll	BUFFER OVERFI
54	12:00:...	printfilterpipeline...	22644	QueryNameInformationFile	C:\Windows\System32\DriverStore\FileRepository\ntprint4.inf_amd64_bf181cc277ada274\Amd64\PDFRenderFilter.dll	SUCCESS
55	12:00:...	printfilterpipeline...	22644	ReadFile	C:\Windows\System32\DriverStore\FileRepository\ntprint4.inf_amd64_bf181cc277ada274\Amd64\PDFRenderFilter.dll	SUCCESS
56	12:00:...	printfilterpipeline...	22644	ReadFile	C:\Windows\System32\DriverStore\FileRepository\ntprint4.inf_amd64_bf181cc277ada274\Amd64\PDFRenderFilter.dll	SUCCESS
57	12:00:...	printfilterpipeline...	22644	ReadFile	C:\Windows\System32\DriverStore\FileRepository\ntprint4.inf_amd64_bf181cc277ada274\Amd64\PDFRenderFilter.dll	SUCCESS
58	12:00:...	printfilterpipeline...	22644	ReadFile	C:\Windows\System32\DriverStore\FileRepository\ntprint4.inf_amd64_bf181cc277ada274\Amd64\PDFRenderFilter.dll	SUCCESS
59	12:00:...	printfilterpipeline...	22644	ReadFile	C:\Windows\System32\DriverStore\FileRepository\ntprint4.inf_amd64_bf181cc277ada274\Amd64\PDFRenderFilter.dll	SUCCESS
60	12:00:...	printfilterpipeline...	22644	CloseFile	C:\Windows\System32\DriverStore\FileRepository\ntprint4.inf_amd64_bf181cc277ada274\Amd64\PDFRenderFilter.dll	SUCCESS
61	12:00:...	printfilterpipeline...	22644	ReadFile	C:\Windows\System32\DriverStore\FileRepository\ntprint4.inf_amd64_bf181cc277ada274\Amd64\PDFRenderFilter.dll	SUCCESS
62	12:00:...	printfilterpipeline...	22644	ReadFile	C:\Windows\System32\DriverStore\FileRepository\ntprint4.inf_amd64_bf181cc277ada274\Amd64\PDFRenderFilter.dll	SUCCESS

A ProcMon Trace Showing Printfilterpipeline Loading the PDFRenderFilter DLL

It should also be noted that Windows also includes a PCLmRenderFilter and PWGRRenderFilter as well in the event these formats are the document-format-default value.

In Chapter 2, "Printer Talk," I detailed the WinRT APIs, which can be used to get the attributes of a targeted printer. When installing an IPP printer through Windows, the Get-Printer-Attributes request is used to gather the attributes the printer supports.

While I would encourage those developing applications on Windows to employ the native Windows libraries. I would also be remiss if I did not mention that there are several different libraries available that descend from or are based on the OpenPrinting IPP CUPS port or from the IPP RFC standards. These include several C#, JavaScript, and

Python libraries available for download from GitHub if you are interested. The issue with any of the alternatives to the OpenPrinting CUPS port is support: will these alternatives be supported several years down the road or even through the next IPP version? You would not want to develop code and then find out the library or framework it relies on is no longer supported or even available. In the event you are developing applications on a Windows platform that sends print to fluid or dynamic printer URIs (in other words, printers not likely to be locally installed), then it might be prudent to stick with the OpenPrinting group's port. As with the OpenPrinting port, it will be incumbent on the developer to convert any unsupported file format to one the printer can natively render if you choose to use the alternative libraries on Windows.

Conversion to PDF

Previously in this chapter, we touched on Mopria and IPP Everywhere as standards for driverless print. You are likely not surprised to find out that both Mopria and IPP Everywhere specify PDF as the default Page Description Language (PDL) for use with IPP printers - the question is why. After all, haven't PCL and PostScript been around for a long time and proven to be robust description languages that printers can employ? The answer to this question revolves around device independence, ease of use, and standardization of PDF as compared to PCL and PostScript.

When compared to PCL, PDF is often seen as more device independent, thus providing a consistent print experience as compared to PCL. This means that output quality can be expected to vary less across manufacturers' print devices when employing PDF as compared to PCL. PDF also supports a more complex graphics capability, including vector graphics, as compared to PCL. Additionally, PDF offers more robust security features such as digital signatures and encryption, which are not universally available in PCL. Finally, PDF can include embedded multimedia and hyperlinks, making it a more complete information-sharing venue.

When comparing PDF to PostScript, ease of use could be described as the salient point for choosing PDF. PDF was derived from the PostScript printer language and included additional navigational features and bookmarks. PDFs are far easier for end-users to create and share compared to PostScript, which requires more technical knowledge to employ. Compatibility across different OS and hardware platforms is another reason to select PDF as the default standard. The PDF format is printer independent, meaning it does not include instructions for a specific printer. Finally, PostScript files are often larger than their PDF counterparts, which would then consume more printer resources to render.

In the end, the combination of the above reasons along with the standardization of PDF by the International Organization for Standardization (of the PDF format) was a factor when choosing PDF as the default format for both Mopria and IPP Everywhere. This ISO standardization allows the PDF format to provide predictable and consistent output across all hardware compliant with ISO standards. Thus, promotion of PDF by both Mopria and IPP Everywhere as the standard PDL for driverless printing appears to be well founded.

Rendering Documents to PDF

In the event you cannot use the built-in Windows print subsystem for IPP/IPPS print (for instance, you are building a network IPP print monitor system), then you may find the need to convert Windows Office files to a format the printer can use. In the event you need to convert file types, your choices are third-party utilities or, if you have Office installed on your Windows machine, some of the built-in Office libraries.

Throughout this book, attempts are made (when possible) to provide low-cost alternatives to commercial products as budgets for development, especially in smaller outfits, are not universally generous. However, for those budgets that will allow, there are some particularly good commercial software packages directed toward conversion of Microsoft Office formats to pdf. Some of these commercial products include Aspose, Spire, and Gembox to name a few.

Using the COM objects exposed for Word and Excel will require you to add some using statements among these Microsoft.Office.Interop.Word and Microsoft.Office.Interop.Excel. For an example of how this might be done, you can load the Document2Pdf solution in Visual Studio to provide an example. The solution is simplistic but does provide a legitimate path for Office file conversion, at least for non-commercial or high-volume applications. A brief description of this process might be in order.

DocumentConversion is a singleton class (can be instantiated only once) that provides access to both Office COM components for conversion and a community edition of FreeSpire [9] that does the same thing. While the FreeSpire version is obviously limited (currently a 3-page limitation), it is very fast as compared to the Office COM route. Converting a doc or docx file (or an xls or xlsv file) is as simple as

```
string Document = @"C:\Temp\TestWordDoc.docx";
DocumentConversion _dc = DocumentConversion.GetInstance;
_dc.engineUsed = DocumentConversion.DOC_CONVERSION_ENGINE.
MS_OFFICE;
_dc._document = Document;
try
{
    if (_dc.engineUsed == DocumentConversion.DOC_CONVERSION_
    ENGINE.MS_OFFICE)
        _dc._pdfdocument = ComOfficeConversion.Convert2Pdf
        (_dc._document);
    else
        _dc._pdfdocument = SpireOfficeConversion.Convert2Pdf
        (_dc._document);
}
catch (Exception ex)
{
    Console.WriteLine($"Document conversion failed, reason:
    {ex.Message}");
}
```

If you use the Office Interop route, take a look at the references for Microsoft. Office.Interop. Word and Microsoft.Office.Interop.Excel in the solution. I found these assemblies in the C:\Windows\assembly\GAC_MSIL folder on my home edition of Windows 11. You do have to have some form of Office installed on your computer for this to work as these assemblies are not automatically exported to the bin\Debug or bin\ Release folders, meaning the host machine will need these as well.

You can get around the above limitations by embedding the interop assemblies directly into your assembly. Locate the office interop assembly you want in the References folder of the solution. Right-click Microsoft.Office.Interop. Word or Microsoft.

Office.Interop.Excel and choose Properties. Now ensure the "Embed Interop Types" property is set to True and recompile the solution.

As of this writing, you can alternatively include the NuGet package **Microsoft. Interop** to the solution, making it easier to distribute and run the solution on other Windows machines without them being required to install Office.

Of course, if you are targeting a printer not locally installed in Windows (and therefore document conversion is an issue), you can at least limit what file types can be used. As described in the previous chapters, the Get-Printer-Attributes request can be used to obtain the document-format-supported attribute, which lists the file types that can successfully be printed. We will provide such a feature in Chapter 6, "Additional Operations," which expands the IPP library.

Chapter Summary

As with previous chapters, a lot of ground was covered in this chapter. While the focus was intended to be on how IPP printing was accomplished using the native Windows print subsystem components, a general introduction into some of the IPP print requests was necessary before covering the IPP class driver. Each request was accompanied by a Wireshark trace to illustrate the composition of request attributes necessary for the printer to correctly process the byte stream. As should be obvious by now, in IPP it is a clever idea to query the capabilities of the printer beforehand to ensure job properties assigned to the print job can be supported on the target printer. Also, the printer should also be checked to ensure it can support any of the IPP operations not explicitly marked as required by the standard.

The chapter then delves into the particulars of the IPP class driver. We explored how the IPP Class driver rendered a print job by creating and sending the validate-job, create-job, and print-document requests to the printer for any given print request. The print subsystem then extracts the print job status from the printer by employing the Get-Job-Attributes request to recover the status of the job. This can be accomplished by polling the printer or subscribing (ideally) to printer notifications. In a perfect world, printer notifications might be the preferred method to receive job status as they are in effect a push or pull event as opposed to the overhead of polling. Unfortunately, notifications are not well supported (yet?) by print manufacturers, and Microsoft itself uses polling to extract job status, at least for now.

While on the IPP class driver, the chapter explored the print pipeline and how document conversion (if needed) is provided. This is a key point to remember: jobs created and processed using the Windows native print path will have document conversion included before the job is submitted to the printer. In the event a developer must use an external library (i.e., for jobs sent to a non-installed local printer), the translation to a suitably supported PDL on the target printer is not automatically provided.

In the event a document conversion is required, there are several paths to take:

1. Insist (programmatically or otherwise) that only supported document types (on the target printer) can be used.
2. If an Office document, use Office conversion assemblies if cost is a mitigating factor.
3. Provide for any document processing event by employing suitable commercial document conversion software.

References

1. How to Use the Internet Printing Protocol, How to Use the Internet Printing Protocol - Printer Working Group, Printer Working Group
2. Process Monitor v4.01, `https://learn.microsoft.com/en-us/sysinternals/downloads/procmon`, SysInternals, 6/2/2024.
3. Wireshark Dissector Tutorial, `https://www.golinuxcloud.com/wireshark-dissector-tutorial/`, Celal Dogan, January 2, 2024
4. Driverless Printing Standards And their PDLS, `https://openprinting.github.io/driverless/01-standards-and-their-pdls/`, OpenPrinting
5. PCLm Overview, `https://www.qualitylogic.com/testing-services/printer-and-pdl-test-tools/pclm-functional-test-suite/`, QualityLogic.
6. o2solutions/pdfview4net, `https://github.com/o2solutions/pdfview4net`
7. JBaarssen/pdflibcore, `https://github.com/jbaarssen/PdfLibCore`
8. IPP: Event Notifications and Subscriptions, RFC 3995, Page 5 – Introduction section.
9. FreeSpire.Doc, `https://www.nuget.org/packages/FreeSpire.Doc/`

CHAPTER 5

IPP Standards Print

In this chapter, we begin building a basic IPP request library in .NET using the C# language. Up to this point in the book, I have recommended using the Microsoft print subsystem (System.Drawing.Printing) framework if you are on Windows printing to install local printers or printers shared off a print server. There are many good reasons for doing this – support, stability, and built-in data translation are but a few that come to mind. However, as you might imagine, not all usability requirements fall into this scenario. For instance, you might want to use a printer not installed on your computer. Maybe you want a library you could plug into existing code bases to print, and the printer is not known or defined for Windows yet. Perhaps you have a requirement to send documents to arbitrary IPP/IPPS printers in your network depending on programmatic states. Whatever your intention or requirements, this chapter will investigate how to develop a solution to fit this scenario. If you are planning to develop or need to support production code using IPP/IPPS print, I would highly recommend you implement the CUPS port to Windows provided by the PWG. However, if you are just interested in learning about IPP in more detail, there is no better instruction into how a system works than participating in the actual construction of the system. This is true for both developers and those wanting to learn more about how the system works – I hope this chapter is instructive for both developers and system engineers.

In many respects, this chapter takes the opposite approach to the one used in Chapter 3, “Deep Dive into the Protocol.” In Chapter 3, “Deep Dive into the Protocol,” the emphasis was on decoding IPP byte streams from the printer; in this chapter we will be encoding byte streams to send to the printer, which will have to interpret them. And lest you assume a smug assurance from this task, know the printer will most assuredly reject most deviations from the IPP RFC standards. In other words, the byte stream sent to the printer must be in the exact format the (IPP-compliant) printer expects: any deviation will result in a failure of the request. Make no mistake: in this endeavor Wireshark, "ipptool," and the RFC standards are your best friends. The RFCs most consulted for this

J. Marion, *Adopting Internet Printing Protocol for Windows*, https://doi.org/10.1007/979-8-8688-2010-6_5

task will be RFC 8010 (Internet Printing Protocol 1.1: Encoding and Transport) and RFC 8011 (Internet Printing Protocol 1.1: Model and Semantics). Together these two form the foundation for understanding the construction of basic IPP 1.1 requests.

To make a comparison of protocol adherence, it is always best practice to enlist a known standard. For the purposes of the test, I used the Microsoft IPP Class driver as the standard to compare Wireshark traces against. This works well, as we can set up the installed IPP/IPPS printers against a known printer for comparison. To get the library working, I used the old trick of setting up my printer to just support IPP, then creating a Windows IPP printer via the GUI. This assures us that our printer will allow unencrypted IPP to be easily dissected by Wireshark. Failure to do this may result in Windows choosing the more secure IPPS service, which requires TLS, which will be opaque/unencryptable in Wireshark traces, making them impossible to read. You would be just as correct to use "ipptool" as the standard to compare your development efforts against. However, I found that using the built-in Windows print subsystem is a bit more convenient - in the end the choice is yours.

I should be clear: you should use existing, well-tested libraries rather than develop your own - it is more efficient to do so and less problematic in the long run. But as you are reading this book, I should assume you also maintain a bit of intellectual curiosity that compels you to explore the details of technology. Thus, while I would always steer developers or technology enthusiasts to using the Printer Working Group's (PWG) library port (for Windows) of IPP, this chapter will be for those developers, technicians, and even computer science folks who desire a deeper understanding of how IPP/IPPS works. Realistically, you can never fully appreciate or understand how any technology works unless you understand the constituent parts that it is composed of and how they interact with each other. Thus, by rolling your own working IPP/IPPS print library, you should better understand how the protocol works, how to emulate it in any development language, and finally how to troubleshoot it when it fails. This is the case for any development language: once the requirements for the standard are carried out within any specific language (here it is C#), it is a matter of emulating the same operation in another language, be it Java, Python, or even a scripting language such as Perl or even Windows PowerShell. With that in mind, let's set up some design considerations.

It would help to temper any expectations of production-level code; the intention is not to compete with the very good existing efforts out there. Rather, building a library on your own will hopefully reinforce the learning experience and produce a better understanding of the protocol itself. That is not to say we will not take basic steps to ensure some degree of thread safety or asynchronous design: these should always be a part of any development project. On the other hand, the code itself should be as easy to follow as possible with minimal abstraction to reduce complexity in a learning environment; this is the course we will pursue. The first thing we should demand of our portable C# IPP print library is ease of use: nobody will use the library if it is cumbersome or if it does not scale well. Additionally, the library should be logical and intuitive to use to ease the developer's burden and make learning technology fun. As mentioned previously, we should require that the library be asynchronous in behavior, especially since it could potentially be used in GUI applications. Nobody likes a GUI that freezes or appears unresponsive - traits that are seen in synchronous (blocking) methods. Coincidentally, C# has a language-level asynchronous programming model that allows you to easily write asynchronous code without having to juggle callbacks or conform to a library that supports asynchrony [4]. Of course, the primary goal of the library is to print documents on the target printer, but being able to successfully cancel an existing job, we no longer want is also important. Finally, we would want descriptive error codes (from the printer) in the event of failure so we could more easily rectify the issue.

With these design goals in mind, I will introduce the CsIppRequests solution, located in the code section of this chapter. The solution is broken into two projects: CsIppRequestLib, the actual library that creates the IPP requests, and the IppPrintRequest console program that employs the library and interacts with the user. In the next chapter, we will add additional functionality as needed, but for now the library will provide basic print and cancellation ability. Our goal is to provide basic print functionality to any IPP/IPPS printer on the network without having to install the printer in Windows. Because of this, we cannot use the WinRT library or the built-in print subsystem, which makes use of the Microsoft IPP Class driver. We will have to build the validate-job, create-job, cancel-job, send-document, and print-job requests to do this, and we will have to format the byte stream that describes these operations for the POST message. As mentioned earlier, this is the opposite of what we were doing in Chapter 3, "Deep Dive into the Protocol." For this book's purposes, library development will be done over the next two chapters.

As mentioned several times in this book, Wireshark is your absolute best friend when working with IPP/IPPS requests. It is, however, not the only tool you should employ in this development effort. Chapter 9, "IPP Tools," introduces some very good tools created to help developers create IPP/IPPS requests. I recommend you look at that chapter if you do not have a test printer that works with IPP/IPPS. There are some virtual IPP printers that can be emulated in software that can be a suitable replacement for real hardware. It is always good to develop against a real printer, but in the event you do not have one, these virtual printers are the next best thing. Returning to Wireshark, my testing brought out flaws in the development of the byte stream that Wireshark was instrumental in identifying.

Capturing from Ethernet (host 10.0.0.215)

File Edit View Go Capture Analyze Statistics Telephony Wireless Tools Help

Apply a display filter ... <Ctrl-/>

No.	Time	Source	Destination	Protocol	Length	Info
16	2.371813	10.0.0.50	10.0.0.215	TCP	54	56637 → 80 [ACK] Seq=435 Ack=736 Win=261888 Len=0
17	4.780491	10.0.0.50	10.0.0.215	TCP	66	56641 → 80 [SYN] Seq=0 Win=64240 Len=0 MSS=1460 WS=256 SACK
18	4.781276	10.0.0.215	10.0.0.50	TCP	62	80 → 56641 [SYN, ACK] Seq=0 Ack=1 Win=2920 Len=0 MSS=1460 W
19	4.781400	10.0.0.50	10.0.0.215	TCP	54	56641 → 80 [ACK] Seq=1 Ack=1 Win=262656 Len=0
20	4.781501	10.0.0.50	10.0.0.215	TCP	172	56641 → 80 [PSH, ACK] Seq=1 Ack=1 Win=262656 Len=118 [TCP F
21	4.791061	10.0.0.215	10.0.0.50	HTTP	79	HTTP/1.1 100 Continue
22	4.791227	10.0.0.50	10.0.0.215	TCP	14654	56641 → 80 [ACK] Seq=119 Ack=26 Win=262656 Len=14600 [TCP F
23	4.798131	10.0.0.215	10.0.0.50	TCP	60	80 → 56641 [ACK] Seq=26 Ack=14719 Win=64240 Len=0
24	4.798147	10.0.0.50	10.0.0.215	IPP	943	IPP Request (Send-Document)
25	4.802057	10.0.0.215	10.0.0.50	TCP	60	80 → 56641 [ACK] Seq=26 Ack=15608 Win=64240 Len=0
26	4.810916	10.0.0.215	10.0.0.50	TCP	591	80 → 56641 [PSH, ACK] Seq=26 Ack=15608 Win=64240 Len=537 [T
27	4.851653	10.0.0.50	10.0.0.215	TCP	54	56641 → 80 [ACK] Seq=15608 Ack=563 Win=262144 Len=0
28	4.852505	10.0.0.215	10.0.0.50	IPP	60	IPP Response (client-error-bad-request)
29	4.893787	10.0.0.50	10.0.0.215	TCP	54	56641 → 80 [FIN, ACK] Seq=15608 Ack=568 Win=262144 Len=0
30	4.894492	10.0.0.215	10.0.0.50	TCP	60	80 → 56641 [ACK] Seq=568 Ack=15609 Win=64240 Len=0
31	4.897260	10.0.0.215	10.0.0.50	TCP	60	80 → 56641 [FIN, ACK] Seq=568 Ack=15609 Win=64240 Len=0
32	4.897272	10.0.0.50	10.0.0.215	TCP	54	56641 → 80 [ACK] Seq=15609 Ack=569 Win=262144 Len=0

Packet-Level View of a Bad IPP Request

The most egregious flaws will be provided to you, consisting of the dreaded Malformed Packet error shown in the next graphic. This means there is something fundamentally flawed in the creation of your byte stream. This could be neglecting the end-of-attributes tag byte, omitting name or value(s) bytes, etc. I have been guilty of all of these and stand convicted thereof. Hopefully, by constructing the libraries in this chapter, you will gain the necessary knowledge to avoid such pitfalls. If you do find yourself mired in the bad request neighborhood after attempting to craft a new operation, compare the Wireshark results from "ipptool" for the same operation you are trying to develop against your own. In most cases, this comparison should throw light on what you have either omitted or erred in creating. Stay patient, and you should see better results as you work through the potential issues.

Wireshark · Packet 9 · Ethernet (host 10.0.0.215)

```
    version: 1.1
    operation-id: Validate-Job (0x0004)
    request-id: 1
  ⌄ operation-attributes-tag
    ⌄ attributes-charset (charset): 'utf-8'
        name: attributes-charset
        charset value: utf-8
    ⌄ attributes-natural-language (naturalLanguage): 'en'
        name: attributes-natural-language
        naturalLanguage value: en
⌄ [Malformed Packet: IPP]
  ⌄ [Expert Info (Error/Malformed): Malformed Packet (Exception occurred)]
      [Malformed Packet (Exception occurred)]
      [Severity level: Error]
      [Group: Malformed]
```

If the Byte Stream Is Severely Malformed, You Might Encounter the Malformed Packet Error

Wireshark · Packet 28 · Ethernet (host 10.0.0.215)

```
> Ethernet II, Src: HewlettPacka_84:af:0f (9c:7b:ef:84:af:0f), Dst: ASUSTekC
> Internet Protocol Version 4, Src: 10.0.0.215, Dst: 10.0.0.50
> Transmission Control Protocol, Src Port: 80, Dst Port: 56641, Seq: 563, Ac
> [2 Reassembled TCP Segments (542 bytes): #26(537), #28(5)]
> Hypertext Transfer Protocol, has 2 chunks (including last chunk)
⌄ Internet Printing Protocol
    [Request In: 24]
    [Response Time: 0.054358000 seconds]
    version: 1.1
    status-code: Client Error (client-error-bad-request)
    request-id: 33554432
  ⌄ operation-attributes-tag
    > attributes-charset (charset): 'utf-8'
    > attributes-natural-language (naturalLanguage): 'en'
    end-of-attributes-tag
```

```
0000  04 42 1a e6 21 bb 9c 7b  ef 84 af 0f 08 00 45 00   ·B··!··{ ······E·
0010  00 2d bd 06 40 00 40 06  68 bc 0a 00 00 d7 0a 00   ·-··@·@· h·······
0020  00 32 00 50 dd 41 1b e4  70 3a f0 6e ba 56 50 18   ·2·P·A·· p:·n·VP·
0030  fa f0 47 3e 00 00 30 0d  0a 0d 0a 00               ··G>··0· ····
```

I left off the last-document Boolean for the send-document request – this was the error

You might also run across the infamous 1024 error, also known as the 'client-bad-error-request'. This is a less egregious flaw than the malformed packet issue and indicates an omission in the byte stream of a necessary attribute for the request. For example, neglecting to include the last-document Boolean attribute from the send-document request will generally cause this error. Hopefully, by understanding the composition of the requests built within this chapter and the next, you can largely avoid these mistakes in whatever development language you may choose to use.

I will go further on reverse-engineering existing IPP libraries later in this book. The straightforward way to do this is to compare the IPP dissector outputs from a good request (i.e., from the Windows IPP Class driver) versus the Wireshark trace taken from any prospective library under development. Another very solid way of reverse engineering the IPP requests is to create them using "ipptool," a fantastic utility explored in Chapter 9, "IPP Tools." For now, the best description of "ipptool" might be "a powerful utility used to issue Internet Printing Protocol (IPP) requests to a printer or print server and receive its responses" [5]. With these constructs in mind, we will take on our first assignment – the basic development model of our library. Since this is primarily an educational exercise, simplicity is key as abstraction tends to obfuscate or lengthen the time to master key points. The basic library will consist of a base class (IppRequest) with derived classes that are inherited from this base class. The base class will make use of the .NET HttpClient class to ease the development of the HTTP/HTTPS request to the IPP/IPPS printer. What makes use of this class (HttpClient) so compelling is essentially its definition: "a class for sending HTTP requests and receiving HTTP responses from a resource identified by a URI" – exactly what we need [6]. We will use HTTP as the protocol for unencrypted (port 631) communications and HTTPS for encrypted (port 631) communications. Thus, the printer URL will be ipps://{printer}:631/ipp/print for IPPS and ipp://{printer}:631/ipp/print for IPP connections.

The library starts with a base object called IppRequest since that is what it is: a basic IPP request. The constructor of this class takes 3 arguments used by all subsequent child objects: the printer's name, whether the connection will be encrypted (port 631 is the RFC standard), and finally the request id.

```
public IppRequest(string printer, bool encrypted, int request_id)
 {
     m_bEncrypted = encrypted;
     //Port 631 per RFC 7472
```

```
    m_sPrinterUri = encrypted ? $"https://{printer}:631/ipp/print" :
    $"http://{printer}:631/ipp/print";
    string m_sIppUri = encrypted ? $"ipps://{printer}:631/ipp/print" :
    $"ipp://{printer}:631/ipp/print";
    m_bRequestId = ToBigEndianBytes(request_id);
    MakeOperationAttributes(m_sIppUri);
}
```

IppRequest also enumerates the various RFC IPP request byte values as specified in RFC 8010 (IPP/1.1: Encoding and Transport). The list is short for now, but in the next chapter we will be adding operational codes to it.

```
public enum RequestType : byte
{
      PRINT_JOB = 0x02,
      VALIDATE_JOB = 0x04,
      CREATE_JOB = 0x05,
      SEND_DOCUMENT = 0x06,
      CANCEL_JOB = 0x08
}
```

All IPP requests will require the “attributes-charset,” “attributes-natural-language," “printer-uri,” and “requesting-user-name" attributes, so we will create one method that builds a buffer of bytes for each attribute in the IppRequest base class.

```
private void MakeOperationAttributes(string printerUri)
{
// Create attributes with dynamic length calculation
m_bAttributesCharset = RequestHelpers.CreatePrinterAttribute(0x47,
"attributes-charset", "utf-8", false);
m_bAttributesNaturalLanguage = RequestHelpers.CreatePrinterAttribute(0x48,
"attributes-natural-language", "en", false);
m_bPrinterUriAttribute = RequestHelpers.CreatePrinterAttribute(0x45,
"printer-uri", printerUri, false);
m_bRequestingUserName = RequestHelpers.CreatePrinterAttribute(0x42,
"requesting-user_name", Environment.UserName, false);
}
```

These attributes are created using the CreatePrinterAttribute method in the RequestHelper file (under the Ipp folder). This method takes (as arguments) one of the enumerated byte attribute tags from the AttributeHelper class, the name of the attribute, and the value of the attribute and creates a byte buffer formatted to RFC specifications. If you look at the CreatePrinterAttribute method, the focus of the conversion is on the last part of the method:

```
return new byte[] { tag }
.Concat(new byte[] { (byte)(nameBytes.Length >> 8 & 0xFF), (byte)
(nameBytes.Length & 0xFF) }) // Name length
.Concat(nameBytes) // Name
.Concat(new byte[] { (byte)(valueBytes.Length >> 8 & 0xFF), (byte)
(valueBytes.Length & 0xFF) }) // Value length
.Concat(valueBytes) // Value
.ToArray();
```

The first line adds the tag byte to the new byte array as required by the RFC - each attribute needs the tag to be included.

```
return new byte[] { tag }
```

Moving to the next line:

```
.Concat(new byte[] { (byte)(nameBytes.Length >> 8 & 0xFF), (byte)
(nameBytes.Length & 0xFF) }) .Concat(nameBytes)
```

The nameBytes (the UTF-8 encoded name of the attribute) is a variable in little-endian format on a Windows machine. This value needs to be formatted in network byte order (big-endian) so the printer can correctly interpret it. The following outlines how this is done.

1. Working left to right, a new byte buffer is created. The value of this byte buffer will be concatenated to the byte buffer's contents with the tag value to form a new byte buffer.

2. The (nameBytes.Length >> 8 & 0xFF) expression right shifts the integer value 8 bits to the right and then ANDs that value with 0xFF. This effectively isolates the high byte of the integer value and places it on the leftmost value of the two-byte buffer (MSB) in step 1.

3. The rightmost value of the resulting integer is formed by (nameBytes.Length & 0xFF), which ANDs the lower byte of the integer. The result of this is placed in the rightmost value of the two-byte buffer (LSB) in step 1.

Perhaps an illustration with an actual integer value of 1234 might help. If we had an integer value of 0x1234, the little-endian representation in memory would be 0x34 0x12. Using the

```
byte highByte = (byte)(value >> 8 & 0xFF); // 0x12
byte lowByte = (byte)(value & 0xFF);       // 0x34
```

The big-endian byte array is created by placing the 0x12 value as the leftmost value in the new byte buffer, while 0x34 is placed in the rightmost value. In other words, byte[] big endian bytes = new byte[] { 0x12, 0x34 }. This effectively reverses the order of the bytes in the buffer relative to the little-endian format, which is exactly what we want. The exact same operation is done on the valueBytes integer, whose resulting byte buffer is again appended to the initial byte buffer whose contents now include the tag byte, the nameBytes (converted to big-endian format), and finally the valueBytes (also converted to big-endian format) integer. The basic operation is illustrated below:

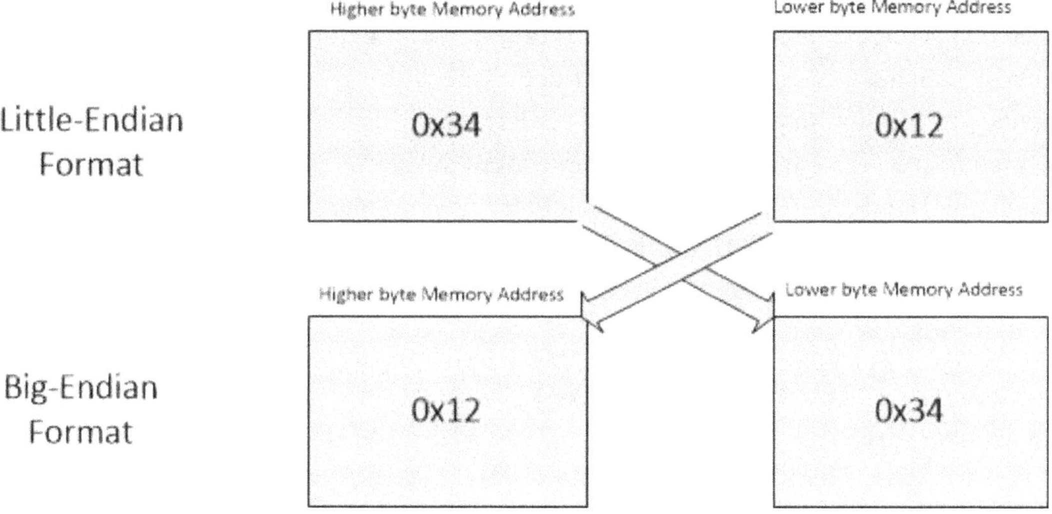

Essentially, creating an IPP request is the creation of a byte stream as opposed to the decoding or deconstruction of the same that we investigated in Chapter 2, "Printer Talk." IPP requests the printers require proper construction of the byte stream in the

exact format required by RFCs 8010 and 8011 so the printer can properly interpret the request. For the CsIppRequests solution, this boils down to using primarily 2 methods: CreatePrinterAttribute and CreateJobAttributesByteArray, both of which reside in the RequestHelper file. The CreatePrinterAttribute method has already been examined; CreateJobAttributesByteArray does the same thing except it works on a list of job attributes rather than a single attribute. These two methods will underpin all the IPP requests created in this and the next chapter of this book.

Sending and Receiving IPP Requests

To send the IPP request, the SendIppRequestAsync method is leveraged in the IppRequest base class. Put simply, this method is the heart of our asynchronous IPP request library. It takes a request type as the argument (i.e., create-job, print-job, etc.) - the signature is shown below:

```
protected async Task<CompletionStruct>
SendIppRequestAsync(RequestType type)
```

You should notice that this method returns an async Task object of type CompletionStruct that asynchronous methods can await. The benefit of the async method is more readily observed in a GUI program where the dispatcher (GUI thread in WPF) will have execution control returned while the awaited method (PostAsync method in SendIppRequestAsync) does the IO piece. This allows the GUI program to remain responsive to input from the user without the tell-tale “freeze” often seen on similar blocking calls. Of course, this benefit is not as noticeable in a console program, but since our library might be used in a GUI application, clever design practice beckons the asynchronous approach. The first part of SendIppRequestAsync might require some explanation.

```
var handler = new HttpClientHandler();
if (m_bEncrypted)
{
handler.ServerCertificateCustomValidationCallback = (message, cert, chain,
errors) => true.
}
```

If this request is sent using IPPS (i.e., TLS for an encrypted connection), the HttpClient object in .NET will need some assurance that the entity on the other end of the connection is who they say they are. After all, what good is an encrypted connection if the other end is a nefarious man-in-the-middle imposter posing as our printer? For this assurance, TLS typically requires the opposite end to provide a certificate that can be trusted. Typically, this is a digital file issued from a certificate of authority the calling party trusts. If the caller trusts the issuer of the certificate, a TLS-encrypted session is allowed.

Unfortunately, in the printer world, many printers have only self-signed certificates whose issuer (the Certificate Authority) is not trusted by the caller. The downside of this is that the HttpClient object will reject the certificate from the printer, and the TLS session will ultimately fail. (Don't ask how I know this to be true!) The code segment above is a way around this by returning true (from a method checking the certificate) for any certificate encountered. While this is hardly optimal, it reflects reality and provides a way for printers without a known trusted certificate authority issuer to participate in an encrypted session (read IPPS). You can, of course, modify this code to comply with your own network requirements. For instance, you might call a certificate check instead of blindly returning true as in the code below.

```
handler.ServerCertificateCustomValidationCallback = (message, cert, chain,
sslErrors) =>
{
    if (sslErrors != SslPolicyErrors.None)
    {
        return false;
    }

    if (cert is X509Certificate2 printer_certificate)
    {
        // Is the cert issuer legitimate?
        if (printer_certificate.Issuer != "CN=YourTrustedIssuer")
        {
            return false;
        }

        // Is this within the date range?
        if (DateTime.Now > printer_certificate.NotAfter)
```

```
        {
            return false;
        }
    }
    return true;
};
```

When it comes to the security of Transport Layer Security (TLS) connections, there are several ways of managing how clients trust the certificates presented to them by the connection. One method is Trust on First Use (TOFU) where the client accepts the certificate from the server (on the first connection) as trustworthy without prior verification. This certificate is then stored for comparison to the certificate received on subsequent connections from the same client. While this is feasible in environments where the devices to trust are relatively unsophisticated (such as smaller IoT devices), it does allow for initial man-in-the-middle attacks. Certificate pinning, on the other hand, involves associating ("pinning") a specific certificate or public key with a server or domain. This does provide a higher degree of security by limiting trust to known certificates. However, management of the certificate is required to avoid service disruption if certificates change.

As an aside, it appears that Microsoft has more lenient policies for IPPS printer TLS session establishment than requiring the certificate issuer to be totally trusted on the client. As an example, the same printer (which uses a self-signed certificate) that failed a TLS session (unless a true is returned from the ServerCertificateCustomValidationCallback) using the HttpClient .NET class appears to work with the IPP Class driver. In the world of an OS supplier such as Microsoft, this might make sense. Without passing the certificate check, configuring printers would be more frustrating and difficult to set up as the process would require the printer certificate issuer to be trusted on the workstation before a TLS session could be initialized. For more on this, see Chapter 7, "Enterprise Conversion," section **Printer Certificate Validation Questions**. Of course, the best practice would be to install a certificate on the printers whose issuer Windows trusts and do the certificate check in the HttpClient. Later chapters in this book will revisit this topic in more detail.

To repeat: A way around a certificate check for TLS is to skip the validation process for SSL certificates completely, i.e., return true always. While useful during development in a test environment, this must never see production use because your application could potentially be subject to man-in-the-middle attacks [7].

Another method would be to implement the TOFU validation code in the ServerCertificateCustomValidationCallback function. You could associate a client URL with the initial certificate using a Dictionary object (in C#) as shown below:

```
Dictionary<string, X509Certificate2>
```

The collection might then be persisted as a binary file using binary serialization or JSON with base64 encoding to save and load the Dictionary collection. You would then have to handle certificate updates: for example, if a certificate changes legitimately, a mechanism would be required to update the stored certificate after verification.

The next few lines of SendIppRequestAsync make use of the .NET HttpClient class and set a TCP timeout value. By default, the timeout is set to 100 seconds (about 3 minutes) or 1.5 minutes. Since this is entirely too long to wait and would make us bad stewards of our computer resources (after all, we cannot expect to be the only IO routines operating concurrently, can we?), we should set this timeout to more than a reasonable 30 seconds.

```
using (var client = new HttpClient(handler) {Timeout = TimeSpan.
FromSeconds(30)})
{
        using (var cts = new CancellationTokenSource (TimeSpan.
        FromSeconds(30)))
```

There are reasons for keeping this setting at 20-30 seconds even though that sounds like a long (relatively) time for a network IO process. Assuming the end printer or computer is in sleep mode or in a low power state, we do want to give prospective machines the necessary time to wake up, process the request, and send back a response. The key is to find a balance between waiting too long and the alternative of wasting resources and limiting the ability for low-power-state entities to respond. You should adjust this time as you see fit - you could even provide this as an argument for the library.

You might also notice that a cancellation token is provided for the PostAsync method, but it is tied to a 30-second timeout value. This is a simplistic but effective way to segregate any thrown exception by the source. You might also notice the ByteArrayContent class exposed by the System.Net.Http namespace being used to hold the composite byte stream (m_b RequestPayload) created for each IPP request child class. This class is particularly useful when creating HTTP content based on a byte array, as we will do here. Make sure the content type is set to "application/ipp" so it aligns with IETF STD 92.

```
var content = new ByteArrayContent(m_bRequestPayload);
content.Headers.ContentType = new System.Net.Http.Headers. MediaTypeHeaderV
alue("application/ipp");
```

Which brings us to the actual request itself, a POST HTTP method with the printer URI as an argument, the binary buffer describing the IPP request data, and of course our cancellation token that will be activated in the event we exceed 30 seconds.

```
var response = await client.PostAsync(m_sPrinterUri, content, cts.Token);
```

Importantly, this method will return a Task<HttpResponseMessage> value, which is awaitable, thus returning execution cycles to the caller during the IO sequence. As explained earlier, this is crucial for GUI threads, most specifically for WPF dispatcher threads to call subsequent async methods from. Of course, if we create an IO request to an entity, we should expect a reply from the same, and the next line of code takes care of this for us.

```
return await GetIppResponseAsync(type, response);
```

As with the PostAsync method, we await the return from the network printer asynchronously, being the polite consumer of computer resources that we should be. The return takes the form of a task of type CompletionStruct. The CompletionStruct contains 2 values: the status (of the IPP request) as returned by the printer and a job id value as determined by the same printer. For those requests that do not expect a job id, this value will be preset to -1.

The next (and final) method in the IppRequest base class is the GetIppResponseAsync method, which, as the name implies, is concerned with the response from the network printer. This method takes as arguments the type of request and, of course, the HTTP response object from the printer. The first point of interest in this method should be where the returned Http stream Task object

```
using (var responseStream = await response.Content.ReadAsStreamAsync()
.ConfigureAwait(false))
```

is returned. The HttpResponseMessage object reads the byte stream content returned from the printer as a Stream object – this allows it to be awaitable for asynchronous operation. Notice that ConfigureAwait is set (by default) to be false. When set false, ConfigureAwait dictates whether the execution context after the await *may* execute on a different thread from the one called GetIppResponseAsync. When set to true and the library was running in a UI thread, the continuation would be marshaled back to that UI thread [8]. This would be especially important to avoid synchronization issues with UI controls or collections. If you encounter issues when running the library in a UI, it might be worth the time to modify ConfigureAwait to properly marshal back to the UI thread. The downside to this is the increased resources incurred and thread context switches.

We can now begin to examine the HTTP response byte by byte to recover requested attributes the printer might have sent us. For starters, we should see if the request was successfully received by the printer – to do this, we need to recover the status code.

```
await responseStream.ReadAsync(buffer, 0, 2).ConfigureAwait(false);
short StatusCode = ByteOrder.Flip(BitConverter.ToInt16(buffer, 0));
```

This allows us to deduce if our print request(s) was successfully accepted on the printer. For now, we only need to worry about recovering the job id from create-job and print-job.

```
if ((type == RequestType.CREATE_JOB) || (type == RequestType.PRINT_JOB))
{
    try
    {
        cs.jobId = await ResponseHelpers.GetIppAttributesAsync(respon
        seStream);
    }
    catch (Exception ex)
   {
       throw new Exception ($"Error retrieving the job id: {ex.Message}");
    }
}
```

At this point, we have the basic architecture created to send IPP requests and recover the printer response. As we add additional functionality and requests in the next chapter, we will expand the operation of this code section to recover more attributes. The current set of requests in the library allows us to create a job, cancel a job, validate a job, send a document, and finally print a job request. While these provide rudimentary functionality, they will shed some light on how IPP requests are formulated, so let us begin to look at them.

Validate-Job

The Validate-Job operation, as you learned in Chapter 4, "The MS IPP Class Driver," is used by a client to check that the target printer can indeed support the job attributes requested. Starting with the arguments supplied to the ValidateJobRequest class constructor:

```
public ValidateJobRequest(string ipp_version, string printerUri, bool
encrypted, int requestId, Dictionary<string, List<object>> jobAttributes) :
base(printerUri, encrypted, requestId)
```

We take an IPP version string, the printer URI string, a Boolean indicating whether this request will be encrypted, the IPP request id, and finally a Dictionary collection that holds job attributes we would like. Some of these values get passed onto the base class as you would expect. This way of creating a request will be replicated for all other requests although the argument will naturally change for each individual request.

To begin with, we will need a byte array to support the IPP version and operational ID, both of which are 2-byte values.

```
byte [] m_bIppVersionAndOperationId = new byte[] {0x01, 0x01, 0x00, (byte)
RequestType.VALIDATE_JOB }; // IPP version and operation ID
```

The reason for this byte buffer being placed in the derived class was to allow for the operational id and IPP version bytes to be modified as needed.

```
if (IppVersions.ContainsKey(ipp_version))
{
    m_bIppVersionAndOperationId[0] = IppVersions[ipp_version][0];
    m_bIppVersionAndOperationId[1] = IppVersions[ipp_version][1];
}
```

```
else
{
    throw new Exception ($"Ipp version: {ipp_version} is not supported");
}
```

If you look in the IppRequest base class, you can see that this looks to see if the ipp_version string supplied (by the user) has a match in the IppVersions dictionary type.

```
protected Dictionary<string, byte[]> IppVersions = new Dictionary<string,
byte[]>()
{
    { "1.0", new byte[] { 0x01, 0x00 } },
    { "1.1", new byte[] { 0x01, 0x01 } },
    { "2.0", new byte[] { 0x02, 0x00 } },
    { "2.2", new byte[] { 0x02, 0x02 } }
};
```

If the string is not included, an exception is thrown to alert the user, but if a match is found, the (2-byte) byte buffer is returned. This returned byte buffer is then placed in the first 2 bytes of m_bIppVersionAndOperationId byte buffer, thereby setting the requested IPP version. The most significant method to understand is the MakeRequestByteBuffer, as this essentially creates the entire byte buffer that will get sent in the POST message for this particular (Validate-Job) request. This job is made much easier within C# by leveraging the LINQ namespace as LINQ makes byte array concatenation significantly less tiresome. To see how easy LINQ makes this, consider how this might be accomplished in more traditional ways:

```
byte[]CombineByteArrays(byte[] a, byte[] b )
{
    byte[] ret = new byte[a.Length + b.Length];
    Array.Copy(a, 0, ret, 0, a.Length);
    Array.Copy(b, 0, ret, a.Length, b.Length);
    return ret;
}
```

Now compare that to LINQ:

```
byte[] newByteBuffer = a.Concat(b);
```

Initially, we ensure the request id and operational attribute tag buffers are concatenated into the m_bRequestPayload byte buffer (this will be placed in the POST message) in the proper order. One of the pleasant things about inheriting from the base class is simply using the byte buffers common to all requests. The MakeOperationAttributes method in the IppRequest base class creates all the byte buffers for the operational attributes (using the RequestHelpers.CreatePrinterAttribute method), and we simply make use of the LINQ Concat method to add these to the m_bRequestPayload byte buffer. The key buffer created (at least for the Validate-Job request) is the buffer of print job attributes created by the CreateJobAttributesByteBuffer utility method in the RequestHelpers.cs file, within the Ipp folder:

```
byte[] concatenatedArray = RequestHelpers.CreateJobAttributesByteArray(_
jobAttributes);
```

which then gets concatenated into the m_bRequestPayload byte buffer in the MakeRequestByteBuffer method of the ValidateJobRequest class:

```
m_bRequestPayload = m_bIppVersionAndOperationId
                .Concat(m_bRequestId)
                .Concat(m_bOperationAttributesTag)
                // Add the attributes
                .Concat(m_bAttributesCharset)
                .Concat(m_bAttributesNaturalLanguage)
                .Concat(m_bPrinterUriAttribute)
                .Concat(m_bRequestingUserName)
                //Add the job-attributes
                .Concat(m_bJobAttributesStart)
                .Concat(concatenatedArray)
                .Concat(m_bEndOfAttributesTag)
                .ToArray();
```

Notice that we have all the requisite tags and attributes necessary to now make the request concatenated into one byte buffer (m_bRequestPayload). The byte buffer now awaits the user to make the request via the SendIppRequestAsync method in each derived class. When viewed from the calling program (in this case the Program.cs file in the IppPrintRequest project), this

```
ValidateJobRequest vjr = new ValidateJobRequest(....
CompletionStruct cs = await vjr.SendIppRequestAsync();
```

is just a line to send the request to the printer and await the reply. This pattern is repeated in all the derived classes. For the balance of the request types, I will not burden you by going over what are the same methods that comprise these request(s) in detail; instead, I will highlight their differences.

Create-Job

The Create-Job request is remarkably like the Validate-Job request, except for a few different variances. One of these is the operational code: Validate-Job uses 0x04 as an op code, while Create-Job uses 0x05 as the operational code. The CreateJobAttributesByteArray utility method from the RequestHelpers file is employed, as in the Validate-Job request, to convert user job preferences into the requisite byte buffer required.

We require a job id to be returned to us if the Create-Job request is successful, as this can be used to cancel the job later if needed. For the Create-Job request, a CompletionStruct should be returned containing the status of the request (success/fail) and the job id to be referenced for later use. Below is from the calling process, namely the Program.cs file in the IppPrintRequest project.

```
try
{
    CreateJobRequest cjr = new CreateJobRequest("1.1", sIppPrinter, false,
request, jobAttributes);
    CompletionStruct cs = await cjr.SendRequestAsync();
    if (cs.status == 0)
    {
        Console.WriteLine($"Job successfully created on {sIppPrinter}");
        Console.WriteLine("Job Id is: " + cs.jobId.ToString());
    }
    else
        Console.WriteLine($"Job validation failed, status returned was {cs.
        status}");
```

As you might recall from Chapter 4, “The MS IPP Class Driver,” the Create-Job request creates (but does not print) a job on the printer. Fundamentally, this request allows the printer to set aside memory for the job and all the requested job attributes required. As mentioned in Chapter 4, “The MS IPP Class Driver,” RFC 8011 Section 4.2.4 stipulates that this request is recommended but not required, meaning that you might find some printers that do not support this operation (although both the Mopria and IPP-Everywhere standards require Create-Job for certification). Also, the RFC states that if a printer supports this (Create-Job) request, it must also support the Send-Document request.

Send-Document

The Send-Document request has a few more variances from the previous requests to account for. Obviously, we have a different operational code, in this case 0x06, to identify (to the printer) that this is a Send-Document request. To begin with, the SendDocRequest class takes arguments for the job id (returned from Create-Job) and the file name of the document to be printed.

```
SendDocRequest(string ipp_version, string printerUri, bool encrypted, int
requestId, int jobId, string fileName)
```

For convenience, we alert the user in the event the file cannot be found:

```
if(File.Exists(fileName) == false)
{
   throw new Exception ($"Error: {fileName} could not be found!");
}
```

and then proceed to create the byte buffer necessary for the Send-Document request in the MakeRequestByteBuffer method. In this method, we create several additional attributes necessary for the request, with the document-format and last-document being the most interesting. The document-format attribute is necessary for the printer to be able to interpret what type of document (txt/pdf/png/jpeg) the blob of bytes in the document file is supposed to be rendered as. The last-document attribute does require some background to understand its use.

All of this was background for the “last-document” attribute and its proper use. Under most conditions, this attribute should be set to true, meaning this is the only document for the printer to process the complete job. In the event you have several documents to process that share similar job-attributes, you might create the job, get the job id back, and proceed to send all the documents to the printer under that one job id. For each of the documents sent (up until the "last document"), the "last-document" would be set to false, indicating more documents to follow. The SendDocRequest class sets this to true by default (obviously in the case of a single document it would be the last one), so in this chapter it is fixed. In the next chapter we will improve on this to make this work as it should.

Cancel-Job

The CancelJobRequest class allows a user to cancel a pending job on the printer if the job id is provided. As you might imagine, the job to be cancelled must be provided by the user to initialize the process.

```
public CancelJobRequest(string ipp_version, string printerUri, bool
encrypted, int requestId, int jobId)
```

In the MakeRequestByteBuffef method, the job id attribute is converted to an attribute to be used in the request:

```
byte[] m_bJobId = RequestHelpers.CreatePrinterAttribute((byte)
AttributeHelper. ValueTag.Integer, "job-id", m_iJobId);
```

Otherwise, this request is remarkably like its siblings. This request can only be appreciated by those who have wasted numerous pages on a job cancelled in Windows. The truth is that if the printer already has the document loaded in memory, cancelling the job in Windows does not stop the printout - in many cases a power cycle is required. The Cancel-Job request is much superior in that the job is removed from memory on the printer itself. The actual time it takes to cancel a job is implementation specific. According to RFC 8011, once a successful response has been sent, the implementation guarantees that the Job will eventually end up in the "canceled" state. Between the time that the Cancel-Job operation is accepted and when the Job enters the "canceled" job-state, the "job-state-reasons" attribute should contain the "processing-to-stop-point" value, which indicates to later queries that although the Job might still be "processing" it will eventually end up in the "canceled" state, not the "completed" state [9].

Print-Job

The PrintJobRequest requires the most arguments from the user to implement.

```
PrintJobRequest(string ipp_version, string printerUri, bool encrypted, int requestId, string fileName, Dictionary<string, List<object>> jobAttributes)
```

This request will always be supported on an IPP printer, even if the Create-Job and Send-Document requests are not. In addition to the normal arguments, the file name to print and the user job preferences are also required.

Section 4.6 of the IPP Implementers Guide v2.0 (PWG) details print job submission options available to IPP clients. Despite the simplicity of the Print-Job operation over the Create-Job/Send-Document model, the latter is the preferred alternative if both models are supported. The reason(s) why are stated in Section 4.6 of the IPP Implementers Guide v2.0 (PWG): better control and recovery of print job errors.

As with the SendDocRequest, we alert the user in the event the file cannot be found:

```
if(File.Exists(fileName) == false)
{
   throw new Exception($"Error: {fileName} could not be found!");
}
```

In the MakeRequestByteBuffer method, we start off by reading in all the bytes from the file to be printed:

```
byte[] fileBytes = File.ReadAllBytes(m_sFileName);
```

Additionally, the document extension is required and is thus processed by the CreatePrinterAttribute method of the RequestHelper utility file.

```
RequestHelpers.CreatePrinterAttribute((byte)AttributeHelper.ValueTag.
MimeMediaType, "document-format", ext);
```

The file byte buffer is added after the end of the attributes tag for the request payload buffer that will be placed in the HTTP packet POST message:

```
•
•
.Concat(m_bEndOfAttributesTag)
.Concat(fileBytes)
.ToArray();
```

which finalizes the request. This is a limited set of requests for our IPP print library, which will be expanded upon in the next chapter. However, basic functionality such as job creation, validation, cancellation, and printing is functional and can be tested.

MORE INFORMATION

In practice, Windows makes the Create-Job and Send-Document calls close in a time span, ranging from a few hundred milliseconds to a few seconds. Of course, many factors explain the variance (of elapsed time) from client processor and memory load to network congestion and even multiple-operation-time-out server load. However, the bottom line is that these calls are sequentially executed in short order within Windows. This observation changes when human reaction is employed, as in the case of a command line utility such as IppPrintRequest. If you take too long between Create-Job and Send-Document, the printer may fail your Send-Document request. Of course, the justification is that printers have a finite number of resources – memory being one of these – whose exhaustion would be catastrophic in terms of reliability. The IPP standard in RFC 8011 stipulates that if a printer supports the Create-Job and Send-Document operations, it must support the "multiple-operation-time-out" attribute [11]. This attribute is the minimum number of seconds the printer will wait between operation requests like Create-Job and Send-Document before it initiates some form of recovery action. What would that recovery action entail? That question is answered by the multiple-operation-time-out attribute, which for my HP test printer defaults to "abort job." Incidentally, my test printer is set to 120 seconds (about 4 minutes) for the multiple-operation-time-out attribute (2 minutes) by default.

Testing the Library

You can test the library out if you have an IPP-compatible printer. The CsIppRequests solution includes a console program called IppPrintRequest that allows a user to employ the various IPP requests built into the library. You must supply a file listing the job attributes desired (which the printer can support). There is a sample list of job attributes in the IppPrintRequest project folder called JobAttributes.txt that should provide a good place to start. The job attributes file needs to be supplied as an argument on the command line. Once that is supplied, the program will ask the user what printer to use and what action to take. The graphic below outlines a user requesting to create a job on printer HPM528.

```
Enter the IPP printer to use:
HPM528
Would you like to validate, create, cancel, senddoc, or print a job?
create
Status: 0
Job successfully created on HPM528
Job Id is: 13
```

Creating a job on the printer

To use Send-Document, create a job and use the returned job id as an argument to Send-Document as shown below.

```
Enter the IPP printer to use:
hpm528
Would you like to validate, create, cancel, senddoc, or print a job?
create
Status: 0
Job successfully created on hpm528
Job Id is: 14
IPP print request completed

C:\Users\jpmsp>"D:\BACKUP\IPP Book\Chap 5 An IPP RFC Library\code\CsIppRequests\IppPrintRequest\bin\Release\IppPrintRequ
est.exe" C:\Temp\JobAttributes.txt
Enter the IPP printer to use:
hpm528
Would you like to validate, create, cancel, senddoc, or print a job?
senddoc
Enter the job id:
14
Enter the file to print:
c:\temp\test1.pdf
Status: 0
Send-Document successful on hpm528 for job: 14
IPP print request completed
```

Creating and sending a document

To cancel a job, you will need the job id returned when the job was created. The next graphic demonstrates creating a job on an IPP printer and then cancelling the job.

```
C:\Users\jpmsp>"D:\BACKUP\IPP Book\Chap 5 An IPP RFC Library\code\CsIppRequests\IppPrintRequest\bin\Release\IppPrintRequ
est.exe" C:\Temp\JobAttributes.txt
Enter the IPP printer to use:
hpm528
Would you like to validate, create, cancel, senddoc, or print a job?
create
Status: 0
Job successfully created on hpm528
Job Id is: 16
IPP print request completed

C:\Users\jpmsp>"D:\BACKUP\IPP Book\Chap 5 An IPP RFC Library\code\CsIppRequests\IppPrintRequest\bin\Release\IppPrintRequ
est.exe" C:\Temp\JobAttributes.txt
Enter the IPP printer to use:
hpm528
Would you like to validate, create, cancel, senddoc, or print a job?
cancel
Enter the job id to cancel:
16
Status: 0
Job 16 successfully cancelled!
IPP print request completed
```

Creating and cancelling a job

Why Chunk?

Ultimately, there are some issues with how SendDocRequest talks to the receiving printer. As you might expect, most modern printers come equipped with enough memory to handle your typical documents sent and render them effectively. There is, of course, a limit to the size of file that can be sent before overwhelming the size of working memory the printer employs. For computers, a lack of physical memory can be mitigated by paging, i.e., swapping memory pages back and forth from a disk backing to working memory. As this is not likely a solution for many printers, another way around a file size limitation needs to be found. The astute reader might conceive of a scenario where the client could send such a large print job to the printer as to overwhelm the receiver.

Printer hardware receiving circuitry design also plays a part in how the printer might handle large print jobs. Older printer models used streaming technology: the data was printed directly as it was received from the client without much storage capability. This design was suitable for small print jobs and immediate printing. Most modern enterprise-level printers are classified as spooling printers, where built-in memory stores the incoming print stream(s). These printers can also handle multiple print jobs sent by clients.

Conceptually, a printer could very well run out of memory in the event the sent job was too large to handle. What happens then could be answered by your math teacher when asked about the result of division by zero: undefined. Optimally, it would be wise to avoid such a situation as the state of the printer in such an event might require a reboot to re-establish operation. Ensuring the printer does not get sent a file larger than it can handle would be the first line of defense. You can find out the limit of file size that can be sent to the printer by consulting the document-supported attribute. It is generally just not practical to limit document size to match the printer's capabilities as users are typically unaware of such technical limitations. Thus, the current iteration of SendDocRequest could potentially cause the receiving printer to run out of memory, and the result would be unpredictable.

In the world of video delivery over the internet, this problem can be solved by chunking a large video file into smaller chunks and sending it to the client. As happens, this method is appropriately called chunking. Think of chunking like slicing a loaf of bread: instead of trying to eat the whole loaf at once, you cut it into slices that are easier to handle [10]. While a full explanation of it is beyond the scope of this book, chunking fundamentally refers to the process of breaking down a large file into smaller, sequenced pieces (chunks) for transmission over the network. By sending a sequence of smaller file chunks to the printer, the receiver can process each constituent chunk from the original file without overflowing the receiver's memory. Chunking also supports data streaming, where the printer can process the chunks while the other chunks are still being transmitted.

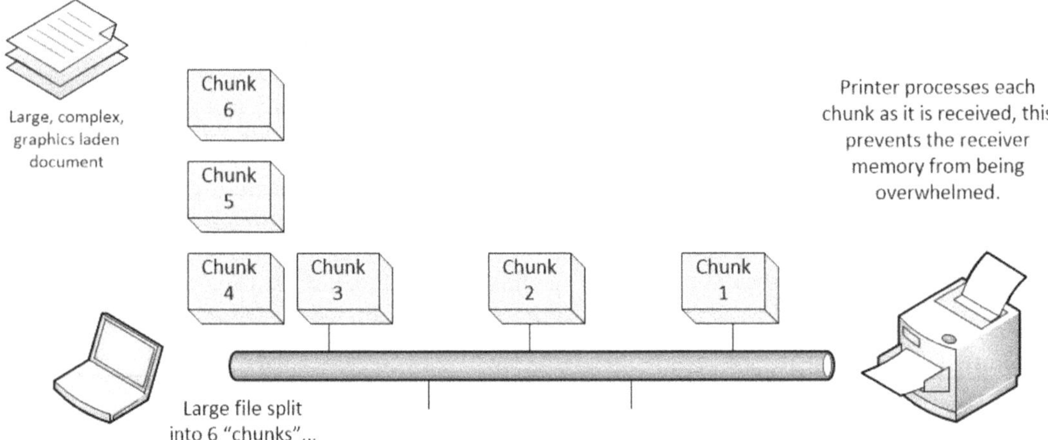

Chunking to prevent receiver overflow

Thankfully, HTTP 1.1 introduced chunking as part of the standard. Thus, newer IPP printers that implement HTTP 1.1 should be able to process chunked data without concern. Even better for us, the HttpClient class used in our library can fully implement chunking if necessary. We will rectify this shortcoming in the next chapter.

There are also issues with error reporting - specifically that users typically want a more detailed reason an operation failed other than a return code. We will address this in the next iteration as well.

A Tale of Two Text Files

As you may recall from Chapter 4, "The MS IPP Class Driver," Microsoft uses Mopria technology to ensure "driverless" print characteristics for IPP/IPPS printing. The default Page Description Language (PDL) for Mopria is PDF, and you may be wondering why. In the Lab folder for this chapter, there is a text file with the name SpoolsMonExport, which has the output of a utility that displays library exports, in this case from the spools.dll library. One thing you should notice is that the text in the file would certainly overflow the standard 8.5" x 11" paper size if the text were not wrapped. As you might remember from the "Why Use a PDL" paragraph in Chapter 1, "Windows Legacy Print," PCL had provisions for word wrapping (\x1B&k2G) to prevent text from "running off" the page.

If you use the new library to print this text file using the Print Job request, you might be a bit perplexed as to the output. Sure, the text file will print, but segments of each line might be missing from the output text file - in other words, the lines will run off the page. The issue is that IPP printers do not automatically wrap long lines when printing plain text. Unlike rich text files or PDFs, plain text does not provide formatting metadata necessary for a satisfactory output. The default baseline document format for Mopria is PWG Raster or PCLm (printers must support both). If the printer supports PDF, the client may use PDF or prefer PDF, but there may be client reasons why it does not use it (including because the printer rejects the job), and the client resends it using one of the baseline formats. Assuming the PDL employed for print is PDF, the page layout is explicitly defined for the printer regardless of the OS source.

If you now convert the same SpoolsMonExport text file to PDF, the results will be more satisfactory. The conversion to PDF sets text wrapping, page size, and font to create a printed output that does not run off the end of the page. I would encourage you to experiment on your own. Recall the Windows print subsystem will automatically convert the format of the file to be printed to the specified format directed by Mopria if the IPP printer is installed in Windows. The users of independent libraries (as we are developing) do not automatically share in that luxury - you will need to provide the conversion.

In summary:

1. **PDF Creates Explicit Page Layout**

   The document is formatted with text wrapping and font(s) used.

   Page size and margins are set, which prevents text runoff.

   Defined print outputs with explicit line breaks are set.

2. **Plain Text (.txt) Has No Layout Information**

   Lacking formatting metadata, raw text does not define page size, word wrapping, or font.

   Printers must rely on default settings, which do not wrap long lines.

   Output from printer to printer is inconsistent, as raw text rendering varies from manufacturer to manufacturer.

3. **Mopria & IPP Printing Standardization**

   Mopria and IPP Everywhere ensure consistent print results across different printers by using application/PDF as the default.

In case you are wondering, there is a limit to the size of the PDF file that any printer can accept, and this limit (constraint in IPP terms) is specified by the "job-k-octets-supported" attribute. This attribute can specify the minimum (yes, there is one as well) and maximum size, measured in 1K octets (1024 bytes or 1KB). In case you were wondering, the "job-k-octets-supported" attribute applies to all document formats, not just pdf types.

Chapter Summary

The chapter started off by stipulating that use of existing, well-tested IPP libraries should be the priority over any development project. However, to the extent this book was developed to promote understanding of the IPP protocol, writing code to emulate the varied requests should promote understanding for technicians and computer science types alike. This is especially true if Wireshark is used to promote development effort(s) as the same trace methodology used in network analysis can isolate issues with production code as well. The output of "ipptool" can also be used to compare with your development effort if you do not want to use the Windows IPP driver as the standard. The chapter introduces packet-level traces in Wireshark of malformed or otherwise bad IPP requests that can otherwise plague development efforts. Patience is a virtue in this regard, especially when consulting the RFCs - especially RFC 8010 and 8011. Finally, do not forget to develop using IPP and not IPPS as the Wireshark IPP dissector makes life much easier.

We next delve into the creation of byte streams necessary to create successful requests. This is not the most exciting concept, and thankfully several methods exist to make this more palatable. The base class in the CsIppRequestLib project is IppRequest, whose job it is to send the request to the printer and then recover the reply. There are 5 requests created in this chapter, all of which use the MakeRequestByteBuffer method to create a suitable binary buffer that will eventually be wrapped in an HTTP POST message. To make the byte buffer a bit easier to manage, the CsIppRequestLib solution contains a class (RequestHelpers) of static functions, two of the most convenient of which are CreatePrinterAttribute and CreateJobAttributesByteArray. A look into how the RequestHelper's CreatePrinterAttribute method works is also touched on, with all the gory endianness included, free of charge.

The business of sending and receiving IPP packets is then reviewed. Since the implementation of the library could be a GUI (i.e., WPF, WinForms, etc.), the need for asynchronous operation must be accounted for. For this book's purposes (i.e., testing against a printer and observing Wireshark traces), asynchronous methods are not explicitly required, but they are best practice, and thus their inclusion. We next go into certificates and why those that come from the printer should be validated against the trusted root certificate publishers of the client. You can do this by invoking certmgr.msc on your Windows machine: this will list the trusted certificate authorities that your printer certificate will need to be created by. The issue of TLS session creation in the HttpClient class when untrusted certs are encountered (as is typical in operation) is approached. The choice is to either pass whatever certs are encountered (for testing only) or implement a Trust on First Use (TOFU) check and storage method.

We created five requests for this chapter next, and the companion project (IppPrintRequest) is provided for testing. This list of requests will be expanded in the next chapter for more functionality. If you do use the IppPrintRequest for testing, make sure you set it as the starting project in Visual Studio. The 5 requests created are validate-job, create-job, cancel-job, send-doc, and print-job.

Next, the chapter covers chunking and the probable reason it might be needed. Chunking prevents overflowing the buffer of a printer if a job is unusually large. In concept, you can think of a video file sent to a receiver where the pertinent chunks are sent and watched by the viewer, eliminating the need to download the entire file at once. We will provide chunking as an update to the library in Chapter 6, "Additional Operations." The chapter finishes by reminding the reader that IPP is a protocol and as such still requires that the print job contain page definitions so the text is properly formatted when rendered. The reason a page layout description is used to format the document is then better understood.

References

1. IPP/1.1: Model and Semantics (RFC 8011), Section 5.1.16, Internet Engineering Task Force (IETF), 2017
2. How to Use the Internet Printing Protocol, How to Use the Internet Printing Protocol - Printer Working Group, Printer Working Group
3. HttpContent.ReadAsStreamAsync Method, Microsoft Learn, `https://learn.microsoft.com/en-us/dotnet/api/system.net.http.httpcontent.readasstreamasync?view=net-9.0`
4. Asynchronous programming scenarios, Microsoft Learn, 03/14/2025, `https://learn.microsoft.com/en-us/dotnet/csharp/asynchronous-programming/async-scenarios`
5. How to use the command 'ipptool' (with examples), CommandMasters, `https://commandmasters.com/commands/ipptool-common/`
6. HttpClient Class, Microsoft Learn, May 19-22, 2025, `https://learn.microsoft.com/en-us/dotnet/api/system.net.http.httpclient?view=net-9.0`
7. Handling SSL Certificate Validation in HttpClient: Solutions and Trade-Offs, Medium, Sep 22, 2024, `https://medium.com/@egbetiimmy/handling-ssl-certificate-validation-in-httpclient-solutions-and-trade-offs-8d7f644c97ac`
8. Task.ConfigureAwait Method, Microsoft Learn, `https://learn.microsoft.com/en-us/dotnet/api/system.threading.tasks.task.configureawait?view=net-9.0`

9. Request for Comments: 8011 (Cancel-Job), January 2017, https://www.rfc-editor.org/rfc/pdfrfc/rfc8011.txt.pdf
10. What is Chunking, and Why Do We Chunk Our Data?, Metric Coders, Mar 29th, https://www.metriccoders.com/post/what-is-chunking-and-why-do-we-chunk-our-data
11. IPP/1.1: Model and Semantics (RFC 8011), Section 4.3.1, Internet Engineering Task Force (IETF), 2017

CHAPTER 6

Additional Operations

In the last chapter, the foundation of an IPP request library was laid out. It could validate jobs using the Validate-Job operation, print using either the Create-Job/Send-Document set of operations or the Print-Job operation, and finally cancel a created job using the Cancel-Job operation. The basics of how this library was created were explored: principally how the byte buffers for each request were built and employed. Fundamentally, Chapter 5, "IPP Standards Print," explored how the byte stream for a request was built, while Chapter 3, "Deep Dive into the Protocol," explored how the byte stream was deconstructed and interpreted. In this chapter, we work to improve the library by adding some key features such as getting information about jobs a user has created on a printer, getting a searchable printer attribute request, sending a request to identify printers, chunking large print job requests, and more. The format used will be like that displayed in Chapter 5, "IPP Standards Print": deconstruct the request in code and view the resulting Wireshark traces the request creates. The goal should be a usable library that can be employed to work with IPP/IPPS printers. Along the way it is hoped that you, the reader, can gain some valuable information about how IPP works.

New Operations

If you recall, the existing library did some rudimentary requests such as creating jobs and printing jobs, but there was some concern about overwhelming the receiver at the printer. Certainly, some documents can be quite sophisticated and be laden with such complex graphics as to be quite large indeed.[1] What is the standard behavior for a printer when memory is overwhelmed by the size of a submitted document? Some

[1] Ironically, some print jobs, such as PDF files that contain complex vector graphics such as multiple layers of transparency, gradients, or shading, can be relatively small but create a large processor workload. Alternatively, a large raster format file - such as a high-resolution bitmap image (e.g., TIFF or BMP) - can be computationally easy for a printer to process.

J. Marion, *Adopting Internet Printing Protocol for Windows*, https://doi.org/10.1007/979-8-8688-2010-6_6

printer hardware might handle this more graciously than others, but in any case, the result would likely be undefined. One should assume the printed output from the overwhelming printer memory would not be satisfactory for the end user, who would likely receive an error. Chapter 5, "IPP Standards Print," went into why chunking for HTTP 1.1 receivers can mitigate the receiver overflow issue and handle these situations properly. The first order of business is therefore to update the IppRequest class to allow the HttpClient class to chunk the data. For the purposes of this discussion, we will be investigating the SendIppRequestAsync method in the IppRequest class – this being in the IppRequest folder of the CsIppRequestLib project.

```
protected async Task<CompletionStruct> SendIppRequestAsync(RequestType type)
{
    var client = HttpClientFactory.GetHttpClient(m_sPrinterUri);
    using (var cts = new CancellationTokenSource(TimeSpan.FromSeconds(30)))
   {
        HttpContent content;
        if (m_bChunkRequest)
       {
            // Chunk the request
            var stream = new MemoryStream(m_bRequestPayload);
            content = new StreamContent(stream);
            content.Headers.ContentType = new System.Net.Http.Headers.MediaTypeHeaderValue("application/ipp");
       }
        else
       {
            content = new ByteArrayContent(m_bRequestPayload);
            content.Headers.ContentType = new System.Net.Http.Headers.MediaTypeHeaderValue("application/ipp");
        }
```

```
        // Create a new HttpRequestMessage and set request-specific headers on it
        var request = new HttpRequestMessage(HttpMethod.Post,
        m_sPrinterUri)
        {
            Content = content
        };

        if (m_bChunkRequest)
        {
            // If needed, set the Transfer-Encoding header directly on the message
            request.Headers.TransferEncodingChunked = true;
        }

        try
        {
            var response = await client.SendAsync(request, cts.Token);
            return await GetIppResponseAsync(type, response);
        }

```

Microsoft makes provision in the HttpResponseHeaders to solve this issue – i.e., the TransferEncodingChunked property indicates if the Transfer-Encoding header for an HTTP response contains chunked data [4]. Thus, the change is straightforward; the key point is to set TransferEncodingChunked to true as shown below:

```
request.Headers.TransferEncodingChunked = true.
```

which clears the content-length size. You cannot use the ByteArrayContent type here as this will automatically set the HttpClient content length, which in this case determines that this request will ***not*** be chunked. Instead, use a MemoryStream type to convert the request buffer and then set the HttpContent to a Stream object. Once done, the TransferEncodingChunked variable can be set to true, which clears the content length and allows for chunking. The crucial point here is that you do not have to implement chunking in your code; let the HttpClient object do this for you. The chunking piece is carried out at a lower OSI level (in the transmit/receive pipeline) where the implementation of IPP on a printer resides. Thus, depending on the state of the m_bChunkRequest variable, the byte contents of m_bRequestPayload will be either chunked or fixed in size during transmission.

I would be negligent if I did not also point out that another Boolean console argument for SendDocRequest must be incorporated into the code. However, it is safe to say that the benefit of chunking far outweighs the additional argument you now must supply.

```
SendDocRequest(string ipp_version, string printerUri, bool encrypted, int
requestId, int jobId, string fileName, bool bChunk, bool bLastDocument)
```

So theoretically, we should have mitigated our file size concern - but how can you tell if the request is being chunked on the network? If you have been following the previous few chapters, you should assume the answer is to do a Wireshark trace - and you would be correct. Initially, we observe an un-chunked request to see that the Content-Length size has been set to the file size. This should be familiar to you as a standard Send-Document request.

```
    TCP payload (39024 bytes)
    TCP segment data (39024 bytes)
> [93 Reassembled TCP Segments (3341664 bytes): #6(120), #8(1460
v Hypertext Transfer Protocol
  > POST /ipp/print HTTP/1.1\r\n
    Content-Type: application/ipp\r\n
    Host: hpm528\r\n
  > Content-Length: 3341544\r\n
    Expect: 100-continue\r\n
    \r\n
    [Response in frame: 194]
    [Full request URI: http://hpm528/ipp/print]
    File Data: 3341544 bytes
v Internet Printing Protocol
    [Response In: 194]
    version: 1.1
    operation-id: Send-Document (0x0006)
    request-id: 33554432
  v operation-attributes-tag
    > attributes-charset (charset): 'utf-8'
    > attributes-natural-language (naturalLanguage): 'en'
    > printer-uri (uri): 'http://HPM528/ipp/print'
    > job-id (integer): 19
    > requesting-user_name (nameWithoutLanguage): 'jpmsp'
    > document-format (mimeMediaType): 'image/jpeg'
    > last-document (boolean): true
    end-of-attributes-tag
  > Data (3341339 bytes)
```

Now take a look at a chunked Send-Document request created by setting the SendDocRequest's **bChunk** argument to true:

```
      [Time since previous frame in this TCP stream: 0.000098000 seconds]
    > [SEQ/ACK analysis]
      TCP payload (5 bytes)
      TCP segment data (5 bytes)
  > [538 Reassembled TCP Segments (3348199 bytes): #6(123), #8(4104), #10(4104), #11(4104),
  Hypertext Transfer Protocol, has 817 chunks (including last chunk)
    > POST /ipp/print HTTP/1.1\r\n
      Content-Type: application/ipp\r\n
      Host: hpm528\r\n
      Transfer-Encoding: chunked\r\n
      Expect: 100-continue\r\n
      \r\n
      [Response in frame: 638]
      [Full request URI: http://hpm528/ipp/print]
    v HTTP chunked response
      v Data chunk (4096 octets)
          Chunk size: 4096 octets
          Chunk data […]: 0101000602000000014700126174747269627574657320636861727365740005
          Chunk boundary: 0d0a
      v Data chunk (4096 octets)
          Chunk size: 4096 octets
          Chunk data […]: 695e7b5679ac0f475624a0f46073f9d73c55ce95a9cf34ba06af7282fada38ae
          Chunk boundary: 0d0a
      v Data chunk (4096 octets)
          Chunk size: 4096 octets
          Chunk data […]: cc6a420006c04918ce73c803342cfa88bb816e068cc876f9ae24195907dfc027
          Chunk boundary: 0d0a
      > Data chunk (4096 octets)
```

Notice that (under Host:) a *Transfer-Encoding: chunked* line (circled in green) appears rather than a *Content-Length* line (with size set to the file size) in the trace. Also notice that an *HTTP chunked response* inset also appears (circled in red) with a listing of each data chunk size. This tells us that the underlying HttpClient object is handling the chunking with the HTTP 1.1 receiver on the printer – exactly as we want it to. You can follow each chunk and add them up to get the initial file size if you study the trace. The last chunk will likely be smaller than the preceding series, as shown in the next graphic. Additionally, the chunking specification calls for the transmitter to send a zero-sized chunk to indicate the end, and this is exactly what we see in the Wireshark trace.

```
      Chunk boundary: 0d0a
    ˅ Data chunk (4096 octets)
      Chunk size: 4096 octets
      Chunk data […]: fa887ea9fcab55a8197a9df79790cd8765c9393c93de
      Chunk boundary: 0d0a
    ˅ Data chunk (3304 octets)
      Chunk size: 3304 octets
      Chunk data […]: 79f55fe9417b8a221193b982e188719e38a6b49098c
      Chunk boundary: 0d0a
    ˅ End of chunked encoding
      Chunk size: 0 octets
    \r\n
  File Data: 3341544 bytes
˅ Internet Printing Protocol
    [Response In: 638]
    version: 1.1
    operation-id: Send-Document (0x0006)
    request-id: 33554432
  ˅ operation-attributes-tag
    > attributes-charset (charset): 'utf-8'
    > attributes-natural-language (naturalLanguage): 'en'
    > printer-uri (uri): 'http://HPM528/ipp/print'
    > job-id (integer): 18
    > requesting-user_name (nameWithoutLanguage): 'jpmsp'
    > document-format (mimeMediaType): 'image/jpeg'
    > last-document (boolean): true
    end-of-attributes-tag
  > Data (3341339 bytes)
```

End of Chunking – Set Chunk Size to 0

It is reasonable to assume that chunking at least mitigates our file size concerns – at least for the more modern printers. As demonstrated, this is a painless addition to the library that should enhance usability.

Another new feature for the SendDocRequest class is handling multiple documents using the same Create-Job id. This allows the client to send multiple documents to the printer to be processed (and possibly collated) for convenience. To do this, the "last-document" attribute is set to false for all but the last document to be processed. On the last document, the "last-document" attribute is set to true to indicate that this is the last document being sent.[2] The job is not finalized and may not be fully processed until the last document is sent with last-document=true. While this feature is recommended, it is not required, and implementation amongst manufacturers can vary. There are also some provisos that need to be heeded:

1. The client must ensure the printer attribute "multiple-document-jobs-supported" is true when reviewing printer attributes. If this attribute is set to false, then multiple document jobs are not supported on the printer.

2. The job attribute "multiple-document-handling" should be set to client specifications. For instance, set this to "separate-documents-collated-copies" to ensure collation amongst the various documents.[3]

3. RFC 8011 stipulates the IPP_STATUS_ERROR_MULTIPLE_JOBS_NOT_SUPPORTED (1289). The error should be returned if the printer does not support multiple documents. However, some printers may not return the IPP_STATUS_ERROR_MULTIPLE_JOBS _NOT_ SUPPORTED error as specified in RFC 8011, so it is best to prepare for any non-standard behavior in your code.

Get Jobs Request

As the name implies, the Get-Jobs request provides a way for a user to retrieve information about print jobs previously created in the printer. This request is required according to RFC8011, so all IPP printers are required to support it. The request does allow for the caller to specify job description and status attributes; some of the more common attributes are shown below:

[2] The client can also send all documents with a "last-document" set to "false" and then close the job with a Close-Job operation.

[3] The "multiple-document-handling" attribute is used to both define how the multiple documents are combined to create a "Set," and then it also interacts with the "copies" attribute, if present and > 1, to specify whether each copy is collated or not.

job-id

job-uri

job-printer-uri

job-more-info

job-name

job-originating-user-name

job-state-reasons

job-state-message

job-detailed-status-message

time-at-creation

time-at-processing

time-at-completed

job-message

A full list of attributes allowed can be obtained via RFC 8011 on pages 5-6 [5]. One of the operation attributes that can be included in a Get-Jobs request is the "which-jobs" attribute. This attribute is optional for the user but must be supported by the printer. Two of the more commonly used values for this attribute can be either "completed" or "not-completed," and the printer must support these. You can verify this by looking at the "which-jobs-supported" attribute returned from a Get-Printer-Attributes request. On my own HP M528 printer, the supported values for this attribute are "completed" and "not-completed." Another job attribute that can be supplied is the "my-jobs" argument. The "my-jobs" argument indicates whether jobs from the requesting user or all users are to be returned in the Get-Jobs request. RFC 8011 stipulates that this attribute may be supplied by the user, and if it is the printer must support it [8]. Additionally, the Get-Job request can specify "which-jobs" and whether you want information on jobs the user originated or for all jobs. The "which-jobs" option allows the caller to specify whether information about completed or not completed jobs is required. Finally, the "limit" attribute sets the threshold of jobs you want returned by the request – this is set to 60 initially.

```
public string[] requestedAttributeNames =
{
```

```
"job-id", "job-uri", "job-printer-uri", "job-more-info","job-originating-user-name", "job-state", "job-state-reasons", "job-state-message", "time-at-completed"
};

```

The GetJobsRequest class employs a string array (requestedAttributeNames) that contains the common job descriptions and status attributes. In the event you want more detail or information for this request, you can add or remove attributes to suit your needs. The next graphic shows the Wireshark trace of a Get-Jobs request with the requested attributes sent circled in red.

```
[Response In: 18]
version: 1.1
operation-id: Get-Jobs (0x000a)
request-id: 16777216
operation-attributes-tag
  attributes-charset (charset): 'utf-8'
  attributes-natural-language (naturalLanguage): 'en'
  printer-uri (uri): 'http://hpm528/ipp/print'
  requesting-user_name (nameWithoutLanguage): 'jpmsp'
  limit (integer): 60
  which-jobs (keyword): 'completed'
  my-jobs (boolean): false
  requested-attributes (keyword): 'job-id'
  requested-attributes (keyword): 'job-uri'
  requested-attributes (keyword): 'job-printer-uri'
  requested-attributes (keyword): 'job-more-info'
  requested-attributes (keyword): 'job-originating-user-name'
  requested-attributes (keyword): 'job-state'
  requested-attributes (keyword): 'job-state-reasons'
  requested-attributes (keyword): 'job-state-message'
  requested-attributes (keyword): 'time-at-completed'
end-of-attributes-tag
```

Wireshark trace of Get-Jobs Request

Most of the operational attributes have been covered previously, with the ones specifically for the Get-Jobs request highlighted in green. The printer replies to this request using a jobs attribute tag (0x02), which is handled in the GetIppAttributesAsync method of the ResponseHelpers.cs file (in the Ipp folder). The job attributes requested are returned for each job as shown in the next Wireshark trace from the target printer being queried. Notice that the Wireshark trace dissector has translated (in the trace) the enumerations for you as a convenience. In your code these may have to be translated, or your user will get the enumerated integer instead of the user-friendly text.

```
v job-attributes-tag
  > job-uri (uri): 'ipp://10.0.0.214/ipp/port1/job-0024'
  > job-id (integer): 24
  > job-printer-uri (uri): 'http://hpm528/ipp/print'
  > job-originating-user-name (nameWithoutLanguage): 'anonymous'
  > job-state (enum): aborted
  > job-state-reasons (keyword): 'job-data-insufficient'
  > job-state-message (textWithoutLanguage): 'job-data-insufficient'
  > time-at-completed (integer): 208555
v job-attributes-tag
  > job-uri (uri): 'ipp://10.0.0.214/ipp/port1/job-0023'
  > job-id (integer): 23
  > job-printer-uri (uri): 'http://hpm528/ipp/print'
  > job-originating-user-name (nameWithoutLanguage): 'anonymous'
  > job-state (enum): completed
  > job-state-reasons (keyword): 'job-completed-successfully'
  > job-state-message (textWithoutLanguage): 'job-completed-successfully'
  > time-at-completed (integer): 208163
v job-attributes-tag
  > job-uri (uri): 'ipp://10.0.0.214/ipp/port1/job-0022'
  > job-id (integer): 22
  > job-printer-uri (uri): 'http://hpm528/ipp/print'
  > job-originating-user-name (nameWithoutLanguage): 'anonymous'
  > job-state (enum): aborted
  > job-state-reasons (keyword): 'job-data-insufficient'
  > job-state-message (textWithoutLanguage): 'job-data-insufficient'
  > time-at-completed (integer): 208153
v job-attributes-tag
  > job-uri (uri): 'ipp://10.0.0.214/ipp/port1/job-0021'
  > job-id (integer): 21
  > job-printer-uri (uri): 'ipps://hpm528:631/ipp/print'
  > job-originating-user-name (nameWithoutLanguage): 'M1795\jpmsp'
  > job-state (enum): completed
  > job-state-reasons (keyword): 'job-completed-successfully'
  > job-state-message (textWithoutLanguage): 'job-completed-successfully'
```

Wireshark Trace Get-Jobs Reply from Printer

A note about the job information returned: while the RFC stipulates what specific job attributes describe, it does not stipulate how that information is stored. Like much else regarding the IPP standard, this is implementation specific. The job information retention period is based in memory, and in many instances, this is volatile, meaning it is lost in a power cycle. Thus, a power cycle is likely to clear out any job information retained, and depending on your circumstances, this could be undesirable. On my own test hardware, an HP M528, an HP M608, an HP M652, and a Lexmark 421, this proved to be the case. Bottom line: if you are counting on retrieving and analyzing job information, be prepared to retrieve this data often (or at least before any power cycles).

I ran into a nasty bug (likely caused by my misreading of the RFC for the Get-Jobs request) that forced me to employ Wireshark to hunt down the issue. The clues to the bug were in the binary stream that the request was sent back to the client. My error – and the ultimate resolution to the issue – is laid out in the section "Using Wireshark to Identify Attribute Recovery Issues" in Chapter 9, "IPP Tools."

Identify Printer Request

While it might be assumed that networked printers are adequately labeled as their host names, the fact of the matter might be a different story. In some instances, printers are moved from office to office to be used as needed, while in other cases they remain inadequately labeled. Either way, inexperienced users are often confused as to the physical location or IP of a targeted printer. For these scenarios, the IdentifyPrinterRequest was (assumingly) created. Employing the Identify-Printer (0x3C) operation ID, this request can manifest itself on the printer in several ways. The actual implementation of the identify action performed (flashing screen, noise) is incumbent on the printer itself. The "identify-actions-supported" attribute returned from a Get-Printer-Attributes request provides the options available to the printer admin – specifically what actions the Identify-Printer will take. For my own test hardware, these actions were display, flash, or sound. The bottom line is to provide a request that can physically identify the target printer when executed. The IdentifyPrinterRequest directs the Identify-Printer (0x3C) IPP request to the target printer to elicit a response, either as an audible alert or a flashing message on the input screen, to identify itself to the user.

This request is the easiest to implement since it requires truly little in the form of requested attributes. Besides the typical requested attributes required of all requests (charset, natural language, printer URI, and requesting username), no other special attributes are needed.

A note about this request – the length of time this request executes (whether beeping, flashing, etc.) is not controlled by an IPP attribute, at least not any I found. Often, the identification signal was too short for me to find the printer unless I was physically close to the hardware.

Get Job Attributes

When a job is sent to an IPP printer, it can return various status messages to the client while the printer processes (and completes) the job. As explained in the section "Print Job Status" in Chapter 4, "The MS IPP Class Driver," the client can either poll the printer - i.e., send out requests intermittently and process the replies until the desired job state is found - or create a subscription for job events from the printer and receive those event updates as they happen. In the event the printer does not support subscriptions, the Get-Job-Attributes (0x09) request can be employed as a polling agent.

Assuming the job rendering time on the printer is not immediate, it is reasonable to assume the printer would elicit various job status messages in response to the GetJobAttributesRequest queries such as

job-pending:	The print job is not yet being rendered and is waiting to be processed.
job-processing:	The print job is now in the state of being processed by the printer.
job-held:	The print job is held for a reason, possibly requesting intervention.
job-stopped:	The print job progress is stopped, possibly due to an error.
job-completed:	The print job has been successfully rendered and is completed.
job-canceled:	The print job has been canceled by the user or the system.
job-aborted:	The print job has been aborted and is no longer being processed.

Thus, assuming a successful print job request, a 0x0000 status code (IPP_STATUS_OK) whilst receiving various status messages (while the job is being processed) is entirely reasonable in response to the GetJobAttributesRequest query. In the library code, this request takes the job id returned by the create-job request and returns a CompletionStruct which contains the status code. The GetJobAttributesRequest query returns the status code, the job state, and the job state reasons. You can see how this happens by looking at the IppPrintRequest project, which provides a convenient way of testing all the various requests in the library via a console program.

```
1. GetJobAttributesRequest gja = new GetJobAttributesRequest("1.1",
   sIppPrinter, false, request, jobId);
2. CompletionStruct cs = await gja.SendRequestAsync();
3. Console.WriteLine(Status.GetIppStatusMessage(cs.status));
```

Using the IppPrintRequest as a way of testing out the various requests, you can retrieve job attribute status information from various job ids created on the computer. For instance, retrieving the job status for job ids 8 and 10 is shown below; one is cancelled and one is successfully completed.

```
Enter the IPP printer to use:
hpm528
Would you like to getattributes, getjobattributes, validate, create,
cancel, senddoc, getjobs, identify, or print a job?
getjobattributes
Enter the job id to query:
8
Status: 0
attributes-charset : utf-8
attributes-natural-language : en
job-state : 7
job-state-reasons : job-canceled-by-user
successful-ok
IPP print request completed
```

```
Enter the IPP printer to use:
hpm528
Would you like to getattributes, getjobattributes, validate, create,
cancel, senddoc, getjobs, identify, or print a job?
getjobattributes
Enter the job id to query:
10
Status: 0
```

```
attributes-charset : utf-8
attributes-natural-language : en
job-state : 9
job-state-reasons : job-completed-successfully
successful-ok
IPP print request completed
```

The GetJobAttributesRequest employs an array of requested attributes:

```
string[] requestedAttributeNames =
{
      "job-state", "job-state-reasons"
};
```

I should elaborate a bit on the job-state, which is an attribute to monitor the progress of a print job. The table below specifies the various job states that are provided for the "job-state" attribute.

Value	Name	Description
3	pending	The job is waiting in the queue and has not yet started processing.
4	pending-held	The job is waiting in the queue but is held (paused) and will not be processed until released.
5	processing	The job is currently being processed by the printer.
6	processing-stopped	The job processing has been stopped temporarily (e.g., paused).
7	canceled	The job has been canceled by the user or administrator.
8	aborted	The job was aborted due to an error or printer failure.
9	completed	The job has finished printing successfully.

The last 3 are "terminal states" – final states the printer will achieve.

Which are then sent to the printer in the request (along with the job id to be queried) in the Wireshark trace shown next.

```
› Transmission Control Protocol, Src Port: 64874, Dst Port: 80, Seq: 14
› [2 Reassembled TCP Segments (372 bytes): #171(140), #173(232)]
› Hypertext Transfer Protocol
⌄ Internet Printing Protocol
    [Response In: 176]
    version: 1.1
    operation-id: Get-Job-Attributes (0x0009)
    request-id: 16777216
  ⌄ operation-attributes-tag
    › attributes-charset (charset): 'utf-8'
    › attributes-natural-language (naturalLanguage): 'en'
    › printer-uri (uri): 'http://hpm528/ipp/print'
    › requesting-user-name (nameWithoutLanguage): 'jpmsp'
    › job-id (integer): 10
    › requested-attributes (keyword): 'job-state'
    › requested-attributes (keyword): 'job-state-reasons'
    end-of-attributes-tag
```

Wireshark Trace of the Get Job Attributes Request

The reply from the printer is shown next...

```
› Internet Protocol Version 4, Src: 10.0.0.214, Dst: 10.0.0.50
› Transmission Control Protocol, Src Port: 80, Dst Port: 64874, Seq: 479,
› [2 Reassembled TCP Segments (609 bytes): #174(453), #176(156)]
› Hypertext Transfer Protocol, has 2 chunks (including last chunk)
⌄ Internet Printing Protocol
    [Request In: 173]
    [Response Time: 0.047114000 seconds]
    version: 1.1
    status-code: Successful (successful-ok)
    request-id: 16777216
  ⌄ operation-attributes-tag
    › attributes-charset (charset): 'utf-8'
    › attributes-natural-language (naturalLanguage): 'en'
  ⌄ job-attributes-tag
    › job-state (enum): completed
    › job-state-reasons (keyword): 'job-completed-successfully'
    end-of-attributes-tag
```

Wireshark trace of get job attributes reply from the printer

Note job subscriptions were not part of the IPP standard until IPP version 2.0 was formalized and accepted. The Microsoft print subsystem itself uses polling to obtain job status as it does not support IPP version 2.0 (yet).

IPP Status Messages

While integer return codes may be sufficient for developers and system engineers, they are not sufficiently descriptive for most users. In fact, lacking the source code or sufficient information relating the returned value to an informative description of the error, return codes are of little use to the average user. The library attempts to correct this in the static Status class GetIppStatusMessage method (Status.cs in the Ipp folder), which takes the status code as a parameter and returns a (more) descriptive error string. The descriptive string is from the CUPS port to Windows code used in the C library. You can use this in your own renditions of IPP software to better inform end users of the status of their requests. This is also a clever idea for support as users are more likely to remember a descriptive string rather than a numerical code when they report issues with your library.

Get Printer Attributes Request

One request conspicuously missing from the library in Chapter 5, "IPP Standards Print," was a way of returning printer attributes, at least to the calling user. This has been addressed with the GetPrinterAttributesRequest, essentially the same code that was used for the first several chapters, only now within the library. A searchable collection of attributes is now available in the event you do not want to view all the returned attributes but do want to know if a particular attribute exists and what the value is.

For instance, using the IppPrintRequest console program to retrieve printer attributes from a printer might look like the following:

```
GetPrinterAttributesRequest gpa = new
GetPrinterAttributesRequest("1.1", sIppPrinter, false, request, true);
CompletionStruct cs = await gpa.SendRequestAsync();
if (cs.status <= (int)Status.IPP_STATUS.IPP_STATUS_OK_EVENTS_COMPLETE)
{
```

```
Console.WriteLine("Enter an attribute to query, leave blank and Enter for none: ");
        string atq = Console.ReadLine();
        if (atq.Length > 0)
        {
            List<string> queriedAttributeValues = gpa.GetAttributeValues(atq);
             foreach (string av in queriedAttributeValues)
             {
                     Console.WriteLine(av);
             }
        }
        else
        {
            IEnumerator<IppAttribute> pas = gpa.GetAttributeValues();
             while (pas.MoveNext())
             {
                     IppAttribute pa = pas.Current as IppAttribute;
Console.WriteLine(string.Format("{0}:{1}", pa.Name, pa.WriteAttributeValuesString()));
             }
        }
}
else
{
Console.WriteLine(Status.GetIppStatusMessage(cs.status));
}
```

Like the Identify-Printer request, the Get-Printer-Attributes request takes few arguments outside of the IPP printer to query. In the background, the RequestHelpers class (which handles the Get-Printer-Attributes request) employs asynchronous methods whenever possible as a best practice for responsive code. As a reminder, the async return type requires at least one instance where a call is awaited, i.e., where it can give up processing time to the calling thread. The next few graphics may help conceptualize the request chain and the asynchronous format it leverages. The first graphic shows the call chain from GetPrinterAttributesRequest through the IppRequest class. The next call chain displays how attributes are decoded by the call chain in the ResponseHelpers class.

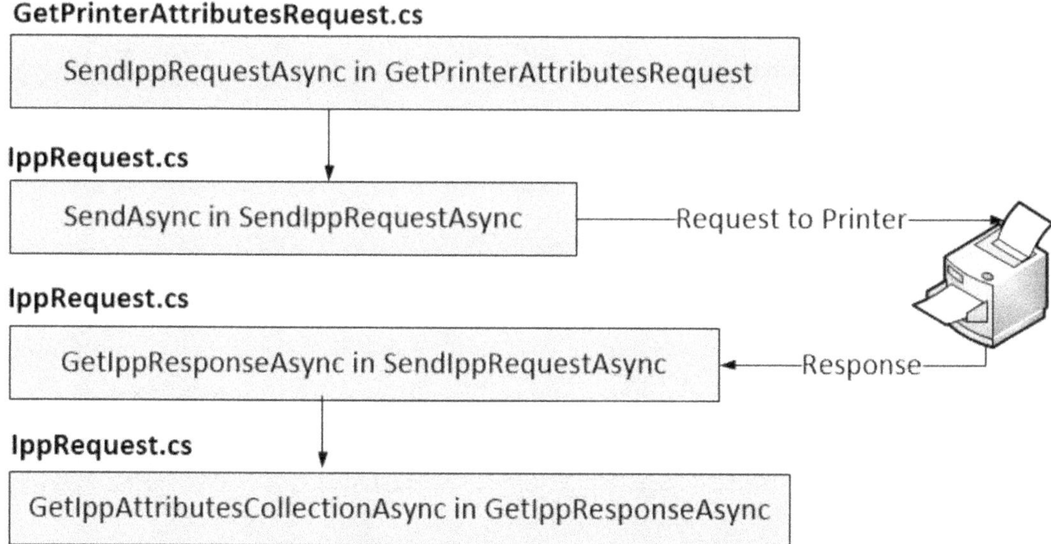

The Request/Response chain formed

The values of each attribute returned are processed in the GetAttributeCollectionAsync method in ResponseHelpers.cs that is called by the IppAttributesCollectionAsync method, which is itself called by GetIppResponseAsync method of IppResponse.cs file. Since this is an IO call, these methods are asynchronous, so the calling thread does not block. Attribute names and values are recovered from the returned byte stream from the printer within the 9 lines of code below:

```
byte[] lenBuffer = new byte[2];
 await stream.ReadAsync(lenBuffer, 0, 2);
 int len = ByteOrder.Flip(BitConverter.ToInt16(lenBuffer, 0));

 byte[] nameBuffer = new byte[len];
 await stream.ReadAsync(nameBuffer, 0, len);
 string name = Encoding.UTF8.GetString(nameBuffer);

 var value = await GetValueTagValueAsync(stream, tag);
```

In the first 7 lines of this code, the attribute name is recovered, while GetValueTagValueAsync method processes the value of the byte stream. These calls are awaited as the processing time to complete is not known and could otherwise be allocated to the calling (GUI) thread. GetValueTagValueAsync delegates the processing to methods determined by the value of the ValueTag byte passed into GetAttributeCollectionAsync.

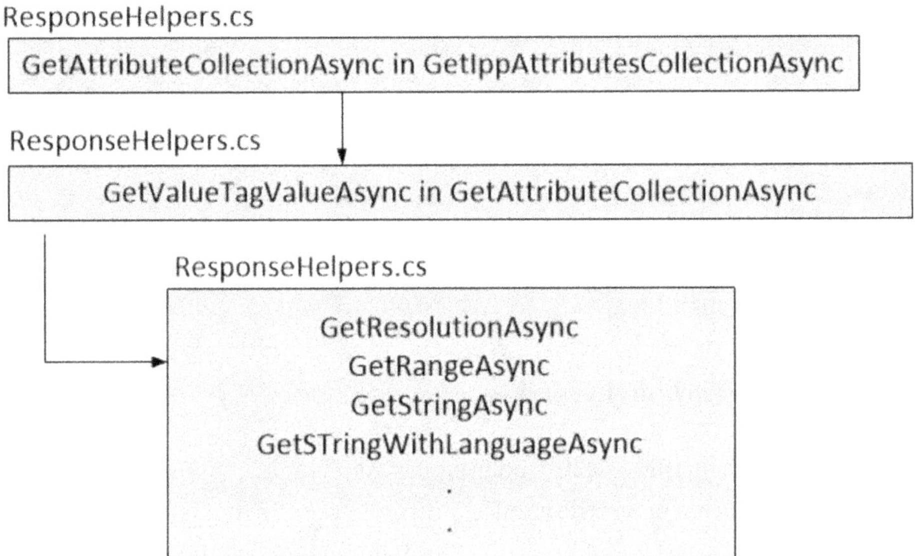

Decoding of Attributes Call Chain

```
⌄ operation-attributes-tag
   › attributes-charset (charset): 'utf-8'
   › attributes-natural-language (naturalLanguage): 'en'
⌄ printer-attributes-tag
   › printer-uri-supported (1setOf uri): 'ipp://10.0.0.214/ipp/print','ipps://10.0.0.214:631/i
   › uri-security-supported (1setOf keyword): 'none','tls'
   › uri-authentication-supported (1setOf keyword): 'requesting-user-name','requesting-user-na
   › printer-name (nameWithoutLanguage): 'HPM528'
   › printer-dns-sd-name (nameWithoutLanguage): 'HP LaserJet Flow MFP M528 [84AF0F]'
   › printer-geo-location (unknown)
   › printer-location (textWithoutLanguage): 'PEB-2J5'
   › printer-info (textWithoutLanguage): 'HP LaserJet Flow MFP M528 [84AF0F]'
   › printer-state (enum): idle
   › printer-state-reasons (keyword): 'none'
   › ipp-versions-supported (1setOf keyword): '1.0','1.1','2.0'
   › operations-supported (1setOf enum): Print-Job,Print-URI,Validate-Job,Create-Job,Send-Docu
   › charset-configured (charset): 'us-ascii'
   › charset-supported (1setOf charset): 'us-ascii','utf-8'
   › natural-language-configured (naturalLanguage): 'en'
   › generated-natural-language-supported (naturalLanguage): 'en'
   › document-format-default (mimeMediaType): 'application/pdf'
   ›  […]document-format-supported (1setOf mimeMediaType): 'text/plain','application/octet-str
   › document-format-preferred (mimeMediaType): 'application/pdf'
   › printer-is-accepting-jobs (boolean): true
   › queued-job-count (integer): 0
   › pdl-override-supported (keyword): 'attempted'
   › printer-up-time (integer): 611891
   › printer-current-time (dateTime): 2025-03-01T23:07:03.1-0500
   › compression-supported (keyword): 'none'
   › pages-per-minute (integer): 45
   › printer-more-info (uri): 'http://10.0.0.214/airprint_mob_status.htm'
   › multiple-operation-time-out (integer): 120
   › copies-default (integer): 1
   › finishings-default (1setOf enum): none,none
   › orientation-requested-default (enum): portrait
   › print-quality-default (enum): normal
```

Wireshark Trace of Get-Printer-Attributes Response from the Printer

Processing the Printer Attributes Byte Stream

Within ResponseHelper.cs, the byte stream from the Get-Printer-Attributes (and other requests) is processed by iteratively reading the stream and processing the returned attributes sequentially from start to end. Once a Delimiter tag is identified in the function GetIppAttributesCollectionAsync, it is processed in GetAttributeCollectionAsync, which recovers the attribute name and calls the awaited function GetValueTagValueAsync. The attribute value is recovered by delegating processing to the constituent function that knows how to best handle the attribute – this is based on the tag. The attribute name, value, and tag are then put into an IppAttribute object, and that object in turn is added to the IppAttributes collection. Processing of the byte stream thus continues until the EndOfAttributesTag (0x03) is identified.

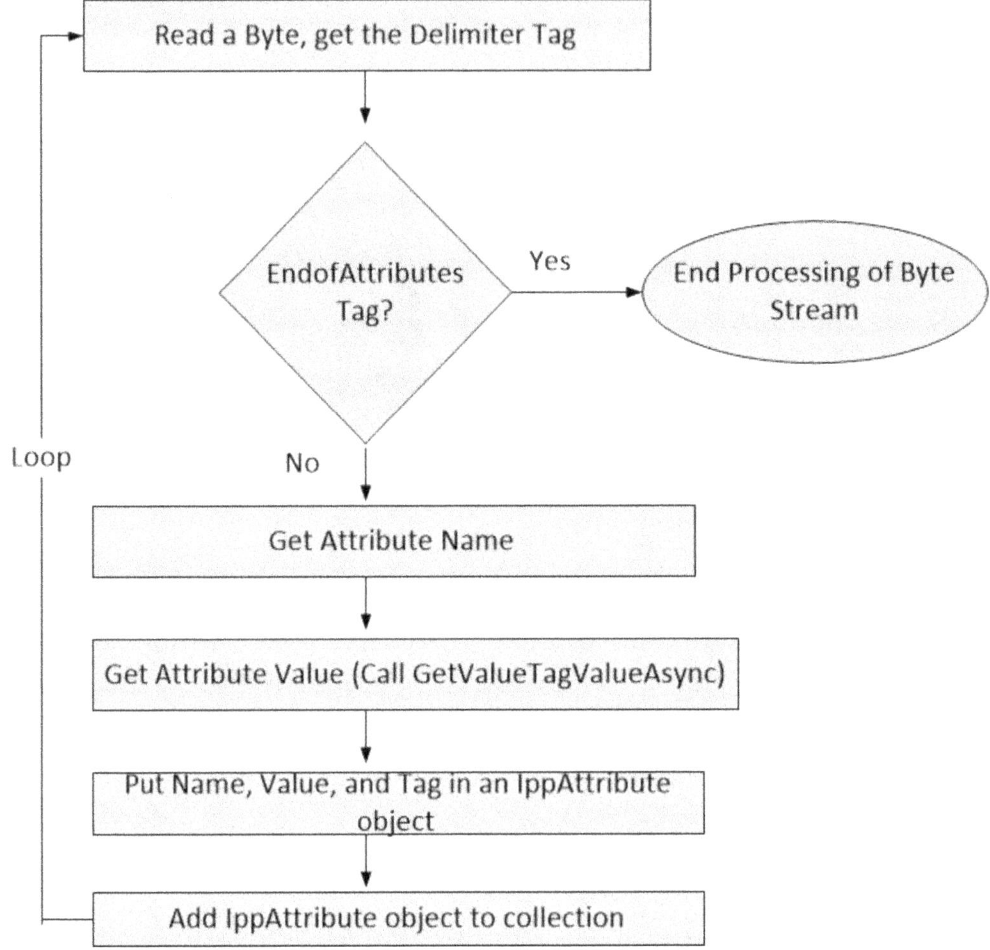

High-Level View of Byte Stream Processing

The result is a collection of IppAttribute objects (name, list of values, tag) stored in a collection housed in the IppAttributes class. This class is then stored in the base IppRequest class, ready for the caller to search through.

Pause and Resume Printer Requests

The last 2 requests added to the library are the pause-printer and resume-printer requests. These are covered in RFC 8011 sections 4.2.7.2 and 4.2.8, respectively. The pause-printer request is optional, meaning some printers will not support this request. In the event the request is sent to a printer that does not support the pause-printer request, the reply should be status code 1281 (error-operation-not-supported). If the pause-printer is supported, RFC 8011 stipulates that the resume-printer must be supported as well, which makes sense. Where a bit of ambiguity creeps in is whether currently processing jobs are stopped or not – apparently this is implementation specific. Interestingly, the printer must still accept job creation (i.e., create-job requests) but will not allow any jobs to enter the processing state.

```
Wireshark · Packet 8 · Ethernet (host 10.0.0.214)

> Frame 8: 195 bytes on wire (1560 bits), 195 bytes captured (1560 bit
> Ethernet II, Src: ASUSTekCOMPU_e6:21:bb (04:42:1a:e6:21:bb), Dst: He
> Internet Protocol Version 4, Src: 10.0.0.50, Dst: 10.0.0.214
> Transmission Control Protocol, Src Port: 62002, Dst Port: 80, Seq: 1
> [2 Reassembled TCP Segments (281 bytes): #6(140), #8(141)]
> Hypertext Transfer Protocol
v Internet Printing Protocol
    [Response In: 11]
    version: 1.1
    operation-id: Pause-Printer (0x0010)
    request-id: 16777216
  v operation-attributes-tag
    > attributes-charset (charset): 'utf-8'
    > attributes-natural-language (naturalLanguage): 'en'
    > printer-uri (uri): 'http://HPM528/ipp/print'
    > requesting-user_name (nameWithoutLanguage): 'jpmsp'
    end-of-attributes-tag
```

Pause-Printer request

My own printer (an HP M528) does not support the Pause-Printer operation, as you can see from the Wireshark traces.

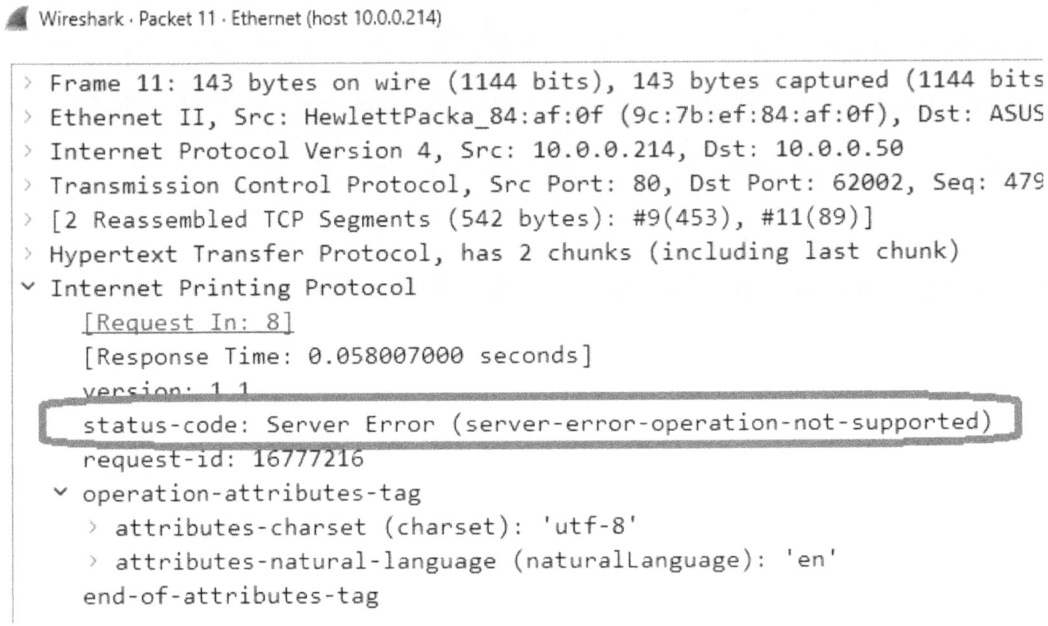

Wireshark · Packet 11 · Ethernet (host 10.0.0.214)

```
> Frame 11: 143 bytes on wire (1144 bits), 143 bytes captured (1144 bits
> Ethernet II, Src: HewlettPacka_84:af:0f (9c:7b:ef:84:af:0f), Dst: ASUS
> Internet Protocol Version 4, Src: 10.0.0.214, Dst: 10.0.0.50
> Transmission Control Protocol, Src Port: 80, Dst Port: 62002, Seq: 479
> [2 Reassembled TCP Segments (542 bytes): #9(453), #11(89)]
> Hypertext Transfer Protocol, has 2 chunks (including last chunk)
v Internet Printing Protocol
    [Request In: 8]
    [Response Time: 0.058007000 seconds]
    version: 1.1
    status-code: Server Error (server-error-operation-not-supported)
    request-id: 16777216
  v operation-attributes-tag
    > attributes-charset (charset): 'utf-8'
    > attributes-natural-language (naturalLanguage): 'en'
    end-of-attributes-tag
```

Pause-Printer reply – operation not supported reply

Despite not supporting the request, the HP M608 printer correctly provides feedback by sending back a 1281 error (server-error-operation-not-supported).

On the newer Lexmark MS421 printer (which does support the Pause-Printer operation), the Pause-Printer operation will stop the printer from accepting any further jobs from clients.[4] This request comes in handy when performing any required maintenance on the printer, such as replacing toner cartridges, adding paper, clearing jams, etc. Once the maintenance tasks are completed, the ResumePrinter request puts the printer back in service.

Adding New Requests

The purpose of adding these requests was to demonstrate how straightforward it is to append to the library any custom requests you might want to support. To create a byte buffer that contains all the necessary attributes, you only need

[4] A spooling printer may continue to accept jobs while the cover is open, etc., but won't be able to process them until those printer states are resolved. Thus, it may not be necessary to manually use the Pause-Printer and Resume-Printer operations in this scenario.

to use either the CreatePrinterAttribute function (for single attributes) or the CreateJobAttributesByteArray function (to create a job attributes array). Below is a rough template of the byte buffer that is created for each request. The attributes in orange are common to all requests and therefore defined in the base class (IppRequest). The attributes in rose are the job attributes that you may or may not need depending on the type of request you want to create. The attribute(s) in green are the custom attributes that may be required for any given request you might want to support.

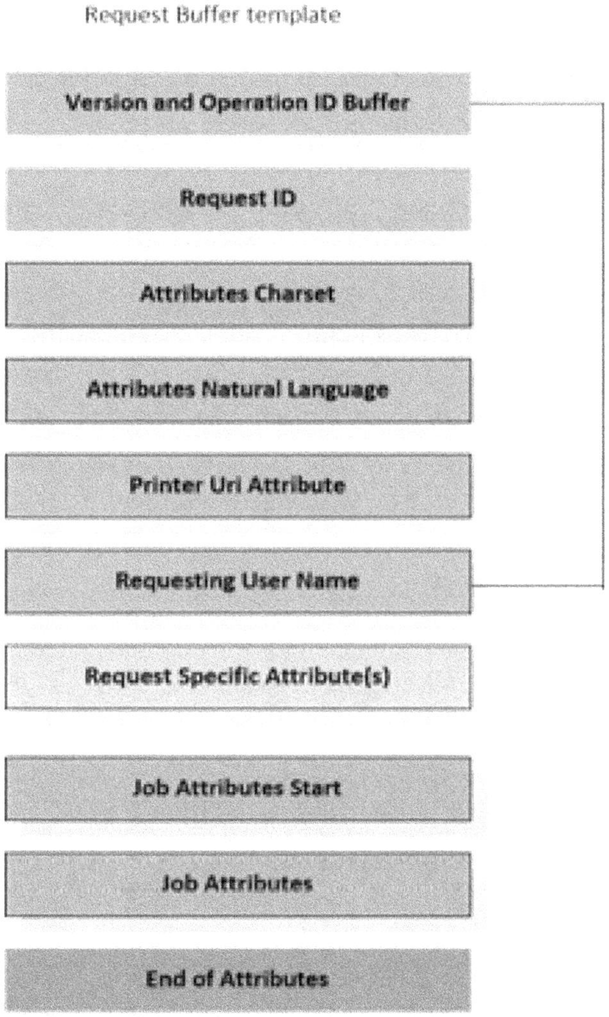

Request Buffer template

Version and Operation ID Buffer

Request ID

Attributes Charset

Attributes Natural Language

Printer Uri Attribute

Requesting User Name

Request Specific Attribute(s)

Job Attributes Start

Job Attributes

End of Attributes

Of course, all of this can be created in the MakeRequestByteBuffer method of the specified request to add. For any request, consult Section 4 (IPP Operations) of RFC 8011, which will annotate all operational attributes required. These will be the attributes in green on the request buffer template and are unique to that request. For instance, when looking at the Cancel-Job request (Section 4.3.3.1 of RFC 8011), the Operational Attributes required are "attributes-charset" and "attributes-natural-language," while either the "printer-uri" plus "job-id" or the "job-uri" operation attribute(s) is required. The “requesting-user-name” is listed as “should be supplied” by the client, whereas a text message may be supplied. If all else fails, you can use IppTool to create the request (if supported) and view the composition in Wireshark. You can discover IppTool (and how to use it) in Chapter 9, “IPP Tools.”

You should also be familiar with the response from the printer. In the case of the cancel-job request, the RFC stipulates “attributes-charset,” and “attributes-natural-language” will be returned. In addition to a required status code, the response may also include a “status-message” attribute as well.

Finally, you will need to know the operation-id parameter, which is listed in table 19 (page 158) of RFC 8011. In the case of Cancel-Job, this value is 0x00008, while the value of Pause-Printer is 0x0010. As with any development intended to traverse the network, Wireshark is your best friend. Just make sure you initially develop using IPP port 631 as the dissector makes things much easier to spot issues with your byte stream of attributes sent in the HTTP post message. As mentioned in Chapter 5, “IPP Standards Print,” if you see the following Wireshark trace, you can be sure that either you have omitted a required attribute, used the wrong byte tag for the attribute, used the wrong operation id, or somehow forgot to add a required tag. Take your time and be patient, review Wireshark traces, and your time invested will eventually pay off.

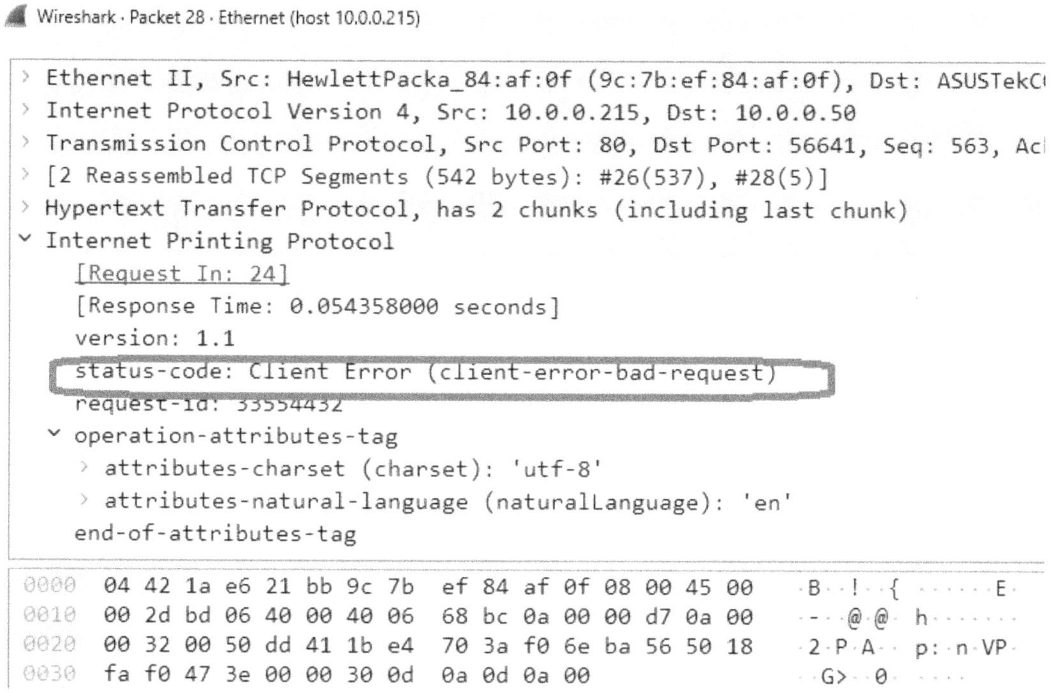

Wireshark · Packet 28 · Ethernet (host 10.0.0.215)

```
> Ethernet II, Src: HewlettPacka_84:af:0f (9c:7b:ef:84:af:0f), Dst: ASUSTekC
> Internet Protocol Version 4, Src: 10.0.0.215, Dst: 10.0.0.50
> Transmission Control Protocol, Src Port: 80, Dst Port: 56641, Seq: 563, Ac
> [2 Reassembled TCP Segments (542 bytes): #26(537), #28(5)]
> Hypertext Transfer Protocol, has 2 chunks (including last chunk)
v Internet Printing Protocol
    [Request In: 24]
    [Response Time: 0.054358000 seconds]
    version: 1.1
    status-code: Client Error (client-error-bad-request)
    request-id: 33554432
  v operation-attributes-tag
    > attributes-charset (charset): 'utf-8'
    > attributes-natural-language (naturalLanguage): 'en'
    end-of-attributes-tag

0000  04 42 1a e6 21 bb 9c 7b  ef 84 af 0f 08 00 45 00   ·B··!··{ ······E·
0010  00 2d bd 06 40 00 40 06  68 bc 0a 00 00 d7 0a 00   ·-··@·@· h·······
0020  00 32 00 50 dd 41 1b e4  70 3a f0 6e ba 56 50 18   ·2·P·A·· p:·n·VP·
0030  fa f0 47 3e 00 00 30 0d  0a 0d 0a 00               ··G>··0· ····
```

Malformed IPP Request

Authentication

Up until this point, our print library has been assuming an entitlement to the extent that it expects to successfully print on whatever IPP printer it chooses. Modern network devices generally require authenticated entities and employ authorization mechanisms, and printers are no exception. First, we should define what authentication and authorization are. In simplistic terms, authentication is the act of verifying an entity is who or whom they claim they are. Put more succinctly: Authentication is the process that companies use to confirm that only the right people, services, and apps with the right permissions can get organizational resources [6]. As you might imagine, printers will delegate this responsibility to the OS the print job emanates from. This is because print protocols do not generally handle user authentication tokens employed as verification during client-server sessions. Lacking this ability, printers rely on the client OS to perform authentication duties. This is certainly not foolproof, but it does provide at least rudimentary protection. Because information security has taken a new prominence, other more promising authentication methods are shown below:

Method	Description	Pros	Cons
Username/Password	Input username and password into device	Simple; Familiarity	Passwords can be lost/stolen/forgotten
PIN Codes	Enter unique code into device	Convenience; Quick access	Can be misused if known by others
Card-Based Authentication	Swipe physical card through reader on device	Easy-to-use; Fast recognition	Cards can be lost/stolen
Biometric Authentication	Use unique biological characteristics (e.g., fingerprints) to verify identity	High security; Can't be easily duplicated or forged	More expensive to implement

*Newer Printer Authentication Mechanisms [**2**]*

Authorization

Authorization is the act of providing access to the device based on the entity they were authenticated as. For instance, you might place one authenticated user in the printer administrator role and another user in the role of a standard print user. As you might expect, the various capabilities, roles, and interfaces vary by vendor but include at least an administrator role, which can manage everything on the printer. Other roles might manage the embedded web server or manage network settings. In the end, these authorization mechanisms are only as good as the entities that were authenticated for the roles.

IPP Authentication

IPP authentication methods are a subject that would require a book itself to adequately cover. I suggest you consult the IPP Authentication Methods documentation from the Printer Working Group if you want to add a more secure authentication method than the Basic authentication level in the library. The Internet Printing Protocol (IPP) provides print job authentication in the form of None, Requesting-User-Name, Basic, Digest, or OAuth methods.[5] The following describes how these authentication mechanisms work and how they stack up against each other:

None (Authentication) indicates that the receiving printer provides no method to accept an asserted identity for the User operating the Client. The user's name for the operation is assumed to be "anonymous" [7].

Requesting-User-Name is considered insecure as none. The printer uses this unauthenticated name as the identity of the User operating on the Client. This method is not recommended if job accounting or access authorization is important, since the printer does not challenge the Client to prove the identity claimed in the "requesting-user-name" [7].

Basic authentication requests the user provide a username and password. While Basic authentication does not encrypt the credentials during transmission, using it in tandem with IPPS (TLS) does provide some level of credential integrity. If IPP is used, the credentials can be read with any network sniffer and are thus vulnerable to network sniffers or packet tracers.

Digest Authentication is more secure compared to Basic Authentication since it encrypts the username and password. Essentially this has the same effect as Basic authentication over IPPS.

OAuth Authorization is the most secure since it allows users to authenticate using third-party services without requiring the user/client to provide the user's credentials directly to the printer. This method provides enhanced scalability and integrity and is the optimal choice if available. OAuth authorization provides a time-limited token used for requests that can be revoked by the issuer in case of a security breach. In mixed security environments where multiple services and heterogeneous devices need to communicate, OAuth's ability to standardize authentication and authorization is a core component. The next graphic displays the basics of the protocol:

[5] IPP leverages and can support any HTTP or TLS authentication method, including those listed, as well as the "negotiate" (Kerberos) and "certificate" (TLS client certificate) authentication methods. These are discussed in "IPP Authentication Methods" (PWG 5199.10 - `https://ftp.pwg.org/pub/pwg/ipp/informational/bp-ippauth10-20190816-5199.10.pdf`).

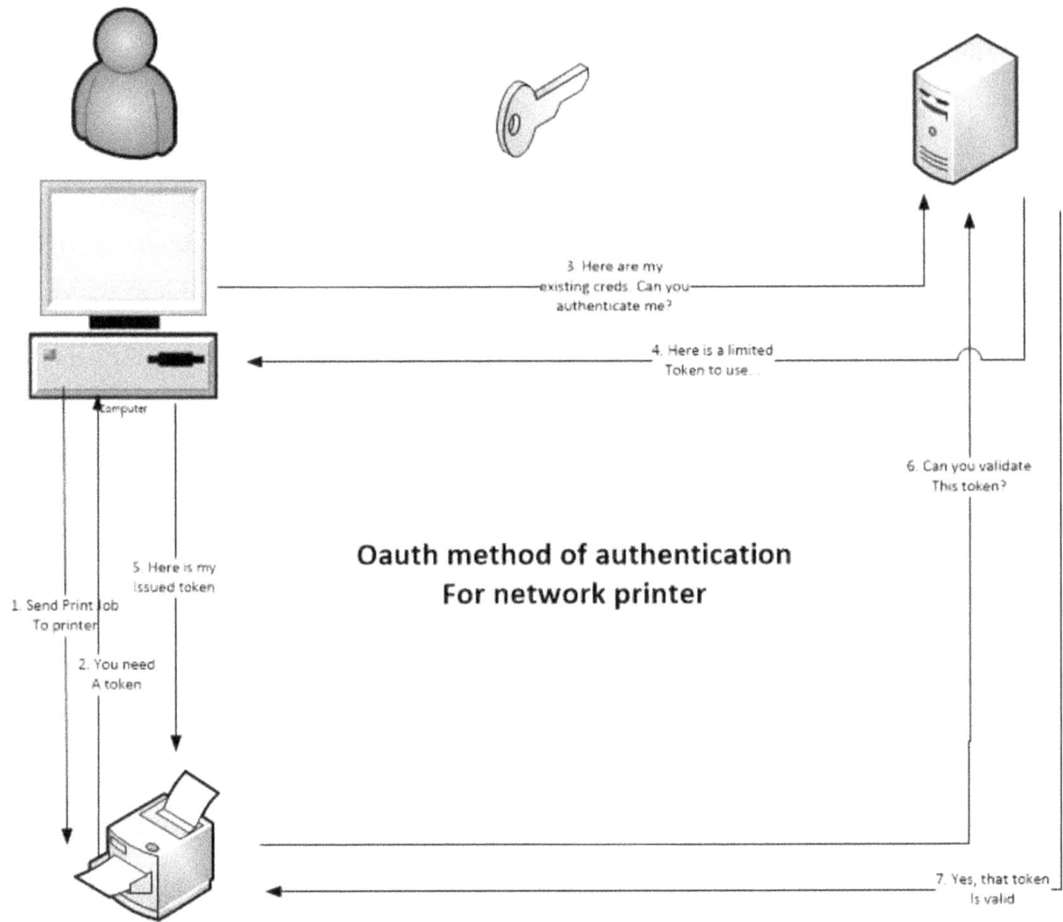

Simplified OAuth interaction for network print

My own HP test printer does not provide an option for Digest or OAuth authentication as it is (the printer) more than 7 years old at the time of this writing. It does offer Basic authentication for IPP, so it might be a clever idea to investigate how this might work. I left my printer as IPP to provide easy-to-read packet traces but keep in mind if you were to do this, you should at a minimum require IPPS so the credentials are encrypted and thus not vulnerable to packet sniffers.[6]

[6] Just for clarity, the PWG recommends that all authentication be done over IPPS.

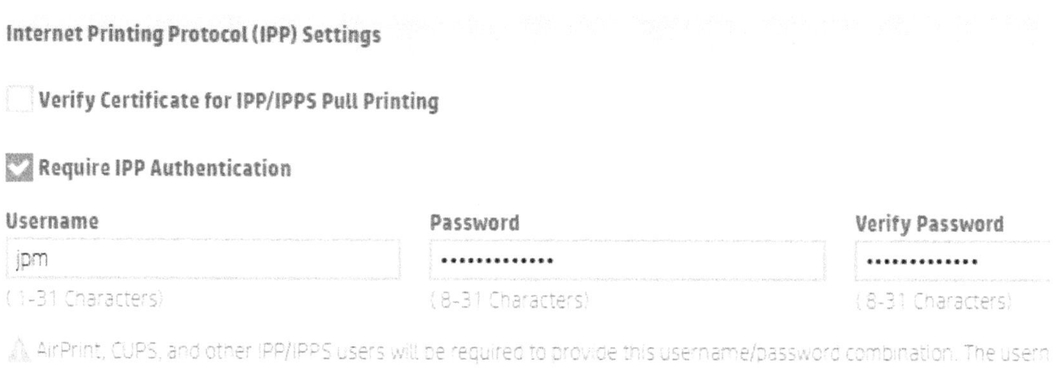

Internet Printing Protocol (IPP) Settings

Verify Certificate for IPP/IPPS Pull Printing

Require IPP Authentication

Username jpm (1-31 Characters)

Password ••••••••••••• (8-31 Characters)

Verify Password ••••••••••••• (8-31 Characters)

AirPrint, CUPS, and other IPP/IPPS users will be required to provide this username/password combination. The usern

Setting up Basic Authentication on my HP M528 printer

Above is how I configured Basic authentication on my HP M528 printer. While each vendor will provide a different look in their Embedded Web Server to configure IPP Basic authentication, all will require some username and password that will need to be matched in order for the IPP request to be passed. I should mention that not all IPP requests will be subject to this check: the get-printer-attributes request does not get checked for credentials as it is essential for the client OS to detect their capabilities during a query.

Updates to the Library

To ensure our print library can at least provide Basic authentication using IPP, we need to update our library a bit. To start off with, a basic console class to request credentials from the user is required. To follow along, open the project in this chapter code folder named BasicAuth_CsIppRequests. To provide Basic authentication, the IppRequest.cs file now has a ConsoleCredentialsProvider class (at the bottom of the IppRequest.cs file). This class takes as an argument a boolean indicating whether the user has been authenticated (bIsAuthenticated) and returns a tuple containing the username, password, and a boolean indicating whether the user wants to cancel the process.

```
public class ConsoleCredentialsProvider : ICredentialsProvider
{
    public Task<(string Username, string Password, bool bCancel)>
    GetCredentialsAsync(bool bIsAuthenticated)
    {
```

```
        if (bIsAuthenticated == false)
        {
            Console.WriteLine("**User is not authenticated or
            authentication failed**");
        }
        string sUserName = string.Empty;
        string sPassword = string.Empty;
        Console.Write("Enter Username: ");
        string username = Console.ReadLine();
        Console.Write("Enter Password: ");
        string password = Console.ReadLine();
        Console.WriteLine("Enter 'q' to cancel, or 'c' to continue:");
        if(Console.ReadLine().ToLower() == "q")
        {
            return Task.FromResult((sUserName, sPassword, true));
        }
        return Task.FromResult((username, password, false));
    }
}
```

The main modification is the new SendIppRequestWithAuthAsync method versus the older SendIppRequestAsync in the IppRequest.cs file. The newer method takes as arguments the RequestType (as did the older method), but now also takes a reference to a method (GetCredentialsAsync, outlined previously) that will request the user to provide the necessary credentials the printer needs as an authentication mechanism. The new method will initially send the user request without any credentials as this is by far the most often encountered scenario.

```
// Send the request
HttpResponseMessage response;
try
{
    response = await client.SendAsync(request, cts.Token);
}
catch (TaskCanceledException)
{
```

```
    throw new Exception("Request timed out.");
}
catch (Exception ex)
{
    throw new Exception($"An error occurred: {ex.Message}");
}
```

If the HttpResponseMessage from this request to the printer is a 401 status (unauthorized), then we request credentials from the user.

```
if (response.StatusCode == HttpStatusCode.Unauthorized)
{
    // Request credentials from the provided provider
    var (username, password, cancel) = await credentialsProvider.GetCredent
    ialsAsync(isAuthenticated);

    // If the user cancels out, then throw exception..
    if (cancel == true)
    {
        throw new OperationCanceledException("User canceled credential
        prompt.");
    }

    // Set the Basic auth header and continue the loop to retry the request
    string credentials = $"{username}:{password}";
    string encodedCredentials = Convert.ToBase64String(Encoding.UTF8.
    GetBytes(credentials));
    client.DefaultRequestHeaders.Authorization = new AuthenticationHeaderVa
    lue("Basic", encodedCredentials);
    continue;
}
```

The credentials provided by the user are then wrapped into the HttpClient headers, so it is ready when the request is submitted to the printer again.

```
client.DefaultRequestHeaders.Authorization = new AuthenticationHeaderValue(
"Basic", encodedCredentials);
continue;
```

Of course, if the response from the printer is successful from the initial attempt (without credentials), then we process the response as before, i.e., passing it onto the GetResponseAsync method. While this works, we must handle the scenario where the user does not know the proper credentials and would therefore be subjected to a never-ending array of requests to provide credentials that he does not know. To handle this scenario, the returned tuple from GetCredentialsAsync has a cancel boolean that the user can elect to use. In the case where the user cancels out, an exception noting this option is thrown, and the loop is broken.

```
var (username, password, cancel) = await credentialsProvider.GetCredentials
Async(isAuthenticated);

// If the user cancels out, then throw exception..
if (cancel == true)
{
    throw new OperationCanceledException("User canceled credential
    prompt.");
}
```

Now if you go back to the new SendIppRequestWithAuthAsync method signature,

```
protected async Task<CompletionStruct> SendIppRequestWithAuthAsync(RequestT
ype type, ICredentialsProvider credentialsProvider)
```

you might wonder where the instantiated credentialsProvider class came from that the method makes use of. That is the other major change, as we need to instantiate this class prior to calling SendIppRequestWithAuthAsync from the SendRequestAsync method of each calling requestor.

```
public override async Task<CompletionStruct> SendRequestAsync()
{
        try
        {
            var provider = new ConsoleCredentialsProvider();
            return await SendIppRequestWithAuthAsync(RequestType.SEND_
            DOCUMENT, provider);
        }
        catch (Exception ex)
```

```
        {
            throw new Exception(ex.Message);
        }
}
```

It might be instructive to see Basic authentication in action via a Wireshark trace. I do want to remind you that the printer to which you are making these requests must have Basic authentication enabled to see the following traces. If you take a look at the initial (without credentials) request for the printer, it looks like any other Print-Job request we have seen before.

```
> Internet Protocol Version 4, Src: 10.0.0.50, Dst: 10.0.0.214
> Transmission Control Protocol, Src Port: 52676, Dst Port: 80, Seq: :
> [3 Reassembled TCP Segments (32878 bytes): #15(142), #17(14600), #1!
v Hypertext Transfer Protocol
  > POST /ipp/print HTTP/1.1\r\n
    Content-Type: application/ipp\r\n
    Host: hpm528\r\n
  > Content-Length: 32736\r\n
    Expect: 100-continue\r\n
    Connection: Keep-Alive\r\n
    \r\n
    [Response in frame: 21]
    [Full request URI: http://hpm528/ipp/print]
    File Data: 32736 bytes
v Internet Printing Protocol
    version: 1.1
    operation-id: Print-Job (0x0002)
    request-id: 16777216
  > operation-attributes-tag
  > job-attributes-tag
    end-of-attributes-tag
```

Step 1: The Job Is Sent to a Printer That Requires Basic Authentication Without Credentials

Assuming the printer (as in these traces) is set up to make use of Basic authentication, it should then reply back that it needs the correct credentials (that you set up on the printer) in order to process the request. More succinctly: "The HTTP 401 Unauthorized client error response status code indicates that a request was not successful because it lacks valid authentication credentials for the requested resource" [3]. You can see the 401-status code returned in the next Wireshark trace from the printer (10.0.0.214) back to the client (10.0.0.50). Since the SendIppRequestWithAuthAsync method sent the initial request, this unauthorized status code will be handled on this line in the method:

```
if (response.StatusCode == HttpStatusCode.Unauthorized)
```

and thus enter the loop that asks the user to provide credentials.

```
> Ethernet II, Src: HewlettPacka_84:af:0f (9c:7b:ef:84:af:0f), Dst: ASUSTekCOMPU_
> Internet Protocol Version 4, Src: 10.0.0.214, Dst: 10.0.0.50
v Transmission Control Protocol, Src Port: 80, Dst Port: 52676, Seq: 460, Ack: 3:
    Source Port: 80
    Destination Port: 52676
    [Stream index: 0]
  > [Conversation completeness: Complete, WITH_DATA (31)]
    [TCP Segment Len: 0]
    Sequence Number: 460    (relative sequence number)
    Sequence Number (raw): 110325121
    [Next Sequence Number: 461    (relative sequence number)]
    Acknowledgment Number: 32879    (relative ack number)
    Acknowledgment number (raw): 4092708535
    0101 .... = Header Length: 20 bytes (5)
  > Flags: 0x011 (FIN, ACK)
    Window: 46104
    [Calculated window size: 46104]
    [Window size scaling factor: 1]
    Checksum: 0xe9e0 [unverified]
    [Checksum Status: Unverified]
    Urgent Pointer: 0
  > [Timestamps]
  > [SEQ/ACK analysis]
> [2 Reassembled TCP Segments (434 bytes): #20(434), #21(0)]
v Hypertext Transfer Protocol
    HTTP/1.1 401 Unauthorized\r\n
    Server: Virata-EmWeb/R6_2_1\r\n
    X-Frame-Options: SAMEORIGIN\r\n
```

Step 2: Printer Sends Back an HTTP Protocol 401 (Unauthorized) Message to the Client

Now assuming the user can successfully provide the requested credentials set on the printer, the next Wireshark trace packet shows the actual authorization credentials sent to the printer. As you can see, these are not encrypted since we are using Basic authentication in IPP (port 631). In production, you would certainly want this transaction to be made using IPPS to ensure it is encrypted. The example created here was made for instructional purposes only; never use Basic authentication on IPP if possible. As you can see, the entire authentication exchange is handled by the HTTP layer, not at the IPP/IPPS level.

```
  TCP segment data (16150 bytes)
> [3 Reassembled TCP Segments (32893 bytes): #28(157), #30(146
v Hypertext Transfer Protocol
  > POST /ipp/print HTTP/1.1\r\n
  v Authorization: Basic anBtOnBhc3N3b3Jk\r\n
      Credentials: jpm:password
    Content-Type: application/ipp\r\n
    Host: hpm528\r\n
  > Content-Length: 32736\r\n
    Expect: 100-continue\r\n
    \r\n
    [Response in frame: 38]
    [Full request URI: http://hpm528/ipp/print]
    File Data: 32736 bytes
v Internet Printing Protocol
    [Response In: 38]
    version: 1.1
    operation-id: Print-Job (0x0002)
    request-id: 16777216
  > operation-attributes-tag
  > job-attributes-tag
    end-of-attributes-tag
  > Data (32408 bytes)
```

Step 3: Print-Job Request Now Has the Necessary Credentials

At this point, you might be thinking that Basic authentication in IPP might be a usable feature – i.e., you can set up a username and password on the printer and thus ensure the printer is a privately shared unit that only you and your friends can make use of. In practice, this is not a practical use case, and the details of the implementation spell out why. For this to be of any use, each user making requests for an IPP printer using Basic authentication would have to share the very same username and password since there is only one set on the printer. The GetCredentialsAsync class within the IppRequest class does allow each user to provide an independent username and password, but this is not always the case with other implementations. In some IPP/IPPS libraries, the username is inferred from the Windows logged-on user – thus, the user can only modify the password. As you might imagine, this could ruin your day.

Making matters even worse, Basic authentication, at least on Windows 24H2 or lower, simply does not work at all. If you set a username and password on an IPP printer installed in Windows, the 401 unauthorized HTTP header does not trigger a callback, and thus the user is blissfully unaware of the authentication failure. This is still an outstanding issue with the Microsoft IPP class driver; hopefully, it will be addressed soon. The result is that print requests to a printer where Basic authentication is configured will fail with no user feedback as to the cause. The bottom line is that at the time of this writing, you should not set Basic Authentication on print hardware if using the MS IPP Class driver.

Additional Options

The library as it sits still lacks a few features, amongst them a way to let the user know that the file they chose to print is not natively supported on the printer. If you remember back in Chapter 4, "The MS IPP Class Driver," the built-in Microsoft IPP class driver will convert most formats to the Mopria standard, which is pdf. While this works for printers installed in the OS and supported by the Microsoft built-in IPP class driver, this feature is lacking for an IPP library that does not go through the MS print subsystem. If you send a document (e.g,, a .docx file) to the printer using our library, all bets are off – most likely it will not be satisfactory and will waste paper in the attempt. A good feature would be to tell the user that the document format they chose is not supported.

In the code section of this chapter, open the folder CsIppRequestsAdditional and load the solution - this will be a helpful solution template for testing the latest ideas out. The new function (CheckFileTypeForSupport) is at the bottom of the Program.cs file in the IppPrintRequest project. This simple addition checks to make sure the document you choose to print can in fact be successfully rendered on the printer you choose. It works by getting the list of **document-format-supported** attribute values from the server and checking the file name against the list. An example of use is in the Print-Job request, where the chosen file to print is checked for compatibility with the printer. If the file is found not to be compatible, an error alerting the user of the problem is provided to the user.

Chapter Summary

Like Chapter 3, "Deep Dive into the Protocol," this chapter covers a great deal of ground. Initially, we explored the reasons it might be a clever idea to chunk the request to a printer, particularly in the event you have a particularly large document to send. For the Microsoft HttpClient, chunking is enabled when the HTTP request buffer content length is not explicitly set, and the TransferEncoding-Chunked variable is set to true. Chunking breaks up the request into chunk sizes and is then sent to the receiver to process a chunk at a time so that memory is not overwhelmed by the sheer size of the file. For instance, the receiver might start printing a graphic based on the content received even while the balance of the graphic object is still in transit.

Another topic for discussion is multiple documents using the same create-job id. In theory this works by setting the "last-document" attribute to false for all but the last document to be processed. On the last document, the "last-document" attribute is then set to true to indicate that this is the last document being sent. As with other features of the IPP standard, this is not required and is not supported on some printer models, my home HP M528 printer being one of them. The printer attribute "multiple-document-jobs-supported" must be true if you plan to use this feature.

We added a few new requests to the original library we started in Chapter 5, "IPP Standards Print." The Get-Jobs, Identify-Printer, Get-Job-Attributes, and finally Pause-Printer and Resume-Printer requests were added to the library. Most importantly, the way to add a new request in the future was covered. The process is straightforward once the required attributes for the request are known - and those (attributes) can be found in the RFCs for IPP online. When you have created a new request, test it against an existing printer that supports the request. To be more accurate, you should test any new request against a virtual IPP printer such as IppServer, since this will confirm conformity to RFC standards. As always, monitoring the network view with Wireshark is necessary for development.

The details of how the returned byte stream is processed for printer attributes are discussed using (tedious) bitwise manipulation code. When possible, this is done asynchronously to try and avoid any GUI hangs typically associated with blocking network calls. I should point out that the code cannot be assumed to be thread-safe nor re-entrant, so beware of this limitation in any testing.

Finally, the chapter touches on working in Basic authentication into the library. While not encrypted itself, paired with IPPS, Basic authentication can be implemented without fear of your password being compromised. Never use Basic authentication with IPP as the password can be compromised by anyone doing a basic packet trace. Traditionally, printers in a network environment rely on the OS for authentication of security principles, although newer biometric and card-based readers can provide some improvement to this. For IPP/IPPS, OAuth promises an improvement for authorization by a token issuer that the network trusts. The time-limited token is used for subsequent requests and can be revoked for any breach of security the issuer detects. This will probably be the authentication protocol of choice in the future.

References

1. Difference Between Authentication and Authorization, Geeks for Geeks, `https://www.geeksforgeeks.org/difference-between-authentication-and-authorization/`
2. Print User Authentication Methods: Your Guide to Improved Security, NPM Awesome, Fabrice Arnoux, `https://www.npmawesome.com/print-user-authentication-methods-guide/`
3. 401 Unauthorized , Mdn Web Docs, `https://developer.mozilla.org/en-US/docs/Web/HTTP/Reference/Status/401`
4. HttpResponseHeaders.TransferEncodingChunked Property, Microsoft Learn, `https://learn.microsoft.com/en-us/dotnet/api/system.net.http.headers.httpresponseheaders.transferencodingchunked?view=net-9.0`
5. Request for Comments: 8011, January 2017, `https://www.rfc-editor.org/rfc/pdfrfc/rfc8011.txt.pdf`
6. What is authentication?, Microsoft Security, `https://www.microsoft.com/en-us/security/business/security-101/what-is-authentication? msockid= 3ac7123563956f5 3338e07eb62386ea5`
7. IPP Authentication Methods, The Printer Working Group, August 16, 2019, `https://ftp.pwg.org/pub/pwg/informational/bp-ippauth10-20190816-5199.10.pdf`
8. Request for Comments: 8011, January 2017, `https://www.rfc-editor.org/rfc/pdfrfc/rfc8011.txt.pdf`

CHAPTER 7

Enterprise Conversion

This chapter is concerned with conversion – the one from legacy print protocols such as port 9100, WS-Print, and LPR to IPPS. While every network or enterprise can benefit by adopting IPP/IPPS as their print protocol, for Windows-based components the incentive to convert is particularly high. Assuming you have convinced management to make the wise leap from legacy print protocols, you will need a way to ensure the change is as seamless a transition as possible. While not a complex task, you will need to do sufficient planning to ensure all bases of print services are covered. For instance, while client-server print transition should be straightforward to plan, have you ensured that mainframe or midrange print services were considered? Have you ensured that no enterprise application or script will be affected by the transition? Have you planned to remove legacy print protocol services from network printers? Have you planned to remove legacy print drivers from the client and server machines in the network, and if so, how will this be done? As expected, planning the conversion is essential to the project's eventual success. Obviously, there is not a singular method that would cover all networks, but there are key points that need to be addressed in any enterprise.

You should plan to canvas all the print service stakeholders in your company or enterprise. Do not omit any component, whether it is Unix, Linux, Mainframe, Mid-Range, or any OS employed in your company. Remember that LPR and port 9100 print span OS platforms, not just the Windows OS. In my own enterprise, we had TN3270 and CICS clients whose standard print requests would normally be fulfilled via existing emulator printer sessions. However, there was also a mainframe component whose VTAM output was routed via a table of LU addresses. These addresses were then dereferenced by a lookup table to a corresponding IP address that allowed for direct print via port 9100. Had we not inquired for all components to discuss existing print services, we might have overlooked this and caused a

J. Marion, *Adopting Internet Printing Protocol for Windows*, https://doi.org/10.1007/979-8-8688-2010-6_7

service outage when physical printers had legacy print protocols removed. As it was, there was a delay of 12 months for the vendor to provide an IPP/IPPS print alternative to their existing product line before we proceeded.

You will also need to canvass your existing print hardware pool within your enterprise. While most printers sold in the last 10-15 years boast IPP/IPPS service capability, the degree to which they comply with the protocol standards may vary. What is the minimum version of IPP you wish to support on your network? The Windows IPP (Internet Printing Protocol) class driver primarily supports IPP versions 1.0 and 1.1, so older printers that support IPP may be fine. These versions enable basic printing functionalities over a network, allowing for features like job management and printer status monitoring. Despite Windows' current support for IPP 1.0/1.1, you might want your hardware printers to support IPP version 1.1 or greater. You should also inquire (of your print hardware vendor) if they plan on providing firmware updates that will provide newer IPP versions as they come out. That is because later IPP versions introduce newer features and services for job management, job status notification, advanced finishing, better media handling, and security enhancements.[1]

How will you find out whether your existing print hardware fleet investment will support a desired version of IPP? Optimally, you would have a homogeneous printer fleet where the IPP version was consistent throughout. Since this is probably not practical, the best way would be to execute IPP Get-Printer-Attributes request(s) at each of the printer(s). Optimally, you might do this by specifying the attribute you want, such as **ipp-versions-supported** in the attributes-requested field of the request. Obviously, printers that do not support the desired level of IPP should either have firmware updates to bring the printer up to desired specs, or failing that, have the printer retired from service. While management might be hesitant to take a functional printer out of service, it should be argued that the operational cost of allowing older print hardware and protocols (port 9100/LPR) to remain in service far outweighs any near-term financial gains.

This chapter covers a broad range of topics essential for ensuring a seamless enterprise-wide conversion to IPP/IPPS and subsequently to Windows Protected Print. Careful coordination and planning are critical for achieving the best possible transition.

---

[1] Note: There isn't really an "IPP/1.1" or "IPP/2.1" certification program - only Mopria, Ipp Everywhere, or AirPrint.

We begin by exploring the evolution of IPP, enabling you to select the minimum version that aligns with your environment's needs. Next, we discuss potential challenges in Pass-through printing and PowerShell IPP printing, providing solutions for these common issues. We also address IPPS and printer certificate management, outlining best practices for secure deployments. Following that, we walk through the necessary steps to transition both print servers (if used) and clients to IPP/IPPS, whether for print connections or direct-printing scenarios. Finally, we conclude the chapter by guiding you through the process of enabling Windows Protected Print on both print servers (if applicable) and client systems.

The Evolution of IPP

Over the years, the IPP protocol has added more operations and advanced operations to its arsenal of capabilities. The first iteration, version 1.0, was primarily focused on validating the job and ultimately printing. Later, more sophisticated operations were added, such as pausing the printer, purging jobs on the printer, and creating subscriptions. While each printer will return a version of IPP supported, that itself might not tell the whole story. We start by looking at the versions of IPP and then look at certification programs that tell a more complete story.

IPP/1.0 (April 1999)

This version was the initial version and set forth the basics of the protocol. Major attention was focused on basic print operations that the client could initiate [9][10][11]. If you observe Wireshark traces from Windows IPP print requests, you should notice that this version pretty much covers what the Microsoft IPP Class driver provides. These Operation Requests included:

1. Print Job
2. Print-URI
3. Validate-Job
4. Create-Job
5. Send-Document
6. Send-URI

7. Cancel-Job
8. Get-Job-Attributes
9. Get-Jobs
10. Get-Printer-Attributes

IPP/1.1 (September 2000)

This version eventually became the accepted standard while adding a few more operations geared towards print operators [12]. It includes everything from IPP/1.0 plus the following requests:

1. Pause-Printer
2. Resume-Printer
3. Purge-Jobs

IPP/2.0 (July 2009)

This version introduced a few more advanced operations like subscriptions, notifications, etc. [13][14].

The following were operations introduced:

1. Hold-Job
2. Release-Job
3. Set-Job-Attributes
4. Set-Printer-Attributes
5. Get-Subscriptions
6. Create-Printer-Subscriptions
7. Create-Job-Subscriptions
8. Renew-Subscription
9. Cancel-Subscription
10. Get-Notifications

IPP/2.1 (July 2009)

IPP/2.2 (February 2011, 2015 Upgrade)[2]

This upgrade added more sophisticated features such as advanced finishing and job management [15][16]. The following were operations introduced:

1. Restart-Job
2. Suspend-Current-Job
3. Resume-Job
4. Promote-Job
5. Schedule-Job-After

Printer Certification/Standards

Alternatively, you may be better off planning printer purchases based on certification standards rather than supported IPP version. In fact, this is the better way to ensure your printer is supported by the OS you plan to employ it in. As this book is concerned primarily with adoption from a Windows perspective, a printer model with Mopria certification is mandatory for Windows Protected Print (WPP); keep this in mind. The following table shows the 3 certification or standards bodies that ensure driverless print.

Certification/Standard	Mopria	IPP Everywhere	AirPrint
Group	Mopria Alliance	PWG (Printer Working Group)	Apple
Transport	IPP over HTTP/S	IPP over HTTP/S	IPP over HTTP/S
Discovery Protocol	mDNS, WS-Discovery	mDNS	mDNS
IPP Print Protocol	IPP 1.1 / 2.0	IPP 2.0 (based on RFC 8011)	IPP 2.0
Required Document Formats	PDF, JPEG, PWG Raster	PWG Raster	PDF, JPEG, Apple Raster (URF)
Authentication	Optional, (must support none)	None (strictly unauthenticated)	Optional, (must support none)
Color / Duplex Requirements	Declared via IPP attribute if supported	Required to report in capabilities	Required to report in capabilities
Driverless Printing	Yes	Yes	Yes
Scanning Support	Yes (Mopria Scan)	No	Yes (AirScan)
Certification Required?	Yes (for Mopria logo)	No (open standard)	Yes (Apple MFi program)
Mobile App Support	Android Print Service Plugin	None	iOS built-in

Thus, if your printer is certified as Mopria-compliant, it will support all the features listed in the table above.

[2] IPP/2.0, IPP/2.1, and IPP/2.2 were all "upgraded" (to full standard) in 2015.

The evolution of the IPP protocol has been a tale of consistent improvements over the original proposal. The minimum version of IPP on your printers, therefore, is tightly coupled with the IPP operations your enterprise requires. For instance, if your enterprise design requires Notifications or Subscriptions, then your print hardware will need to support IPP 2.0 at a minimum. If, however, you only require the basic IPP functionality of version 1.0, then you might be able to repurpose older existing print hardware that supports this version. However, keep in mind that *Windows requires printers to be Mopria certified in the event you plan on enabling WPP*. The issue becomes a bit murkier in regard to OS support. For instance, Wireshark traces reveal that while the IPP Class Driver supports Validate-Job, Create-Job, and Send-Document, the status of the job is recovered via Get-Job-Attributes called repeatedly (polling) until job completion. While Mopria supports IPP version 2.0, I have never seen the IPP Class Driver in Wireshark register for Subscriptions or receive Notifications.

Planning decisions should also revolve around whether IPP will be the exclusive print protocol allowed on the network or not. Do you wish to completely remove other print protocols (such as port 9100, WS-Print, and LPR) from the printers, or do you wish to run legacy print protocols simultaneously with IPP? The former choice requires much more detailed planning and cooperation from client sites since planners must ensure all print processes can operate using IPP/IPPS. The latter allows you to slowly implement IPP in the enterprise without inadvertently causing print service outages but could inhibit the implementation schedule of Windows Protected Print (WPP). Remember, to implement WPP, all V3 drivers must be removed from active service on the Windows machine. If you do not plan on implementing WPP, then your job of introducing IPP to the enterprise is much easier. However, this is certainly not a best practice that Microsoft would approve of, as it may ultimately compromise your network and expose your printer fleet (unnecessarily) to malicious exploits.

Going further, you might also want to think about ancillary protocols that provided feature detection and information for the legacy protocols, particularly port 9100 and LPR. For instance, it is well documented that SNMPv1 and SNMPv2c are not secure. This is because both versions use plain text “community strings” that are vulnerable to discovery via network sniffers. This leaves printers implementing these versions open to reconfiguring the printer using SET commands via the hijacked private community string. At the very least, you should consider upgrading the SNMP version to SNMPv3, which supports a user-based security model (username and password), authentication, and encryption [24].

Are My Printers Compatible with Modern Print?

For your conversion to IPP/IPPS and then ultimately to Windows Protected Print (WPP) to be successful, your printers must be compatible with Microsoft's Modern Print standards. According to Microsoft documentation, "Modern print does not require the installation of drivers from the printer manufacturer. Since drivers from the printer manufacturer do not need to be installed, it provides a simple, streamlined, and secure printing experience compared to traditional printers, regardless of the Windows device architecture. Modern print is designed to work with Mopria-certified printers, and many existing printers are already compatible with modern print" [20]. While the need to comply with IPP standards is intuitive, it is also imperative that your printers support Mopria as well. The Windows Protected Print mode is designed to work with Mopria-certified printers only [20]. You can consult the list published by the Mopria Alliance to see if existing or prospective hardware meets the standard. The link is here:

```
https://mopria.org/certified-products
```

to check for Mopria certification. If there is any doubt as to the capability of your hardware, you can always check using the IppCheck tool in the code section for the addendum to this book.

Pass-Through Printing

Speaking of any TN3270 or 5250 clients, are you sure your emulation software can use the Microsoft IPP class driver? Have you tested this capability for all the mainframe applications used in your enterprise? For example, some of the earlier mainframe applications had PCL encoded in their print session data – this ensures the mainframe print job is already preformatted for print. For the IBM PCOMM emulator, this was handled by using a PCOMM PDT (Printer Definition Table) file for data conversion (also EBCDIC to ASCII conversion) along with Windows pass-through code to send the print stream directly to the printer without providing additional print driver processing. This works for printers that listen for port 9100 as the print stream was essentially "RAW" and ready for print. However, this type of print stream will not work on IPP printers as they will likely not understand the encoded PCL characters, and there will be no IPP print requests (Create-Job, Send-Document) created. A different approach needs to be found for pass-through printing using an IPP printer. A good start might be converting the previous EBCDIC/PCL data stream (from the mainframe) to ASCII and then PDF. As of this writing, IBM has provided a new library for PCOMM emulators that is compatible with IPP/IPPS printers. The lesson here is to be wary of any applications that employ pass-through printing. Pass-through printing is a method where a print stream (from an application or outside process) sends raw print data to the printer directly through Windows with little or no processing by the print driver. Thus, the print stream bypasses additional processing or modification from the Windows print subsystem, ensuring that the raw stream is sent to the printer exactly as it left the source.

Of course, for this to work, you would need a printer that could interpret the PCL stream correctly, so port 9100 print would have to be enabled and active. Additionally, Windows must allow passthrough printing and not alter the print stream, and finally, the Windows port monitor must channel the print stream to the intended target. If you are interested in how this could be done programmatically, the URL below describes how to send data directly to a printer [8].

`https://learn.microsoft.com/en-us/windows/win32/printdocs/sending-data-directly-to-a-printer`

A useful method to uncover potential IPP/IPPS conversion issues is to take all print protocols off the physical printer, leaving only IPP and IPPS print services available. Start with just one printer on the network and ask selected test users to send jobs to that printer. Of course, this test assumes you have installed the Microsoft IPP class driver on all the clients. If you start having complaints about certain applications not printing (whether client-server, mainframe, Linux, etc.), you can quickly narrow down the issue and (if necessary) convert the printer configuration back to its original state. In this manner, you can process the outcome of iterative development tests with continuous refinement based on client feedback to obtain the best implementation strategy based on your unique network requirements. Remember, however, that any exception should be temporary with the understanding that a solution must be reached: your ability to implement Microsoft WPP requires IPP/IPPS implementation without type 3 print drivers loaded. While doing these tests, you should also be vigilant for any irregularities such as extra pages printed, illegible characters, or other problems that end users might object to. In some cases, you might need the developer(s) to step in and make modifications to rectify any issues that arise.

One of the most pressing matters is automation – IPP is implemented in Windows on WSD ports. My company needed a way to automate installing IPP/IPPS printers on user workstations with the preferred network printers. If your network relies primarily on print connections (i.e., Point and Print), then your job is significantly easier to accomplish. If your company uses direct printers, your job is a bit more involved. Either way, this book provides code written in C# (PowerShell as well) that you can use to accomplish these tasks if you do not relish doing this on a per-machine basis via the GUI. You will need to provide the printer connections or names to install on the user machine, and just as likely, the printer to remove. You do not want to go through this conversion (IPP/IPPS) only to find out holdouts are still printing on leftover port 9100 printers or print connections. Remember that users may not know (or care) about what type of printer is used if it works.

PowerShell Printing Issues

Many printing issues regarding Windows (when using the IPP Class Driver) come down to documents or files not formatted in a Page Description Language (PDL) the printer can natively understand. When a document is sent to the printer using the GDI spooling path (in other words, using the in-box IPP class driver), the format is likely to meet the PDL set required by the IPP/IPPS printer. This is because the versions of PDF supported on the printer are returned to Windows 11 via the Get-Printer-Attributes request (and set by Mopria), so the IPP class driver can then format the document to meet that standard. For instance, my HP 528 printer returns a supported MIME type of application/pdf as one of the MIME types the printer can natively handle. When trying to print a test PDF file using PowerShell's Get-Content cmdlet, I discovered the print output was incorrectly formatted, with a lot of extraneous characters embedded in the output. In PowerShell ISE, I had been using the Get-Content cmdlet and piping out the results to Out-Printer to print. For instance, the following might be used to print a file to the network printer: **Get-Content -Path C:\Temp\Test.pdf | Out-Printer HPM528.** What I was unaware of is that the Get-Content cmdlet processes the test.pdf as text (rather than binary for PDF) by default, even if the file is binary. This means Get-Content wants to process the binary data of a PDF file as a UTF-encoded text. You can imagine what this does - sending a mess of garbled ASCII characters to the printer. In this case, the printer did not recognize the file as a PDF, resulting in the incorrect formatting that I was experiencing. Equally confusing was the Wireshark trace that showed good request handling – i.e., Get-Printer-Attributes, Validate-Job, Create-Job, Send-Document, and finally a slew of Get-Job-Attributes until the final "job-completed-successfully" result was returned to the sender. While the IPP requests succeeded and the job was successfully printed, the outcome was not as expected. Bottom line: Do not use the PowerShell Get-Content cmdlet to process binary files like PDFs (to print on IPP printers) as it may interpret the file as text, and the results are disappointing at best.

If you need to send a PDF to an IPP/IPPS printer in PowerShell, the following script (using the same file as above) will work:

```
# Start the print process and get the process object
$process = Start-Process -FilePath "C:\Temp\GroupPolicy.pdf" -Verb
PrintTo -ArgumentList "HPM528" -PassThru

# Wait for the printing process to complete
$process.WaitForExit()

# Check the exit code (if needed)
Write-Output "Printing completed with exit code: $($process.ExitCode)"
```

In the code section of this chapter there is a PowerShell script (PdfPrint.ps1, in the PowerShell folder) that allows you to pass the file to print and the IPP printer name in as below:

```
.\PdfPrint.ps1 -file "C:\Temp\GroupPolicy.pdf" -printer "HPM528"
```

IPPS and Printer Certificates

As you know, IPP is based on the HTTP protocol, inheriting the security model composed therein. HTTPS, and by association IPPS, both use TLS encryption as a way of ensuring message integrity on the network. TLS is the successor to SSL and features a handshake protocol that is more efficient and secure as compared to SSL. Even so, TLS has undergone several upgrades to keep it current, the latest being version 1.3, the current standard. The main attribute of TLS is the ability to defeat man-in-the-middle attacks, where a nefarious agent impersonates the intended communication partner. This is accomplished by exchanging digital certificates to identify the printer, ensuring the client is communicating with the intended target. Additionally, TLS ensures data integrity by using message authentication codes (MACs) to detect any tampering during transmission and message encryption to prevent eavesdropping on the network.

Printer Certificate Validation Questions

Why does the browser connecting to a printer embedded web server (using a self-signed certificate) issue a warning, but IPPS connections still appear to work correctly on Windows? The reason may be that Windows accepts the printer's certificate as legitimate for establishing a TLS session despite the issuer not being trusted due to more lenient policies or concentration on confidentiality and integrity of the print job rather than strict identity verification. It is also possible that Windows might have cached or pre-approved the printer certificate or fingerprint, bypassing the strict CA trust check.

Obviously, the client must trust the Certificate Authority (CA) that creates the certificate employed by the printer during the exchange. In the event the browser or printer client cannot or does not trust the certificate authority that created the certificate being presented as evidence that the printer is the intended target, IPPS setup will fail. You can clearly see this happen if you connect to an embedded web server on the printer - if the certificate being presented by the printer web server is not trusted, you will see a warning and caution not to continue the communications session. The HttpClient being used for the C# IPP/IPPS library created back in Chapter 5, "IPP Standards Print," requires proper certification trust, or the TLS setup will fail and any IPPS communication attempt will throw an exception. Microsoft does provide a workaround to this, albeit at the expense of communications security and integrity.

```
if (m_bEncrypted)
{
    //Note: the following trusts all certs from all printers - you might
    want to change this for production.
    handler.ServerCertificateCustomValidationCallback = (message, cert,
    chain, errors) => true;
}
```

Above you can see that the function returns true regardless of the certificate being presented by the printer. While this allows for the IPPS communication setup to continue, it is obviously not good practice. On this note, I should state an observation: it appears that the Microsoft IPP Class driver does succeed in TLS session setup even though the very same printer will cause the HttpClient class TLS session setup to fail (if the callback is not coded to return true). This would suggest a more lenient certificate validation policy (by Windows OS) on network printer objects to reduce configuration complexity. On the surface, this appears reasonable as most network printers are within the corporate firewall (or should be) and thus do not pose the risk that outside-the-firewall web connections might.

A better result can be obtained by having a private CA to generate a certificate that can be used by all enterprise printers. Then, you can instruct the clients to trust the CA root certificate (and thus all certs derived from the authority). To do this:

1. Have a Private Certificate Authority (CA) to generate a certificate that can be used by all the printers in the enterprise. Better yet, have a unique cert for each printer from the same CA.

2. Install the printer certificate (issued by the CA) created in step 1 and the corresponding private key on all the printers. This allows the printer to present a valid certificate during TLS negotiation. This method assumes:

    A. The certificate is signed by a trusted CA.

    B. The certificate is not expired or revoked.

    C. The hostname matches the certificate Common Name (CN) or Subject Alternative Name (SAN).

3. The printers will present this certificate during secure connections (HTTPS, IPPS, etc.).

4. Export the CA root certificate for client(s) to trust.

5. Create or modify a group policy that installs the public root CA certificate to the client machines. Once the GPO is applied, the client machines should trust any certificate issued by your internal CA, including the certs that are used by the printers.

The above can be visualized as shown below:

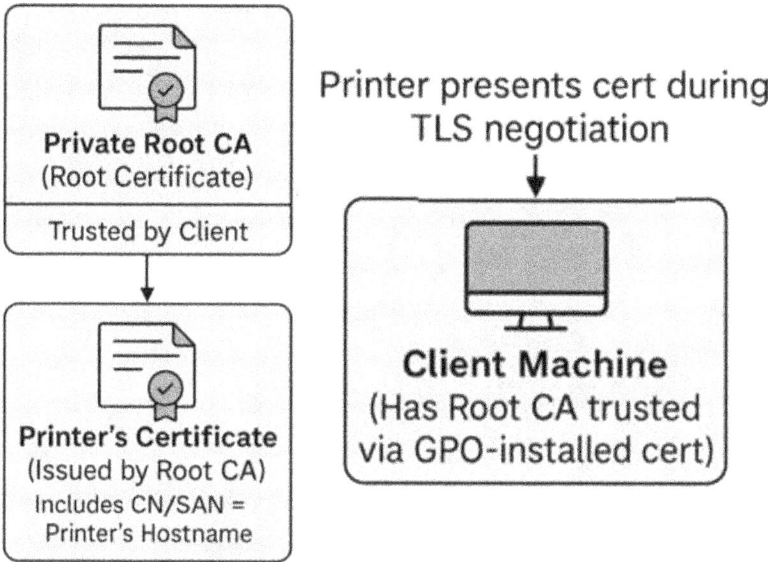

Printer Certificate Issued by Root CA That Is Trusted on the Client

A bonus obtained by this setup would be that clients should not see the trusted certificate warning when connecting to the printer's embedded web server. Short of this, you can also upgrade the HttpClient code for the C# IPP/IPPS library to at least check a few parameters within the printer certificate. Instead of returning true to all certificates received by the client, you could implement a few checks as shown below:

```
var handler = new HttpClientHandler();
handler.ServerCertificateCustomValidationCallback = (message, cert, chain,
sslPolicyErrors) =>
{
    if (sslPolicyErrors != SslPolicyErrors.None)
    {
        return false;
    }

    if (cert is X509Certificate2 certificate)
    {
        // Check the issuer
        if (certificate.Issuer != "CN=Your Trusted Issuer")
```

```
        {
            return false;
        }

        // Check the subject
        if (certificate.Subject != "CN=Your Printer")
        {
            return false;
        }

        // Check the expiration date
        if (DateTime.Now > certificate.NotAfter)
        {
            return false;
        }
    }

    return true;
};

var client = new HttpClient(handler);
```

The choice of implementation is yours, but the most flexible and secure would be to issue a certificate from a trusted private Certificate Authority as, in the end, this is the most secure.

Getting the Printers Configured

While most new printers support IPP/IPPS, you will have to ensure that these services are enabled. While briefly discussed in the section "Preparing Your Printer" in Chapter 2, "Printer Talk," it is impractical to handle this task without some form of automation. The purpose of this is obvious: reduction in manual configuration errors and providing documentation that the printer configuration was in fact modified. Depending on your printer vendor, several print management software frameworks exist to aid in IPP/IPPS configuration.

I loosely use the term "print management software frameworks" to describe vendor-based or provided solutions intended to optimize management of the vendor print hardware in enterprise environments. Some of these solutions are free, and some are fee-based, but all are specifically optimized for an intended product line. Examples include HP Web JetAdmin or Lexmark MarkVision software offerings. These offerings may also perform SNMP queries and provide general information about rival products using RFC 3805 MIB.

Hewlett-Packard provides the Web Jet Admin utility to configure HP print devices; MarkVision can do the same for Lexmark printers. Additionally, most print vendors now provide an embedded web server (EWS) to configure and maintain their print hardware. While it is feasible on smaller networks to connect to each printer individually (using the embedded web server) and make the necessary configurations to enable IPP/IPPS, on a larger enterprise this might prove impractical.

If you currently have Print Fleet Management Software (PFMS) installed or are planning to install a solution for your network, there are a few things to consider. The vast majority of PFMS solutions, whether vendor-supplied or universal, use SNMP for printer status and monitoring. As touched on in Chapter 1, "Windows Legacy Print," SNMP requires Management Information Base (MIB) files to gather detailed information from a base of OIDs. For a more universal look at print metrics, the RFCs 1759 and 3805 MIBs can be used on all vendor models, although the information gleaned is limited to standardized metrics stipulated in the RFC. If information and metrics about items such as toner usage, supply, serial numbers, etc. are all that you require, any of the PFMS solutions should suffice.

Ultimately, the needs of enterprise management, especially concerning networked printers, are typically much more demanding. Security and configuration settings are typical management needs, while firmware versioning is essential. Unfortunately, while vendors can agree to standardize SNMP metrics (at times), there is little standardization incentive for firmware updates or configuration settings. Market considerations conveyed by perceived design advantages means that each vendor provides firmware updates and configuration setting services in a proprietary manner. For corporate customers, this means islands of vendor fleet management software are required for any meaningful comprehensive network management solution. Thus, if you have purchased best-in-breed network printers from various manufacturers over the years, you are going to require several Print Fleet Management (PFMS) solutions to provide an automated approach to IPP/IPPS provisioning. I wish this were not the case, but these are the current market realities. In Chapter 10, "Additional Information," I will outline a few IPP extensions that can provide some universal standardization, provided the vendor supports the PWG recommendations. For now, a partial list of Print Fleet Management Software solutions that exist is shown below.

Available Print Management Solutions by Vendor

Vendor	Fleet Management Software
Hewlett-Packard	Web JetAdmin
Lexmark	MarkVision
Kyocera	Device Manager
Konica Minolta	Fleet RMM
Epson	Print Admin
Brother	BRAdmin Professional

My test network uses primarily HP hardware; thus, my provisioning examples employ HP Web JetAdmin to provision existing printers to IPP/IPPS. However, the concept of provisioning network printers remotely is a feature provided by many fleet management software suites. Typically, once printers are discovered by the PFMS suite, you may modify the particulars of their configuration.

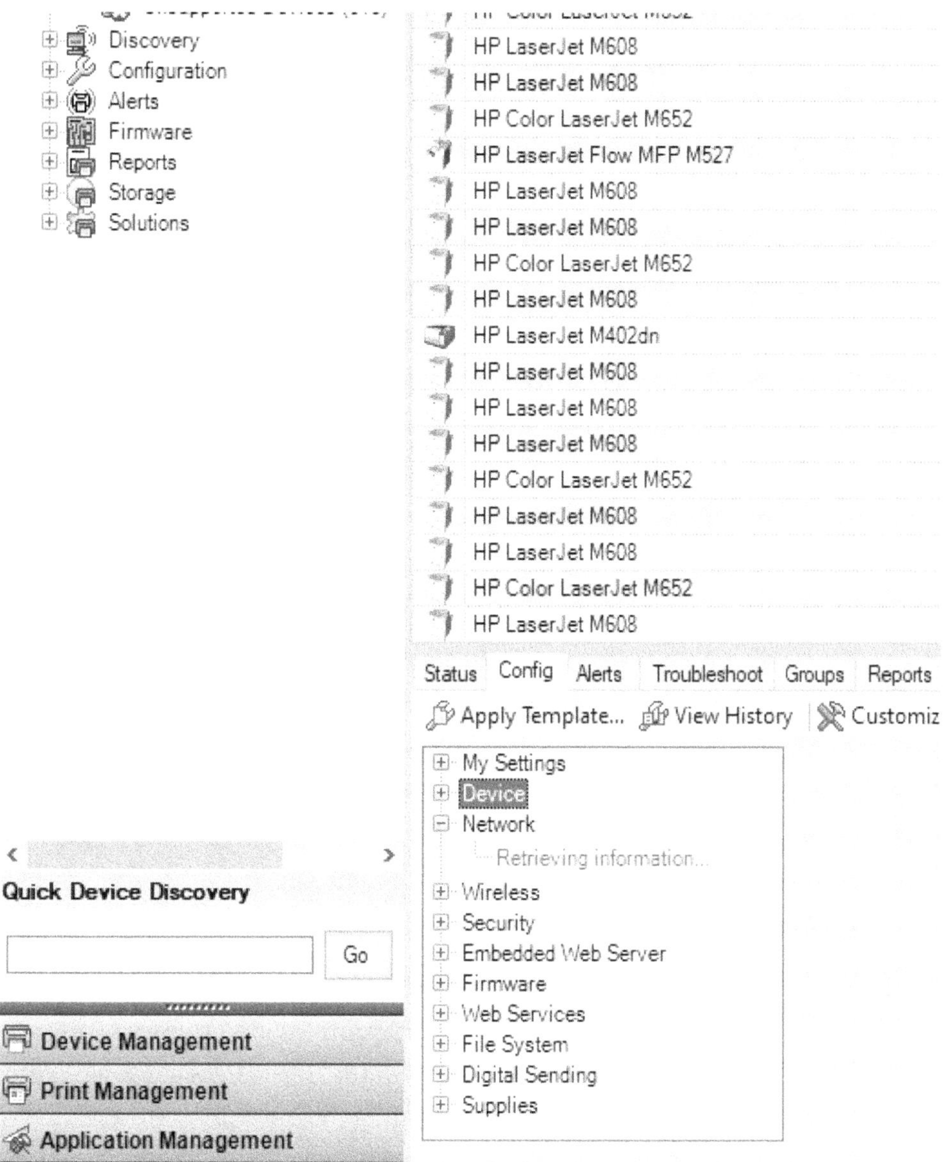

HP Web Jet Admin: Reading Printer Configuration Items

Depending on how fast your network is, the act of changing configuration items from the PFMS for any given printer may test your patience. Still, the ability to group printers by device type, physical location, firmware revision, IP address range, etc. makes project management a bit easier. Even better, most PFMS solutions provide comprehensive reporting ability, so queries on IPP/IPPS configuration status are available for management to peruse.

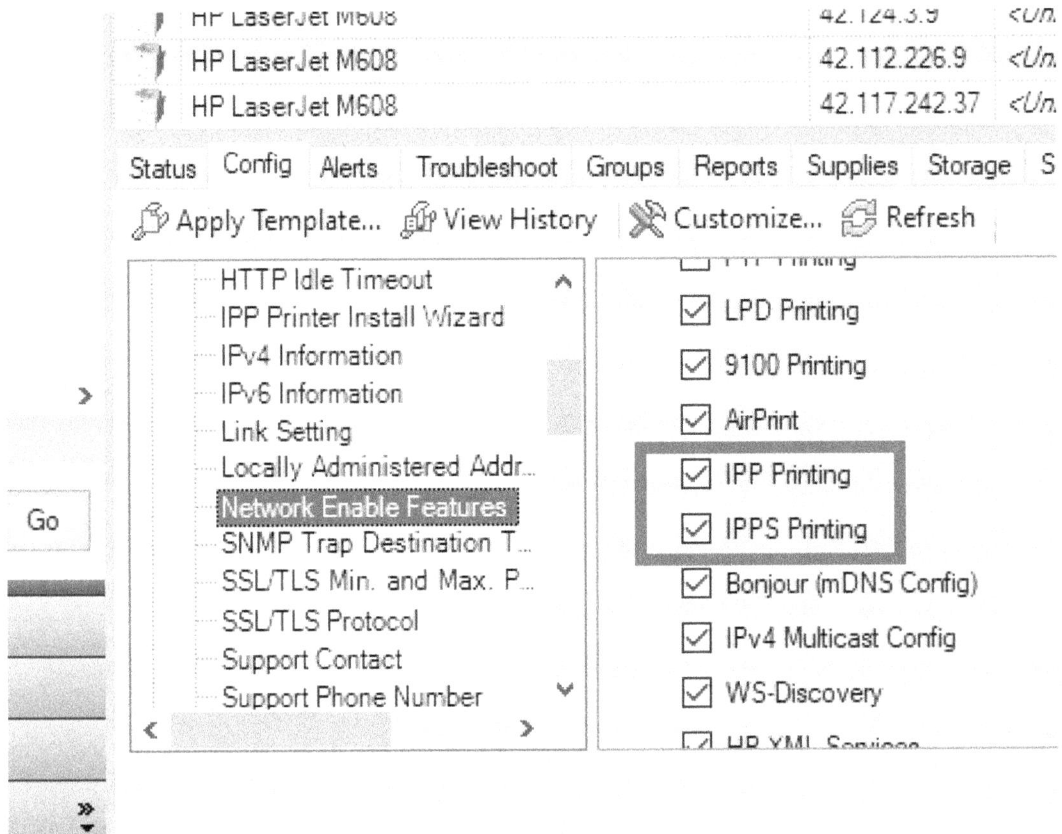

Web Jet Admin: Enabling IPP/IPPS Services

I would encourage you to engage in pilots prior to wholesale rollout of IPP/IPPS. As mentioned earlier in this chapter, you are likely to identify at least one application or vendor print system that is not fully compatible with IPP/IPPS. Pilot sites that represent prototypical print patterns and hardware representing the enterprise are a terrific way to identify these issues. While it is certainly possible to leave some legacy print protocol, such as port 9100 services, enabled on the printers, it is not always optimal. For instance, leaving port 9100 enabled on the printer assures that legacy print jobs can potentially continue to use unencrypted data streams, providing nefarious listening entities with a security vector to exploit. Furthermore, leaving legacy protocols enabled on the printer(s) does not provide incentive to remove legacy drivers; in the end, this will be a maintenance nightmare.

The maintenance nightmare scenario of leaving port 9100 enabled on printers is not a trivial issue. Consider that enabling Windows protected print mode (which is best practice to reduce vulnerability concerns) only provides printing to Mopria-certified printers that support a subset of inbox Windows print drivers [7]. If any of your clients continues to rely on the port 9100 protocol print, you will then be forced to delay WPP adoption. Optimally, the application developers would fix the issue promptly; otherwise, the adoption of WPP could potentially stall.

Windows 11 Print and Standard Users

There are a few idiosyncrasies in what operations Windows 11 allows a standard user to perform for printer management. First, I should define what a "standard user" is - at least for the purposes of this book. For our purposes, a standard user is one who does not possess elevated security credentials - i.e., this user is not an admin on the machine and has only basic user rights. Oddly, Windows 11 does not provide a convenient way to remove local printers but is allowed to add a local IPP or IPPS printer using the AddIppPrinter utility.

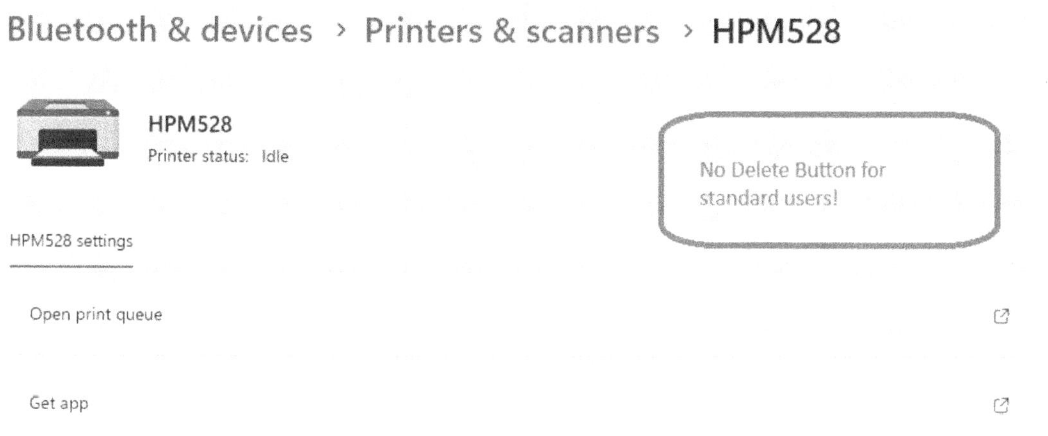

Bluetooth & devices › Printers & scanners › HPM528

HPM528

Printer status: Idle

No Delete Button for standard users!

HPM528 settings

Open print queue

Get app

A Standard User in Printers and Scanners Does Not See a Remove or Delete Button for Legacy Local Printers

```
C:\Users\Tester>"D:\BACKUP\IPP Book\Chap2\Code\AddIppPrinter\bin\Release\AddIppPrinter.exe" /p=HPM528 /s=631
Success: IPP printer created from HPM528
```

As you can see above, running the AddIppPrinter utility as a standard user is successful provided the printer is online and has not been created. This is in stark contrast to removing existing legacy printers, which a standard user cannot do. Keep this in mind when dealing with local printer removal (or addition) when working on client machines. Print connections from the server, of course, can be added/removed without issue.

I should clarify why the observed behavior is true. The restrictions on (local) legacy printers are due to the type V3 printer driver(s) and potential network port(s). Adding or removing printer ports required of legacy printers involves changes to system settings that potentially require administrative privileges. This is because printer ports affect how the operating system communicates with the hardware and thus impact system stability and security. In the context of IPP, the "port" does not refer to a physical port like those used in traditional networked or USB connections. Instead, it represents a network endpoint (usually an IP address and a port number, such as 631 for IPP) that the client employs to communicate with the printer. IPP printers utilize the modern driver model V4, which are typically installed per user under HKCU\printers\connection and do not require elevation, as they are not kernel mode drivers.

Converting Existing Installed Printers to IPP/IPPS on Client Machines

Because most IT networks have large bases of existing Windows clients to convert to IPP/IPPS, the process of replacing the existing print services on these clients may appear formidable. This is especially true for those clients who have local printers already installed. For those clients using connections from a print server, the process is a bit easier to complete. Users need no special security context to either add or remove print connections. In the world of IPP/IPPS printer conversion, print connections are the low-hanging fruit.

I should add a proviso here for networks that have employed print nightmare restrictions via group policy – in those networks clients that run Type 3 print drivers may not be able to add print connections if the print server is not in the "trusted" server list distributed by group policy. Luckily, IPP clients use the MS IPP Driver, which is a Type 4 driver and thus not restricted as Type 3 drivers were. This is true since they do not download third-party configuration files and libraries that have proven to be vulnerable to exploits. Just another reason to convert to IPP/IPPS – escape from cumbersome print nightmare restrictions.

While there are several ways to get IPP/IPPS print connections on the client, for the purposes of this chapter, the focus will be on systematic and programmatic ways to accomplish this. While it is possible to manually remove unwanted legacy print connections and add IPP/IPPS print connections on each client machine in an enterprise, the time and labor to do this make this unreasonable. Thus, converting entire offices of Windows clients to IPP/IPPS print connections really boils down to several options. This chapter will cover conversion of printer connections (from the print server) as a separate task from conversion of client local (direct) printers as they differ in how they are handled.

Client Side: Conversion of Print Connections via Group Policy

An administrator can provide group policy to specify which print connections an office will use. In this case the Windows policy would be a user-based policy (as opposed to a machine policy) since print connections are stored in the HKCU registry hive for each user. This also means that, assuming unique printer DNS names throughout your enterprise, the policy created should be customized (and attached) for each Organizational Unit (OU) in your enterprise. Group policy is a relatively robust technology and well-integrated into Windows, so this approach is certainly worth investigating.

For fine-grain control, it might be advantageous to employ group policy preferences. In the Group Policy Management Console (GPMC), you would need to edit (or create) a Group Policy Object (GPO). The printer deployment section should be used:

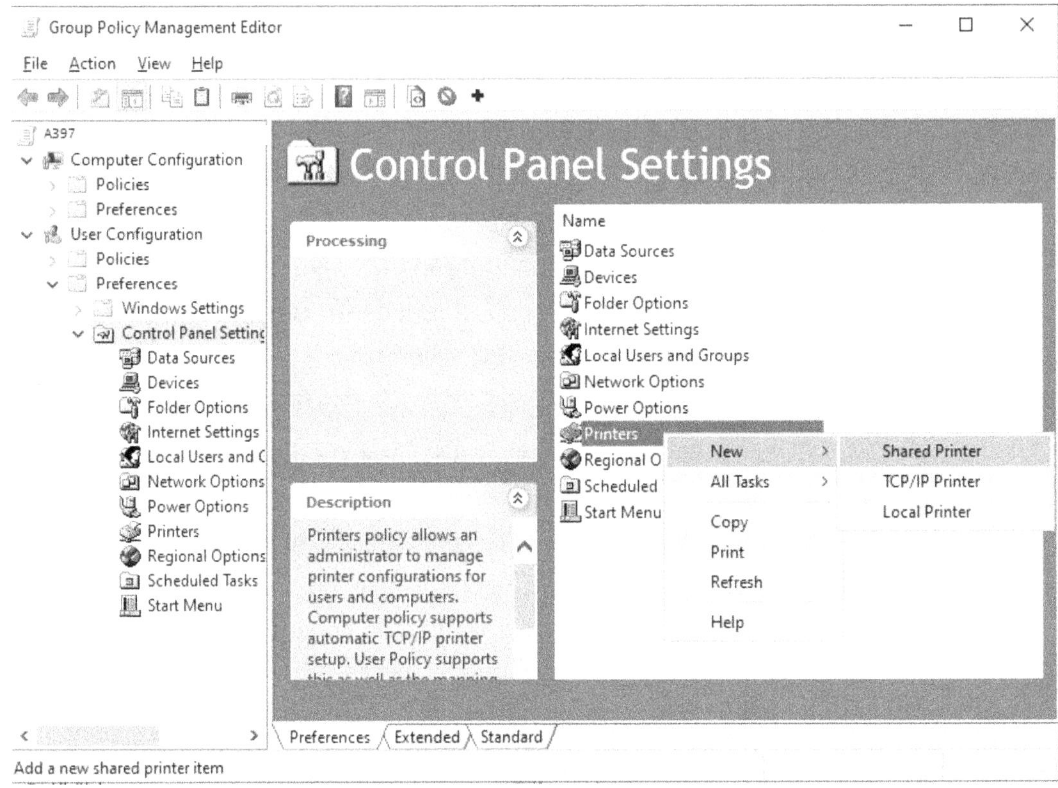

Create a Group Policy Printer Deployment

In GPMC, navigate to: User Configuration ➤ Preferences ➤ Control Panel Settings ➤ Printers. Here you will add a shared printer. To do this:

1. Right-click **Printers ➤ New ➤ Shared Printer**.
2. "Update" or "Create."
3. In the Share Path, enter the printer UNC path (i.e., \\ServerName\PrinterName)
4. Optionally, check "Set this printer as default" if needed.
5. Repeat for all printers you want to add.

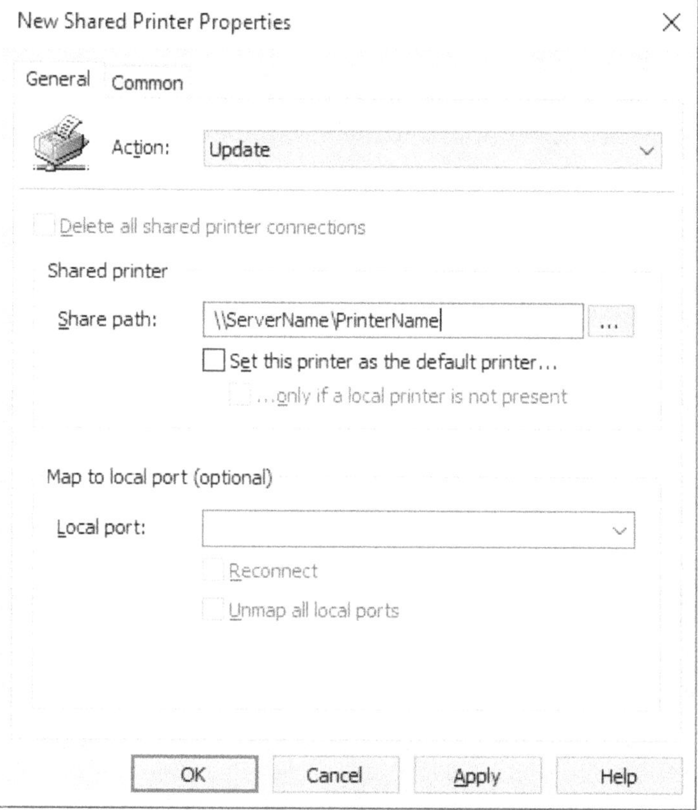

Add the Server and Printer Name to the Share Path

Once all the printers are created, you will have to scope the policy to target users or groups. To do this, check **item-level targeting** to designate the users, computers, or security groups to filter how the GPO is applied. Finally, you will need to link the GPO to an Organizational Unit (OU), which houses the targeted users. To test, log onto a machine in the targeted OU as a user specified in the GPO. Run **gpupdate /force** to ensure the policy is applied – now check to see if the correct printers appear.

This approach works well for small or highly structured domain architectures where printer names are derived from a central logical framework. For instance, if the first printer in Site A would thus be named PrinterA1, the second PrinterA2, and so forth, a group policy could easily be created to cover this scenario. But what if the printer names were not derived from such a structured approach, and the enterprise was on a larger scale? In this case, the creation of such group policies, at least from a centralized authority, might prove cumbersome and difficult to maintain. Also, any changes to the locally targeted environment would not be reflected (to the clients) until the GPO was modified.

For these reasons, another approach might warrant your consideration as a solution.

Client Side: Conversion of Print Connections via Customized Script or Code

In some cases, the application of customized scripts or software might be a better approach - especially for larger, dynamic environments prone to intermittent changes or modifications. In this case, it would be ideal if the script or utility would dynamically discover shared printers from a print server and then reflect those changes to the clients. Of course, this approach is not novel to IPP/IPPS environments, and as a result I had created such a utility years ago for legacy applications. This approach allows for high scalability and flexibility and is especially applicable in larger, less structured environments. If this scenario might be advantageous to your network, consider the AddSharedIppPrinters solution available in the code section of this chapter. The program requires a Windows print server name (from the local network) to which the utility will query for shared IPP/IPPS printers.

Optionally, the utility can filter the IPP/IPPS print connections returned (and installed) by location. However, since you have the source code, you may implement whatever changes your own environment might require. The utility does provide a way to remove old print connections by the **purge** option, which allows the client to remove all legacy print connections and install new IPP/IPPS print connections in one action. Note that the program uses the print server name set by the /ps option on the command line. The core of the utility is in the MiniPrintLib class, under the Print folder of the solution. Here, the Interop functionality necessary to implement the utility is defined. Central to this is the ServerEnumPrinters function that takes as arguments the print server name and a reference to the PrinterConnections class. This function does the actual print connection enumeration on the target print server using the Windows EnumPrinter API. Feel free to debug this and modify the source code as you wish. The AddSharedIppPrinters solution uses p/Invoke methods from the Win32 APIS to perform the shared printer addition, but you can investigate the .NET System.Printing namespace as well.

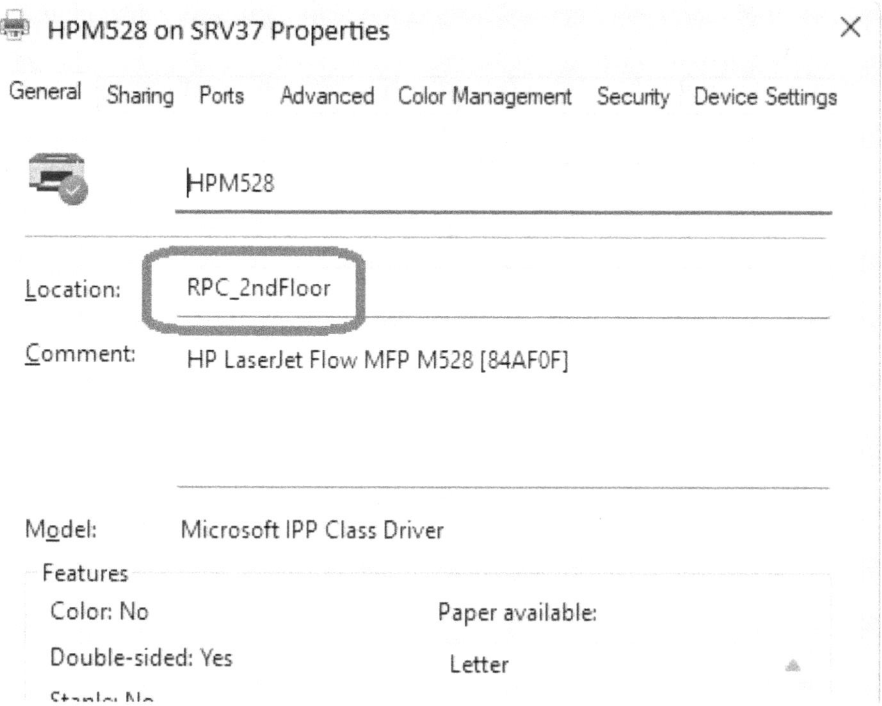

Location Field on Shared Printer

Specifying /pl option with comma-delimited location string(s) will provide filtering based on the Location entry value seen when reviewing printer properties on the server. The utility will then add only print connections whose location field string (see above) matches one of the comma-delimited strings from the /pl option on the command line.

When new IPP/IPPS printer connections are added to the client, they are stored in the **HKEY_CURRENT_USER\Printers\Connections** registry hive for each user. Thus, connections persist through power or logon cycles, so the utility or script only needs to be run once to add (or modify) connections. However, if the user were to travel to another office, or new printers were added to the existing environment, the utility would have to be run again to reflect the network modifications. Luckily, Windows clients need no special rights to run the utility as all changes affect only their personal user profile.

It might be a good idea to run the utility from a central location (like a file server). This way, users can update their print environment to IPP/IPPS after you have added IPP/IPPS printers to the print server.

Create a shared folder (on a server) that contains the utility and a batch file the users can run. For instance, if your server was named SRV57 with a shared folder called IppUpgrade, you might create a batch file with the command:

```
\\SRV57\IppUpgrade\ AddSharedIppPrinters.exe /ps=MyPrintServer /purge
```

To remove all previous print connections and add all the IPP/IPPS print connections to the client from the server. In a larger environment, you might create several batch files with location filtering that adds only the closest shared printers for a user based on location. For instance:

```
\\SRV57\IppUpgrade\ AddSharedIppPrinters.exe /ps=MyPrintServer /purge /
pl=flr2A, flr2B
```

which would add only the IPP/IPPS print connections from the server printer whose location field included flr2A or flr2B to the local client.

Client Side: Conversion of Local Printers via Customized Script or Code

Conversion of existing local network printers on the client to IPP/IPPS is not nearly as dynamic as with print connections. That is because the changes made to shared printers on the print server are replicated to the clients via the "Point and Print" connection. That does not mean the task is insufferably difficult or tedious; it does mean you need a bit more planning to accomplish this successfully. To start off with, you will need to know the DNS names of all the printers (both old and new) that you either plan to convert or install on the network. A good step would be to put this information in an accessible location (in the cloud or on a server) for the clients or admins of the site to access when needed. You should plan who (or what computers) requires local printers and which printers are closest to where the user of the computer sits. Decide if your users are technical enough to manage local IPP/IPPS printer installation. If your users cannot or should not handle this responsibility, then you will need to allocate help for the site to manage this task. One issue that might arise is one of security context: simply put, most standard (non-administrative) users are not able to delete the local (non-IPP) printers. Keep this in mind as you consider your conversion options.

Decide whether you will remove the existing legacy local (networked) printers or will leave them in place. Best practice will be to remove them, and long term that should be your goal. The help desk will thank you for not leaving local printers (on the client) with ports to printers that no longer accept legacy print connections (or even exist). To aid in this task, look into the Code folder for this chapter for a C# solution called RmLocalPrinters. This project can remove local printers from local or remote machines that do not use the IPP Class driver and tests each printer port so as not to delete software printers. As always, you should test this utility out in a lab and make any adjustments you might require for your own network. The utility will require the caller to have sufficient rights on any machine it is expected to remove printers from. You can call this utility in this manner:

```
RmLocalPrinters /c=<remote_computer> /u=<secs for connection
timeout> /r //l
```

Where the remote_computer is the target computer, you want to remove local printers that do not employ the MS IPP Class driver. This argument is required, while the /l, /u, and /r switches are optional. The /u switch (when used) sets the number of seconds before the connection attempt is considered timed out. If you add the /r switch, the utility will remove the printers that do not employ the MS IPP Class driver. The utility will ask the user if they want to remove any named printer that appears to be a local, legacy (non-IPP) printer – they should respond yes or no for each identified printer. If this switch is not specified, the utility prints out the removed printers. If the /l switch is used, the utility logs all actions to the RmLocalPrinters.log file that is created (and appended thereafter) in the user's Documents folder. This utility uses WMI as the connection agent, and thus the target must have WMI services running (by default Windows does). You will also need sufficient rights to remove printers on another machine, or the dreaded access denied (5) will rear its ugly head. You can run the utility in standard (non-admin) mode if you just want a list of non-conforming printers (don't specify the /r switch). The order of the switch arguments is not important.

If you plan on using this utility, I will direct your attention to the ProcessPrinterEntry method of the RemotePrinter class in the Collections folder of the project.

```
if((string.Compare(port_name, "nul:", true) == 0) ||
     (string.Compare(port_name, "PORTPROMPT:", true) == 0) ||
    (string.Compare(port_name, "FILE:", true) == 0) ||
    (string.Compare(port_name, "SHRFAX:", true) == 0))
    {
        IsSoftwareOnlyPrinter = true;
    }
```

This bit of code tests the known software-only printer ports typically seen on Windows. Please ensure there are no other types of (software-only) printer ports to consider on your MS Windows clients. This bit of code ensures these software-only printers are not added to the collection of printers that are scheduled to be removed. The project is in the code section of this chapter and can be modified as required for your needs.

I should mention that removing local printers that do not use the MS IPP Class Driver after the IPP/IPPS conversion but before Windows Protected Print (WPP) is enabled is recommended. Once WPP is enabled, printers that use type 3 drivers will no longer work and, in effect, become zombies on the machine. These printers do not work but will show up in Printers and scanners for each user on the machine, creating a potential help desk issue. To make matters worse, RmLocalPrinters *will no longer detect these (zombie) printers* as the associated port (e.g., TCP/IP or vendor-specific) has been deleted, breaking the communication path to the printer. The good news is that these zombie printers do not show up in application print dialogs.

Anticipating the more involved configuration nature of local (networked) IPP/IPPS printers on the client, and in an attempt to make this as painless as possible, the AddIppPrinter utility (introduced back in Chapter 2, "Printer Talk") was developed. It can be run under a non-elevated security context, so standard users can run it successfully. However, the utility does require knowledge of the IP address or DNS name of the printer being created, and it must be told to create either IPP or IPPS local printers. Thus, placing this information (about the IPP/IPPS printers) in an accessible location really comes in handy. The utility can be used to add a single printer or multiple printers in one shot, but when used in bulk mode, the /s argument (used to determine IPPS creation) holds for all the printers being created. If you use the bulk mode (with a list) to create the printers, you must also specify the path and name of the input file specifying the printers to be created.

To add a single IPP printer to the Windows client:

```
AddIppPrinter /p=<printer IP address> /s=<ipp or ipps>
```

Adds an IPP/IPPS printer via IP address or via hostname.

To add multiple IPP printers to the Windows client:

```
AddIppPrinter /l=<text file of IP addresses or hostname> /s=<ipp or ipps>
```

Opens the list and adds IPP/IPPS printers based on IP addresses or hostnames.

When creating an IPP or IPPS printer via AddIppPrinter (or manually via the GUI), understand that Windows Workstation only permits adding any IPP/IPPS printer once per client. Attempting to add an additional IPP port to the same physical printer will fail. In contrast, for legacy protocols (like port 9100), you may add an additional IP address multiple times – on the condition that the printer's name is unique. This is a way to add tandem printer instances with alternate default settings (like duplexing or collating). Unfortunately, as of now, this flexibility is not available for IPP/IPPS printers on Windows workstation platforms: only Windows Server allows this. Chapter 10, "Additional Information," has a method of adding tandem print instances on Windows Server to the same physical printers. You can mitigate this by creating tandem IPP print instances on the print server and then sharing them out with different share names (to reflect alternate default settings) if desired.

Server Side: Converting Existing Legacy Printers to IPP/IPPS Printers

Assuming you have an investment in legacy port 9100 printers shared off your print servers, finding a way to repurpose these printers might well be a priority. Further, preparing alternate plans for occasional instances where print operations do not work with the newer IPP/IPPS printers (very few conversion projects work as planned) might be a clever idea. One option to consider during the conversion is to un-share (or pause) existing legacy printers on the print servers. This way, users will not be able to print to the legacy (shared) printers, but in the event an issue is revealed that requires legacy print for an application or system (that was overlooked in the planning process), you can bring the legacy printer back online for service quickly by re-sharing (or un-pausing) it. You can do this easily in the Print Management utility on the server. Open Print Management, and on the left-hand side, click the **Printer Servers** drop-down list and choose your print server. Next, choose **Printers,** and then pause the legacy printers shared out to the users on your network.

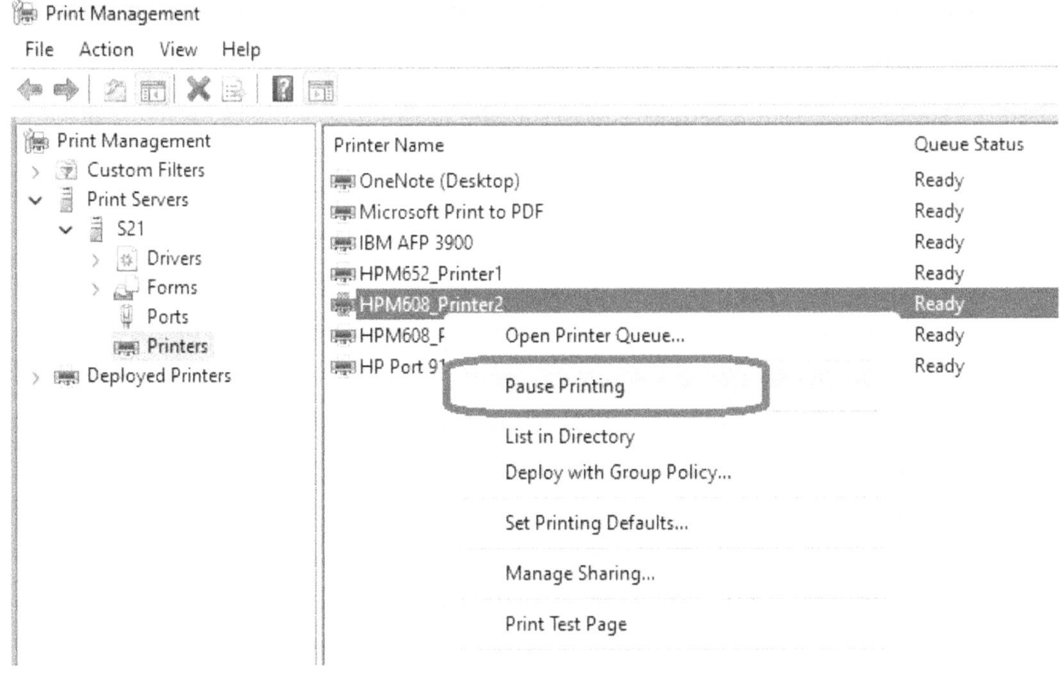

Pause a Printer in Windows Print Management

The next graphic shows all legacy (in this case, port 9100) printers on the print server as paused.

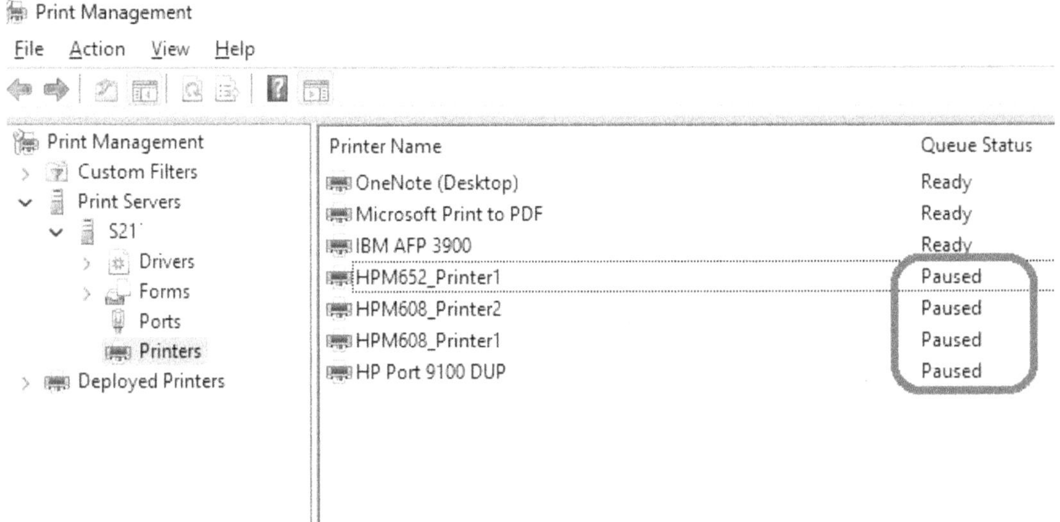

Port 9100 Printers Paused

Removing legacy print drivers from Windows clients and servers is another step you might consider taking after you are sure the conversion to IPP/IPPS is successful. While not necessary, it removes some confusion for users if they have the right to install printers on their machines. I would only recommend this step (removal of legacy drivers) for those enterprises sure the print environment is satisfactory. The good news for print system architects is that the move to WPP removes the ability of users to load these legacy components, so if you are planning to convert to WPP, legacy print driver removal might not be necessary at all.

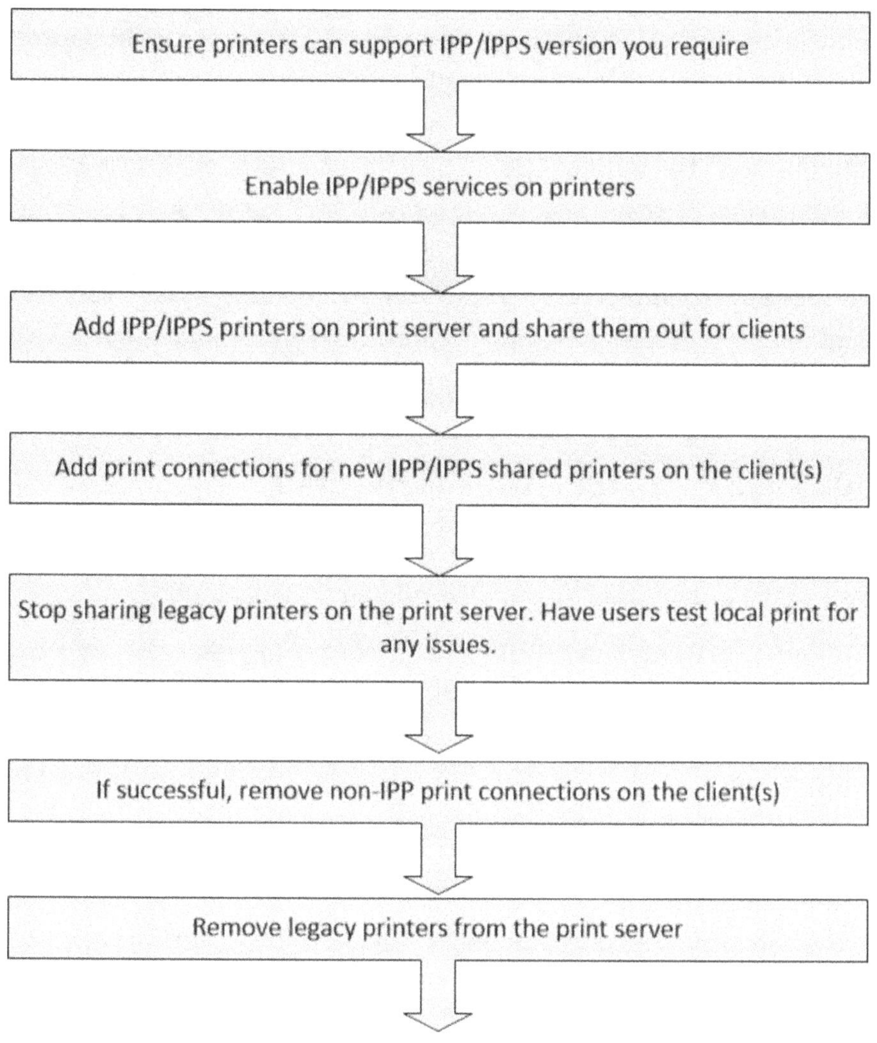

High-Level Diagram of IPP/IPPS Site Conversion Steps

Windows Protected Print

Besides security considerations, your network should work towards Windows Protected Print as early as possible. Windows Protected Print Mode (WPP) is a security-enhanced printing platform for Windows that runs with lower privileges and uses IPP/IPPS paired with Mopria to eliminate the need for third-party drivers. Together, these remove significant security risks that can lead to attackers gaining SYSTEM-level access [18]. This is especially true for those enterprises where print nightmare restrictions were only alleviated by group policy trusted print server lists. These are cumbersome to incorporate at best and a downright maintenance nightmare at worst. Your administrators and customers will thank you for removing them from the print nightmare restrictions. There are many compelling reasons to plan the conversion to WPP in your business. The most convincing: Microsoft has stated that 9% of all security issues reported to the Microsoft Security Response Center were caused by print stack-related issues [18]. The fact that the spooler runs with system-level privileges and loads software over a network connection makes the entire operating system vulnerable to exploits. You can bet that this issue (gain of control exploits against the Windows spooler service) will only get more sophisticated in execution and damaging to data in the future.

How Does WPP Protect Your Network?

Below are just a few of the reasons WPP provides an added degree of protection against rogue agents trying to gain control or exploit your client's machines.

1. Because WPP employs IPP/IPPS as the core print protocol along with Mopria, no third-party drivers are required. This significantly reduces the vulnerability of embedding malware on client machines.
2. In addition to the printer drivers, the loading of other software such as third-party print providers is not allowed.
3. Point and print can only employ V4 drivers - older V3 drivers are not allowed to run.
4. Most print spooler tasks now run at a lower privilege level, reducing the ability of attackers to gain control of your machine.

The benefits of Windows protected print mode include [21]:

1. Increased Windows device security
2. Simplified and consistent printing experience, regardless of the Windows device's architecture
3. Removes the need to manage print drivers

There are, of course, some basic requirements before you can enable WPP in your enterprise. You will need to have Windows 11, 24H2, or later installed. If your client machines are not at 24H2 or greater, they will not see the option to go to Windows Protected Print in Windows Workstation Settings in Printers and Scanners. You will also need to have the MS IPP Class driver installed (comes by default with later versions of Windows 11). Microsoft also highly recommends using IPPS over IPP as well - this for reasons of message integrity (encryption) during print.

Additional WPP Considerations

Feature	Requirement
IPP Class Driver	Required
Windows 11 (24H2 or later)	Required
Microsoft Account or AD	Required for user-authenticated release
Printer supports IPPS	Recommended (IPPS)

Requirements for WPP

In summary:

Protocol	WPP Compatible	Encrypted	Recommended for WPP
IPP	Yes	No	Not recommended
IPPS	Yes	Yes	Recommended

Note Several references on Microsoft sites and on the web allude to being able to upgrade versions of Windows 11 prior to 24H2 to Windows Protected Print. In my own testing, this is *not correct* as the V3 drivers installed on printers for the test continued to operate with no error messages on Windows 11 23H2. I can attest that version 24H2 of Windows 11 operates in WPP as touted by Microsoft.

Which Print Drivers Are Type V3 Drivers

If you are unsure if any of the print drivers on a machine are V3 technology, you can always consult the Printers & scanners ➤ Print Server Properties ➤ Drivers tab on the machine in question to check. This dialog provides a list of the print drivers on the machine with Type 3 clearly indicated. Any printers using these drivers will be disabled when WPP is enabled.

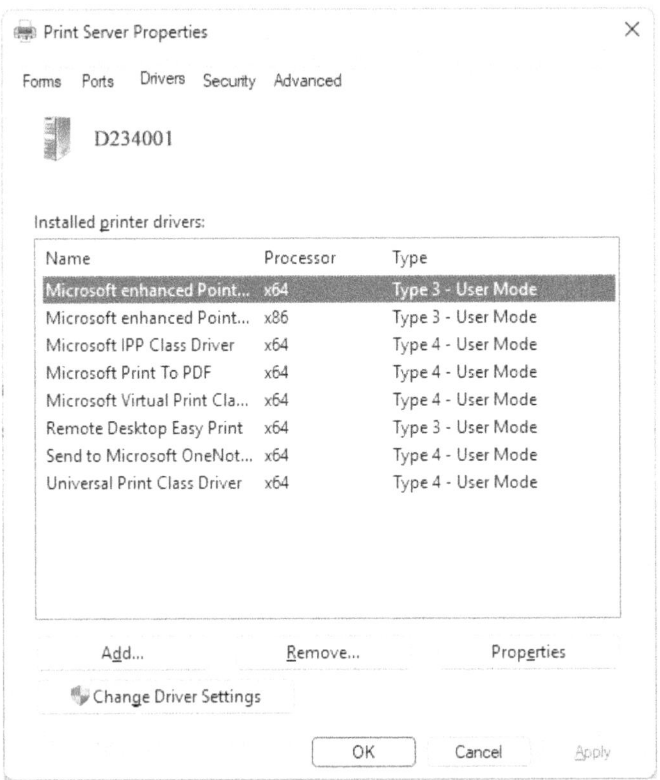

Listing the Print Driver Types

Back Up Your Print Environment

It is highly recommended that users back up their print environment prior to enabling WPP on the computer. Chapter 10, "Additional Information," includes PEBackup.bat and PERestore.bat files in the Code\Scripts folder for this purpose. While you may have painstakingly researched all aspects of your company's print environment, one missed detail could ruin your day - better safe than sorry.

Enabling WPP

You can enable Windows Protected Print in several ways, some more amenable to enterprise conversion than others. The most straightforward method would be simply enabling WPP by using the Windows 11 Settings App [17].

1. Open the Settings app by pressing the WIN+I keys together or using the Start Menu.
2. Go to the Bluetooth and Devices ➤ Printers and Scanners page.
3. In the right-side pane, look for the Windows protected print mode option. Click on the Setup button and follow the wizard. It will enable the WPP mode on your Windows 11 device. As a reminder, the machine needs to be at 24H2 to see this option in Printers & scanners.

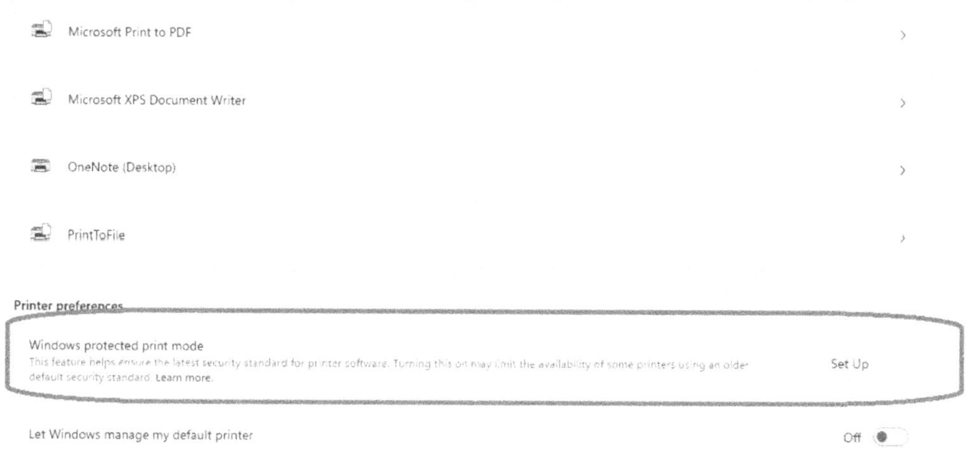

Open Bluetooth and Devices ➤ Printers and Scanners to See the Upgrade Option

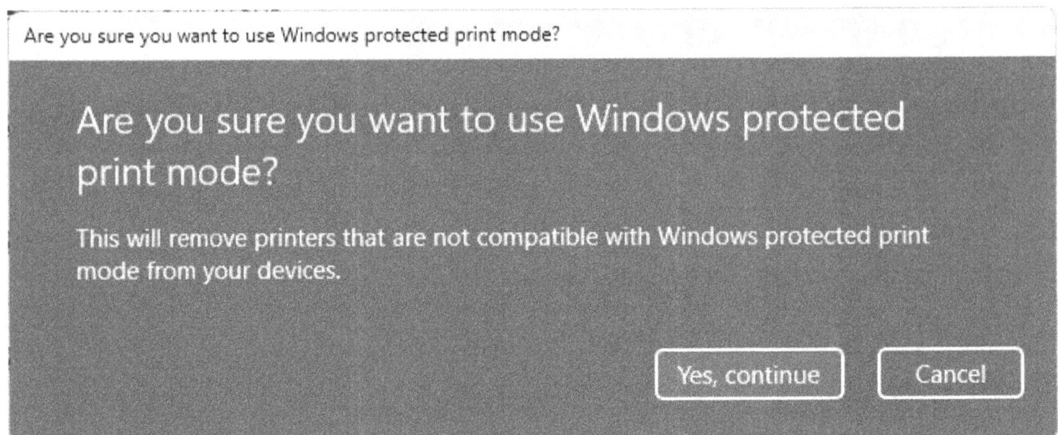

Click Yes to Begin the Upgrade Process

The user will need administrative rights to do this – standard users cannot complete this task. Of course, while this method may be the most direct, it is certainly not an efficient way to upgrade a large network. The next method involves modifying the registry via a script.

1. In the Windows 11 Search box, type in Regedit and press Enter. This should open the registry editor.

2. Navigate to the following key: HKLM\SOFTWARE\Policies\Microsoft\Windows NT\Printers\WPP. You should create the following registry name/value pairs, all of them with DWORD values:

```
EnabledBy = 2
WindowsProtectedPrintGroupPolicyState = 1
WindowsProtectedPrintMode = 1
WindowsProtectedPrintOobeConfigComplete =1
```

Note on some machines the hive beyond HKLM\SOFTWARE\ Policies\Microsoft\Windows NT does not exist and may need to be created.

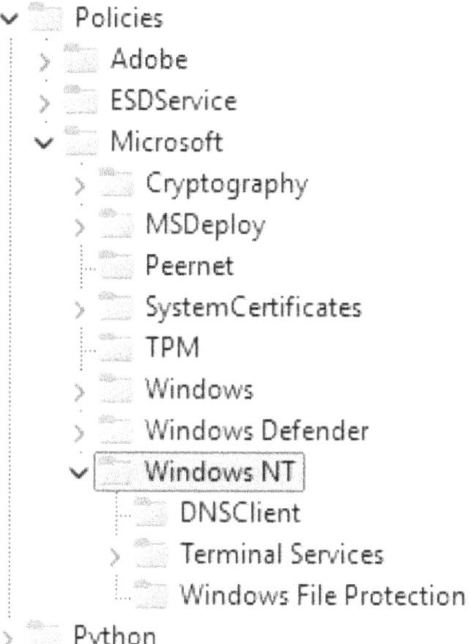

You can disable WPP mode by setting EnabledBy to 0 again. You should then delete the remaining registry options [19]. However, print driver configuration data is lost and will have to be recreated – in other words ensure you have backups of the print environment before you start. Chapter 10, "Additional Information," provides a script to backup and restore print environments on the client and server.

If you need a REG file:

```
Windows Registry Editor Version 5.00
[HKEY_LOCAL_MACHINE\SOFTWARE\Policies\Microsoft\Windows NT\
Printers\WPP]
"EnabledBy"=dword:00000002
"WindowsProtectedPrintGroupPolicyState"=dword:00000001
"WindowsProtectedPrintMode"=dword:00000001
"WindowsProtectedPrintOobeConfigComplete"=dword:00000001
```

The above registry script should do the trick. While this is certainly a better option for large enterprises than the first option, there is still a much better option. For convenience, there are WPP enable and disable reg files in the Code\Registry section of this chapter.

Activating WPP via Group Policy

For larger networks or enterprises, this is the best way to go. You can activate the policy globally or on an OU-by-OU basis. To do this:

1. In Windows 11, open the Group Policy Editor. Obviously, this is something that needs to be planned as you do not want to enable this setting globally for sites not yet ready to convert.
2. Navigate to the following setting:
   Computer Configuration ➤ Administrative Templates ➤ Printers
3. In the right-side pane, look for the "Configure Windows protected print" option. Double-click on the option, select the Enabled radio button, and apply changes.

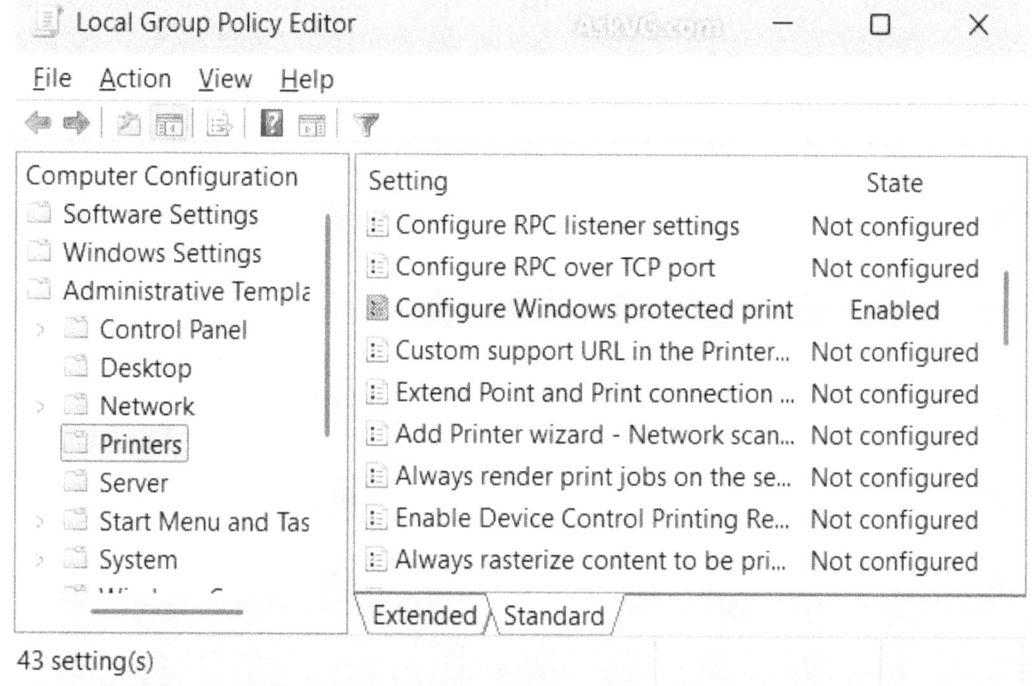

*Setting WPP to Enabled in Group Policy [**17**]*

This activates the WPP mode feature in your Windows 11 device when applied to the machine.

Note To deactivate WPP mode, set the policy (Configure Windows protected print) to not be configured.

After WPP Activation

If you enable WPP on your client machines, there are some changes in the client print system you need to consider. For starters, activation of WPP will disable any printers on your machine that requires type V3 printer drivers to operate. The process does not do this without your consent - the WPP wizard (When run interactively) will ask you if you want to go through with the process and displays the printers that will be disabled. If you choose to back down at this moment, you can cancel the process and there are no consequences. If you choose to proceed, the WPP conversion process takes some time to complete - the amount of time is proportional to the number of printers to query on the client. Once the process completes, you will clearly see the **Not connected** string indication below any of the disabled printers as shown below.

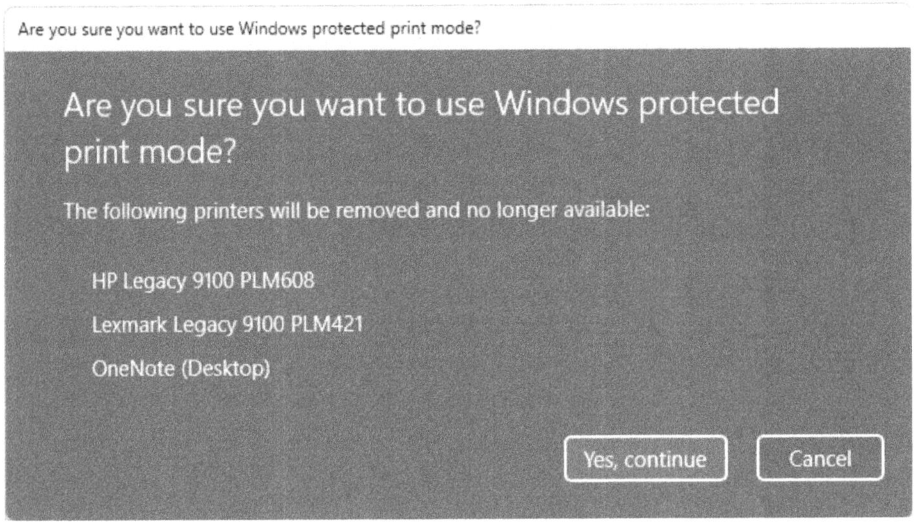

WPP Will Disable Any Printers on the Client That Uses V3 Print Drivers

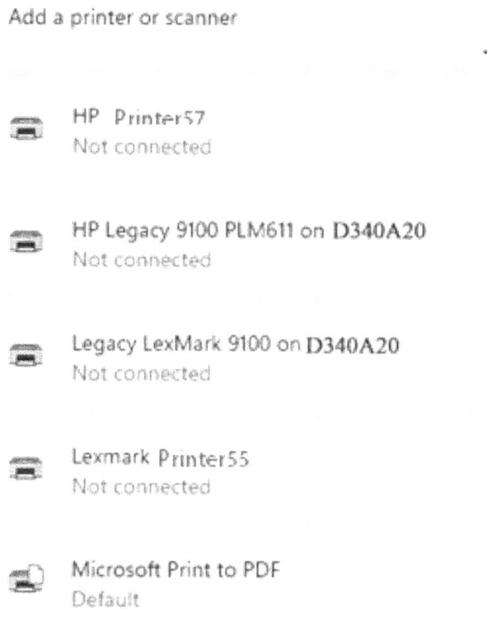

Disabled Printers, Both Local and Server Connections

Note that the process disables both local printers and print connections that employ type V3 print drivers - they will no longer work. If you try to print a test page from these disabled printers, you will see the following error:

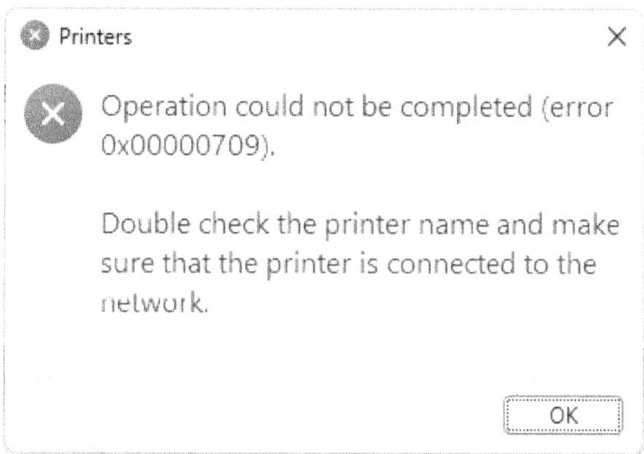

Attempting to Print a Test Page Using Disabled Printer

If you attempt to review any of the printer properties, you will see another error like that shown below:

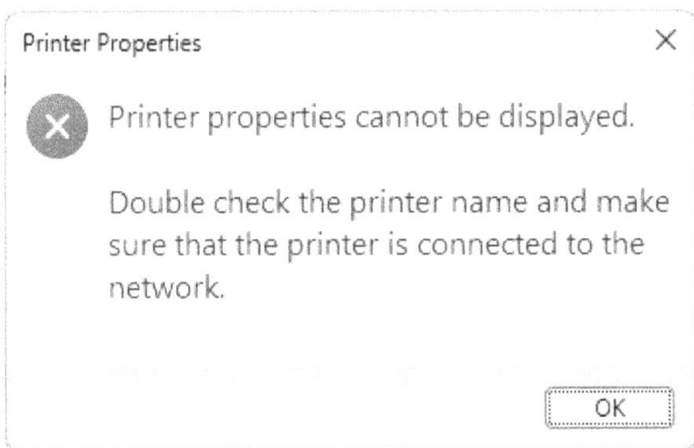

Attempting to Look at Properties on Disabled Printer

Finally, if you attempt to look at the hardware properties, you will get an error indicating the hardware is no longer connected to the computer.

Technically, MS removes the printer port instance from the printer when WPP is enabled, severing the communications channel from the client to the hardware printer. In addition, MS disables the Type 3 print driver connection to the printer instance. By taking these steps, the printer is left disabled and registers "Not Connected" when viewed in Printers & scanners.

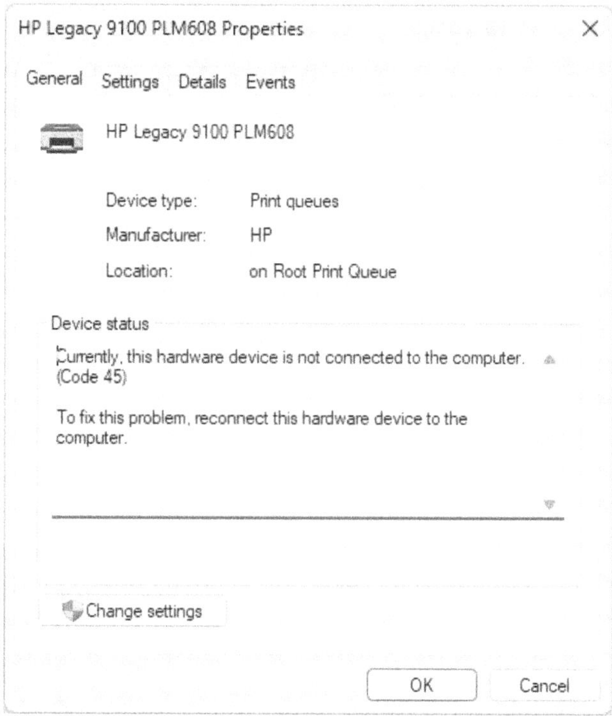

Hardware Is Not Connected Error

Of course, all of this is by design – type 3 drivers are a security vulnerability that Microsoft wants to protect their customers from. Overall, you are likely to significantly reduce the attack vector on your enterprise print environment.

One annoying issue with how MS implemented WPP activation is the fact that the disconnected or disabled printers (that used type V3 drivers) are left on the machine in a disabled state and are not removed. This will cause complaints and trouble tickets if users (in Printers & scanners) invariably click on the printer to look at its properties or create a Test page. While print connections can easily be removed by the user, local or direct printers cannot – at least by standard users. It might be a clever idea to remove the disable local printers left after WPP is enabled. Thankfully, these zombie printers do not show up in application print dialogs.

The Issue with Zombies

When WPP disables a printer due to non-compliance with Modern Print standards, the print subsystem does the following:

- The printer's driver is disconnected from the printer, so the system cannot load the necessary software to process print jobs.
- The associated port (e.g., TCP/IP or vendor-specific) is deleted, breaking the communication path to the printer.
- The printer queue is invalidated, and the system marks the printer as non-functional, displaying "Not Connected" to indicate that it cannot be used in the current WPP configuration.

The issue relates to the fact that the "zombie" printer still shows up in Printers & scanners. As mentioned earlier, if you try to look at the properties of the printer or print a test page, an error is displayed to the user. Obviously, this is likely not the scenario you would desire for your users after WPP is enabled. As mentioned earlier in the section "Client Side: Conversion of Local Printers via Customized Script or Code" in this chapter, it is highly advisable to remove the non-conforming local printers before WPP is enabled.

If these zombie printers are causing you grief, there is a scripted way to remove them. A PowerShell script, WppCleanup.ps1, is available in the code section of this chapter. While this script will remove the "Not Connected" printers, it must be run in the context of the user. This is inelegant at best and an inconvenience to enterprises. Hopefully, Microsoft will address this issue in a more enterprise-friendly manner.

Reverting from WPP

In the event you experience print issues after the conversion, you can disable WPP on the machine, rolling back *some* of the changes. The key word here is some, as not all the changes are reversable, and thus the admonition to thoroughly test the print environment before you commit to this change.

Printer preferences

Windows protected print mode
This feature helps ensure the latest security standard for printer software. Turning this on may limit the availability of some printers using an older default security standard. Learn more.
Turn Off

Let Windows manage my default printer
Off

Download drivers and device software over metered connections
Data charges may apply
Off

Turn WPP Off in Printers and Scanners

If you need to revert, you will find the **Turn Off** button under Printers & scanners ➤ Printer Preferences in Windows Settings. As with enabling WPP, you will need administrative rights to revert from WPP– standard users cannot complete this task.

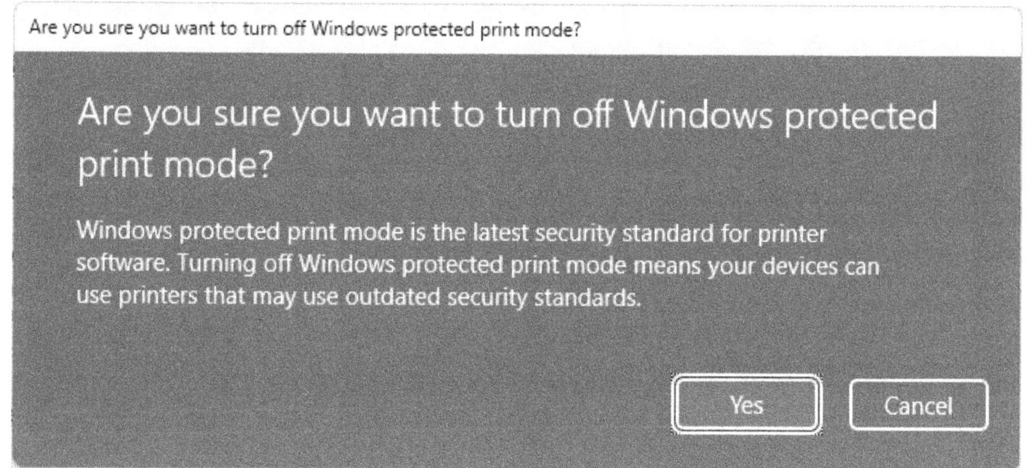

Dialog Displayed When Reverting WPP Activation

Once you click Yes, WPP is disabled and reverts from the earlier changes. From testing this process, it appears that print connections will revert back to operation, but local printers do not. Thus, you will end up with an environment that looks similar to the next graphic. In this case, the print connections (in green) have been successfully put back in service whilst the local printers (in red) still appear disabled. These printers will have to be re-installed if a print environment backup is not available.

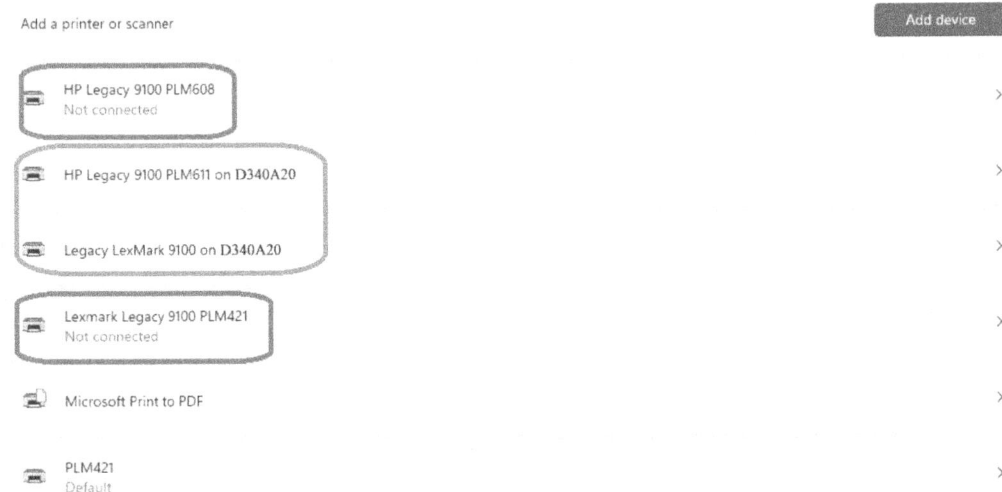

Print Connections (in Green) Were Restored, Local Printers (in Red) Stayed Disabled

If you are testing how WPP will affect printing in your organization and want the status of any machine in your lab or test environment, there is a utility in the code section of this chapter that allows you to determine this remotely. CheckWppEnv takes the name of the computer to check and will display the IPP printers found on the machine and the status of Windows Protected Print. It will also allow you to enable or disable WPP on remote machines, provided you have the right to do so.

Chapter Summary

This chapter covers the techniques and tools to help Windows engineers or administrators make the transition from legacy print protocols to IPP/IPPS. Because printing may cover multiple OS platforms and applications, proper planning is key to a successful transition. Ensure that all components of your enterprise, even ones who would not appear to have a direct stake, are involved in the planning process. Many times, in these conditions, you might learn about applications or scripts that assume RAW printability. Ensure the IPP version hosted on your printer fleet will adequately meet your needs or IPP/IPPS request requirements – if not, inquire if there is an update for those printers that do not meet the minimal requirements. The Microsoft IPP Class Driver implements IPP version 1.0, so older IPP printers may still be salvageable. Additionally, be on the lookout for any scenarios where Windows "pass-through" printing is employed – ensure these will work with IPP/IPPS.

A good technique is to test the entire application suite employed by your enterprise with test printers using only IPP and IPPS print services. This prevents testers from assuming the application passes when it processes the print on legacy print protocol(s). Ensure your transition team has conversion to Windows Protected Print (WPP) in their plans. Employing IPP/IPPS is important, but without WPP you will be missing the chance to further protect your network against newer exploits. While there are several ways of enabling WPP, group policy is likely the most reasonable method for large enterprises. You can do this on a site-by-site basis, and if there is an issue, it can be rolled back via group policy as well. If you do plan to implement WPP, ensure you have performed print environment backups on all clients and print servers. Once WPP is enabled, you typically cannot successfully revert back to local printers without reinstalling them. Print connections, on the other hand, do appear to recover full operation after reverting.

While on WPP, it is highly recommended that you use IPPS versus IPP for message integrity. If you are planning on IPPS, you will want to ensure your printers have a certificate installed that is in the trusted root certificate authorities in the Windows **certmgr** utility on the client. This is not required, as Windows 11 seems to use IPPS connections even with printers whose certificate issuer is not trusted on the computer. However, this is best practice, and Microsoft could potentially change this behavior in the future – better to be prepared than not.

Of course, there is a matter of configuring the printers in your enterprise, and the method used is highly dependent on the size of your printer fleet. If your printer fleet is small, i.e., 5–50 printers in total, you could probably get away with manual configuration. This would involve connecting to the printer via the embedded web server and configuring IPP/IPPS to enable and (optimally) disable other legacy protocols such as LPD and port 9100. For larger printer fleets, the best method would be to use a vendor print management software suite such as HP's Web Jet Admin or Lexmark's MarkVision. Just ensure that IPP/IPPS printing works with all your enterprise applications before making the jump.

We also covered some idiosyncrasies with PowerShell print commands. The bottom line is to not use the PowerShell Get-Content cmdlet to process binary files like PDFs as it may interpret the file as text, which will not work for IPP print. In the event you need to work with IPP/IPPS in PowerShell, a workaround is provided. In the event all else fails, you could also use the code from Chapters 5, "IPP Standards Print," and 6, "Additional Operations," and wrap it into a PowerShell cmdlet. Additionally, Chapter 10, "Additional Information," provides a C# utility that can be employed to print PDF files on disk to a print connection or a local printer.

Finally, we arrive at the conversion of existing printers on a print server and their corresponding print connections that appear on the client(s). This conversion can be done manually or automatically, and the route you take will undoubtedly be determined by the size of your printer fleet. Regardless of how this is accomplished, you will want to do this site by site and only after extensive testing. If you find that, despite the best planning, an application or system cannot work with IPP/IIPS, you could leave a few printers on the site with a legacy print protocol enabled to allow them to work. Just remember that WPP cannot be enabled on the client unless it employs the V4 MS IPP Class driver as V3 print drivers are not supported. If WPP is enabled, existing V3 drivers, print ports, and preconfigured printer settings will be removed. Most specifically, while WPP does support IPP, this is certainly not recommended as this leaves the transport of data unencrypted and vulnerable to snooping. Instead, ensure you use IPPS with WPP to provide the most secure environment possible.

Finally, the IT world is one of never-ending one-upmanship between those tasked with protecting the integrity of data and those determined to undermine the same. The successful implementation of IPPS and WPP on your enterprise, being a major blow for the former, gives yourself a much-deserved pat on the back.

References

[1] BRAdmin Professional, Brother Printers, `https://brotherb2bportfolio.com/categories/device-management-deployments/bradmin-professional-4`

[2] Business Printing Solutions, Epson Printers, `https://epson.com/business-printing-solutions`

[3] Printer Software and Utilities, LexMark Publications, `https://publications.lexmark.com/publications/pdfs/lexmarkc720/eng/mkvision.pdf`

[4] Flett Remote Monitoring & Management, Konica Minolta, `https://www.konicaminolta.eu/eu-en/digital-workplace/software-services/fleet-remote-monitoring-management`

[5] HP Web JetAdmin, Hewlett-Packart, https://h20195.www2.hp.com/V2/GetPDF.aspx/4AA5-2718ENW.pdf

[6] Kyocera Device Manager, Kyocera Document Solutions, https://www.kyoceradocumentsolutions.us/en/products/software/KYOCERADEVICEMANAGER.html

[7] Enable or Disable Windows Protected Print Mode in Windows 11, Windows Eleven Forum, https://www.elevenforum.com/t/enable-or-disable-windows-protected-print-mode-in-windows-11.20670/

[8] How To: Send Data Directly to a GDI Printer, Microsoft Learn, https://learn.microsoft.com/en-us/windows/win32/printdocs/sending-data-directly-to-a-printer

[9] Internet Printing Protocol/1.0: Model and Semantics, RFC 2566, Network Working Group, April 1999, https://www.rfc-editor.org/rfc/rfc2566

[10] Internet Printing Protocol/1.1: Encoding and Transport, Internet Engineering Task Force, RFC 8010, January 2017, https://www.rfc-editor.org/rfc/rfc8010.html

[11] Internet Printing Protocol/1.1: Model and Semantics, Internet Engineering Task Force, RFC 8011, January 2017, https://www.rfc-editor.org/rfc/rfc8011

[12] Internet Printing Protocol/1.1: Implementor's Guide, Network Working Group, November 2001, https://datatracker.ietf.org/doc/html/rfc3196

[13] Internet Printing Protocol (IPP):Event Notifications and Subscriptions, Network Working Group, March 2005, https://www.rfc-editor.org/rfc/rfc3995

[14] Internet Printing Protocol (IPP): Job and Printer Set Operations Network Working Group, September, 2002, https://www.rfc-editor.org/rfc/rfc3380.html

[15] IPP Version 2.0, 2.1, and 2.2, The Printer Working Group, October 30, 2015, https://ftp.pwg.org/pub/pwg/standards/std-ipp20-20151030-5100.12.pdf

[16] Internet Printing Protocol (IPP):Job and Printer Administrative Operations, Network Working Group, March 2005, https://datatracker.ietf.org/doc/draft-ietf-ipp-ops-set2/04/

[17] Tip: How to Enable Windows Protected Print Mode in Windows 11, VG, October 14, 2024, https://www.askvg.com/tip-how-to-enable-windows-protected-print-mode-in-windows-11/

[18] The complete guide to Windows Protected Print Mode (WPP), PaperCut, https://www.papercut.com/discover/the-complete-guide-to-windows-protected-print-wpp

[19] Configuring Windows Protected Print, Windows OS Hub, https://woshub.com/enable-windows-protected-print-mode-wpp/

[20] Modern Print Platform, Microsoft Support, https://support.microsoft.com/en-us/windows/modern-print-platform-4f59fa38-3419-41c7-a6a7-8ca4e21f70bc

[21] Modern Print Platform, Microsoft Support, "Windows Protected Print Mode, https://support.microsoft.com/en-us/windows/modern-print-platform-4f59fa38-3419-41c7-a6a7-8ca4e21f70bc#bkmk_windows_protected_mode

[22] Invoke-Command, Microsoft Learn, https://learn.microsoft.com/en-us/powershell/module/microsoft.powershell.core/invoke-command?view=powershell-7.5

[23] Use PowerShell Invoke-Command to run scripts on remote computers, 4sysops, https://4sysops.com/archives/use-powershell-invoke-command-to-run-scripts-on-remote-computers/

[24] What is SNMPv1, SNMPv2c, and SNMPv3?, DPS Telecom,https://www.dpstele.com/snmp/v1-v2c-v3-difference.php

CHAPTER 8

A Print Support App

In this chapter, we will cover Printer Support Apps (PSAs) that vendors are likely to develop to better integrate their products into the Windows IPP (Modern Print) environment. Users will download these apps (optimally) from the Microsoft Store to provide better integration of vendor features that may not have a standard IPP RFC attribute. At first glance, this might sound like a bit of regression – writing vendor-specific code to better integrate their products. After all, wasn't IPP/Mopria supposed to do away with having to install third-party drivers and software – wasn't that one of the major selling points for this venture? Officially, Microsoft touts the PSA as an "architecture that was introduced to help Independent Hardware Vendors (IHVs) add customization to IPP printers without the use of legacy third-party drivers" [1]. The crux of the issue can be found in vendor product differentiation – in this case, product features that may help sell their printers. Let's face it: vendors need to market and sell their products, and standout features help provide an edge on the competition. Against this backdrop we have a consortium of vendors involved with creating a print protocol that standardizes the most common print hardware attributes. How can vendors integrate unique product features into a Windows environment that uses IPP/Mopria as the new print protocol? This chapter will delve into how this is accomplished without requiring the inclusion of vendor-specific drivers.

You might be wondering where you fit into all of this. Why would you need to know how or why a PSA is created and operates if it is primarily designed for vendor integration of their products? The short answer to these questions is support – managers, network engineers, and system admins will need to know how to troubleshoot user complaints that will invariably arise when IHV features don't work as advertised. If you can make sense of a Wireshark trace to ensure the vendor-specific attributes are actually configured as they should be, you will be ahead of the game. You should also be aware of how the OS calls any given PSA on the system – essentially how it links printer hardware IDs to Universal Window Apps (UWA) PSA software. Finally, while PSAs are primarily for

J. Marion, *Adopting Internet Printing Protocol for Windows*, https://doi.org/10.1007/979-8-8688-2010-6_8

IHVs, they also exist so enterprises can ensure basic print job attributes (such as print quality and duplexing) are set for any print operation. Yes, your company's developers can write a PSA to ensure default print standards are provided with every print job.

I should set some basic expectations from the outset. The idea in this chapter is to provide how a PSA can be built and what to look out for when creating one rather than churning out a usable PSA you can deploy for multitudes of printer hardware. We will explore how the OS triggers your PSA to activate when the targeted printer is selected in an app like Notepad - in this case, when the "More settings" link is clicked in the standard print dialog. Alternatively, your PSA can also be called when the user clicks the "Printer Preferences" button in the "Printers and Scanners" section in Setup. Finally, the PSA can be called by the more mundane "Open Printer App" button in the "Printers and Scanners" area as well. How your PSA is called will reflect what you show to the user as information. The PSA is connected to the print subsystem by "contracts," which are essentially subscribed callbacks into defined methods. I hope by the end of this chapter you will have a good idea of why PSA apps are needed for IPP printing in the Windows world and at least a bit of understanding of the basic print flow they modify.

Windows driver-docs provides a document entitled "Print support app association" [15] that details the steps you will need to take to associate a PSA to a printer queue using a Hardware ID. If your PSA is destined for production, you will be required to provide a PSA extension INF file. We will cover the test linkage in this chapter; you can find information on creating an INF file for production code online. Because this chapter is more concerned with how the PSA operates rather than creating a production PSA, we will work on linking the test PSA with the printer hardware ID in the registry. Windows allows developers to do this (and forgo creating an INF file to deploy) to aid in the development and debugging process. Finally, this chapter deviates from the concepts of the previous chapter, where usable code examples were provided. Although an example PSA is provided, its hardware-specific nature renders it compatible only with the printer it was designed for and may not work with others.

Get It at the Store

As PSA apps are written using UWP or WinUI3 technology, they are loaded (as all store apps are) into the local folder C:\Program Files\WindowsApps under a GUID. The idea was for the OS to automatically detect that the Hardware ID from your newly installed IPP printer is not associated with a Package Family Name in the registry and go up to the MS store and download one that could work with your printer. This would make integration into the MS print system seamless and secure. If you navigate to C:\Program Files\WindowsApps, you might notice a few things that are rather different about this folder. In the first place, the folder is (by default) hidden. You can rectify this by navigating (in Explorer) to View ➤ Show and then checking "Hidden items." However, what you will then notice is that you do not have (by default) the right to list any of the contents of this folder. Further, even if you are an administrator of the machine, you are not the owner; the security principal **Trusted Installer** is.

While these might seem like impositions to developing a PSA, they are not. Visual Studio will take on the task of deploying your development PSA app to the WindowsApp folder at your behest. However, you will have to ensure the Package.appmanifest is appropriately configured for this to work. Visual Studio will do a check on this file every time you debug, and if there are issues, the app will fail to deploy. Fortunately, the test PSA being developed in this chapter (BasicPsa) can serve as a guide.

Developer Mode

To create or debug a UWP PSA app, you will need to enable Developer Mode. The reason this is required is for side-loading, a technique to install Windows Apps outside of the Windows Store. We will go into the reason this is necessary in the later part of this chapter, but for now ensure you have Developer Mode enabled. To do this, go to Settings ➤ System ➤ For Developers, and you will see the Developer Mode button near the top of the menu as shown below. Ensure this option is enabled so you can debug and develop Windows Apps.

Developer Mode Enabled

There are other reasons you need this enabled: PSAs may need to handle XPS-to-PDL conversion or interact with the print stack via APIs, which requires a development environment set up with Developer Mode.

Getting Printer Hardware ID

No matter what a PSA is designed to accomplish, it needs to be linked to the printer hardware it will support. Ensuring this ID is correct is absolutely tantamount to proper operation of the PSA. While there are several ways to accomplish this, I prefer to employ Device Manager to obtain the proper Hardware ID for any printer. To get the Hardware ID of your IPP printer, ensure your printer is online and open Device Manager in Windows.

While I don't want to offend readers with trivial information, it can sometimes be more difficult than it should be to find older utilities in the newer Windows 10/11 user layout. To avoid wasting time searching for Device Manager, I prefer to type in "Device Manager" in the Windows search box to make it easy.

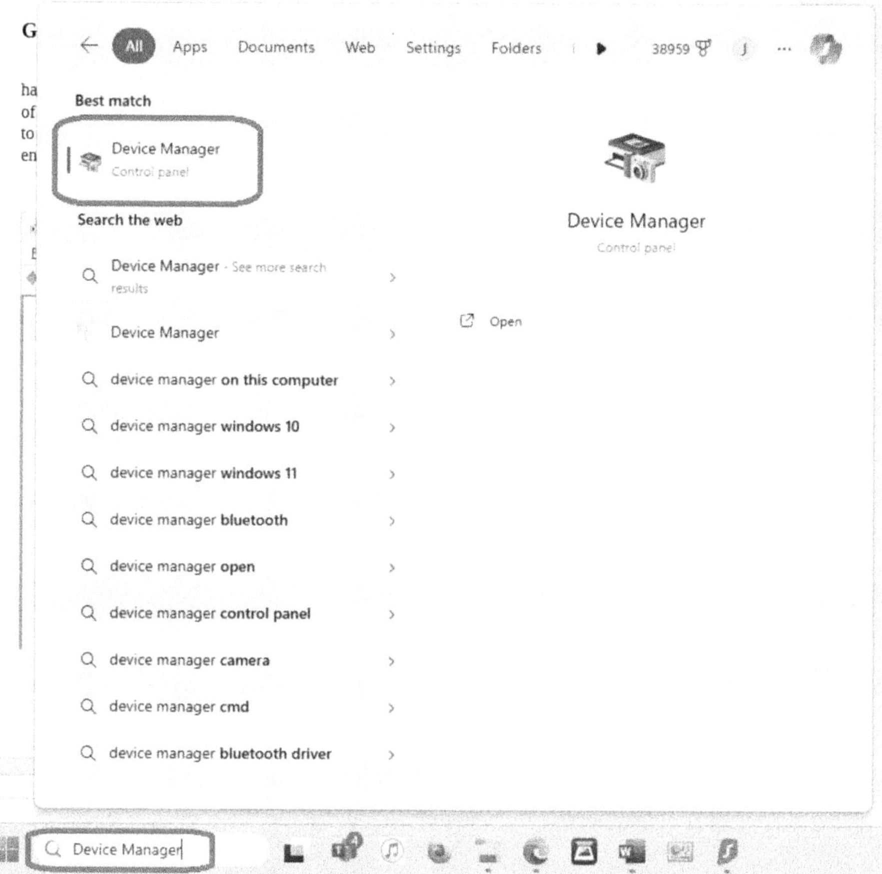

The Easy Way to Find Utilities in Windows 11

Once you have Device Manager open, click the View menu item at the top and ensure this is set to "Device by Type." Expand the **Printers** node to reveal the list of enumerated printers known to Windows.

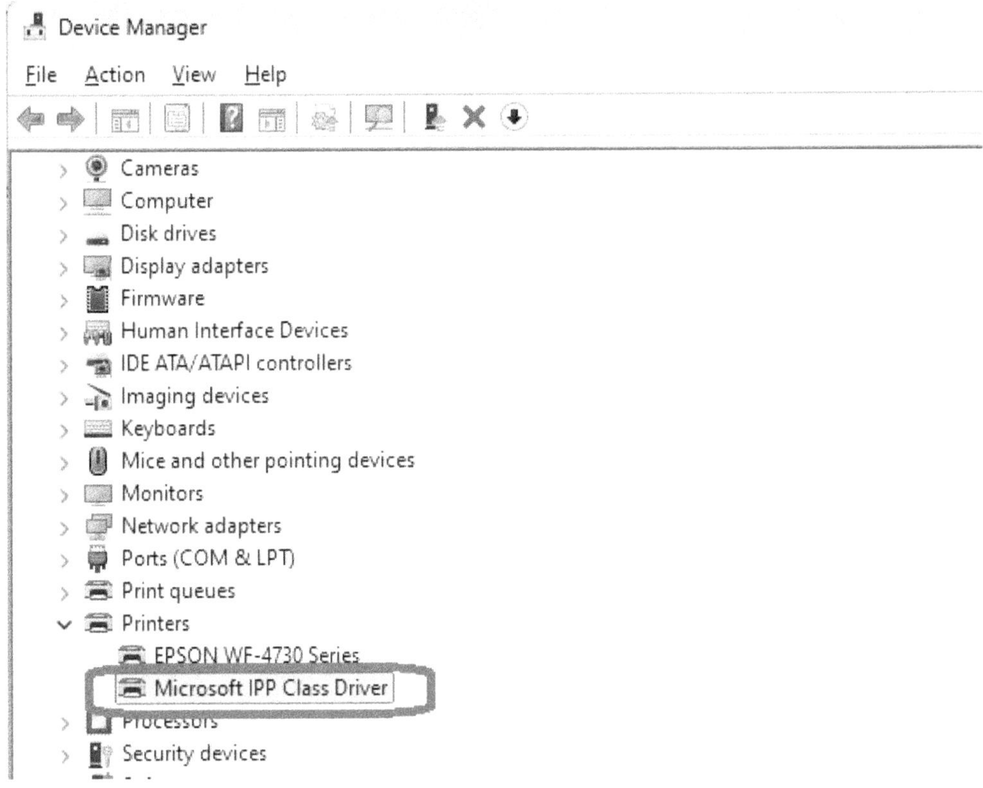

Locating the Microsoft IPP Class Driver Virtual Printer

There can be several Microsoft IPP Class Driver instances under the Printers root node, and each will be associated with a unique printer hardware IDs.

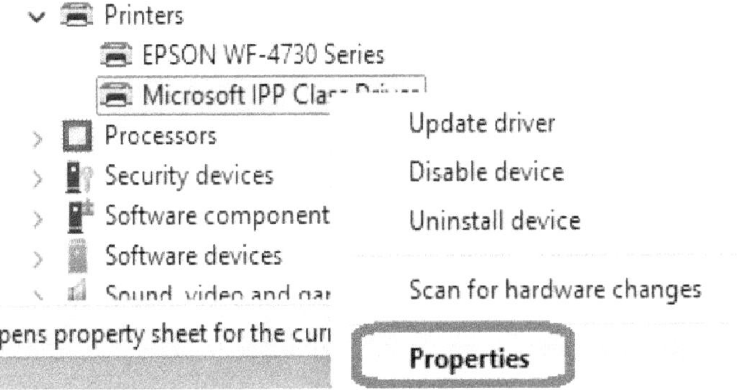

Right-Click Microsoft IPP Class Driver and Choose Properties

Right-click the Microsoft IPP Class Driver instance and choose properties, and then select the **Details** tab. In the Details tab, select the **Property** drop-down and select **Hardware Ids** to then find

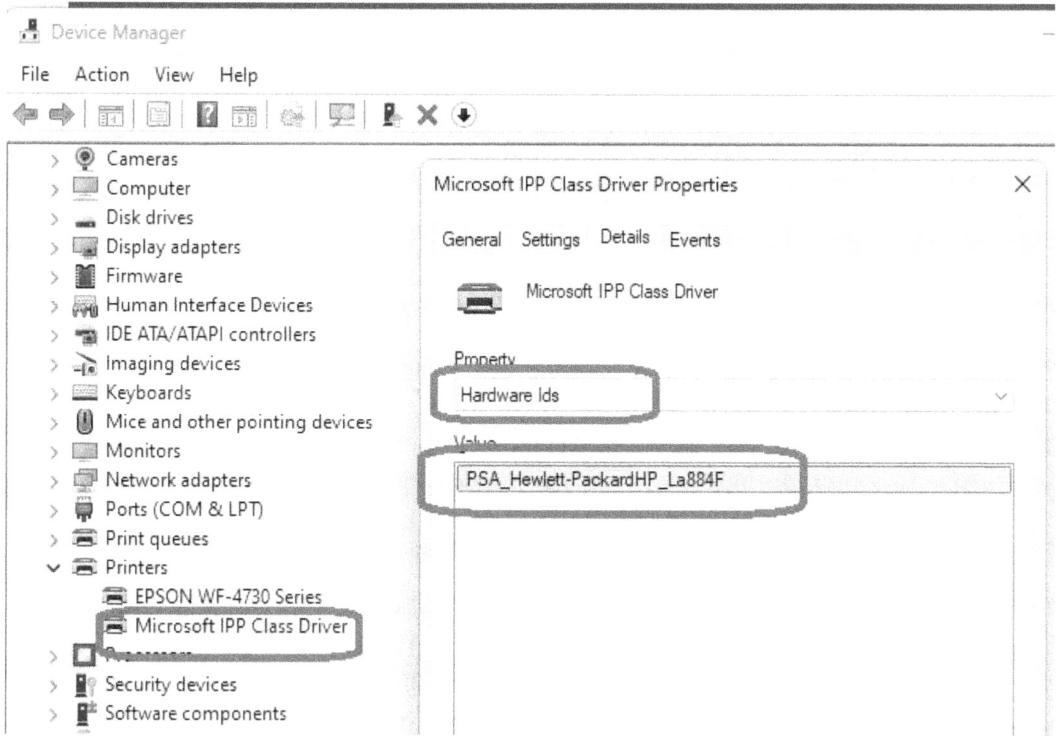

The Hardware ID Can Be Found in the Details Tab

the hardware ID of your printer. You can right-click the entry in the Value list box and choose Copy to load the hardware ID value string in Cut/Paste memory.

Property
Hardware Ids
Value
PSA_Hewlett-PackardHP_La884F
Copy
Select All

Components of the PSA Extension INF File

A PSA is associated with a printer by using an extension INF file. The PSA INF file is similar to other INF files in construction except for some select components. Below is the [Strings] section that highlights these components [4]:

```
[Strings]
ManufacturerName = "Microsoft"
SoftwareName = "Microsoft Print Support App"
Device.ExtensionDesc = "Print Support App Extension"
MicrosoftStoreType = 2
PackageFamilyName = "dd5de805-d9bb-4785-88e9-399cbff2130e_ph1m9x8skttmg"
AUMID = "dd5de805-d9bb-4785-88e9-399cbff2130e_ph1m9x8skttmg!App"
PrinterHardwareId = "PSA_CanoniP110_seriesD84F"
PrinterHardwareId2 = "PSA_XeroxAltaLink_B8055C036"
PrinterHardwareId3 = "PSA_BrotherMFC-J775DWF678"
```

Some clarification should be provided: the PackageFamilyName is a unique identifier string that represents the app package and is generated by Visual Studio when the PSA is created. The PackageFamilyName uniquely identifies the app software package installed in the Windows OS. The AUMID (AppUserModelId) is a combination of the PackageFamilyName with an additional (short) identifier string that specifies a particular app or app component within the package.

The order of INF file creation for a PSA is provided below:

1. Update the **PrinterHardwareId** in the psa.inf file with your Hardware ID or Compatible ID. (For demonstration purposes, there are other PrinterHardwareIds shown – you can have one PSA associated with multiple hardware printers.)

2. Update the **PackageFamilyName** and **AUMID** (AppUserModelId) for your PSA application.

3. Create a catalog file.

4. Sign the psa.cat file sample extension INF.

The PSA extension INF file is contained in a signed catalog file. The signed catalog file proves the PSA files haven't been tampered with by containing a signed list of hashes for each file. The Inf2cat executable can be used to create this cat file. The command to do this:

```
Inf2Cat /driver:<PSA dfile_folder> /os:<OS_list>
```

Where /os switch is the target OS platform – in the case of Windows 11 64-bit, this would be 11_X64. At this point, you have an unsigned catalog file. You can use the SignTool to then sign the catalog file and complete the process.

In this chapter, we will not create a production PSA, so no INF file or catalog file will be used. Instead, we will create an association (for testing purposes) between the Package family name and the printer Hardware ID you wish to associate your PSA with. This is done in the registry and is the primary way to test or debug your PSA.

To begin with, Microsoft is working to prod vendors so they publish PSAs to the Microsoft Store. The idea is when a client attempts to use an IPP printer, Windows would automatically provide a link to download the necessary PSA from the store. This is the preferred way to install PSAs, but vendors can also host the software on their own websites to be downloaded and installed by the user. Either way, PSAs are hardware-specific; each PSA will be linked to one or more vendor printer hardware IDs the client has installed. While there can be a one-to-many relationship between PSA software and printer hardware, each piece of hardware is associated with only one PSA. If no PSA is available, the IPP printer will still function but might lack some vendor-specific features the PSA provides.

Virtual Printers

In the PSA context (when working with IPP/IPPS printers), Microsoft makes use of virtual printers. These are not physical printers as might be represented in the legacy print world; they represent a logical abstraction of IPP printers for the Windows print subsystem. You might think of this as a proxy between the print subsystem and the actual physical printer. You can see this in Device Manager, where instances of printers are labelled "Microsoft IPP Class Driver" instead of the physical printer's name provided by legacy protocols (with print drivers). This idea also has an operational context: the print ticket settings created from the user registry defaults are converted into IPP job attributes that will be provided to IPP requests (Validate-Job, Create-Job, Send-Document) in the same manner for all IPP printers.

Print Tickets

In Windows, users store their default settings for a printer (i.e., duplex mode, print quality, page orientation, etc.) in the HKEY_CURRENT_USER (HKCU) registry hive. Per-printer preferences for items such as paper size and print quality are stored in the HKCU\Printers\DevModesPerUser and DevModes2 paths. As mentioned in Chapter 1, "Windows Legacy Print," these settings are stored in binary format, which can make it somewhat difficult to work with. The important point is that these per-user default print settings are converted into an abstraction called a print ticket by the Windows print subsystem. During print job creation or preview, the XPS Print Pipeline Manager converts the binary information from the registry devmode hive into a file containing these settings in XML format - this is termed the "Print Ticket." These settings are then converted into IPP job attributes by the IPP Class Driver as described in the Virtual Printers section. A listing of some of the Windows components that create the Print Ticket is shown below:

Component	Function
PrintConfig.dll	Converts DEVMODE ↔ PrintTicket (v4 drivers, IPP)
PrintTicketManager.dll	Interfaces with apps and settings UI
XpsPrint.dll	Manages XPS printing and PrintTicket flow

Conceptually then, we could modify the Print Ticket contents before it reaches the IPP Class Driver, whose job it is to convert the user request and job settings into a binary stream and place that into the HTTP/HTTPS packet payload. This modification is done via a common print dialog where the user can choose which, if any, of the print job settings they wish to modify. The system can then store those choices in a per-user file format on the computer so that they appear as the default choice for the next print job on the targeted printer. Vendor features expressed as attributes can then be exchanged (along with RFC standard attributes) back and forth to the targeted printer. The diagram below represents a basic print job settings flow that the IPP Class Driver consumes.

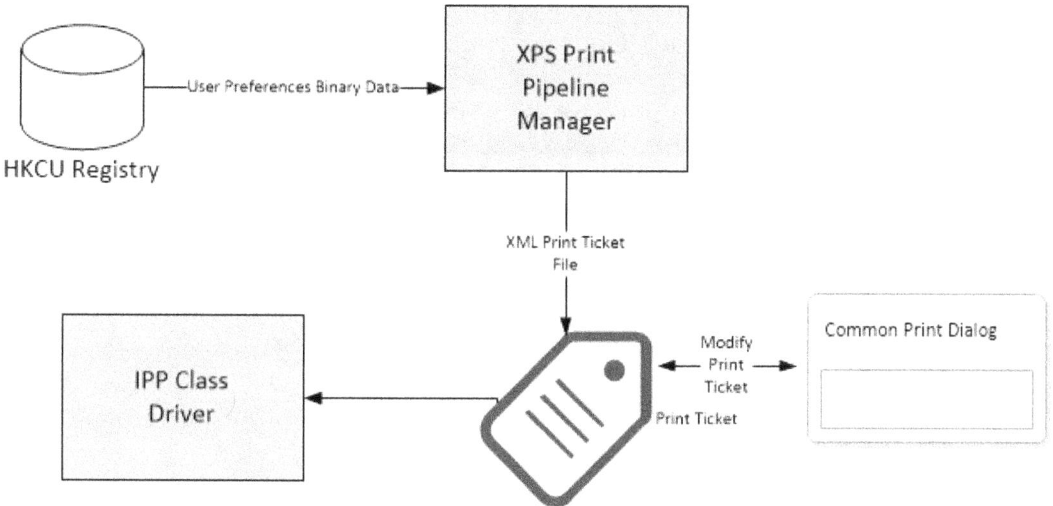

Conceptual Diagram of Print Ticket Creation

Visual Studio Requirements for PSA

There are some prerequisites you should have installed in Visual Studio to explore how Print Support Apps (PSA) are created. My test machine has Visual Studio 2022 (64-bit) version 17.13.6 installed. To develop a PSA with UWP in Visual Studio 2022, you should have installed the Windows 11 SDK (minimal version 22000.1) before any development can commence. If you open Visual Studio Installer, ensure WinUI application development is checked as well. The very minimum level of Windows 11 SDK required is **Windows 10 SDK (10.0.10240.0),** but the recommendation is to use **Windows 11 SDK (10.0.22000.0)** or greater. Microsoft also advises that to leverage the latest security APIs and ensure compatibility with Windows 11, Windows version 24H2 should be installed. To check this on your machine, the fastest way is to open Windows Settings ➤ click **System** (on the left) ➤ **About**. Check the entries under the **Windows Specifications** section to ensure your version is at least 24H2. On my own machine I have the following Windows 11 SDKs installed:

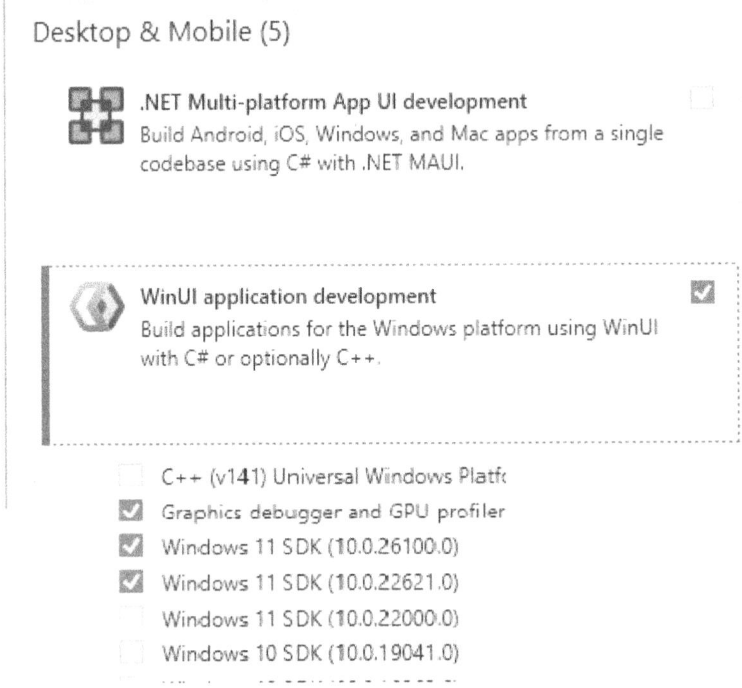

View of Visual Studio Installer SDK components

On the right should appear various Windows SDK versions. I started the project using Windows 11 SDK (10.0.22621.0), which is compatible with the development of BasicPsa.

Creating a New UWP Application

PSA apps can be created using UWP or WinUI3 – our example will then be a UWP version of a PSA called BasicPsa. One of the standout features of UWP applications is their ability to use a common API on all devices that run Windows – something Microsoft was looking to provide [7]. Some key advantages of UWP apps over the existing Win32 application development are

1. Ability to run across all Windows platforms with a consistent user experience.
2. Limited access to Win32 resources (registry access, drivers, network access) unless specifically allowed (in the manifest file) to do so.
3. Sandboxed environment that limits application access to the native hardware.

In the code section of this chapter is a UWP PSA called BasicPsa, you can refer to this or load this in Visual Studio 2022. If you want to create your own PSA, follow the instructions below:

1. Open Visual Studio 2022.
2. Navigate to **File ➤ New ➤ Project**
3. To the right of "**Create a new project,**" type in "**Universal Windows**" in the textbox.
4. In the project templates that appear, choose **"Blank App (Universal Windows)"** and click **Next**. (Note: You might also see UWP Blank App as the template name.)
5. Name your PSA project and choose the folder you want to place it in.
6. Click Create to start a new PSA project.
7. You will be prompted to choose a target version (take the default) and a minimum version you want to support for your clients. Click OK to start.

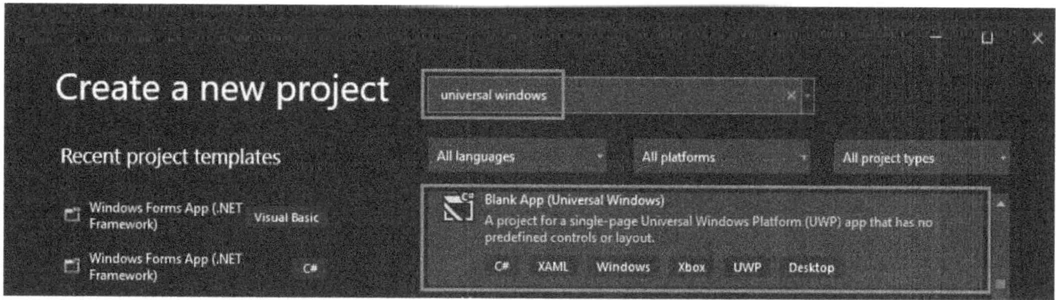

Create a New UWP Project

Once your new UWA application is created, you will want to note the package family name. This GUID uniquely identifies your application on the system it is running on. It will be paired with the target printer's hardware ID and link the 2 together for operational purposes. To get the package family name, do one of the two below:

1. Right-click the **Package.appxmanifest** in Visual Studio Solution Explorer and choose View Designer in the context menu.
2. Double-click **Package.appxmanifest** in Visual Studio Solution Explorer.

Making the Association

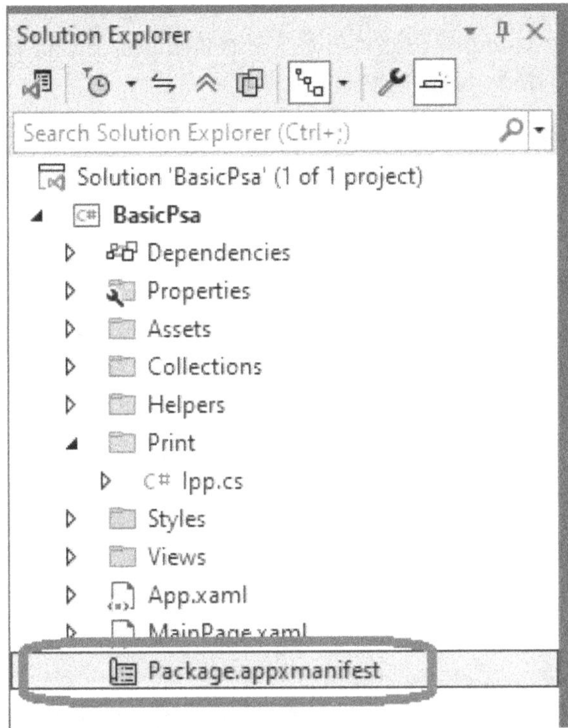

Package.appxmanifest in Solution Explorer

Once the designer view has been opened, click the **Packaging** tab – the Package family name is the last entry on this page. Copy this string as it will be paired with the Hardware ID of the printer for testing.

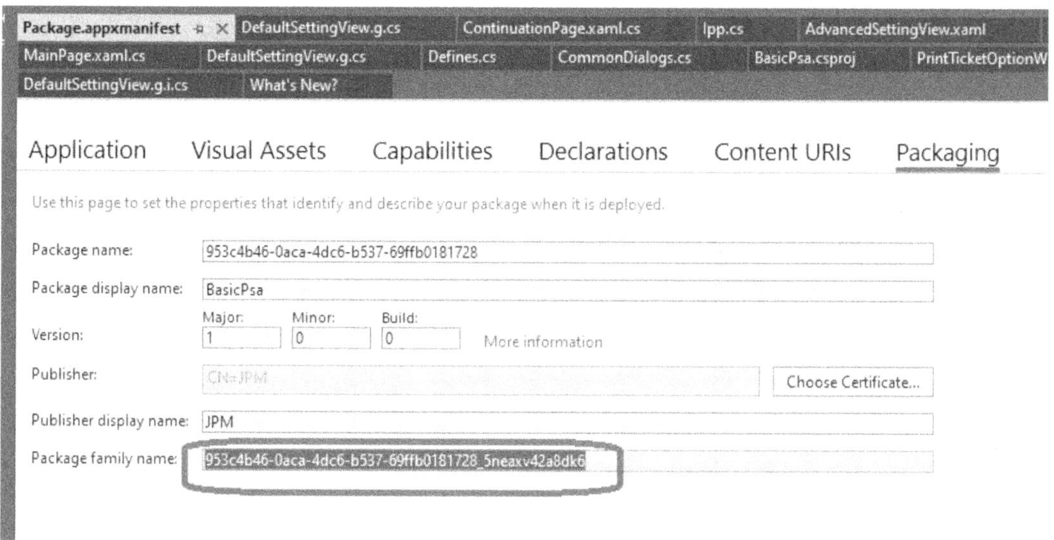

Once you have the package family name, you will want to open the Package. appmanifest file in code view. To do this, right-click Package.appmanifest in Solution Explorer and choose "View Code." You will see something like that shown below – in this case, take a look at the <Applications> section, and in particular the first entry, "Application ID." This value is the label that is appended to the package family name, i.e., **<packagefamilyname>!<Application Id>** to comprise the full string that will be used to associate the PSA to the hardware.

```
<Resources>
  <Resource Language="x-generate"/>
</Resources>

<Applications>
  <Application Id="App"
    Executable="$targetnametoken$.exe"
    EntryPoint="BasicPsa.App"
    uap10:SupportsMultipleInstances="true">
    <uap:VisualElements
      DisplayName="BasicPsa"
      Square150x150Logo="Assets\Square150x150Logo.png"
      Square44x44Logo="Assets\Square44x44Logo.png"
      Description="BasicPsa"
      BackgroundColor="transparent">
      <uap:DefaultTile Wide310x150Logo="Assets\Wide310x150Logo.png"/>
      <uap:SplashScreen Image="Assets\SplashScreen.png" />
    </uap:VisualElements>
    <Extensions>
```

An example might be helpful. The BasicPsa solution had a Package family name in the Package.appxmanifest of 953c4b46-0aca-4dc6-b537-69ffb0181728_5neaxv42a8dk6, and an Application Id (as seen in the previous graphic) of "App." Assuming a Hardware ID of PSA_Hewlett-PackardHP_La884F (from Device Manager), the registry association would be as shown below:

Registry View of Association

Name	Type	Data
(Default)	REG_SZ	(value not set)
PSA_Hewlett-PackardHP_La884F	REG_SZ	953c4b46-0aca-4dc6-b537-69ffb0181728_hp80dpmwedp4j!App

This is made in the HKEY_LOCAL_MACHINE\SYSTEM\CurrentControlSet\Control\Print\PSA\Association hive. Effectively, this links the printer hardware to the application that will be called when the print ticket is being processed. Initially, this will be one PSA to one printer or one PSA application to several printers. If you have to make another association, it will be done in the exact same hive (HKEY_LOCAL_MACHINE\SYSTEM\CurrentControlSet\Control\Print\PSA\Association) that this example was created in.

Going back to the Package.appxmanifest in Visual Studio Solution Explorer, we will need to add the printsupport namespace to the top as shown below.

```
<Package
  xmlns="http://schemas.microsoft.com/appx/manifest/foundation/windows10"
  xmlns:mp="http://schemas.microsoft.com/appx/2014/phone/manifest"
  xmlns:uap="http://schemas.microsoft.com/appx/manifest/uap/windows10"
  xmlns:uap10="http://schemas.microsoft.com/appx/manifest/uap/windows10/10"
  xmlns:printsupport="http://schemas.microsoft.com/appx/manifest/
  printsupport/windows10"
  IgnorableNamespaces="uap mp printsupport">
```

You will also have to add the printSupportSettingsUI contract extension in the manifest file as well. In BasicPsa, this gets added after the VisualElements section in the <Applications> node.

```
<Extensions>
 <printsupport:Extension Category="windows.printSupportSettingsUI"
EntryPoint="BasicPsa.App"/>
</Extensions>
```

There are a good many moving parts to getting the UWP PSA to build correctly; my best advice would be to follow along by using the BasicPsa UWP application as a guide. If you look at the contract extension, you should notice that your entry point should be the name of your PSA, in this case, BasicPsa. Your name will likely differ, so make sure you get that set correctly.

PrintSupportSettingsUI Launch Types

In the Package.appxmanifest file, you should take notice of the Extensions node in the Applications section as mentioned above. In effect, this extension allows the application to integrate with the Windows printing system by informing the UWP framework that your app can handle the print support settings UI. More specifically, the UWP framework recognizes the extension and routes the activation to the appropriate handler (EntryPoint), in this case, the handler found in the test app, BasicPsa. When the UWP PSA app is activated, the OnActivated method (in the App.xaml.cs file) receives a PrintSupportSettingsActivatedEventArgs object that provides access to information about the print support UI session [11].

This is important as the PSA is triggered or activated based on particular user actions within the OS. Two of these events, viewing default printer properties and/or viewing print job properties, are represented by the **UserDefaultPrintTicket** and **JobPrintTicket** launch actions in the OnActivated method within the App.xaml.cs file of BasicPsa. Armed with this information, you can set breakpoints on these launch types (in code) to learn what user events trigger their activation. For instance, if your intention was to change basic printer default settings for an IPP printer, you would navigate to the Settings App ➤ Bluetooth & devices ➤ Printers & scanners ➤ <your target printer>. At this point, you would click **Printing preferences.**

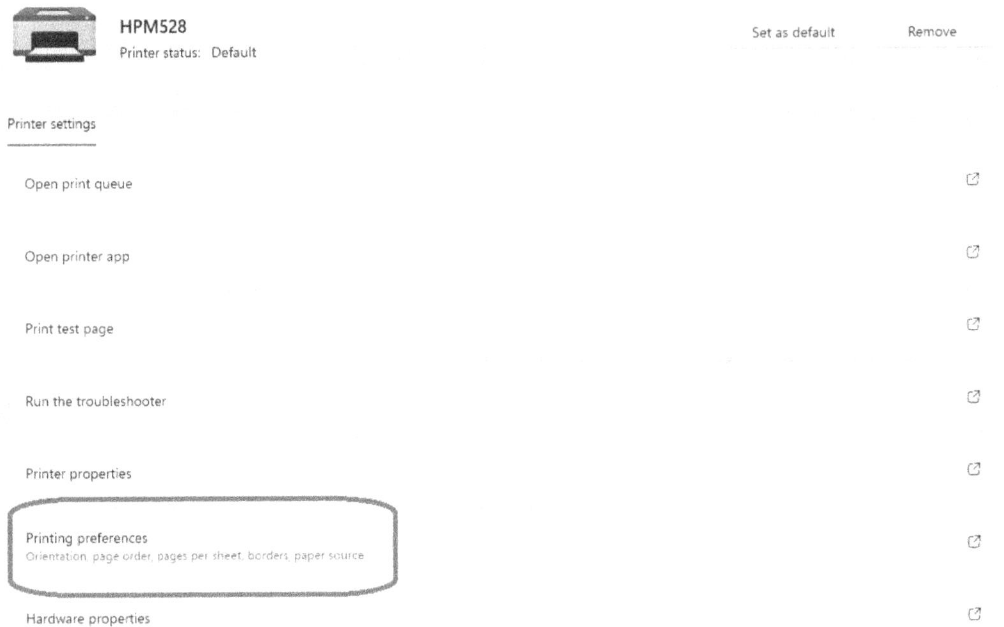

...which then should trigger a breakpoint set at the **SettingsLaunch. UserDefaultPrintTicket** LaunchKind of the **OnActivated** Method housed in the **App. xaml.cs** file of BasicPsa.

```
switch (settingsSession.LaunchKind)
{
    case SettingsLaunchKind.UserDefaultPrintTicket:
        // Navigate to the default settings page
        rootFrame.Navigate(typeof(DefaultSettingView), settingsEventArgs);
        break;
    case SettingsLaunchKind.JobPrintTicket:
        // Navigate to the advanced settings page
        rootFrame.Navigate(typeof(JobPrintTicketView), settingsEventArgs);
        break;
}
```

On the other hand, if your intention was to change the print job settings, you might open a print dialog used by most Windows applications. Ensure your target hardware printer is selected in the Printer combo box. At this point, you should see the default print dialog settings, which are filled in by the default settings provided to the current PrintTicket.

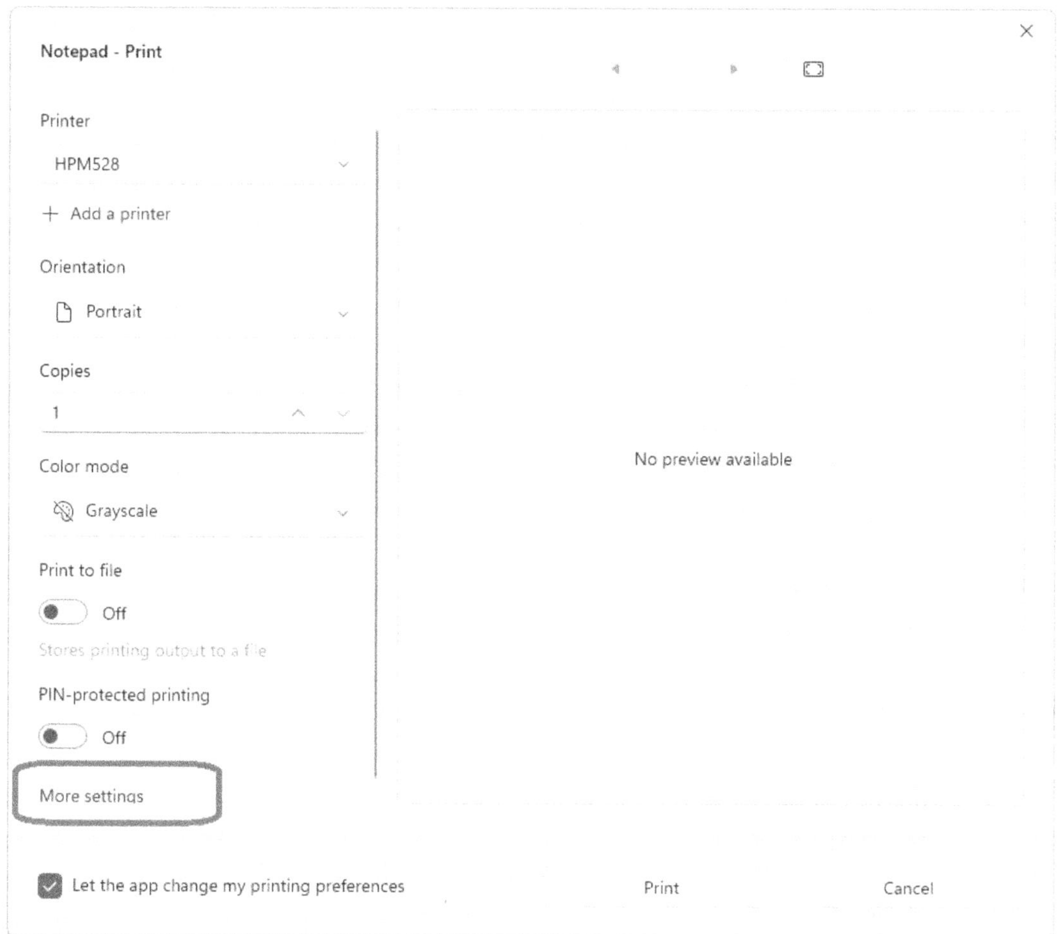

More Settings for the Default Notepad Print Dialog

In Notepad, when you click the More settings link (located near the bottom of the dialog), you signal your intentions to pursue additional available printer job settings. This in turn should trigger a breakpoint set in the SettingsLaunchKind.JobPrintTicket LaunchKind shown below.

```
switch (settingsSession.LaunchKind)
{
    case SettingsLaunchKind.UserDefaultPrintTicket:
        // Navigate to the default settings page
        rootFrame.Navigate(typeof(DefaultSettingView), settingsEventArgs);
        break;
    case SettingsLaunchKind.JobPrintTicket:
        // Navigate to the advanced settings page
        rootFrame.Navigate(typeof(JobPrintTicketView), settingsEventArgs);
        break;
}
```

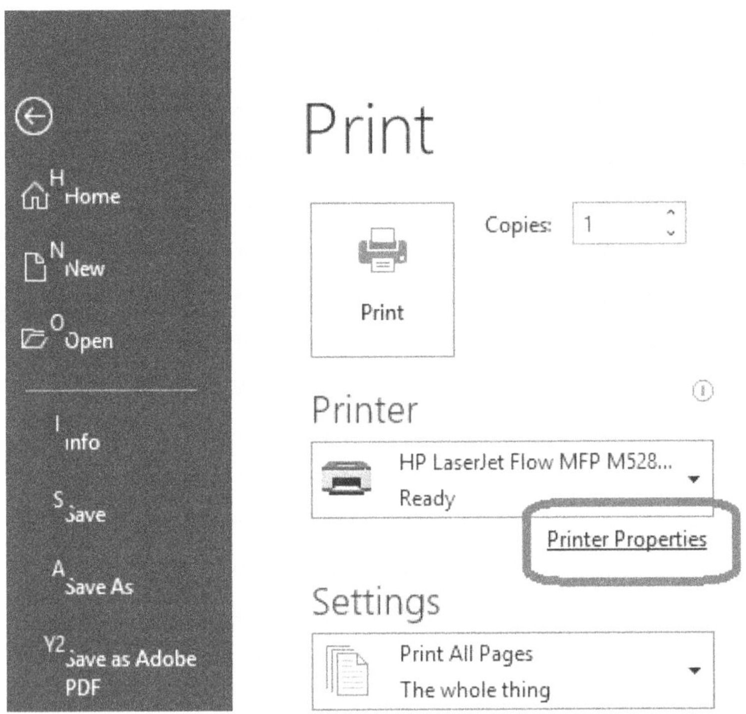

For Word, Print Job Settings Are Called When the Printer Properties Link Is Clicked

If you are using Microsoft Word, the **JobPrintTicket** Page is called when you click the **Printer Properties** link in the Print dialog.

There is another method called by the print subsystem – this one when the user clicks the "Open Printer app" button that appears on the selected printer in Printers

& scanners when the relationship between the Hardware ID and the Application ID is created. When a user clicks this button, the **OnLaunched** method is called. This is the same method called when a standard

Open Printer App Button

```
protected override void OnLaunched(LaunchActivatedEventArgs e)
```

UWP application starts up, and as such this book will not devote much time to it. It is nevertheless good to know about it and why it exists.

Deployment Information

As mentioned earlier, Windows Apps, including UWP PSA apps, differ considerably from their Win32 brethren, most specifically in what they are allowed to do and how they are installed. The intent from Microsoft is to have them installed by the Windows Store into a specific location, in this case, the C:\Program Files\WindowsApps folder. This folder is marked as hidden by default, so you will have to check Explorer's View ➤ Show ➤ Hidden items to be able to see the folder. Even if you make this folder visible, you will (by default) not be able to view or list files within the folder. Trusted Installer is the security principal that has full control of this folder structure as Microsoft wanted to control the installation of apps to this folder. When you build your PSA successfully, it will get deployed (by Visual Studio) into this folder so the system can access it as needed.

The obvious question then is how does Visual Studio deploy updated app information to this folder if the security context or principal that Visual Studio is running under is the developer? The answer for local deployment from Visual Studio is AppX deployment service. The Windows Application Deployment (WinAppDeploy) tool, which is part of the UWP development environment, is used for remote deployment. For Windows 11, Visual Studio uses the Windows Application Model APIs (part of the Windows SDK) to deploy and register apps [8]. These APIs communicate with the AppX deployment service (formerly known as the Windows Package Manager service) to handle app installation and updates in the WindowsApps folder. For remote deployment (to another machine), Visual Studio uses the Windows Application Deployment (WinAppDeploy) tool, which is part of the UWP development environment. WinAppDeploy communicates with the AppX deployment service on the target device, which performs the actual installation and registration. WinAppDeployCmd requires elevated permissions to initiate the deployment process and interact with the remote device's AppX deployment service, but the folder access is handled by the service, not the tool directly.

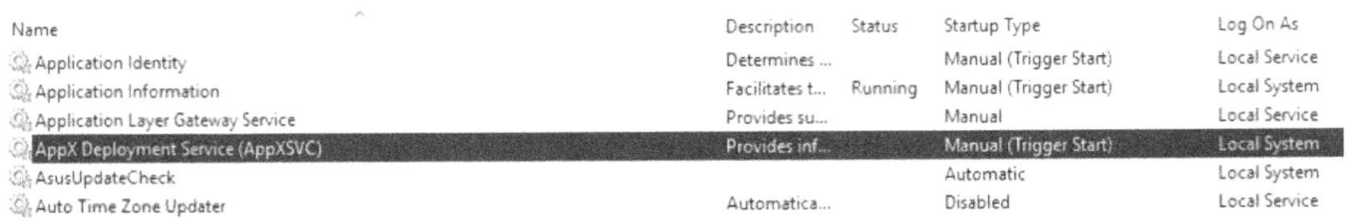

Name	Description	Status	Startup Type	Log On As
Application Identity	Determines ...		Manual (Trigger Start)	Local Service
Application Information	Facilitates t...	Running	Manual (Trigger Start)	Local System
Application Layer Gateway Service	Provides su...		Manual	Local Service
AppX Deployment Service (AppXSVC)	Provides inf...		Manual (Trigger Start)	Local System
AsusUpdateCheck			Automatic	Local System
Auto Time Zone Updater	Automatica...		Disabled	Local Service

AppX Deployment service within the Windows Services applet

The Appx Deployment Service runs under the local SYSTEM account, and as you can see from the next graphic, the ACL for the C:\Program Files\WindowsApps folder allows this security context Full Control of the folder structure.

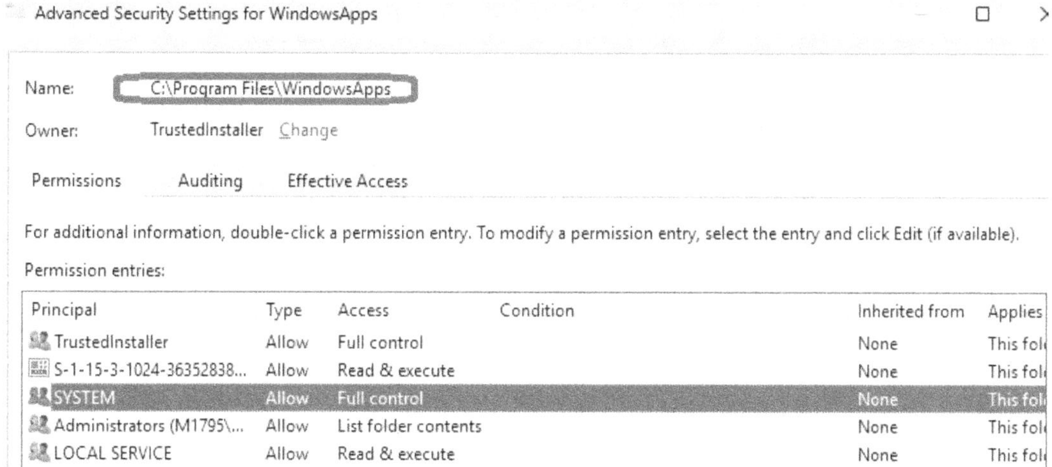

ACL list for C:\Program Files\WindowsApps folder

Thus, while you as a developer do not have rights to directly access the Windows Store, a proxy service running on the machine allows Visual Studio to deploy your debug binaries. You should know that Visual Studio uses a temporary certificate to sign the (to be) deployed app. This certificate is not trusted on other machines, only the native machine where the app is being developed. If the app is destined for the Microsoft Store, the app must be re-signed by the Microsoft trusted store certificate. During development, the certificate used to publish to the local store must be in the computer's trusted root or trusted publishers.

Target Framework Identification

If you forget the target framework initially requested, you can always find this in your project. Click the Solution tab in your project and then double-click the Project Name at the top – in this case, BasicPsa. This will open up an XML file where the TargetFramework property can be viewed.

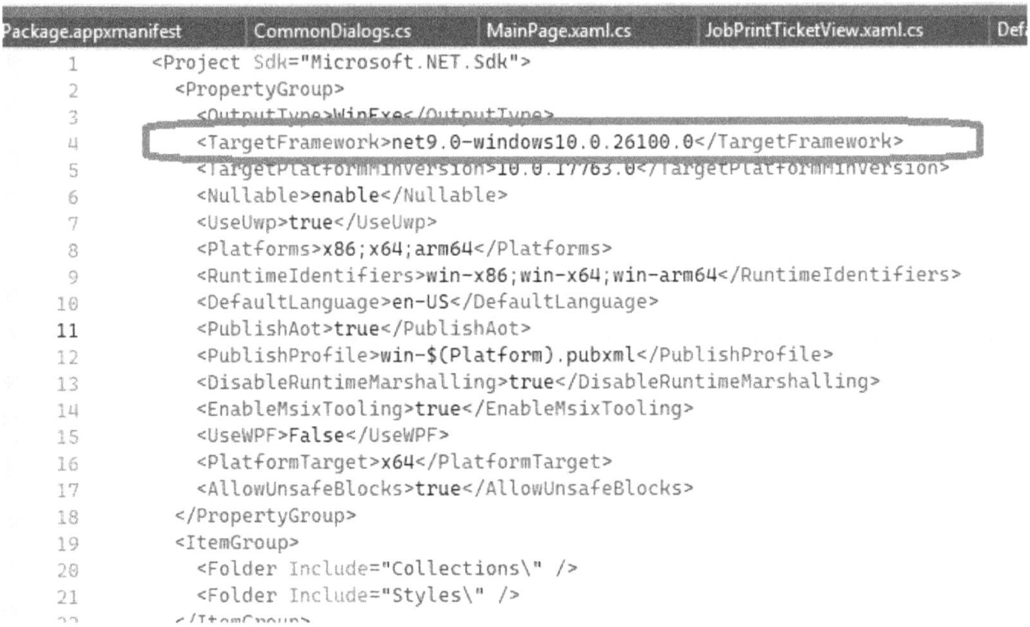

Package.appxmanifest | CommonDialogs.cs | MainPage.xaml.cs | JobPrintTicketView.xaml.cs | Def

```xml
<Project Sdk="Microsoft.NET.Sdk">
  <PropertyGroup>
    <OutputType>WinExe</OutputType>
    <TargetFramework>net9.0-windows10.0.26100.0</TargetFramework>
    <TargetPlatformMinVersion>10.0.17763.0</TargetPlatformMinVersion>
    <Nullable>enable</Nullable>
    <UseUwp>true</UseUwp>
    <Platforms>x86;x64;arm64</Platforms>
    <RuntimeIdentifiers>win-x86;win-x64;win-arm64</RuntimeIdentifiers>
    <DefaultLanguage>en-US</DefaultLanguage>
    <PublishAot>true</PublishAot>
    <PublishProfile>win-$(Platform).pubxml</PublishProfile>
    <DisableRuntimeMarshalling>true</DisableRuntimeMarshalling>
    <EnableMsixTooling>true</EnableMsixTooling>
    <UseWPF>False</UseWPF>
    <PlatformTarget>x64</PlatformTarget>
    <AllowUnsafeBlocks>true</AllowUnsafeBlocks>
  </PropertyGroup>
  <ItemGroup>
    <Folder Include="Collections\" />
    <Folder Include="Styles\" />
  </ItemGroup>
```

Getting target framework from project file

Getting Ahead of Time

If you have previously written any code for WPF applications, you are likely familiar with binding properties to the UI in XAML. For WPF, this was accomplished with the {Binding} attribute. For UWP, an alternate to {Binding}, {x:Bind}, is available that runs in less time and less memory than {Binding} and supports better debugging [13]. The difference is generally in when the code from XAML is converted to equivalent C#. When using {Binding}, this happens after runtime inspection using Reflection. Conversely, {x:Bind} shines as this generation happens at compile-time, allowing for faster application startup and reduced memory footprint. Although the binding objects created by {x:Bind} and {Binding} are largely functionally equivalent, {x:Bind} provides compile-time validation of your binding expressions, allowing instant feedback about issues relating to any binding failures.

The compile-time validation of {x:Bind} thus provides feedback on errors when your application is compiled. This has the advantage over {Binding} expressions that are resolved at run time, which makes debugging more difficult to understand and rectify. Regardless of the choice you make, there are some basic distinctions you should be aware of. To start off, {x:Bind} has a default binding mode of OneTime, where the default for {Binding} is OneWay. In addition, {x:Bind} does not use the DataContext as a default source - it will look in the code-behind of your page or user control for properties or fields.

While this is a potential improvement, I should point out an issue that may cause frustration (and needless wasted debugging time) for developers. The PublishAot (Publish Ahead-of-Time) setting produces a fully native executable that can run on machines that don't have the .NET runtime installed [14]. This is especially significant for high-performance applications and environments. Native AOT deployment model uses an ahead-of-time compiler to compile IL to native code at the time of publish. The native AOT apps don't use a just-in-time (JIT) compiler when the application runs [14]. To do this, certain features such as reflection (System.Reflection.Emit) are scaled back or stripped out for this performance gain. Unfortunately, metadata about certain bindings (in the case of Combobox, it was DisplayMemberPath) is lost, and the binding is not resolved - in this case, item text did not appear as it should.

There are several remedies to this:

1. Set the **<solution name>.csproj** file **PublishAot** entry to false to turn off Ahead of Time (AOT).

   ```
   <PublishAot>false</PublishAot>
   ```

   While this will work, it will also increase the wait time before the app starts as the JIT compiler will be called. However, Reflection metadata is saved; thus, your application works as it would under WPF.

2. Leave PublishAOT as true, but create strongly-typed bindings using x:Bind along with a DataTemplate. This compiles the bindings ahead of time and complements AOT, providing a win-win scenario. This is the direction I took for the BasicPSA app.

When referring to "loosely typed" binding versus "strongly typed" binding, the distinction is specifically whether the compiler will check if a property actually exists or not. For instance, if a WPF binding was created as shown below:

```
<TextBlock Text="{Binding Path=ApplicantName}" />
```

In a loosely typed binding (Standard WPF Binding), the compiler does not check to see that the string literal "ApplicantName" exists. Thus, if there was a typo in the ViewModel, this will not be caught until runtime, where the error would then manifest itself. In x:Bind, the binding is checked at compile time, for instance:

```
<TextBlock Text="{x:Bind ViewModel.ApplicantName, Mode=OneWay}" />
```

is checked at compilation; thus, if ApplicantName was a mistype, the developer would know before runtime errors are created.

Getting and Setting Standard Printer Attributes

If you recall, Windows stores standard print properties common to most printers in the registry for each user. When you click Printing Preferences in the Settings App for the associated printer, this triggers a call into the OnActivated (overridden) method in the App.xaml.cs class. Recall the contract in Package.appxmanifest file:

```
<Extensions>
<printsupport:Extension Category="windows.printSupportSettingsUI"
EntryPoint="BasicPsa.App"/>
</Extensions>
```

which informs the OS you want to receive that contract as your entry point in the named (BasicPsa in this case) PSA. The first code line in OnActivated (in the App.xaml.cs file):

```
if (args.Kind == ActivationKind.PrintSupportSettingsUI)
```

can thus be used to control the flow of execution depending on the activation mechanism. In the case of standard print properties, this is

```
SettingsLaunchKind.UserDefaultPrintTicket
```

thus, we navigate to this page. As an argument to the DefaultSettingView Page, we pass a PrintSupportSettingsUISession object, which provides the session print ticket we need to examine and modify (if necessary) [11].

Navigation in UWP Apps

If you have previously been exposed to WPF applications, a very brief synopsis of UWP PSA navigation might be in order. UWP apps navigate between frames, which host pages and manage navigation history. In UWP, there is typically a single Frame that hosts other pages. You can navigate between those pages using the root frame's Navigate method, which replaces the current page with a new page. (There is generally only one active Frame, and changing pages replaces the contents of each page.) After Navigation, OnNavigatedTo event handler is called by the UWP framework and gets the NavigationEventArgs object from the previous page. A Parameter object passed from the caller and URI are amongst the properties passed [10].

Examining the Print Ticket

We should now examine the BasicPsa app in operation - the first assignment is to examine the default print ticket properties and (if necessary) to modify them to meet our print requirements. In **DefaultSettingView.xaml.cs** file, the OnNavigatedTo method is called (from App.xaml.cs) with the PrintSupportSettingsUISession object set as a parameter. This is cast into the PrintSupportSettingsUISession object from which we extract a WorkflowPrintTicket (printTicket). From this value we can get the list of print ticket capabilities in the LoadFeatures method:

```
PrintTicketCapabilities printTicketCapabilities = this.printTicket.
GetCapabilities();
```

We can then load the Combobox controls in the XAML page with the values from each PrintTicketOption object we extract from the print ticket and display them.

At this point, the user is free to rummage through the controls and select the values that suit their printing requirements. For demonstration purposes, BasicPsa displays the print orientation, page resolution, and duplex and collate settings. You are free to add/subtract as you please from the properties typically provided by the default print ticket. Keep in mind that these properties originated in the per-printer user preferences stored in binary format in the registry location(s) HKCU\Printers\DevModesPerUser and DevModes2. Once satisfied that their selections will meet their print requirements, the user can click OK to set the choices in the print ticket. The print ticket can then be used (in IPP printers) as a basis for the IPP request job attributes that the IPP Class Driver creates. Recall the IPP Class Driver must convert the print ticket values to applicable RFC job attributes for the IPP printer. The choices are also stored back in the per-user preferences for the next print request.

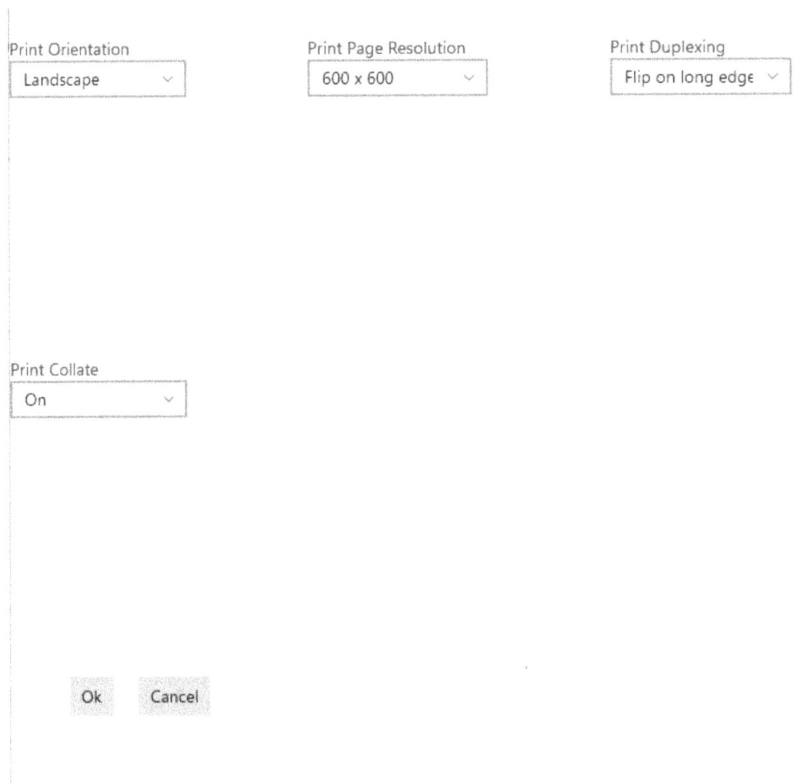

DefaultSettingView and PrintTicket Values

While looking at (or modifying) the default print ticket values may seem rather ordinary, it does hold some value for organizations that might benefit by "steering" their print clients to settings that align with corporate values. For instance, you might want to filter out the 1200x1200 print page resolution and provide only 300x300 and 600x600 page resolutions. Perhaps your organization would like to encourage users to select only duplexing to save paper – this is your chance to do so. If this is considered, then remember that only one PSA can service and print any Hardware ID.

When the OK button is selected, the OkClicked event handler is called. Most of the code here is rather intuitive, but I would like to direct your attention to the way in which the print ticket is validated and updated. Once this is accomplished, the print ticket is then sent to the IPP Class Driver and converted into IPP requests with job attributes that align with the validated print ticket options.

```
// Validate and submit PrintTicket
WorkflowPrintTicketValidationResult result = await printTicket.
ValidateAsync();
if (result.Validated)
{
    // PrintTicket validated successfully - submit and exit
    this.uiSession.UpdatePrintTicket(printTicket);
    this.application.Exit();
}
```

Note The UpdatePrintTicket modifies the in-memory print ticket and does not specifically store the values you modify. However, in practice it appears that the last used print ticket is persisted to the registry as settings do appear to persist between sessions.

Getting Special Vendor Attributes

At the time of this writing, no major print manufacturer has supplied a Print Support App that can be used in production. This makes a demonstration of intent a bit more difficult, but we can display *how* this would be accomplished even if the example is a bit contrived. As you are aware, one of the purposes of a PSA is to allow the user to interact with special vendor attributes that may not be specified in the IPP standards [5]. In other words, users can access features not defined by standard IPP registrations. In this regard, you will have to allow a bit of leeway for the demonstration in this chapter. This is because each vendor is tasked with providing the special feature attributes, and at the time of this writing, no particular attributes are yet forthcoming. Nevertheless, for demonstration purposes, I noticed my HP M528 had a few non-standardized attributes returned when requesting Get-Printer-Attributes. Those attributes were:

hp-edge-to-edge-support

hp-enhanced-mixed-orientation-supported

hp-tabbed-printing-supported

None of these are intended as IPP special attributes – this coming from our HP print engineer. Nevertheless, they have boolean values attached to them and as such will have to suffice for demonstration purposes. Conveniently, the WinRT APIs leveraged in Chapter 2, "Printer Talk," will work just as well in our demo PSA. If you look in the Print folder of the BasicPsa app, you should find the Ipp.cs file. This file houses the GetVendorSpecialAttributesAsync method, which calls get-printer-attributes using WinRT and provides the resulting IDictionary<string, IppAttributeValue> collection as the return value if successful. You can limit the return collection by specifying just the special attributes you desire, in this case, our pseudo-special attributes outlined earlier.

```
public static string atts = "hp-edge-to-edge-support,hp-enhanced-mixed-
orientation-supported,hp-tabbed-printing-supported";
```

We split the string along the "," char and place the result in a list of strings that the IppPrintDevice object's GetPrinterAttributes method can use. As these are network calls, we should await this call, especially for methods housed in GUI apps as our PSA is. The result should be our special attributes along with their values. The center of action lies in the Ipp.cs file, specifically the following code line in the GetVendorSpecialAttributesAsync method. This method uses the Windows.Devices. Printers namespace and the very same GetPrinterAttributes call used in Chapter 2, "Printer Talk," for the WinRtIppTest project.

```
return await Task.Run(() => printer.GetPrinterAttributes(requested_
attributes));
```

Which handles the collection of IDictionary<string, IppAttributeValue> values that are returned (as a Task) from GetPrinterAtributes.

If you choose to modify this code, you can request different attributes to return. Depending on the attributes you choose to return, you may have to deal with a different variable type than the boolean types returned for these special attributes. If you get a bit confused, you can always refer to the DisplayPrinterAttributes method of Chapter 2's, "Printer Talk," WinRtIppTest project for guidance on handling other variable types.

I will draw your attention to JobPrintTicketView, which is the code behind for the XAML UI that will present the "special" attributes: hp-edge-to-edge-support, hp-enhanced-mixed-orientation-supported, and hp-tabbed-printing-supported. As mentioned earlier, the HP engineer had advised me that these IPP attributes are not intended to be used as special vendor attributes and are essentially a leftover from the old V3 driver info. Regardless, they will serve as an example of how to recover any special attributes from the printer and present them for modification in the UI. If you look at the GetVendorSpecialAttributesAsync return, you will notice that the collection of IDictionary objects is returned from the Awaited method and thus is likely filled by a thread other than the dispatcher thread. A note of warning: If you attempt to modify a UI control in this context, there is likely to be trouble.

```
IDictionary<string, IppAttributeValue> attributes = await Ipp.GetVendorSpec
ialAttributesAsync(printer.PrinterName);

await Dispatcher.RunAsync(Windows.UI.Core.CoreDispatcherPriority.Normal, ()
=>foreach (var attribute in attributes)
{
    if (attribute.Key == "hp-edge-to-edge-support")
    {
        EdgeToEdge = (bool)attribute.Value.GetBooleanArray().
FirstOrDefault();
    }
```

Because of this, we call the Dispatcher thread to modify the UI controls rather than the awaited thread, thus safely completing the Ipp.GetVendorSpecialAttributesAsync method. If you are running this example and using anything but an HP printer, you can easily modify this code to suit your needs.

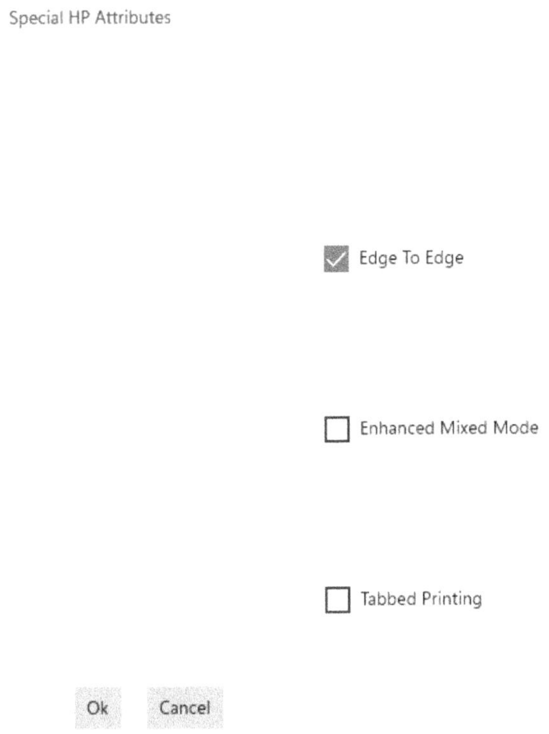

Special HP Attributes

Edge To Edge

Enhanced Mixed Mode

Tabbed Printing

Ok Cancel

HP "Special" Attribute Values Displayed for the User

As mentioned previously, the "special attributes" I used in this demo are neither special nor even normal IPP attributes. In fact, these are non-modifiable from the user end and thus hardly qualify to be used as such. Therefore, you should notice that the OkClicked event handler in the JobPrintTicketView file does absolutely nothing - it does not have provisions to send the modified "special attributes" back to the printer as you would assume it should. This, unfortunately, is a limitation, but hopefully enough of the concept was provided for you to understand how that would be done.

UWP Storage

UWP apps can leverage the UWP Storage APIs to persist data between sessions. The **Storage.cs** file in the IO folder of the project has several ways to persist data. For instance, you might use something like the following to store individual settings:

```
ApplicationData.Current.LocalSettings.Values["MySettings"] = propertyValue;
```

To store a list of application setting strings:

```
public static async Task WriteSettings(List<string> appSettings)
{
    try
    {
        Windows.Storage.StorageFolder storageFolder = Windows.
        Storage.ApplicationData.Current.LocalFolder;
        Windows.Storage.StorageFile file = await storageFolder.
        CreateFileAsync("BasicPsaStorage.txt", Windows.Storage.
        CreationCollisionOption.ReplaceExisting);
        await Windows.Storage.FileIO.WriteLinesAsync(file,
        appSettings);
        // Log the written items
        System.Diagnostics.Debug.WriteLine("Written items: " +
        string.Join(", ", appSettings));
    }
    catch (Exception ex)
    {
        // Handle exceptions (e.g., log them)
        System.Diagnostics.Debug.WriteLine("Error writing settings:
        " + ex.Message);
    }
}
```

And finally, to store a list of Print Ticket Options:

```
public static async Task StorePrintTicketOptionsAsync(List<PrintTicket
Option> printTicketOptions)
{
    // Get the local folder
    StorageFolder localFolder = ApplicationData.Current.LocalFolder;
    // Create or replace the file
    StorageFile file = await localFolder.CreateFileAsync("PrintTicket
    OptionStorage.txt", CreationCollisionOption.ReplaceExisting);
```

```
        // Serialize the list of PrintTicketOptions to JSON and write to
           the file
        string jsonString = JsonSerializer.Serialize(printTicketOptions);
        await FileIO.WriteTextAsync(file, jsonString);
    }
```

Chapter Summary

The Print Service App is specifically designed to allow clients to modify the print ticket prior to the Microsoft IPP Driver converting these settings to their constituent IPP request components. It also allows clients to interact with printer attributes not specifically supported by the IPP RFC standards but necessary for interaction with unique vendor features. It requires that the developing machine have developer mode enabled in order for side loading to handle XPS-to-PDF conversion or interact with the print stack via APIs. When debugging, the PSA is deployed to the WindowsApps folder, which is specifically permissioned by default to allow only the Trusted Installer to accomplish this task. Windows provides the AppX deployment service as a proxy to update or modify the local Windows Store without allowing users direct access.

Developing or Debugging a PSA requires an association be made between the UWP application's Package family name and the IPP printer hardware id. It is by this association that Windows knows which PSA to activate when any particular IPP printer is selected. In development mode, this association can be made manually in the registry, but in the event of production code, an extension INF file contained in a signed catalog file is required. The signed catalog file proves the PSA files haven't been tampered with by containing a signed list of hashes for each file.

Only one PSA application can be associated on any Windows system with a given Hardware ID provided by the manufacturer. On the other hand, multiple Hardware IDs can be associated with a PSA application, these being associated within an INF file or (in the case of development) in the registry. The Package.appmanifest file specifies the PackageFamilyName that uniquely identifies the PSA software package and any contract extensions supported by the PSA. Finally, while a PSA is typically developed by a vendor to support features not specifically supported in the IPP RFCs, it can also be used by organizations to limit the feature options shown to the user community to encourage print usage behaviors.

References

1. Print Support App v4 API design guide, Microsoft Learn, 01/13/2025, https://learn.microsoft.com/en-us/windows-hardware/drivers/devapps/print-support-app-v4-design-guide
2. Print Support App v1 and v2 design guide, Microsoft Learn, May 19-22 2025 , https://learn.microsoft.com/en-us/windows-hardware/drivers/devapps/print-support-app-design-guide
3. Windows.Graphics.Printing.PrintSupport Namespace, Microsoft Learn, May 19-22 2025, https://learn.microsoft.com/en-us/uwp/api/windows.graphics.printing.printsupport?view=winrt-26100&viewFallbackFrom=winrt-insider&preserve-view=true
4. Print support app association, MicrosoftDocs, https://github.com/MicrosoftDocs/windows-driver-docs/blob/staging/windows-driver-docs-pr/devapps/print-support-app-association.md
5. Internet Printing Protocol (IPP) Registrations, IANA, 7/15/2002, last updated 10/9/2024, https://www.iana.org/assignments/ipp-registrations/ipp-registrations.xhtml
6. How to SideLoad apps on Windows 11/10, TheWindowsClub, https://www.thewindowsclub.com/sideload-apps-windows-10
7. What's a Universal Windows Platform (UWP) app?, Microsoft Learn, 8/20/2024 , https://learn.microsoft.com/en-us/windows/uwp/get-started/universal-application-platform-guide
8. Windows.ApplicationModel Namespace, Windows Learn, https://learn.microsoft.com/en-us/uwp/api/windows.applicationmodel?view=winrt-26100
9. Navigate to a new page, RIP Tutorial, https://riptutorial.com/uwp/example/26308/navigate-to-a-newest-page
10. NavigationEventArgs Class, Windows Learn, https://learn.microsoft.com/en-us/uwp/api/windows.ui.xaml.navigation.navigationeventargs?view=winrt-26100
11. PrintSupportSettingsUISession Class, Windows App Development, https://learn.microsoft.com/enus/uwp/api/windows.graphics.printing.printsupport.printsupportsettingsuisession?view=winrt-26100
12. Install apps with the WinAppDeployCmd.exe tool, Microsoft Learn, https://learn.microsoft.com/en-us/windows/uwp/packaging/install-universal-windows-apps-with-the-winappdeploycmd-tool

13. {x:Bind} markup extension, Microsoft Learn, 10/20/2022, https://learn.microsoft.com/en-us/windows/uwp/xaml-platform/x-bind-markup-extension
14. Native AOT deployment, Microsoft Learn, https://learn.microsoft.com/en-us/dotnet/core/deploying/native-aot/?tabs=windows%2Cnet8
15. Print Support App Association, Windows Learn, https://learn.microsoft.com/en-us/windows-hardware/drivers/devapps/print-support-app-association https://developer.microsoft.com/en-us/windows/downloads/windows-sdk/ https://learn.microsoft.com/en-us/windows/uwp/get-started/create-uwp-apps https://learn.microsoft.com/en-us/windows/apps/get-started/system-requirements https://learn.microsoft.com/en-us/windows/uwp/launch-resume/how-to-create-and-consume-an-app-service

CHAPTER 9

IPP Tools

In this chapter, we will explore some great software development and learning aids you might employ to gain a better understanding of IPP/IPPS. By now, you are well versed with Wireshark, likely the best diagnostic tool for IPP you can use. The tools in this chapter take it up a notch and create or accept stricter enforcement of the IPP RFC standards. For instance, if you develop against a hardware vendor whose enforcement of IPP is a bit loose, you might find that your code will not work on another vendor's print hardware. If you are a print hardware manufacturer, you might want to develop an IPP/IPPS network services stack or server-side implementation of IPP. In short, engineers might want to

1. Test IPP compliance (simulate how their printer responds to real IPP clients).
2. Verify printer behavior without needing physical hardware.
3. Develop and debug IPP-based features before deploying them on the actual embedded OS.
4. Validate conformance with IPP standards (for example, IPP Everywhere, Mopria).

Whatever your reason for testing, one of the best tools for learning IPP or developing for IPP is "ippserver," developed and made available by the ISTO Printer Working Group. The basic idea was to create a virtual IPP printer that would respond to IPP requests as an IPP printer should (and just as importantly, exactly as the RFC standards dictate). The upshot is that a technician or developer could learn or develop without the need for actual hardware printers. There are several ways to get this utility, and there are several OS versions it can run on. In this chapter, we will explore these tools on both Linux and Windows 11.

J. Marion, *Adopting Internet Printing Protocol for Windows*, https://doi.org/10.1007/979-8-8688-2010-6_9

As you are reading this book about running IPP on Windows, I'll assume that you (like myself) might be less than an expert on Linux. Thus, the next few recommendations are for those users eager to get the virtual IPP server up and running and less interested in compiling the binaries on the Linux platform. Of course, if you are comfortable with Linux, you probably already know how to compile and build these apps natively. This chapter also includes an executable version of "ippeveprinter," which is similar to "ippserver" yet can be operated on a Windows platform (natively) as it is compiled for Windows x64 architecture. Either way, you can use a virtualized IPP printer to test, develop, or debug issues you may encounter moving to IPP or developing IPP software.

Windows Native Utilities

The Linux Foundation OpenPrinting group created a Windows port of the CUPS project, which provides many of the tools used for testing on Windows. One of the tools called "ippeveprinter" emulates a printer that supports IPP Everywhere. The idea is to test prospective IPP Everywhere clients against a lightweight server to test basic functionality. A second IPP print emulation utility is called "ippserver," and while this utility is more difficult to set up, it provides a more comprehensive test environment as it adheres more closely to the RFC specifications. While "ippserver" in its native Linux environment seems to run with fewer issues, the Windows version works for those more comfortable within the Microsoft world. The final utility we will visit is "ipptool," which provides an RFC-compliant IPP client. The idea is to submit RFC-compliant IPP requests and test printer response. This also pays dividends when you want to develop IPP client software and compare your request against a known good standard. "ipptool" is included in the Windows Utilities folder of this chapter; the ipptool-20130731-windows MSI file works on both x64 and x86 platforms. Both "ippserver" and "ippeveprinter" come in the Windows Utilities folder as well and can be run from that location if desired.

"ipptool" on Windows

Ipptool sends IPP requests to the specified printer-uri and tests and/or displays the results. Each named test file defines one or more requests, including the expected response status, attributes, and values. Output is either a plain text, formatted text, CSV, or XML report on the standard output, with a non-zero exit status indicating that one or more tests have failed [7]. The first order of business should be to run the "ipptool" MSI and install the utility. For convenience, you might want to add a Windows Path statement - as this is not done during the installation. Two of the most common switches are -t (produce a test report) and -v (be verbose), and of course they can be combined (-tv). The utility uses a <requestname>.test file for configuration purposes: thus, the get-printer-attributes request would expect a get-printer-attributes.test file, a print-job request would expect a print-job.test file to be available, etc. Argument position on the command line is important; thus, entering **ipptool -t get-printer-attributes.test ipp://HPM528/ printer/print** on the command line will get you a view of help, while **ipptool -t ipp://HPM528/ printer/print get-printer-attributes.test** will run perfectly fine. Let's try a simple get-printer-attributes request and ask the utility to just provide a test result.

```
ipptool -t ipp://HPM528/printer/print get-printer-attributes.test
```

For this test, the following brief test reply with PASS or FAIL will be shown as below:

```
"C:/Program Files (x86)/ipptool/ipptool/get-printer-attributes.test":
    Get printer attributes using Get-Printer-Attributes          [PASS]
```

To return the actual printer attributes (as you typically would want to), use the verbose (-v) switch:

```
ipptool -t -v ipp://HPM528/printer/print get-printer-attributes.test
```

Which will provide a much more verbose response back, including all the requested attributes:

```
    Get-Printer-Attributes:
        attributes-charset (charset) = utf-8
        attributes-natural-language (naturalLanguage) = en
        printer-uri (uri) = ipp://HPM528:631/printer/print
    Get printer attributes using Get-Printer-Attributes                [PASS]
        RECEIVED: 13828 bytes in response
        status-code = successful-ok (successful-ok)
        attributes-charset (charset) = utf-8
        attributes-natural-language (naturalLanguage) = en
        printer-uri-supported (uri) = ipp://HPM528:631/ipp/print
        uri-security-supported (keyword) = none
        uri-authentication-supported (keyword) = requesting-user-name
        printer-name (nameWithoutLanguage) = HPM528
```

```
        printer-dns-sd-name (nameWithoutLanguage) = HP LaserJet Flow MFP
        M528 \[84AF0F]
        printer-geo-location (unknown) = unknown
        printer-location (textWithoutLanguage) = PEB-2J5
```

The actual response is much lengthier, but for brevity it was truncated. Notice the first positional argument after options on the command line is always treated as the URI, and this value gets assigned to $uri in the *.test file.

The next request tested will be a get-jobs request, and more specifically, the get-completed-jobs test. As you can see, this request looks for the get-completed-jobs.test file. The ipptool command line for this test is shown below:

```
ipptool -t -v ipp://HPM528/printer/print get-completed-jobs.test
```

The response from the printer is what you might expect – it provides all the completed jobs on the printer under the username that made the request.

```
job-id job-state job-name                            job-originating-user-name
job-media-sheets-completed
------ --------- ------------------------------ ----------------------- -
4      completed ipp://110.0.0.214/ipp/port1-0004 jpm1962                   1
3      aborted   ipp://110.0.0.214/ipp/port1-0003 jpm1962                   0
2      completed ipp://110.0.0.214/ipp/port1-0002 jpm1962                   1
1      completed ipp://110.0.0.214/ipp/port1-0001 anonymous                 1
```

As you might imagine, a print-job test is just as easy to do. In this case, you must use the -f switch to indicate the file you want to print, but otherwise the syntax is similar to all the other requests.

```
ipptool -tv -f "C:\Temp\test.pdf" ipp://HPM528/ipp/print print-job.test
```

The reply from the printer indicates that this request passed the test ([PASS]}, and the job-id is provided (although by this time the job has already been printed out).

```
  Print-Job:
        attributes-charset (charset) = utf-8
        attributes-natural-language (naturalLanguage) = en
        printer-uri (uri) = ipp://HPM528:631/ipp/print
        requesting-user-name (nameWithoutLanguage) = jmsp
```

```
        document-format (mimeMediaType) = application/pdf
        copies (integer) = 1
    Print file using Print-Job                                    [PASS]
        RECEIVED: 205 bytes in response
        status-code = successful-ok (successful-ok)
        attributes-charset (charset) = utf-8
        attributes-natural-language (naturalLanguage) = en
        job-uri (uri) = ipp://110.0.0.214/ipp/port1/job-0005
        job-id (integer) = 5
        job-state (enum) = processing
        job-state-reasons (keyword) = none
        job-state-message (textWithoutLanguage) = none
```

The uses for this tool are obvious: you can not only compare your development efforts against the tool via Wireshark, but hardware manufacturers can test their server-side implementation of IPP as well.

A few other tests you can do:

For testing IPP Everywhere conformance of a printer:

```
ipptool -tv ipp://HPM528/ipp/print ipp-everywhere.test
```

For subscriptions to a printer:

```
ipptool -tv ipp://HPM528/ipp/print get-subscriptions.test
```

For notifications from a printer:

```
ipptool -tv ipp://HPM528/ipp/print get-notifications.test
```

For testing IPP 2.0 conformance of a printer:

```
ipptool -tv ipp://HPM528/ipp/print ipp-2.0.test
```

Depending on the printer hardware you test against, not all of the tests will be successful. For instance, since my HP528 printer does not support notifications, you should expect the request to fail, and it does. Having the -v switch set can really help here as the printer error will be verbose and easier to diagnose:

```
Get events using Get-Notifications          [FAIL]
status-code = server-error-operation-not-supported (server-error-operation-
not-supported)
```

When the request fails, you should also receive a status code that aids in finding out the reason. As my printer hardware does not support notifications, the "server-error-operation-not-supported" status code is entirely expected.

IppEvePrinter

The "ippeveprinter" tool is a simple Internet Printing Protocol (IPP) server conforming to the IPP Everywhere (PWG 5100.14) specification. It can be used to test client software or act as a very basic print server that runs a command for every job that is printed [8]. You can use it to test your IPP library for conformity to the IPP Everywhere standard. The command line to run the virtualized printer is similar to that of ippserver. You can find the x64 executable in the section "Windows Native Utilities" of this chapter under the "ippeveprinter" folder. As with the "ippserver," you might want to create a Windows Path statement so you can easily call it on the command line. When you start ippeveprinter, you should be aware that it will not automatically start up on port 631 - you must tell it to do so. For instance, entering the following on the Windows command line:

```
ippeveprinter.exe MyFakePrinter
```

Without specifying the port resulted in the virtual printer listened on port 8631 instead of 631. Thus, if you want to start your ippeveprinter utility on a port that real printers listen on (for IPP), you should enter the following:

```
ippeveprinter.exe -p 631 MyFakePrinter
```

To ensure a more realistic test environment. After entering the last command line, I received the following prompt from Windows. Clicking **Allow** will tell the firewall to let the utility run without restrictions, so you can test.

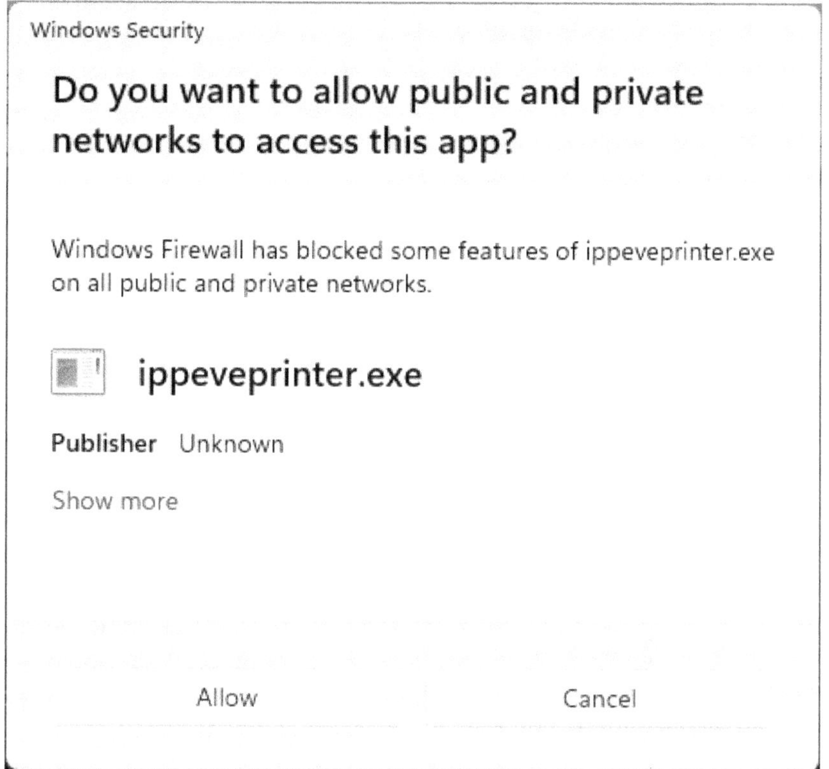

Windows Firewall Prompt

Oddly, when performing an IPP Everywhere test from my Linux machine (using "ippserver") against my Windows ippeveprinter listening on port 631, the IPP everywhere test fails. Apparently ippeveprinter does not support all the required attributes the IPP Everywhere test file requires. That should not be a surprise as ippeveserver was not designed for strict compliance verification. Rather, it was more intended as a lightweight quick test for connectivity.

If you are patient, you can run both ipptool (as the client) and ippeveprinter (as the virtual IPP printer) from the same Windows machine. The following graphics were taken from my Windows machine serving as client and printer at the same time. The client does a get-printer-attributes request, and the printer returns back (virtual) attributes it supports. While ippeveprinter can do some testing, I would recommend testing against ippserver. On my Windows box, the ippeveprinter would close after one request from the client, making testing a bit cumbersome.

```
Command Prompt

C:\Users\jpmsp>ipptool -tv ipp://110.0.0.5/ipp/print get-printer-attributes.test
"C:/Program Files (x86)/ipptool/ipptool/get-printer-attributes.test":
    Get-Printer-Attributes:
        attributes-charset (charset) = utf-8
        attributes-natural-language (naturalLanguage) = en
        printer-uri (uri) = ipp://10.0.0.50:631/ipp/print
    Get printer attributes using Get-Printer-Attributes                    [PASS]
        RECEIVED: 7193 bytes in response
        status-code = successful-ok (successful-ok)
        attributes-charset (charset) = utf-8
        attributes-natural-language (naturalLanguage) = en
        color-supported (boolean) = false
        copies-default (integer) = 1
        copies-supported (rangeOfInteger) = 1-1
        finishing-template-supported (keyword) = none
        finishings-col-database (collection) = {finishing-template=none}
```

"ipptool" on Windows as an IPP Client

```
cmd.exe - Shortcut

C:\Windows\System32>"D:\BACKUP\IPP Book\Chapter 9\Windows Utilities\ippeveprinter.exe" -p 631 "MyVirtua
lPrinter"
110.0.0.5  POST /ipp/print
110.0.0.5  Continue
110.0.0.5  Get-Printer-Attributes successful-ok
           OK
110.0.0.5  Client closed connection.

C:\Windows\System32>
```

"ippeveprinter" on Windows as a Virtual IPP Printer

Ippserver

If "ippeveprinter" was designed as a lightweight, quick-test virtual printer, "ippserver" is a heavyweight RFC-compliant tool. You can find the x64 executable in the section "Windows Utilities" of this chapter.

"ippserver" on Windows Subsystem for Linux

Windows Subsystem for Linux (WSL) is a feature of Windows that allows you to run a Linux environment on your Windows 11 machine without the need for a separate virtual machine or dual booting [2]. You can run various distros (on my machine it was Ubuntu) and use Linux applications, utilities, and Bash command-line tools directly on Windows, unmodified, without the overhead of a traditional virtual machine or dual boot setup [3]. For our purposes, this setup allows the use of many of the CUPS tools running in their native (albeit virtualized) environment they were designed to work in. If you are not comfortable running "ipptool" on a Linux box (or the cost of a second computer is prohibitive), this might be a good way to make requests against a real printer or even a virtual (read "ippserver" or "ippeveprinter") printer. The advantage here is comparing the IPP traces they create on Wireshark to a development project request or even to an existing software utility having issues with an IPP printer. While I would recommend comparing Wireshark traces to existing Windows 11 IPP Class Driver output, when possible, there are likely requests (Pause-Printer, Resume-Printer, Get-Jobs, etc.) that the IPP Class Driver does not currently support.

Why might you want to use Windows Subsystem for Linux when there are native Windows binaries for "ipptool," "ippserver," and "ippeveprinter"? The easiest answer is to learn Linux in the same box you use Windows on. My own experience was that WSL, while an interesting alternative, is not yet robust enough to fully rely on.

IppServer on Linux

The easiest way to download and get the software running is to install it on a Linux box and use that as your virtual printer. For those not fully versed in Linux, there are ways to make this as painless as possible. For ease of installation and use, I decided to go the AppImage route, which is described as an "elegant and efficient way to make (packaged applications) run across a large range of Linux distributions" [1]. You can find the link to this download here:

```
https://github.com/KurtPfeifle/ippsample/releases/
download/continuous/ippsample-xperimental-x86_64.
AppImage
```

In the event the link changes, you can search for "ippsample-xperimental-x86_64. AppImage," which should take you to the right place. Download the appimage and place it in a folder you want to run it from. You can even keep it in your Downloads folder if you like. Once downloaded on your Linux box, you must make it executable – this should do it:

```
chmod +x ippsample-xperimental-x86_64.AppImage
```

Which should make it ready to run or execute. In truth, this AppImage is a bit different in that it lets you run the command line interfaces for ippfind, ippserver, ipptool, and ippproxy from one file. For the purposes of this book, we will concentrate on ippserver, as it will play an important role in learning and developing on IPP, but feel free to explore the others as well. If all goes well, you can open a command line and navigate to the location where you copied the AppImage file and run it from there.

```
./ippsample-xperimental-x86_64.AppImage ippserver MyVirtualPrinter
```

And after you hit Enter, you might see something like:

```
Starting IPP Everywhere Printer: MyPrinter
Listening on port 8000...
```

Or, in my case:

```
Ignoring Avahi state 2
```

Both of which tell you that "ippserver" is up and listening for requests. The second line indicates the app tried to talk to the Avahi Daemon but didn't get a response, so it will skip auto-announcement. I would direct you to the port it is listening to – by default this is port 8000. If you are comfortable testing your IPP software with the default (8000) port, you are set. However, as IPP by default uses port 631 (we won't go into IPPS on your Linux machine, as that would entail creating a certificate to present to your client, which would be out of the scope of this discussion), it might be best to test your software on the port it was designed to use. Thus, we have to tell ippserver to use port 631 rather than the default port. We can do this by using the -p <port to use> option for ippserver.

```
./ippsample-xperimental-x86_64.AppImage ippserver <Your Printer
Name> -p 631
```

Hopefully that works on your box, but it complained as shown on my box:

```
Unable to listen on address "0.0.0.0": Address already in use
Unable to listen on address "[V1.::]": Address already in use
```

For whatever reason, CUPS still blocked ippserver from using port 631. You can change the config file for CUPS so it does not do this, but as this is for testing purposes, there is a less intrusive method. You can stop CUPS for the time being, run ippserver for testing purposes, and then restart CUPS.

To do this, type the following on the command line in the path where the ippsample-xperimental-x86_64.AppImage file resides:

```
sudo systemctl stop cups
./ippsample-xperimental-x86_64.AppImage ippserver <Your Printer
Name> -p 631
```

When you are done, you can restart CUPS:

```
sudo systemctl start cups
```

And things are back to normal. If all goes well, you can start testing your code against the virtual printer. You might be asking why go through all the trouble of setting up a virtual IPP printer on a Linux box, but if you perform a simple get-printer-attributes query, you will see why:

```
operations-supported : 2
operations-supported : 3
operations-supported : 4

operations-supported : 5
operations-supported : 6
operations-supported : 7
operations-supported : 8
operations-supported : 9
operations-supported : 10
operations-supported : 11
operations-supported : 12
operations-supported : 13
operations-supported : 16
operations-supported : 17
operations-supported : 19
operations-supported : 20
operations-supported : 21
operations-supported : 22
operations-supported : 23
operations-supported : 24
operations-supported : 25
```

```
operations-supported : 26
operations-supported : 27
operations-supported : 28
operations-supported : 34
operations-supported : 35
operations-supported : 36
operations-supported : 37
operations-supported : 38
operations-supported : 41
operations-supported : 42
operations-supported : 43
operations-supported : 45
operations-supported : 51
operations-supported : 52
operations-supported : 53
operations-supported : 55
operations-supported : 56
operations-supported : 57
operations-supported : 59
operations-supported : 60
operations-supported : 61
operations-supported : 63
operations-supported : 64
operations-supported : 65
operations-supported : 66
operations-supported : 67
operations-supported : 68
operations-supported : 69
operations-supported : 71
operations-supported : 72
operations-supported : 73
operations-supported : 70
```

In other words, the virtual IPP printer, unlike the real hardware versions, supports practically all operational requests. This makes developing or debugging the virtual printer much more complete. You should still use real hardware printers to test against, as your software will need to handle cases where the operation(s) are not supported. As you test the full suite of requests your software supports, you will undoubtedly reveal some idiosyncrasies. For instance, a validate-job request that uses the following job attributes works fine on my HP M528 printer but fails against the virtual ippserver:

```
copies=1
print-color-mode=monochrome
output-bin=face-down
print-quality=4
orientation-requested=3
media=iso_a4_210x297mm
```

Here was the request as it was sent to the virtual printer on Wireshark:

```
> Frame 11: 380 bytes on wire (3040 bits), 380 bytes captured (3040 bits) on
> Ethernet II, Src: ASUSTekCOMPU_e6:21:bb (04:42:1a:e6:21:bb), Dst: HP_44:63:
> Internet Protocol Version 4, Src: 10.0.0.50, Dst: 10.0.0.19
> Transmission Control Protocol, Src Port: 55813, Dst Port: 631, Seq: 149, A
> [2 Reassembled TCP Segments (474 bytes): #8(148), #11(326)]
> Hypertext Transfer Protocol
v Internet Printing Protocol
    [Response In: 13]
    version: 1.1
    operation-id: Validate-Job (0x0004)
    request-id: 1
  v operation-attributes-tag
    > attributes-charset (charset): 'utf-8'
    > attributes-natural-language (naturalLanguage): 'en'
    > printer-uri (uri): 'ipp://ubuntu2024:631/ipp/print'
    > requesting-user_name (nameWithoutLanguage): 'jpmsp'
  v job-attributes-tag
    > copies (integer): 1
    > print-color-mode (keyword): 'monochrome'
    > output-bin (keyword): 'face-down'
    > print-quality (enum): normal
    > sides (keyword): 'two-sided-long-edge'        Works on HP M528 printer
    > orientation-requested (enum): portrait
    > media (keyword): 'iso_a4_210x297mm'
    end-of-attributes-tag
```

And the reply from the virtual printer, which was very descriptive about what exactly caused the problem. As you can see, it was the sides attribute with a value of 'two-sided-long-edge' that caused the issue. As soon as I removed that attribute from the job attributes, the request was successful.

```
> Frame 13: 207 bytes on wire (1656 bits), 207 bytes captured (1656 bits) on ir
> Ethernet II, Src: HP_44:63:6a (04:0e:3c:44:63:6a), Dst: ASUSTekCOMPU_e6:21:bt
> Internet Protocol Version 4, Src: 10.0.0.19, Dst: 10.0.0.50
> Transmission Control Protocol, Src Port: 631, Dst Port: 55813, Seq: 321, Ack:
> [2 Reassembled TCP Segments (448 bytes): #12(295), #13(153)]
> Hypertext Transfer Protocol
v Internet Printing Protocol
    [Request In: 11]
    [Response Time: 0.001322000 seconds]
    version: 1.1
    status-code: Client Error (client-error-attributes-or-values-not-supported)
    request-id: 1
  v operation-attributes-tag
    > attributes-charset (charset): 'utf-8'
    > attributes-natural-language (naturalLanguage): 'en'
    > status-message (textWithoutLanguage): 'Unsupported sides keyword value.'
  v unsupported-attributes-tag
    > sides (keyword): 'two-sided-long-edge'
    end-of-attributes-tag
```

Now in my case, the answer wasn't hard to track down: in the get-printer-attributes return from ippserver, the cause of the request failure was found:

```
sides-default : one-sided
sides-supported : one-sided
```

To correct this, the default behavior of ippserver needs to be changed. In this case, we want to have the virtual printer support duplexing, so we need to create a config file that allows for that.

You can also simulate sending a document to ippserver as a print job. Here is create-job and send-doc series using the ippserver (virtual) printer from a Chapter 6, "Additional Operations," command line (IppPrintRequest) test utility:

```
C:\Users\jmsp>"D:\BACKUP\IPP Book\Chap6 Additional RFC IPP Operations\
Code\CsIppRequests\IppPrintRequest\bin\Debug\IppPrintRequest.exe" C:\temp\
JobAttributes.txt
Enter the IPP printer to use:
```

```
ubuntu2024
Would you like to getattributes, validate, create, cancel, senddoc,
getjobs, identify, or printjob?
create
Status: 0
successful-ok
Job successfully created on ubuntu2024
Job Id is: 1
IPP print request completed

C:\Users\jpmsp>"D:\BACKUP\IPP Book\Chap6 Additional RFC IPP Operations\
Code\CsIppRequests\IppPrintRequest\bin\Debug\IppPrintRequest.exe" C:\temp\
JobAttributes.txt
Enter the IPP printer to use:
ubuntu2024
Would you like to getattributes, validate, create, cancel, senddoc,
getjobs, identify, or printjob?
senddoc
Enter the job id:
1
Enter the file to print:
c:\temp\test.pdf
Is this the last document: Y/N?
y
Status: 0
successful-ok
IPP print request completed
```

"ipptool" on Linux

On the other end of the IPP request spectrum is the client itself. Having a tool able to create RFC standard IPP requests to monitor (on Wireshark, of course) or develop against is a great asset. For instance, if you are unsure of how the request for a send-document would look like, here is the way to simulate that request (or any other). For engineers wanting to test how their hardware responds to RFC-compliant IPP requests, this tool is ideal. I should inject here that my distro is Ubuntu Linux, so keep that in mind for the next few paragraphs. This tool ("ipptool") does come with the standard CUPS installed on most Linux distros. To see if ipptool is installed, enter the following on an open terminal session:

```
which ipptool
```

which should reply with the folder structure it is housed in. If you get no path, try:

```
dpkg -L cups-client | grep ipptool
```

If nothing is returned, you might have to do what I did, which was to reinstall the cups package.

Wireshark

While all the utilities or tools are good to develop or learn IPP with, Wireshark is almost indispensable. It is the go-to tool for working out kinks in development or for trying to spy on how networked applications behave. Being able to see in packet format what your development project creates is indispensable to correcting any issue that may arise. That said, you will want to troubleshoot print issues or development snags using IPP versus IPPS simply because it is much easier to read the packet trace. Recall that the Windows client will by default take the most secure transport option (IPPS) offered when a new printer is being created.

Wireshark Quick Use Guide

This is a quick and simplistic way to get Wireshark up and going for those unfamiliar with the tool. To be sure, you should read the many online references for Wireshark to become adept at using the tool. However, as the tool can be somewhat complex at times to get going for beginners, the following steps should at least get you to the point where you can capture packet traces of your communication sessions with your printer. While the installation of Wireshark is straightforward, I would suggest you choose to install USBPcap as an option in the event you want to monitor any USB activity on your computer.

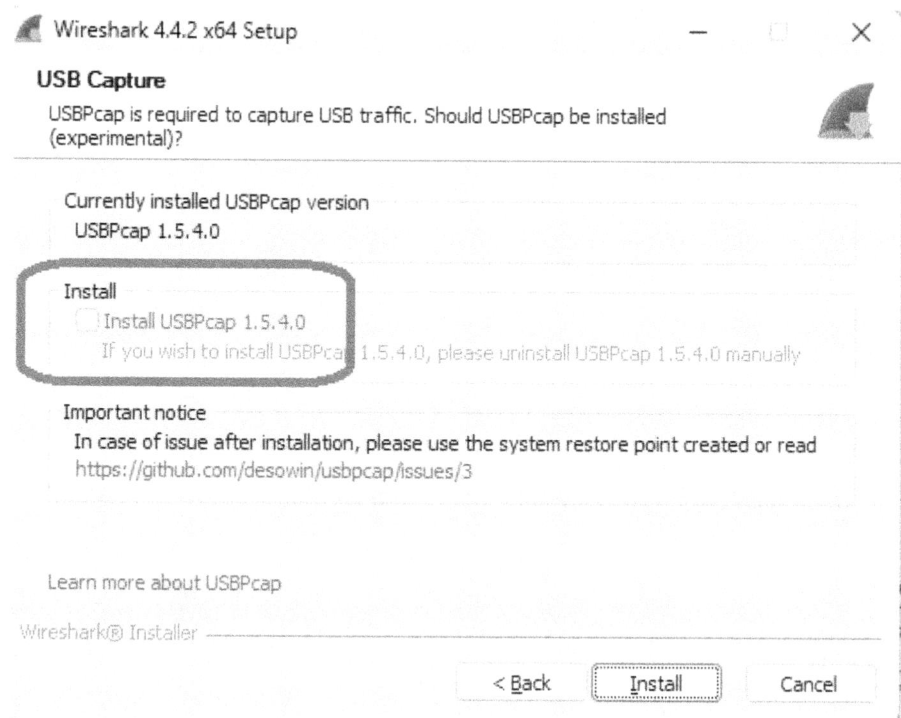

For maximum flexibility, you might want to ensure USBPcap is installed

Once installed, the following steps should give you a good idea of how to do a basic packet trace similar to one you would perform on IPP print operations:

Quick Setup

Open Wireshark and look at the network activity the utility picks up. You will see several network interfaces but concentrate on those showing activity (circled in red in the graphic). If you are connected by Ethernet, you would then select that option or another option that is relevant.

Capture

...using this filter: Enter a capture filter ...

Ethernet
SurfsharkWireGuard
Adapter for loopback traffic capture
Local Area Connection* 10
Local Area Connection* 9
Local Area Connection* 8
Local Area Connection* 2
Local Area Connection* 1
OpenVPN Data Channel Offload for Surfshark
Ethernet 2

The Network Interfaces Showing Activity Are Shown

Now enter the target IP address (your printer) into the capture filter test box as shown. For instance, if your IPP printer is 10.0.0.214, enter ***host 10.0.0.214*** as shown in the graphic.

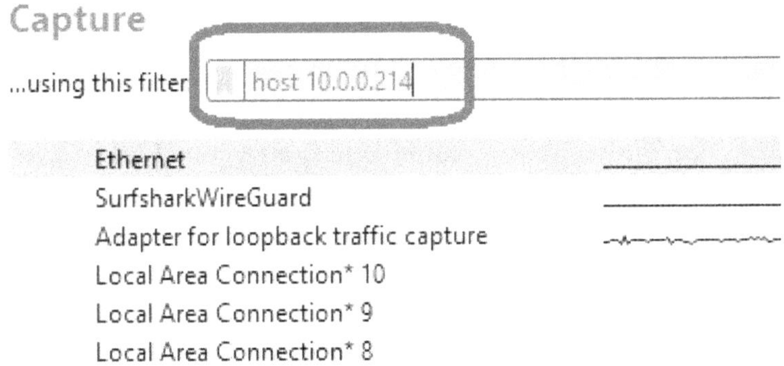

Enter the IP Address of Your Target

Now simply hit Enter, and Wireshark should start monitoring the target. Any network activity going to or from your target will be recorded.

Capture Filter Setup

Once Wireshark has been installed, you should create a capture filter as a convenience for your test printer. This will eliminate much of the traffic seen on the tool to just the communication between your computer and test printer.

1. Open Wireshark and click **Capture** from the menu, then choose **Capture Filters** from the drop-down menu.

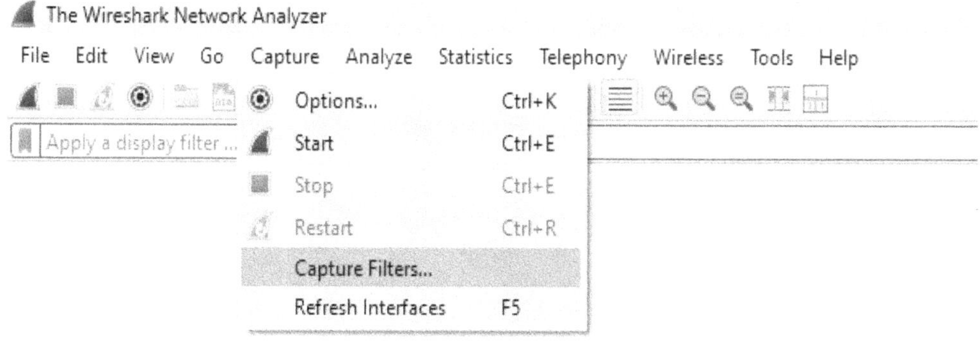

2. This will open a Capture Filter dialog. We are going to create a new capture filter, so on the bottom left-hand side, click the + symbol to add a new filter.

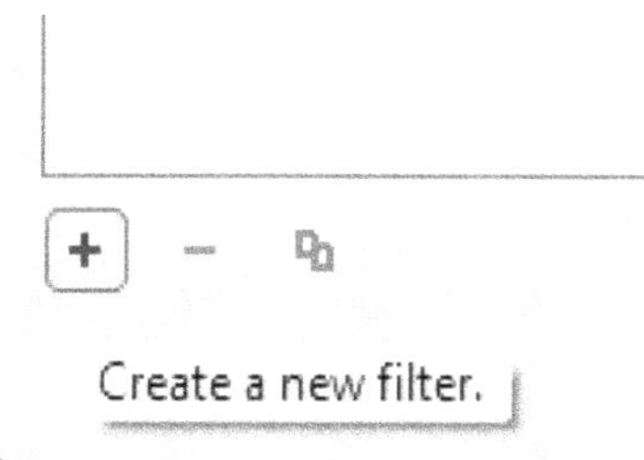

3. We need to name this capture filter and then enter the capture filter expression. The syntax of the capture filter could take an entire chapter itself, so for expediency we will enter a filter expression that will limit traffic to a known host (the test printer) and our computer. Name the filter after your printer, and on the right-hand side, delete the default value and enter the following **host <IP address of your printer>**. For example, if your printer's name was PrinterA and its IP address was 10.0.10.234, you would enter **host 10.0.10.234**. My printer was named HPM528, and the IP address was 10.0.0.215, so you can see why I entered the values in the filter expression as I did.

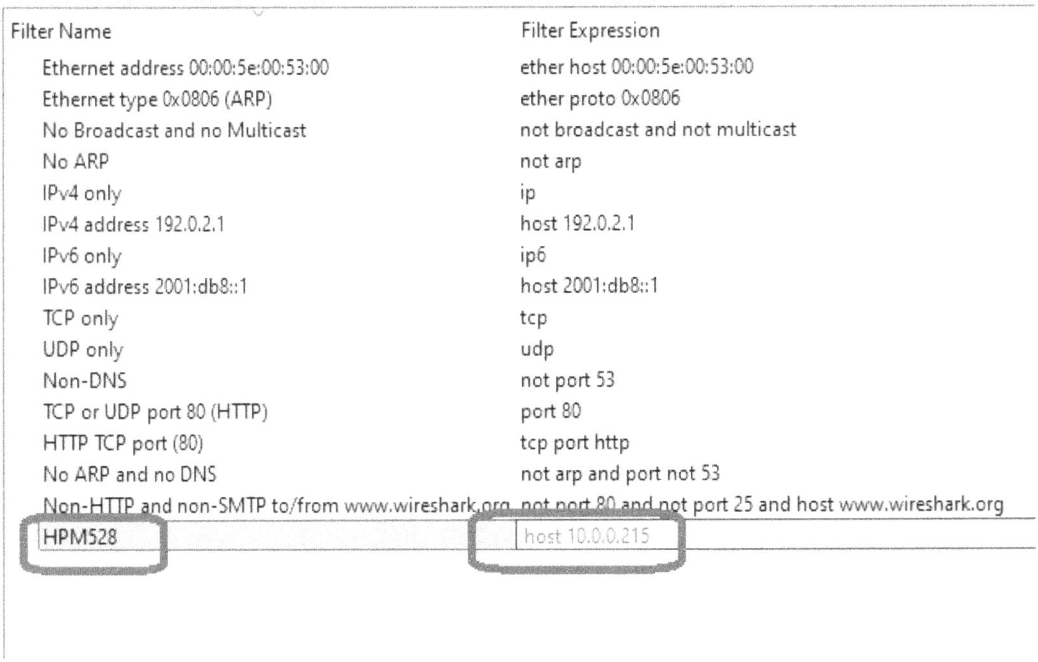

Filter Name	Filter Expression
Ethernet address 00:00:5e:00:53:00	ether host 00:00:5e:00:53:00
Ethernet type 0x0806 (ARP)	ether proto 0x0806
No Broadcast and no Multicast	not broadcast and not multicast
No ARP	not arp
IPv4 only	ip
IPv4 address 192.0.2.1	host 192.0.2.1
IPv6 only	ip6
IPv6 address 2001:db8::1	host 2001:db8::1
TCP only	tcp
UDP only	udp
Non-DNS	not port 53
TCP or UDP port 80 (HTTP)	port 80
HTTP TCP port (80)	tcp port http
No ARP and no DNS	not arp and port not 53
Non-HTTP and non-SMTP to/from www.wireshark.org	not port 80 and not port 25 and host www.wireshark.org
HPM528	host 10.0.0.215

4. Select OK to save this capture filter for future use.
5. Now that we have a capture filter, let's start the capture process. Click the green icon in the Capture "***using this filter:***" text box. Select the name of the capture filter you created (my filter was named HPM528) and then double-click the active interface.

Open

D:\BACKUP\IPP Book\WireShark\HP Printer Discover USB.pcapng (1520 KB)

D:\BACKUP\IPP B

Save this filter

Remove this filter

Manage Capture Filters

Ethernet address 00:00:5e:00:53:00: ether host 00:00:5e:00:53:00

Ethernet type 0x0806 (ARP): ether proto 0x0806

No Broadcast and no Multicast: not broadcast and not multicast

No ARP: not arp

IPv4 only: ip

IPv4 address 192.0.2.1: host 192.0.2.1

IPv6 only: ip6

IPv6 address 2001:db8::1: host 2001:db8::1

TCP only: tcp

UDP only: udp

Non-DNS: not port 53

TCP or UDP port 80 (HTTP): port 80

HTTP TCP port (80): tcp port http

No ARP and no DNS: not arp and port not 53

Non-HTTP and non-SMTP to/from www.wireshark.org: not port 80 and not port 25 and host www.wireshark.org

Capture

HPM528: host 10.0.0.215

...using this filter: Enter a capture filter ...

Ethernet

Adapter for loopback traffic capture

Local Area Connection* 1

OpenVPN Data Channel Offload for Surfshark

Ethernet 2

Notice: if you are having difficulty figuring out the active network interface, you can reduce the choices a bit to make it easier. My machine is connected via Ethernet, so I wanted to reduce my choices to just wired connections. To do this, you can click the **n interfaces shown, y hidden** button on the right-hand side, and uncheck all but the type of interface you will be using. For example, I cleared all but the wired interfaces.

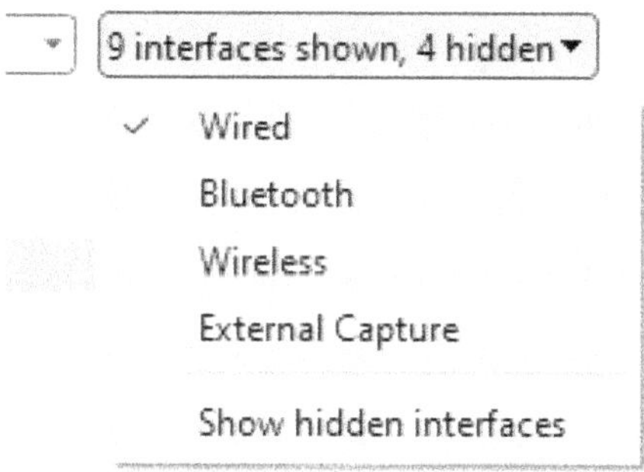

6. You should also note the mini-trace icons shown next to the available adapters.

   Choose an adapter that shows traffic seen by Wireshark as shown in the red box below.

Capture

...using this filter: Enter a capture filter ...

Ethernet

Adapter for loopback traffic capture

Local Area Connection* 10

Local Area Connection* 9

Basic Operations

1. When you double-clicked the desired interface, the packet capture should have started. Don't worry if nothing is shown yet since you will have to send data in order for the packet trace to display any activity. If you need to stop or restart a capture, you can do that with the menu buttons shown below. Notice the ***Capturing from Ethernet (host w.x.y.z)*** notification at the top of Wireshark letting you know an active capture operation is underway.

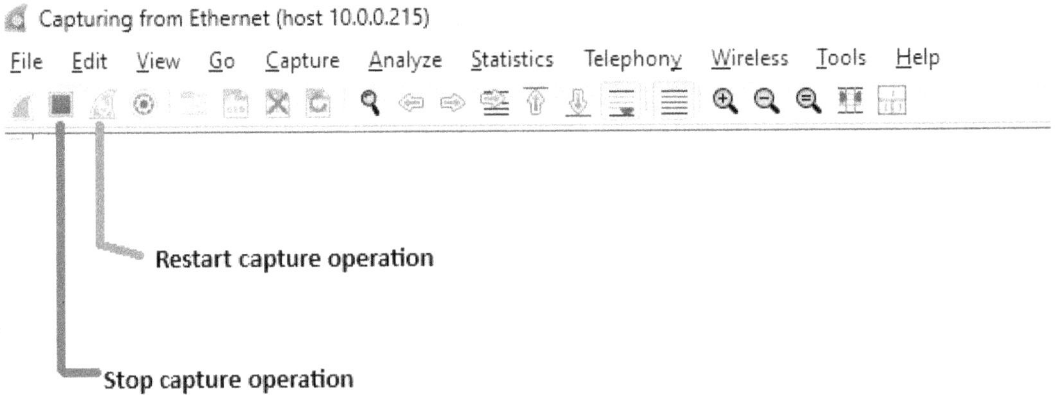

2. You can test your setup by pinging your test printer. To do this, open a command window and enter ping <IP address of printer> on the command line and hit Enter. Once the ping traffic starts, you should see activity on your Wireshark main window if you have the proper IP address, capture filter, and network interface chosen.

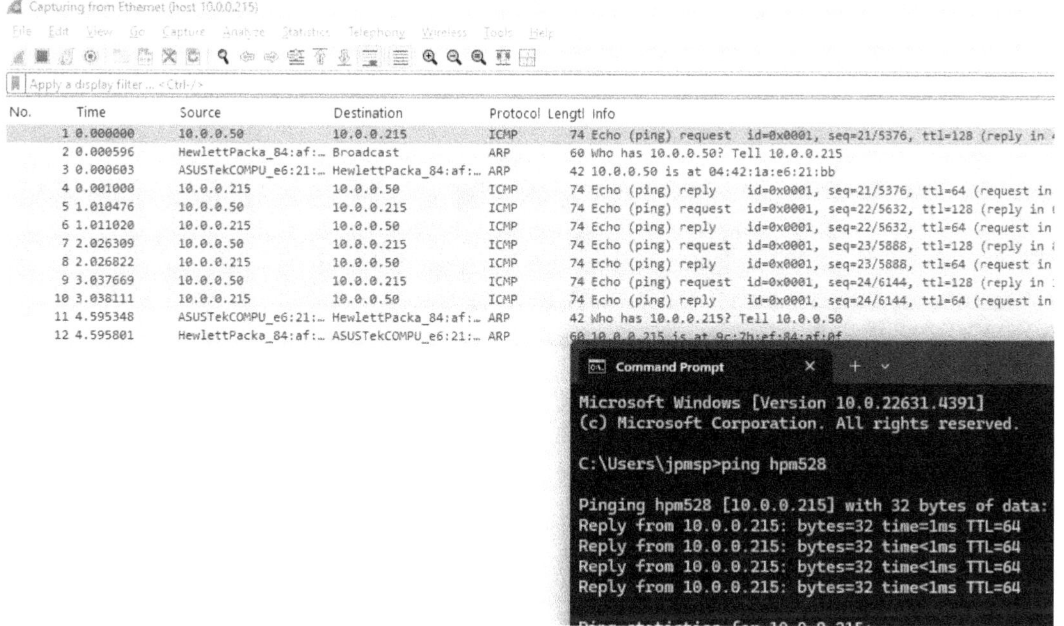

In the above graphic, ping relies are displayed on the command window and the Wireshark main window. This lets you know you have set up the network capture correctly.

3. If you do not see activity with a test ping of your printer, you most likely have entered the wrong IP address in the capture filter, or you have chosen the wrong interface to monitor.

A bit about IP sessions and how they show up on Wireshark. Generally, IP sessions start with a SYN (synchronize) packet as part of the three-way handshake to establish a connection (SYN, SYN-ACK, ACK) and end with a FIN (finish) packet. The packets between these packets should draw your interest for display. In the graphic below, I circled the SYN packet in green to signify the session start and in red to show the session end. The IP address of the packet source and the IP address of the packet destination will tell you who the sender and receiver of the packet are. If you click on a packet of interest, the details of the packet will be shown in another window.

No.	Time	Source	Destination	Protocol	Lengtl	Info
1	0.000000	10.0.0.50	10.0.0.215	TCP	66	52370 → 9100 [SYN] Seq=0 Win=64240 Len=0 MSS=1460 WS=256 SACK_PERM
2	0.000715	HewlettPacka_84:af:…	Broadcast	ARP	60	Who has 10.0.0.50? Tell 10.0.0.215
3	0.000722	ASUSTekCOMPU_e6:21:…	HewlettPacka_84:af:…	ARP	42	10.0.0.50 is at 04:42:1a:e6:21:bb
4	0.000977	10.0.0.215	10.0.0.50	TCP	62	9100 → 52370 [SYN, ACK] Seq=0 Ack=1 Win=1460 Len=0 MSS=1460 WS=1
5	0.001038	10.0.0.50	10.0.0.215	TCP	54	52370 → 9100 [ACK] Seq=1 Ack=1 Win=262656 Len=0
6	0.001148	10.0.0.50	10.0.0.215	TCP	194	52370 → 9100 [PSH, ACK] Seq=1 Ack=1 Win=262656 Len=140
7	0.001178	10.0.0.50	10.0.0.215	TCP	54	52370 → 9100 [FIN, ACK] Seq=141 Ack=1 Win=262656 Len=0
8	0.001294	10.0.0.50	10.0.0.215	TCP	66	52371 → 9100 [SYN] Seq=0 Win=64240 Len=0 MSS=1460 WS=256 SACK_PERM
9	0.001892	10.0.0.215	10.0.0.50	TCP	60	9100 → 52370 [ACK] Seq=1 Ack=142 Win=1320 Len=0
10	0.001962	10.0.0.215	10.0.0.50	TCP	62	9100 → 52371 [SYN, ACK] Seq=0 Ack=1 Win=1460 Len=0 MSS=1460 WS=1
11	0.001994	10.0.0.50	10.0.0.215	TCP	54	52371 → 9100 [ACK] Seq=1 Ack=1 Win=262656 Len=0
12	0.002029	10.0.0.50	10.0.0.215	TCP	278	52371 → 9100 [PSH, ACK] Seq=1 Ack=1 Win=262656 Len=224
13	0.002046	10.0.0.50	10.0.0.215	TCP	54	52371 → 9100 [FIN, ACK] Seq=225 Ack=1 Win=262656 Len=0
14	0.002621	10.0.0.215	10.0.0.50	TCP	60	9100 → 52371 [ACK] Seq=1 Ack=226 Win=1236 Len=0
15	0.005584	10.0.0.215	10.0.0.50	TCP	60	[TCP Window Update] 9100 → 52370 [ACK] Seq=1 Ack=142 Win=64240 Len=0
16	0.006522	10.0.0.215	10.0.0.50	TCP	60	9100 → 52370 [FIN, ACK] Seq=1 Ack=142 Win=64240 Len=0
17	0.006561	10.0.0.50	10.0.0.215	TCP	54	52370 → 9100 [ACK] Seq=142 Ack=2 Win=262656 Len=0

I used the RawPrintStreamTest solution from Chapter 1, "Windows Legacy Print," as a source of network traffic, as it sends a stream of non-PCL-formatted text first and then a stream of PCL-encoded text next to compare. You can see the captured packet results below. Notice the PCL coding in the second packet.

```
0000  9c 7b ef 84 af 0f 04 42  1a e6 21 bb 08 00 45 00   ·{·····B ··!···E·
0010  00 b4 3a ad 40 00 80 06  00 00 0a 00 00 32 0a 00   ··:·@··· ·····2··
0020  00 d7 cc 92 23 8c ae 26  9e c1 14 60 65 c1 50 18   ····#··& ···`e·P·
0030  04 02 15 af 00 00 49 20  6c 6f 76 65 20 63 6c 61   ······I  love cla
0040  73 73 69 63 20 63 61 72  73 2c 20 65 73 70 65 63   ssic car s, espec
0050  69 61 6c 6c 79 20 65 61  72 6c 79 20 61 6e 64 20   ially ea rly and
0060  6c 61 74 65 20 36 30 73  20 4d 75 73 74 61 6e 67   late 60s  Mustang
0070  73 20 61 6e 64 20 43 6f  72 76 65 74 74 65 73 0a   s and Co rvettes·
0080  20 61 6e 64 20 43 68 61  72 67 65 72 73 2e 20 54    and Cha rgers. T
0090  6f 20 6d 65 2c 20 74 68  65 73 65 20 72 65 70 72   o me, th ese repr
00a0  65 73 65 6e 74 20 74 68  65 20 65 70 69 74 6f 6d   esent th e epitom
00b0  65 20 6f 66 20 36 30 27  73 20 73 74 79 6c 69 6e   e of 60' s stylin
00c0  67 2e                                              g.
```

```
0000  9c 7b ef 84 af 0f 04 42  1a e6 21 bb 08 00 45 00   ·{·····B ··!···E·
0010  01 08 3a b1 40 00 80 06  00 00 0a 00 00 32 0a 00   ··:·@··· ·····2··
0020  00 d7 cc 93 23 8c 70 d7  87 d9 6c 5b db d9 50 18   ····#·p· ··l[··P·
0030  04 02 16 03 00 00 1b 26  6c 36 30 46 1b 26 6b 32   ·······& l60F·&k2
0040  47 1b 28 73 31 53 1b 20  49 20 6c 6f 76 65 20 63   G·(s1S·  I love c
0050  6c 61 73 73 69 63 20 63  61 72 73 2c 20 65 73 70   lassic c ars, esp
0060  65 63 69 61 6c 6c 79 20  65 61 72 6c 79 20 61 6e   ecially  early an
0070  64 20 6c 61 74 65 20 36  30 73 1b 28 73 30 53 20   d late 6 0s·(s0S
0080  1b 28 73 33 42 4d 75 73  74 61 6e 67 73 1b 28 73   ·(s3BMus tangs·(s
0090  30 42 20 1b 28 73 31 53  61 6e 64 1b 28 73 30 53   0B ·(s1S and·(s0S
00a0  20 1b 28 73 33 42 43 6f  72 76 65 74 74 65 73 1b    ·(s3BCo rvettes·
00b0  28 73 30 42 2c 0a 1b 28  73 31 53 61 6e 64 1b 28   (s0B,··( s1Sand·(
00c0  73 30 53 20 1b 28 73 33  42 43 68 61 72 67 65 72   s0S ·(s3 BCharger
00d0  73 1b 28 73 30 42 2e 1b  28 73 31 53 20 54 6f 20   s·(s0B.· (s1S To
00e0  6d 65 2c 20 74 68 65 73  65 20 72 65 70 72 65 73   me, thes e repres
00f0  65 6e 74 20 74 68 65 20  65 70 69 74 6f 6d 65 20   ent the  epitome
0100  6f 66 20 36 30 27 73 20  73 74 79 6c 69 6e 67 2e   of 60's  styling.
0110  1b 28 73 30 53 0a                                  ·(s0S·
```

*If you want to clear the display window and run another capture, you must first stop any existing capture.

*If you want to save this capture to a file (to review later), the following menu button(s) can be used to close the existing capture file, reload an existing capture file, or save the existing capture to a file.

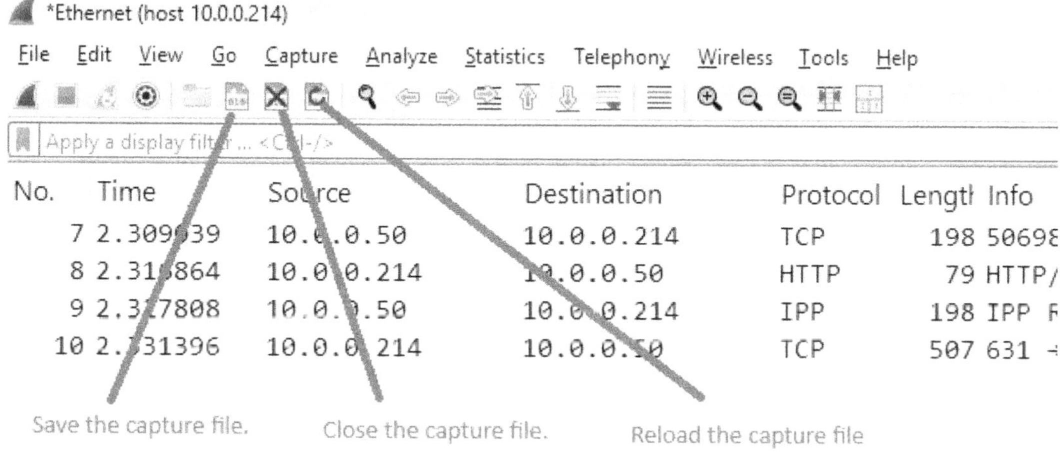

Capture File Action Buttons in Wireshark

For a more detailed operation of Wireshark, I would encourage the reader to consult any of the excellent tutorials on the web. However, a real issue encountered while writing the Get-Jobs request (back in Chapter 6, "Additional Operations") might provide an idea of how to use Wireshark to investigate similar issues that might arise. Keep in mind that you do not have to be a developer to appreciate the uses of the tool; many perplexing issues can be resolved with the greater insight provided by a Wireshark trace. For instance, you might troubleshoot a PSA developed by a vendor to see whether the attributes sent to/from the printer do in fact correctly engage the features on the printer advertised.

Using Wireshark to Identify Attribute Recovery Issues

Wireshark can be employed to analyze some critical issues that might be difficult to track down. One such issue plagued the development process of the Get-Jobs request, and I was not easily able to isolate the cause using just Visual Studio. This issue manifested itself in some of the potential job properties that can be requested with the Get-Jobs request. When attributes such as "job-name" or "user-name" were included in the property sets to be returned for each job in the request, the list of jobs was truncated. In practice, I would receive about half the jobs I thought I should get back, and use of "ipptool":

```
ipptool -tv ipp://printer1/ipp/print get-completed-jobs.test
```

confirmed my suspicions that something was awry in my ResponseHelper file. Since "ipptool" received back all the jobs, I needed to take a look at the formatting of the NameWithLanguage and TextWithLanguage attributes in my code as these appeared to be where my issue lay. Upon further investigation, it was apparent that the original function was simplistically calling GetStringAsync twice, once for the language value and once for the actual value.

```
public static async Task<StringWithLanguage> GetStringWithLanguageAsync
(Stream stream)
        {
            //get language
            var language = await GetStringAsync(stream);
```

```
        //get value
        var value = await GetStringAsync(stream);
        return new StringWithLanguage(language, value);
    }
```

The problem manifested itself in the 2nd call – the one that would retrieve the language value. My suspicions that I was not reading the byte stream correctly arose in the GetStringAsync call, where the length read was quite a bit larger than the number of bytes allocated for that value in the byte stream.

```
public static async Task<string> GetStringAsync(Stream stream)
        byte[] lenBuffer = new byte[2];
        await stream.ReadAsync(lenBuffer, 0, 2);
        int len = ByteOrder.Flip(BitConverter.ToInt16(lenBuffer, 0));

        byte[] stringBuffer = new byte[len];
        await stream.ReadAsync(stringBuffer, 0, len);
        return Encoding.UTF8.GetString(stringBuffer);
    }
```

In other words, I was reading well past the proper size of the returned value and causing chaos in the process. For these matters, you can get a trace using Wireshark of the Get-Jobs request and examine the hex value of the returned stream from the printer. To do this, use Wireshark as you normally would to track an IPP request (in this case Get-Jobs) to the printer. Select the packet where the Get-Jobs request is successful to examine the return stream of bytes.

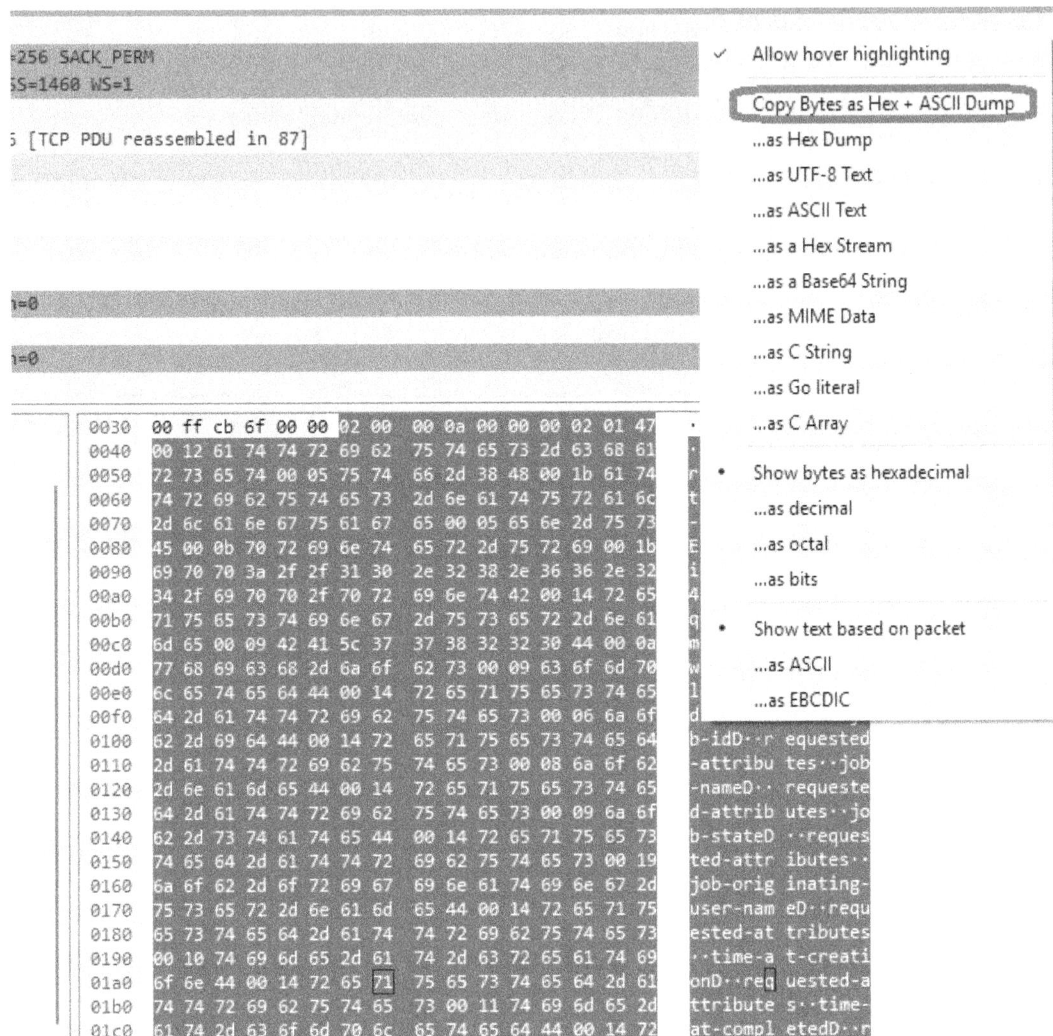

To examine the binary stream, right-click on the hex representation of the request that was returned and then choose **Copy Bytes as Hex + ASCII Dump**. Now you can paste this into Word for further investigation.

```
0090  64 00 04 00 00 00 01 36 00 08 6a 6f 62 2d 6e 61  d......6..job-na
00a0  6d 65 00 29 00 05 65 6e 2d 75 73 00 20 69 70 70  me.)..en-us. ipp
00b0  3a 2f 2f 36 30 2e 32 38 2e 36 36 2e 32 34 2f 69  ://60.28.66.24/i
00c0  70 70 2f 70 6f 72 74 31 2d 30 30 30 31 36 00 19  pp/port1-00016..
00d0  6a 6f 62 2d 6f 72 69 67 69 6e 61 74 69 6e 67 2d  job-originating-
00e0  75 73 65 72 2d 6e 61 6d 65 00 12 00 05 65 6e 2d  user-name....en-
00f0  75 73 00 09 42 41 5c 37 37 38 32 32 30 23 00 09  us..DZ\705230#..
0100  6a 6f 62 2d 73 74 61 74 65 00 04 00 00 00 09 44  job-state......D
0110  00 11 6a 6f 62 2d 73 74 61 74 65 2d 72 65 61 73  ..job-state-reas
0120  6f 6e 73 00 1a 6a 6f 62 2d 63 6f 6d 70 6c 65 74  ons..job-complet
```

Sample Wireshark Trace

For dissection purposes, the sequence of bytes starts at the down arrow (pointing to 36H) in the trace. Each byte field is separated from the next with a different color. Below we walk through the byte stream created by the dump.

1. 36 H is the ValueTag for TextWithLanguage
2. (Yellow) 00 08 H (in network byte order) is 8 bytes in size that will be read.
3. (Red) Translating the bytes (6a,6f,62,2d,6e,61,6d,65 H) to UTF-8, we get the Name "job-name."
4. (Aqua) The 00, 29 H bytes were the unknown entities that I did not properly handle (and the cause of my issues). The crux was 0x29 = 41 bytes and is supposed to signify the total length of the TextWithLanguage value.

5. (Yellow) The 00,05 H (**2**) bytes represent a length to read of 5 for the language.

6. (Red) The **5** bytes (65,6e,2d,75,73 H) were read and translated into UTF-8 to "en-us," the language.

7. (Black) The next **2** bytes (00,20 H) were for the length of the string (32 bytes).

8. (Olive) The string "ipp://60.28.66.24/ipp/port1-00016" is indeed **32** bytes.

Thus, the (00,29 H) value = 41 bytes total in the TextWithLanguage attribute (2 + 5 + 2 + 32 bytes = 41 bytes total). Once I realized how I had mishandled the decoding of TextWithLanguage, the fix was straightforward.

The final resolution is provided below – this fixed the issue I was encountering.

```
public static async Task<StringWithLanguage> GetStringWithLanguageAsync(Str
eam stream)
        {
            //read 2 bytes of the encoding type..
            byte[] lenBuffer = new byte[2];
            await stream.ReadAsync(lenBuffer, 0, 2);
            int encoding = ByteOrder.Flip(BitConverter.
            ToInt16(lenBuffer, 0));

            //get language
            var language = await GetStringAsync(stream);

            //get value
            var value = await GetStringAsync(stream);
            return new StringWithLanguage(language, value);
        }
```

Using ProcMon to Investigate the IPP Print Process

Using ProcMon as a tool to analyze an IPP print job can provide a compelling insight into how Windows processes an IPP print job request. Process Monitor is an advanced monitoring tool for Windows that shows real-time file system, Registry, and process/thread activity [5]. The utility is distributed by Sysinternals, a company that specializes in tools and utilities for Windows. The latest version (as of this writing) is Process Monitor v4.01 and is available on the Sysinternals website. ProcMon is specific to the CPU architecture, so you must run either the 32-bit or 64-bit version depending on your own machine. If you are curious as to how the Windows print subsystem works when processing an IPP print request, ProcMon might be the tool to explore. A test IPP trace can demonstrate the value of this tool to determine how Windows processes IPP print from an application such as Word and converts the native file format into something the IPP printer can successfully render. As a reminder, the Word native file format is .docx, while an IPP printer prefers a PDF format. That means that Windows must create the print ticket for the request, perform the format conversion, and place the (properly formatted) job on the spooler to be routed to the printer. We will try to capture this operation on a high level and identify some components that provide this service along the way.

As an example, create a document in Word with the intent to print to an IPP printer you have previously set up and installed in Windows. Hold off printing the file for now; we need to set up ProcMon first. Open ProcMon64 (if you are on a 64-bit machine) and go to the Filter tab, then select Filter. Add the following processes and operations to monitor:

> Process: Winword.exe, spoolsv.exe, splwow64.exe, rundll32.exe, printisolationhost.exe
>
> Operations: CreateFile, ReadFile, WriteFile, Process Create

When you are done, it should look like the following filter matches:

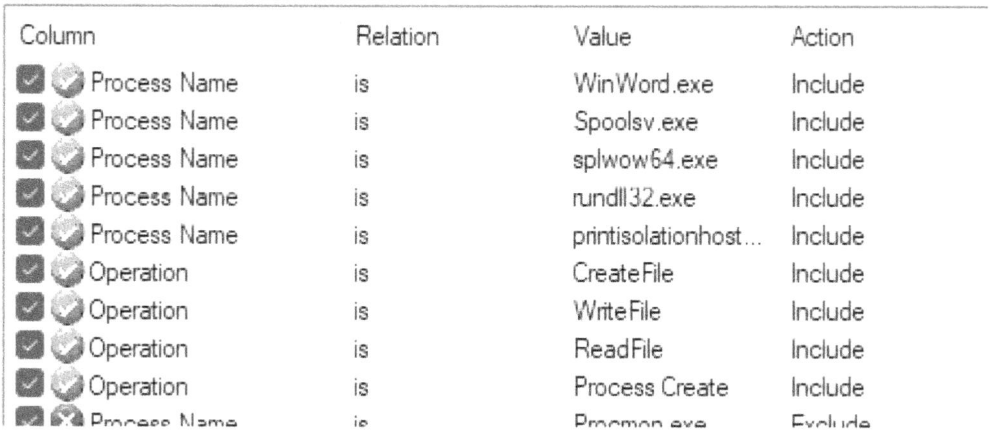

Column	Relation	Value	Action
Process Name	is	WinWord.exe	Include
Process Name	is	Spoolsv.exe	Include
Process Name	is	splwow64.exe	Include
Process Name	is	rundll32.exe	Include
Process Name	is	printisolationhost...	Include
Operation	is	CreateFile	Include
Operation	is	WriteFile	Include
Operation	is	ReadFile	Include
Operation	is	Process Create	Include
Process Name	is	Procmon.exe	Exclude

Filter Application

Click Apply, and you will be ready to monitor the IPP print request. In Word, click Print to start the trace on the document you created a few minutes ago. ProcMon should start loading filtered entries as your print job moves through the print subsystem and finally gets printed. The icon in the red box below stops/starts captures, while the icon in the green box brings up the filter dialog.

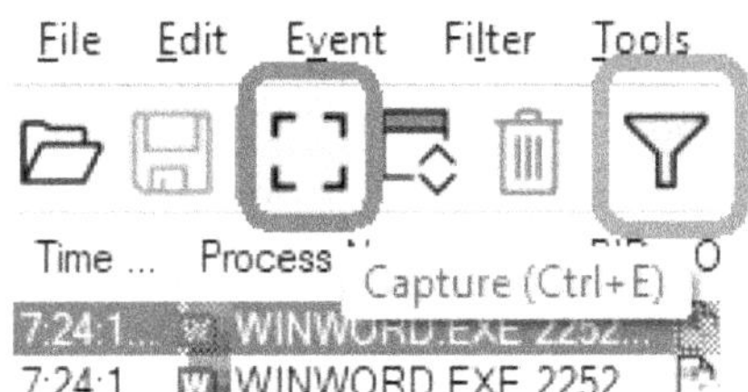

Snapshot of Wireshark Menu Choices

A word of advice: ProcMon will display all events that match your capture filter, and in many cases this is significant. Once your document starts to print on the device, you can stop the capture to save memory and reduce the legion of captured entries you will undoubtedly be inundated with. One of the first things you might notice is that the print subsystem opens and reads the MSIPP-manifest.ini file.

Upon examination of MSIPP-manifest.ini in the Driver Store's file repository, the contents are:

```
[DriverConfig]
DataFile=MSIPP.xml
DataFileType=application/vnd.ms-PrintDeviceCapabilities+xml
RequiredFiles=PDFRenderFilter.dll,PWGRRenderFilter.dll,PCLmRenderFilter.
dll,TiffRenderFilter.dll
PrinterDriverID={B71661F4-A4DC-43DF-BC16-39D337D15A95}
RetrievePrintDeviceCapabilitiesFromDevice=true
RetrievePrintPageDescriptionLanguageFromDevice=true
DriverCategory=PrintFax.Printer

[DriverRender]
OutputFormat=application/pdf
XpsFormat=OpenXPS
```

The data for print ticket defaults appears to be retrieved from the MSIPP.xml file. In this context, the MSIPP.xml file is populated with information that can be obtained from the printer itself, typically through a Get-Printer-Attributes request. The communication often involves sending requests to the printer to gather information about its supported features, such as

Supported media sizes

Print resolutions

Color capabilities

Finishing options (e.g., duplex printing)

The information retrieved from these requests is then used to populate the MSIPP.xml file. While details on exactly how the default data is populated are not public knowledge, the entry **RetrievePrintDeviceCapabilitiesFromDevice=true** would appear to support this statement. Armed with information from the MSIPP-manifest.ini and MSIPP.xml files, the system can piece together a good idea as to the capabilities of the printer and what files are needed to process the print to completion. For instance, the **OutputFormat=application/pdf** entry appears to provide the preferred format the printer desires - in this case, pdf. After the MSIPP-manifest file is processed, the pdc.xml file is then processed.

The next step in the trace appears to access an XML in the C:\Windows\System32\spool\V4Dirs folder path. The "pdc" in pdc.xml typically stands for "Printer Description Configuration" [4]. This file format is used to describe the capabilities and features of a printer, allowing the operating system and applications to understand how to interact with the printer and what options are available for print jobs. This file (pdc.xml, located in the V4Dirs folder of the spool directory) has what appears to be default printer settings, likely to standardize the default print ticket that the system provides:

```
<!-- orientation-requested-default, orientation-requested-supported -->
<psk:PageOrientation psf2:psftype="Feature">
<psk:Portrait psf2:psftype="Option" psf2:default="true"/>
<psk:Landscape psf2:psftype="Option" psf2:default="false"/>
</psk:PageOrientation>

<!-- print-quality-default, print-quality-supported -->
<psk:PageOutputQuality psf2:psftype="Feature">
<psk:Normal psf2:psftype="Option" psf2:default="true"/>
<psk:Draft psf2:psftype="Option" psf2:default="false"/>
<psk:High psf2:psftype="Option" psf2:default="false"/>
</psk:PageOutputQuality>
```

```
<!-- multiple-document-handling-default, multiple-document-handling-supported -->
<psk:DocumentCollate psf2:psftype="Feature">
<psk:Uncollated psf2:psftype="Option" psf2:default="true"/>
<psk:Collated psf2:psftype="Option" psf2:default="false"/>
</psk:DocumentCollate>
```

At the very bottom, the following entries:

```
<!-- Printer = HP LaserJet M608 -->
<!-- Preferred PDL = application/pdf -->
```

Appear to suggest the preferred format (PDL) to use on the named print hardware. Moving on with the dissection of the trace, the creation of the print ticket and subsequent spooling of the file are evident in the following trace capture.

7:24:3...	splwow64.exe	2191...	ReadFile	C:\Windows\System32\DriverStore\FileRepository\prnms012.inf_amd64_17bb82cc430e1f2e\MSIPP-manifest.ini
7:24:3...	splwow64.exe	2191...	CreateFile	C:\Windows\System32\spool\V4Dirs\C3323C20-CB9D-4740-8437-C8F9274CB07C\pdc.xml
7:24:3...	splwow64.exe	2191...	ReadFile	C:\Windows\System32\spool\V4Dirs\C3323C20-CB9D-4740-8437-C8F9274CB07C\pdc.xml
7:24:3...	splwow64.exe	2191...	ReadFile	C:\Windows\System32\spool\V4Dirs\C3323C20-CB9D-4740-8437-C8F9274CB07C\pdc.xml
7:24:3...	splwow64.exe	2191...	ReadFile	C:\Windows\System32\spool\V4Dirs\C3323C20-CB9D-4740-8437-C8F9274CB07C\pdc.xml
7:24:3...	splwow64.exe	2191...	ReadFile	C:\Windows\System32\spool\V4Dirs\C3323C20-CB9D-4740-8437-C8F9274CB07C\pdc.xml
7:24:3...	splwow64.exe	2191...	ReadFile	C:\Windows\System32\spool\V4Dirs\C3323C20-CB9D-4740-8437-C8F9274CB07C\pdc.xml
7:24:3...	splwow64.exe	2191...	ReadFile	C:\Windows\System32\spool\V4Dirs\C3323C20-CB9D-4740-8437-C8F9274CB07C\pdc.xml
7:24:3...	splwow64.exe	2191...	ReadFile	C:\Users\778220\AppData\Local\Temp\fnt6A5B.tmp
7:24:3...	splwow64.exe	2191...	CreateFile	C:\Users\778220\AppData\Local\Temp\fnt6A5B.tmp
7:24:3...	splwow64.exe	2191...	CreateFile	C:\Windows\System32\DriverStore\FileRepository\ntprint.inf_amd64_c9c90c6b723b165b\Amd64\MXDWDRV.DL
7:24:3...	splwow64.exe	2191...	CreateFile	C:\Windows\System32\DriverStore\FileRepository\ntprint.inf_amd64_c9c90c6b723b165b\Amd64\MXDWDRV.DL
7:24:3...	splwow64.exe	2191...	CreateFile	C:\Windows\System32\DriverStore\FileRepository\ntprint.inf_amd64_c9c90c6b723b165b\Amd64\MXDWDRV.DL
7:24:3...	splwow64.exe	2191...	WriteFile	C:\Windows\System32\spool\PRINTERS\00002.SPL
7:24:3...	splwow64.exe	2191...	WriteFile	C:\Windows\System32\spool\PRINTERS\00002.SPL
7:24:3...	spoolsv.exe	6412	CreateFile	C:\Windows\System32\spool\PRINTERS\00002.SPL
7:24:3...	spoolsv.exe	6412	CreateFile	C:\Windows\System32\spool\PRINTERS\00002.SHD
7:24:3...	spoolsv.exe	6412	CreateFile	C:\Windows\System32\spool\PRINTERS\00002.SHD
7:24:3...	spoolsv.exe	6412	CreateFile	C:\Windows\System32\spool\PRINTERS\00002.SHD
7:24:3...	spoolsv.exe	6412	WriteFile	C:\Windows\System32\spool\PRINTERS\00002.SHD

The MXDWDRV.dll file is a dynamic link library (DLL) associated with the Microsoft XPS Document Writer (MXDW) printer driver. Here are some key points about its function:

XPS Document Writer: The Microsoft XPS Document Writer is a virtual printer that allows users to create XPS (XML Paper Specification) documents from any application that supports printing [6]. When you print to this virtual printer, it generates an XPS file instead of sending the output to a physical printer.

The MXDWDRV.dll file contains the necessary code and resources for the XPS Document Writer to function properly. It handles tasks such as rendering the print job into the XPS format and managing the print settings.

From there, the file gets written into SHD (shield) and SPL (spool) file formats.

The primary role of PrinterCleanupTask.dll is to facilitate the cleanup of printer-related tasks and resources. This can include removing unused printer drivers, clearing print queues, and managing other printer-related maintenance tasks. This library is used to remove the SHD (shadow) and SPL (spool) files from the spooler after the print is completed.

As you can see, ProcMon is a powerful tool that has a steep learning curve. While there are many good references on the web to aid or help you, the truth is that this tool will take time to learn to use it properly. Because ProcMon can provide such a vast source of trace activity, a tight display filter is imperative.

A few quick examples of display filters:

To view registry keys that the spooler service is using:

```
Process Name     is     spoolsv.exe    =>    Include
```

To view file activity such as file reads:

```
Operation        is     ReadFile        =>    Include
```

Finding access issues for a process or file:

```
Result           is     ACCESS DENIED   =>    Include
```

Monitor registry activity or changes to a known key:

```
Path      begins with     HKLM\SYSTEM\CurrentControlSet\Enum\
SWD     =>      Include
```

To use Display Filters Effectively, follow the following steps:

1. Use **Include** filters to show only matching items.
2. Use **Exclude** filters to hide extraneous trace input activity generators.
3. Use the **Reset** button to clear all filters and start again.

Chapter Summary

This chapter was about introducing the reader to some of the excellent tools available to develop, troubleshoot, or learn about the IPP protocol. These are free tools that I would encourage the reader to download and explore as they will ultimately make working with the IPP protocol much easier as well as expand your knowledge about the inner workings. IppEveServer emulates an IPP Everywhere printer and is available on both Linux and Windows. It was intended more as a quick connect tester rather than a complete RFC request tester as "ippserver" is. Make sure you tell the utility that you want to use either port 631, as the default setup will not listen on this port unless you tell it explicitly. This can save you time trying to figure out why the server is not responding to your IPP code on the client, which is set on either 631.

"ippserver" is the more complete IPP print emulator, as it was designed to allow developers to test against the full RFC implementation, up to and including the latest version of IPP. It is a good idea to test any IPP software against this utility rather than physical printers as the implementation on some printers may be more relaxed than on others. This means that code that works on one vendor may not necessarily work on another. If your script or code works with "ippserver," you can be assured that it works against printers that support the IPP protocol. "ippserver" is available for Linux distros (I tested it on Ubuntu) and comes as a Windows binary as well. I should add that the Linux version worked a bit better than the Windows version, as might be expected for a utility created initially on Linux.

The "ipptool" differs from the above 2 utilities as it was designed as a client to make requests for a printer. In this capacity, it is a great tool for hardware developers or engineers trying to create IPP software. Printer hardware engineers no doubt can use this to test the server-side implementation of IPP on the printer. It also can be paired with Wireshark to provide an idea of how an operational request that conforms to the RFC specification should look.

Next up is Wireshark, undoubtedly one of the best tools available for network trace requirements. While Wireshark provides a much higher degree of diagnostic capability than just IPP/IPPS trace abilities, the IPP dissector is particularly adept at displaying the structure of the HTTP POST binary buffer. Wireshark, when used in conjunction with "ipptool," is a very good way of tracking down issues. Comparing the "ipptool" traces to client print traces can reveal issues in development very quickly.

Finally, we end with ProcMon, a tool that provides insight into the Windows OS and how it handles processes. This tool could potentially help with issues where print document processing fails. As an example, access errors or missing (or corrupted) file dependencies such as MSIPP-manifest.ini, pdc.xml, etc., may be discovered here. Look for registry errors, CreateFile failures, or printfilter-pipelineprxy.dll access issues as a potential cause for print job issues. The tool does take some time and patience to weed through the potentially many entries it may capture. However, there are display filters, component (registry, file, network, and process) activity buttons to filter events, and search options to help narrow down or find what you are looking for.

References

1. "What is an AppImage?", Brian Potkin, `https://github.com/apple/cups/wiki/IPP-(Everywhere)-Mini-Tutorial`
2. What is the Windows Subsystem for Linux?,Microsoft Learn , `https://learn.microsoft.com/en-us/windows/wsl/about`
3. How to install Linux on Windows with WSL. Microsoft Learn, `https://learn.microsoft.com/en-us/windows/wsl/install`
4. Getting capabilities for the printer registered through Universal Print connector, Microsoft Learn, `https://learn.microsoft.com/en-us/universal-print/fundamentals/universal-print-connector-getting-print-options`
5. Process Monitor v4.01, Microsoft Learn, `https://learn.microsoft.com/en-us/sysinternals/downloads/procmon`
6. Microsoft XPS Document Writer (MXDW), Windows Learn, `https://learn.microsoft.com/en-us/windows/win32/printdocs/microsoft-xps-document-writer`
7. ipptool, Apple Inc., `https://www.cups.org/doc/man-ipptool.html`
8. ippeveprinter, Apple Inc, `https://www.cups.org/doc/man-ippeveprinter.html`

CHAPTER 10

Additional Information

This chapter covers subject matter not covered in the first nine chapters of this book but tangential to the implementation of IPP/IPPS in a Windows environment. The first thing covered will be additional Windows Protected Print (WPP) information. As you know, WPP seeks to significantly reduce the security vulnerabilities or footprint present in your print network. Think of this as a bit of insurance against the realm of nefarious agents always waiting to gain control or wreak havoc on your network. In a way, Windows Protected Print is the complement to the implementation of IPPS and the culmination of security improvements Microsoft recommends you take.

The next item we cover is not part of the official IPP standard but is fundamental to lowering the cost of ownership your company may bear. It helps to upgrade firmware more easily in a vendor-neutral fashion that, to this date, has not yet been available. If you feel that the security threats to the printing world will recede over time or are not yet convinced that implementing the latest printer firmware is to your benefit, then this feature might not be worth your interest. However, if you are responsible for a network of heterogeneous printers from multiple vendors and need to implement the latest firmware, then the IPP Printer Firmware Extension standard should carry your interest. Unfortunately, vendor implementation of the proposal is not yet widespread, so working code is not available to test as of this writing.

Included is the implementation of multiple printer instances using the same IPP port on Windows Server. While this has always been supported on Windows Server, the method slightly differs for IPP/IPPS printers. A notable difference is the fact that Windows Workstation no longer supports multiple printer instances using the same IPP port. Multiple print instances on the server can aid in reducing confusion arising from multiple print preferences clients must make. While multiple instances of the same physical printer exclusively for convenience may not appear efficient, user expectations should always be considered – thus, the inclusion here.

J. Marion, *Adopting Internet Printing Protocol for Windows*, https://doi.org/10.1007/979-8-8688-2010-6_10

Additional Windows Protected Print Information

As mentioned previously in this book, Windows Protected Print (WPP) is an optional feature available for enterprises wishing to reduce their exposure to print system exploits. While Chapter 7, "Enterprise Conversion," was concerned with the implementation of WPP, this chapter is concerned with more detailed analysis. To summarize the key points of WPP:

1. *Permanent Transition for Local Printers*: When enabled, non-IPP print configurations are deleted.
2. *Exclusive IPP-Based Printing*: No V3 or third-party drivers are allowed.
3. *Runs with Lower Privileges*: Reduces escalation of privilege attacks.

Backing Up the Current Print Environment

Before any major change to the Windows print environment, it is essential to secure a good backup in the event the change must be rolled back. This is especially true for the conversion to Windows Protected Print as enabling WPP permanently remove third-party driver configuration and traditional TCP/IP print queue configuration entries from the workstation. This means that if your organization depends on legacy printer configurations, their configuration will be lost and cannot be recovered by simply disabling WPP [3]. Before you execute an enterprise conversion to WPP, execute backup and restore operations to your print environment to ensure it is recoverable. The good news here is that all Windows 11 versions (except Windows Home) include the Printer Migration wizard, which you can use to export the essential elements of your print environment [4].

To back up your environment using the Printer Migration wizard, open a Run command and enter **printbrmui.exe** and then hit enter. This opens a wizard that walks the user through the print environment backup process. You will be prompted to export/import a backup set, the location and name of the file containing the backup data, etc. An important point to understand: the wizard does not actually back up the print driver files and support DLLs – it expects them to be present on the machine in the event it needs to restore the environment. Instead, the tool backs up (and restores) the print environment configuration. This can be accomplished utilizing a batch file with the following command:

```
C:\Windows\System32\spool\tools\PrintBrm.exe -b -f %TEMP%\%USERNAME%.
printerExport
```

where %TEMP%\%USERNAME%.printerExport represents the name and path of the backup file. Of course, you might modify this to suit your own requirements. To restore the previous print environment, use the following command:

```
C:\Windows\System32\spool\tools\PrintBrm.exe -r -f %TEMP%\%USERNAME%.
printerExport
```

where the file to restore information is located at %TEMP%\%USERNAME%
.printerExport or wherever you placed the backup file. I cannot emphasize enough that reasonable diligence should compel administrators planning the conversion to WPP to conduct frequent testing to ensure successful restoration of print configuration information is possible. While standard users can back up printer configuration information on their machine, they likely do not have the necessary rights to restore that same information - keep that in mind.

During testing, I have observed that PrintBrm does not appear to handle spaces in the file path specified. The utility also does not work even if quotes are used to surround the file path specified – keep this in mind when planning the file to back up or restore from.

Other Points to Consider

Once converted to WPP, third-party drivers will no longer work, thus raising the potential that advanced print features will be lost. You should ensure your vendor can deliver a Printer System Application (PSA) that is designed to work with your hardware (as outlined in Chapter 8, "A Print Support App") as these features may not function without a PSA. You should test all features out prior to converting the enterprise to WPP to avoid user complaints about lost feature compatibility. Obviously, this assumes the print hardware you plan to use after the conversion would have a vendor-supported PSA installed. It is also important to ensure all the printers you plan to use post WPP support Mopria as the IPP Class driver will not function properly on printers that do not have this support. You can check to see if your printer supports Mopria by going to

`https://mopria.org/certified-products`,

which maintains a database of certified Mopria-compliant printers. Under WPP, scanner hardware must also be Mopria certified, or it will cease functioning properly. Moreover, multi-function devices should have complete functionality tested as Mopria certification for the printer function of an MFD may not carry over for the scanner. In this case, when the device is installed, the printer is installed, but the scanner driver is not [5]. Be aware that turning on Windows protected print mode uninstalls all unsupported (read V3 print drivers) software printers on Windows, which includes OneNote (Desktop). This should be conveyed to your user base so an appropriate replacement of functionality can be realized. For those using the PCOM emulator access, the IBM AFP 3900 driver (a V3 driver) will no longer work when WPP is enabled, so make plans if a replacement process is required. The salient point is to test your workstation image for compatibility with WPP mode to ensure you are not left scrambling for a resolution to an unforeseen issue.

WPP Reduces Threat Vector

WPP employs various modifications to the print subsystem to reduce the threat of malicious code causing harm to the Windows host. A few of the improvements made to the Windows print subsystem to restrict or reduce the attack vector:

> *Removal of V3 Drivers*: Since vendor print drivers were loaded into the Microsoft print subsystem, any vulnerability they introduced would potentially compromise the system. The system is only as strong as the weakest link, and some of the older drivers have not been updated to leverage binary mitigations Microsoft has added to the OS. One issue identified was driver parsing logic that could lead to injection attacks, which might allow full control of a process (Spooler) that runs in the SYSTEM security context. Having the IPP driver written and deployed by Microsoft ensures the latest security mitigations will be present.

Ancillary Modules Written by Vendors: Legacy print drivers typically make use of ancillary code such as printer ports and monitors that are typically written as DLLs. These were also targeted for attack and could compromise the system. To combat this, legacy APIs were updated to restrict the configuration to values that make sense only when using IPP. This will limit the opportunity for attackers to leverage the Spooler to modify files on the system [7]. Additionally, restrictions in WPP ensure only Microsoft-signed binaries required for IPP are loaded.

Reduced Security Context: Formally, XML Paper Specification (XPS) rendering was done using SYSTEM privileges; this is now done in the principle of least privilege, which reduces the potential attack surface. The new Spooler Worker process has a new restricted token that removes many privileges and no longer runs at the SYSTEM level [7].

Reduction of PDLs Supported: While IPP provides the printing framework, it does not necessarily stipulate driverless printing. Driverless printing comes from a reduction in the number of PDLs supported to a limited set such as PWG Raster and PDF. This limitation reduces the conversion code parsing job and thereby reduces the errors incurred that can potentially be exploited.

If you use the registry or the GUI to enable WPP, Windows may not update dynamically and show WPP as enabled to the user currently logged on. I found that opening a console window as Administrator and then stopping and starting the spooler service fixes the issue. This can be accomplished as shown below:

net stop spooler

net start spooler

after which the GUI should update.

Updating Firmware

I should emphasize that at the time of this writing, the firmware extension proposal has not yet been accepted by the PWG, and thus nothing is finalized, and no IANA entries are formalized. While many of the details are still in the planning stages, several forward-thinking vendors, such as HP and Lexmark, have indicated early support.

Of all the responsibilities system administrators and engineers have, keeping the hardware components entrusted with data safe from security vulnerabilities ranks high. Of course, this means keeping the firmware that printers use to ensure peripherals talk to the OS properly on the latest patch levels. Unfortunately for the printer world, this is not as easy as it might first sound. That is because the printer ecosphere has historically been vendor-specific regarding management software and, most importantly, how firmware updates are executed. For instance, vendor A may provide a method to update their firmware over the network, but that same method will not work with vendor B. Keep in mind that we are talking about update methods, not firmware binaries, which are also generally hardware specific. The result has been a segmentation of print management software (except SNMP queries that, by design, span vendors) in the enterprise. Thus, if you own 200 printers from vendors A, B, and C, you might require 3 separate printer management islands to facilitate their timely firmware updates for your enterprise. While many vendors do offer their management software for free, the cost of installation, server licensing, computer hardware, and overall management costs (patches and updates for the components of the management software) can prove expensive to maintain. Additionally, many enterprises want to feel as if they can pick the best-in-breed printer hardware at the time of purchase or lease without feeling tied to any vendor software for firmware updates. Of course, many vendors might also offer outsourcing solutions for the above scenarios, but this comes at a cost as well. What was needed (for firmware updates) was a vendor-neutral operation to update firmware on the printer fleet.

The proposal for a standard to address the issue is being furnished by the Printer Work Group (PWG) via the IPP Firmware Update Extensions. This extension to the IPP standard proposes an IPP request that would start a firmware update cycle on the targeted printer [1]. The advantage here is that the Firmware Update Extensions proposed are independent of vendor printer management methods that have been required in the past. Thus, the same IPP request that triggers vendor A printers to update their firmware should theoretically work with vendor B or vendor C. Note that the actual firmware binaries remain specific to vendor and hardware type. The actual firmware binary differences do not matter - what does matter is *how* the firmware update trigger is called. For enterprises, the real benefit lies in the universal methods of updating that the proposed IPP standard provides. At the time of this writing, concrete examples of code to test the proposals are not yet outlined as some of the details are still in the planning stages. This should change as vendors adopt the extension for their existing product lines.

The IPP Firmware Update Extension v1.0 documentation from the Printer Working Group offers several classifications of firmware update methods, which can essentially be broken down to

1. *Agent-Initiated Firmware Updates*: This method has an agent running on a management console discovering (from a firmware repository) new firmware packages. This package is then sent to the printer (or output device) for installation. This method requires no human intervention.

2. *Autonomously Initiated Firmware Updates*: This method allows the printer (or, as the documentation describes them, output devices) to initiate the firmware update process when it discovers (and acquires) a firmware package from a firmware repository. The printer then installs the new firmware without human intervention. The printer can then signal (via IPP) the new firmware status, although this is not mandatory.

3. *Triggered Autonomous Firmware Updates*: In this method, an IPP client requests that the IPP printer initiate a firmware update process. The installation of the new firmware can be installed immediately or later at a designated time.

New Operations Proposed for Firmware Updates

Check-For-Firmware-Update: This request is required to be supported and entails the printer checking for firmware updates. When the printer finishes this request, it updates the "printer-firmware-update-last-checked" attributes with the current time and updates the "printer-firmware-update-last-status" attribute to indicate the status of the request. If the operation was successful, a printer is required to return the following status attributes:

1. printer-firmware-update-urgency
2. printer-firmware-update-version
3. printer-firmware-update-string-version

The Check-For-Firmware-Update request requires that the following attributes must be supplied (by the client):

1. attributes-charset
2. printer-uri
3. requesting-user-name

You have seen these exact attributes in Chapters 5, "IPP Standards Print," and 6, "Additional Operations," so they should be familiar to you now. In the event you must write a Check-For-Firmware-Update request, a similar method of encoding these attributes into a byte buffer as used in Chapters 5, "IPP Standards Print," and 6, "Additional Operations," should suffice.

The Check-For-Firmware-Update Response (from the printer) supplies the following attributes. In all cases the printer must supply, and the client must support these attributes.

1. attributes-charset
2. printer-firmware-update-last-status
3. printer-firmware-update-last-checked
4. printer-firmware-update

Update-Printer-Firmware: This operation (operation code 0x0068) compels the Printer to perform a firmware self-update (if there is a firmware update available) from the vendor repository. The client can monitor the firmware update status using the familiar Get-Printer-Attributes operation as performed in Chapter 6, "Additional Operations." This operation requires that the authenticated account requesting the update of firmware must be an operator or administrator of the printer, or the printer must reject the request with the "client-error-forbidden" or "client-error-not-authenticated" status code.

Operationally, the Update-Printer-Firmware Request specifies the following operational attributes from the client. In all cases, if the client supplies the attribute, the printer must support the attribute. However, from the client perspective, only "printer-uri" and "requesting-user-name" are required attributes.

1. attributes-charset
2. printer-uri
3. requesting-user-name
4. printer-firmware-update-name
5. printer-firmware-update-uri
6. delay-update-until
7. delay-update-until-time

The Update-Printer-Firmware Response provides the status message providing the success or failure of the update operation. The "attributes-charset" attribute is required to be supplied/supported by the printer/client, respectively. The printer must also supply a status-code and, optionally, a status-message operational attribute. Additionally, the following attributes must also be supplied/supported by the printer/client, respectively:

1. printer-firmware-name
2. printer-firmware-patches
3. printer-firmware-string-version
4. printer-firmware-version

Creating Multiple Printer Instances Using Existing IPP Port on Windows Server

Using legacy print protocols, Windows has in the past allowed administrators to create several print instances on Workstation or Server using the same printer port. This allowed clients to create one printer instance with default settings (such as Duplexing and Collating) while another print instance may contain different default settings, each using the very same printer port. This allowed clients to deploy several default print profiles using the exact same hardware printer. For IPP, the workstation can no longer provide this option, but Windows Server 2022 still provides this convenience. Technically, this involves using the same printer port to create a "tandem" printer targeting the same print hardware. Traditionally, many Windows shops used this as a convenience, providing users with desired printer settings without the user having to select options such as duplexing mode. As mentioned previously, this can still be done in Windows Server 2022, and the following steps outline the method to accomplish this.

On Windows Server 2022, start Server Manager. Choose Tools ↗ Print Management.

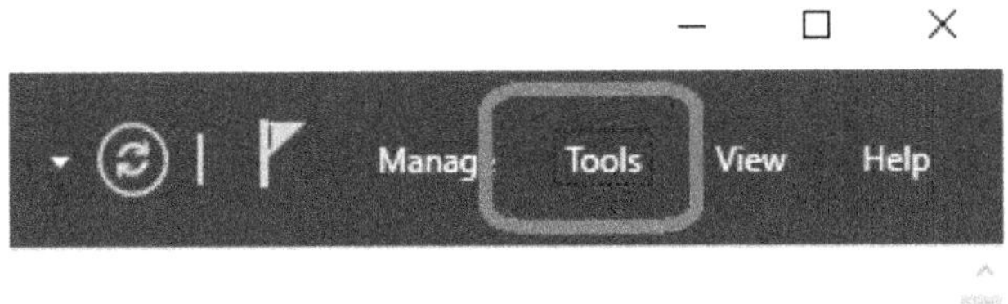

In Server Manager, at the Top, Choose Tools

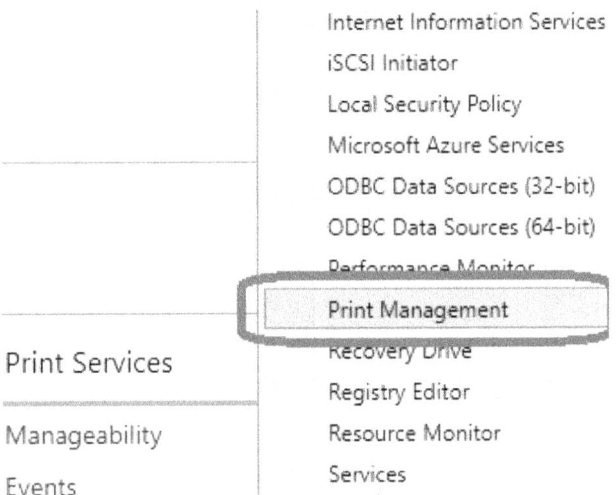

Choose Print Management from the Menu

This should display the Print Servers managed; you need to choose your print server if that is not already chosen by default.

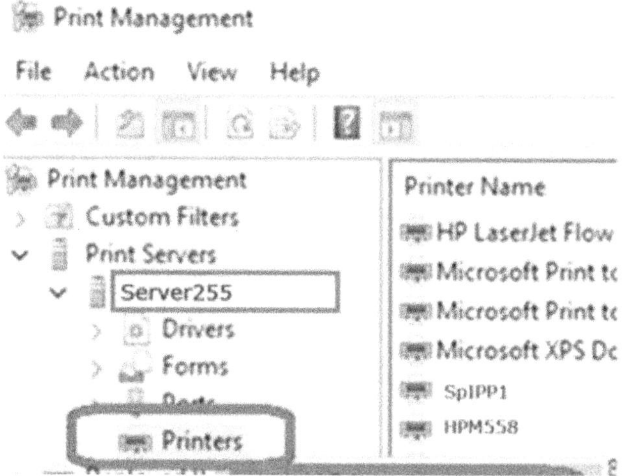

Select Printers If Not Already Selected

In the right-hand pane, right-click the printer whose port you wish to use and create a tandem printer instance. Select Properties ➤ Ports tab to view the port this printer uses. Denote this port as you will have to select it from a list in a few moments.

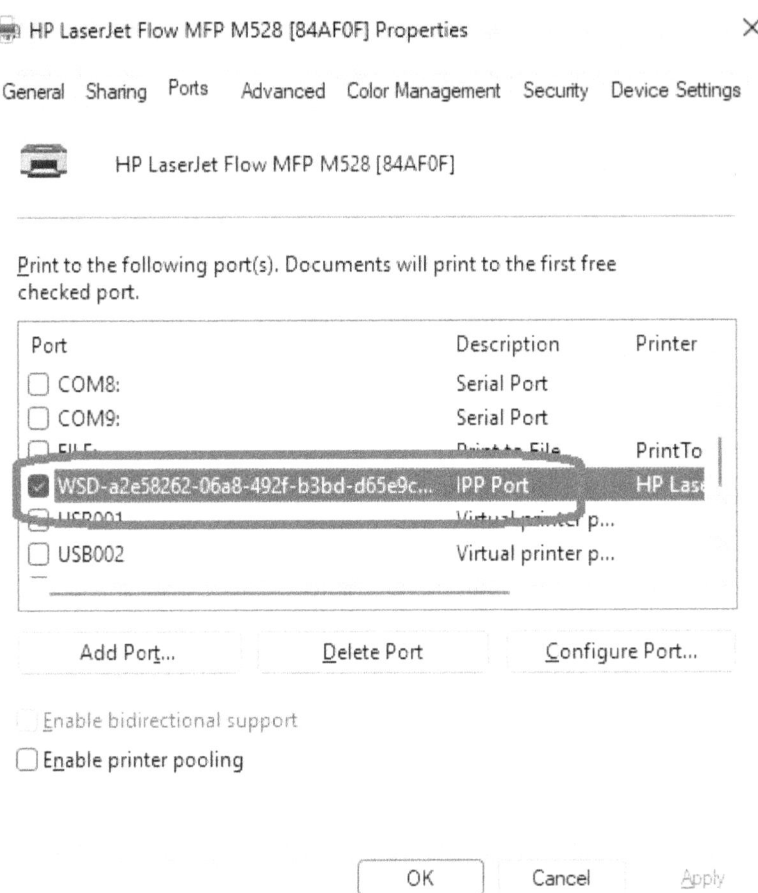

You can now add a new printer: right-click on the Printers selection under Print Servers in the left-hand pane. In the context menu, select **Add Printer**.

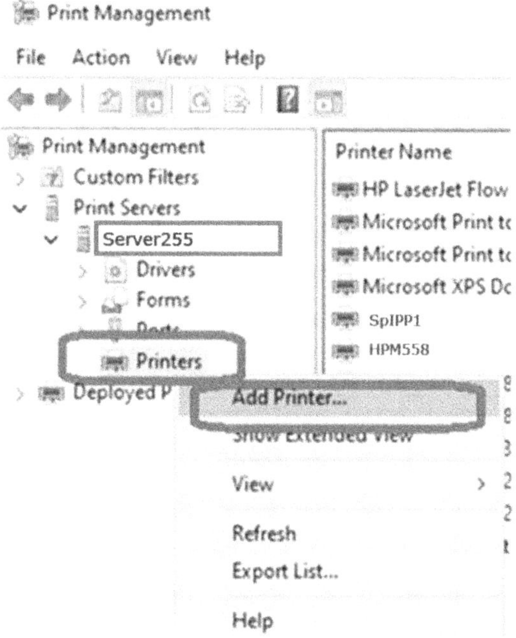

Start the Add Printer Process

The key is to add a new printer using an existing port – in this case, the port denoted earlier. You can select this port from the dropdown of available ports as shown below.

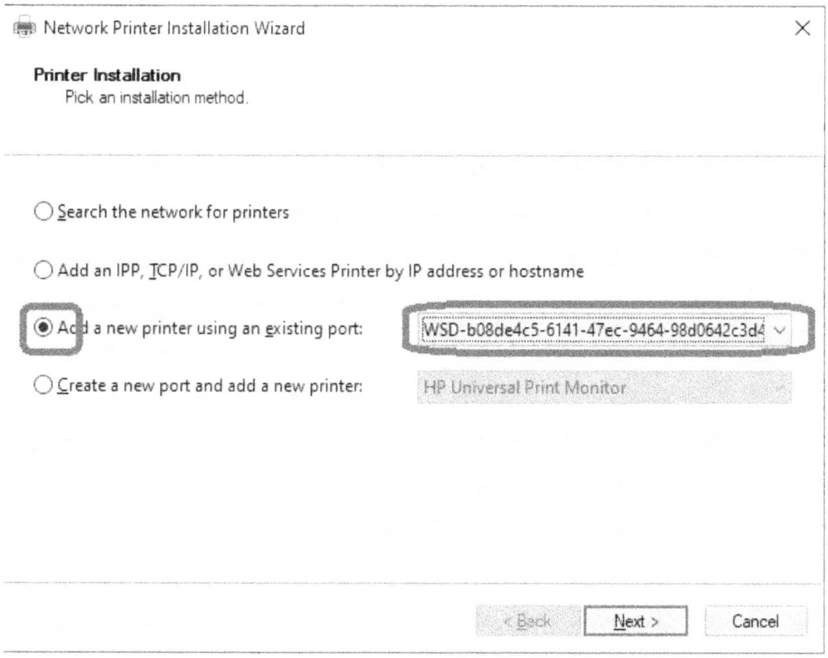

After clicking Next, the wizard will ask you to select an existing print driver. As this is an IPP printer, choose the Microsoft IPP Class Driver.

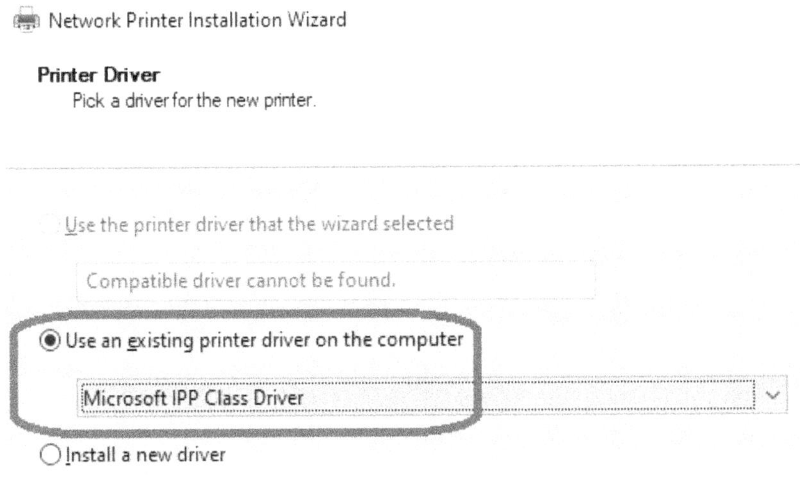

Finally, you will be asked for a printer name and whether you want to share the printer.

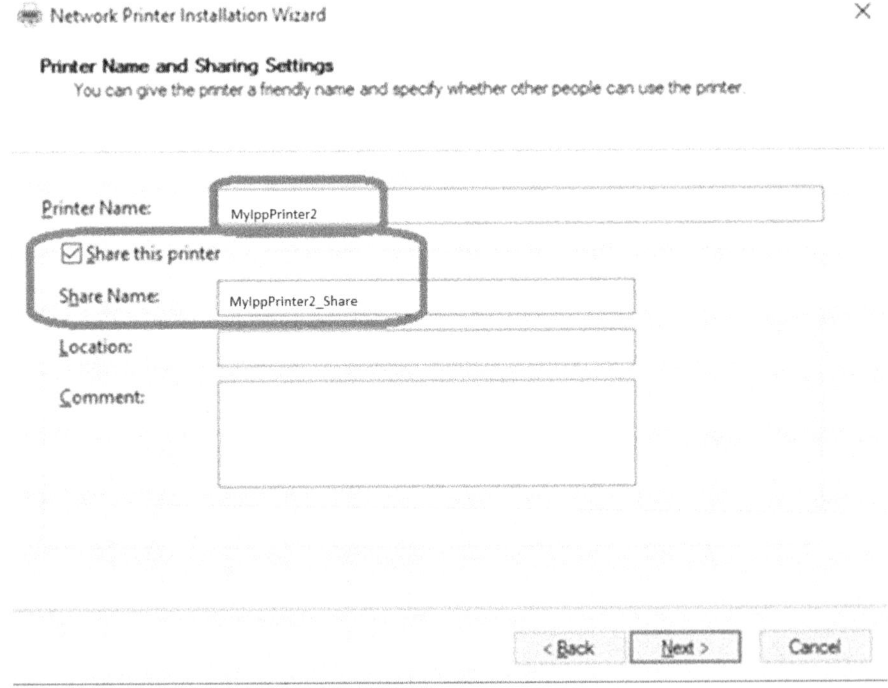

When the printer has been created, make sure the default settings you want all users to inherit (i.e., duplexing or print quality) are set. You can do this by opening Printers and Scanners and selecting your printer. Now follow the following instructions so all users connecting to the shared printer get the desired default settings.

1. Click **Printer properties**.
2. Go to the **Advanced** tab.
3. Click **Printing Defaults**.
4. Change your settings.

PDF Console Print Utility

While creation of print through Windows applications (to an IPP printer installed in Windows) was covered back in Chapter 4, "The MS IPP Class Driver" (BasicIppPrint solution), we have not covered how to programmatically process and print a pdf file on disk. For example, you might be required to programmatically print pdf files created by other applications or processes. Obviously, if you had Adobe Acrobat Pro, you would use its COM interface with .NET to accomplish this task, or perhaps if you preferred PowerShell, you might use the free Acrobat Reader to do the same. There is also another alternative that does not require the installation of Adobe Acrobat Pro and has a high degree of process control.

If you look in the code section of this chapter, you will find the ConsoleIppPrint project, which houses the CSPrint utility. What makes this intriguing is the high degree of control you have on the printed document - i.e., number of pages, types of duplexing, etc. This utility uses the PdfiumViewer: a project available on Git that provides the libraries to load, process, and print pdf files [5]. PdfiumViewer makes printing pdf files a breeze and provides an elevated level of control to boot.

Loading and printing a pdf file on disk using PdfiumViewer

```
using (var document = PdfDocument.Load(sPdfFilePath))
 {
     using (var printDocument = document.CreatePrintDocument())
     {
```

```
            printDocument.PrinterSettings.PrinterName = sPrinterName;
            printDocument.PrintController = new StandardPrintController();
            printDocument.PrinterSettings.Duplex = Duplex.Vertical;
            printDocument.PrinterSettings.Copies = 1;
            printDocument.Print();
        }
    }
```

Once the engine to load and process pdf files is included, the rest of the assignment is easy. If you need precise control on how the document is formatted or printed, look at the **printDocument.PrinterSettings** option values - perhaps you could include options for those in command line arguments, providing more flexibility to the utility. As it is, the GetArguments function asks the user for the printer (for instance, HPM528 or \\servername\sharename, etc.) and then the full path to the pdf file on disk. Once these are loaded, the utility then prints the expected document on the given printer. One caveat is that the printer (or print connection) must exist on Windows. If the printer is not installed in Windows, a more appropriate option would be to use the library created in Chapters 5, "IPP Standards Print," and 6, "Additional Operations," or a commercial version of the same.

Spooling Around

This subject, while potentially suited to Chapter 4, "The MS IPP Class Driver," or 9, "IPP Tools," is more appropriately aligned with the material in this section, as it does not fit neatly anywhere else. Regardless, it is essential to have a comprehensive understanding of network printing and therefore warrants inclusion in this book. Whatever term you use - Point and Print, Print Connection, or Server-Based Printers - the use of printers shared off a server is so pervasive in the Windows world as to be ubiquitous. Their use has allowed centralized control of printers, drivers, and print queues, which significantly helps reduce operating costs. From the user perspective, print connections reduce the need for end-user intervention or local setup. But just how does the print job that originated on a workstation eventually get queued and printed on the print server? Even more interesting, how would you troubleshoot an issue in this print flow?

We touched on this subject matter a bit in Chapter 1, "Windows Legacy Print," albeit from a developer's point of view. At a very high level, you might conceptually understand this as copying the print job to the server spooler, which then processes and delivers it to the printer. In the IPP world, the print job is typically rendered at the client side, often into PDF (or PWG-Raster, Apple Raster, etc.), before it is sent to the server. When the spooler service starts processing the job, the IPP requests Validate-Job, Create-Job, and Send-Document to finish the job delivery to the printer. In effect, the process of submitting a print job to a print connection (rather than a local printer) can be thought of as a split process: the job submission from the client to the print server spooler and then the culmination of the IPP print request from the print server to the printer. The following graphic provides a high-level fundamental process breakdown about the entire IPP print connection job submission flow.

To understand the process of conveying print job data to the server, you will need an overview of the network protocols used. While an in-depth explanation is beyond the scope of this book, a high-level view is essential to understanding what is going on. DCERPC (Distributed Computing Environment/Remote Procedure Calls) are employed to call print operations (Win32 APIs) remotely via the SPOOLSS interface. DCERPC will use the established named pipe (as a transport to the print server) to route calls to SPOOLS. Think of the named pipe (\\PIPE\Spoolss) as the "highway" back and forth to the server while DCERPC is the protocol used on the highway to call APIs. Server Message Blocks then do the actual file transfer (over RPC) to send data, and the server spooler writes it to the spool file(s) on disk.

When a client uses a shared print connection to print via an application installed on the machine, such as Word or Notepad, local spooler APIs are employed, such as OpenPrinter, StartDocPrinter, WritePrinter, etc. The local spooler on the workstation knows the shared printer (\\print_server\share) is a remote printer via the print redirector. The client-side spooler service uses DCERPC over a named pipe (the "highway") to communicate with the server spooler service (SPOOLSS). The \PIPE\spoolss service is a well-known endpoint that uses SMB over TCP port 445 to relay DCERPC calls. Thus, the client can initiate OpenPrinterEx, StartDocPrinter, and WritePrinter RPCs over this link to the listening SPOOLSS service on the print server. On the server end, it will write the created spool files (.SPL and .SHD) to the print server disk. After this is completed, the job can be routed to the IPP printer for a hard printout.

From the client's perspective, there is no direct communication with the printer. Instead, the client Windows machine communicates with the Windows Server 2022 print server using Remote Procedure Calls (RPC) — specifically SPOOLSS (Spooler Subsystem RPC Interface) over the established named pipe transport. Spoolsv.exe is the spooler's API server. It is implemented as a service that is started when the operating system is started and exports an RPC interface to the server side of the spooler's Win32 API [8]. The Print System Remote Protocol uses RPC over named pipes ([MS-RPCE] Section 2.1.1.2) for RPC sequences.

The well-known endpoint \pipe\spoolss is used for RPC calls made from the print client to the print server [9]. The initial objective from the client perspective, then, is to ascertain if the print server SPOOLS interface is available. You will see the following on a Wireshark trace to indicate the spooler service is up and available:

```
Map Request, SPOOLSS, 32-bit NDR
```

This marks the point in the communication stream where the client asks the Endpoint Mapper service on the server (port 135) to identify the appropriate named pipe for SPOOLSS [6]. For example, a high-level sequence might be

- Connect to \\remote_print_server\PIPE\epmapper
- Returns: use \\PIPE\spoolss for the server SPOOLSS interface

The Wireshark trace below highlights the communication from the client to the print server.

Source	Destination	Protocol	Lengtl	Info
Client	Server	DCERPC	466	Request: call_id: 1250, Fragment: Single, opnum: 0, Ctx: 3
Server	Client	TCP	60	53912 → 54090 [ACK] Seq=672 Ack=5760 Win=2096896 Len=0
		TCP	60	53912 → 54090 [FIN, ACK] Seq=672 Ack=5760 Win=2096896 Len=0
Client	Server	TCP	54	54090 → 53912 [ACK] Seq=5760 Ack=673 Win=130560 Len=0
Client	Server	DCERPC	194	Response: call_id: 1250, Fragment: Single, Ctx: 3
		DCERPC	210	Request: call_id: 1251, Fragment: Single, opnum: 20, Ctx: 3
		DCERPC	194	Response: call_id: 1251, Fragment: Single, Ctx: 3
		TCP	54	54089 → 135 [ACK] Seq=1505 Ack=1485 Win=131328 Len=0
Client	Server	DCERPC	290	Request: call_id: 1252, Fragment: Single, opnum: 16, Ctx: 3
		DCERPC	1218	Response: call_id: 1252, Fragment: Single, Ctx: 3
		DCERPC	274	**Request: call_id: 1253, Fragment: Single, opnum: 16, Ctx: 3**
		DCERPC	1218	Response: call_id: 1253, Fragment: Single, Ctx: 3
		DCERPC	290	Request: call_id: 1254, Fragment: Single, opnum: 16, Ctx: 3
		DCERPC	1218	Response: call_id: 1254, Fragment: Single, Ctx: 3
		TCP	54	54102 → 53912 [ACK] Seq=[illegible] Ack=672 Win=130560 Len=0
Client	Server	EPM	222	Map request, SPOOLSS, 32bit NDR
Server	Client	EPM	226	Map response, SPOOLSS, 32bit NDR
		TCP	66	54103 → 53912 [SYN] Seq=0 Win=64260 Len=0 MSS=1428 WS=256 SACK_PERM
		TCP	66	53912 → 54103 [SYN, ACK] Seq=0 Ack=1 Win=65535 Len=0 MSS=1460 WS=256 SACK_PERM
		TCP	54	54103 → 53912 [ACK] Seq=1 Ack=1 Win=131328 Len=0
		TCP	1482	54103 → 53912 [ACK] Seq=1 Ack=1 Win=131328 Len=1428 [TCP PDU reassembled in 728]
		TCP	1482	54103 → 53912 [ACK] Seq=1429 Ack=1 Win=131328 Len=1428 [TCP PDU reassembled in 72
		TCP	1482	54103 → 53912 [ACK] Seq=2857 Ack=1 Win=131328 Len=1428 [TCP PDU reassembled in 72
		DCERPC	724	Bind: call_id: 2, Fragment: Single, 3 context items: SPOOLSS V1.0 (32bit NDR), SP
		TCP	60	53912 → 54103 [ACK] Seq=1 Ack=2857 Win=2097664 Len=0
		TCP	60	53912 → 54103 [ACK] Seq=1 Ack=4955 Win=2097664 Len=0
		DCERPC	340	Bind_ack: call_id: 2, Fragment: Single, max_xmit: 5840 max_recv: 5840, 3 results:
Client	Server	DCERPC	274	Alter_context: call_id: 2, Fragment: Single, 1 context items: SPOOLSS V1.0 (64bit
		DCERPC	159	Alter_context_resp: call_id: 2, Fragment: Single, max_xmit: 5840 max_recv: 5840,
Client	Server	SPOOLSS	498	OpenPrinterEx request
Server	Client	SPOOLSS	194	OpenPrinterEx response
Client	Server	SPOOLSS	194	ClosePrinter request
Server	Client	SPOOLSS	194	ClosePrinter response

Client Communication with the Print Server

Once established, the client can now make the following calls:

OpenPrinterEx – Opens a handle to the IPP printer shared off the server.

GetPrinter, EnumJobs – Queries the printer status and relays this back to the client.

StartDocPrinter, WritePrinter – Sends the rendered print data to the IPP printer.

ClosePrinter – Closes the handle opened by OpenPrinterEx.

So now we can put together a high-level flow of a print job submitted to a print connection as

1. Windows 11 client binds to \\PIPE\spoolss to issue Win32 print API commands.
2. Client sends a DCERPC call: OpenPrinter/GetPrinter/StartDocPrinter/WritePrinter/ClosePrinter. This goes over SMB (as a write to the named pipe).
3. Server receives this RPC call and: Writes the buffer to a .SPL file in its spool folder and updates any job metadata written to the .SHD file.

Of course, the return value from these Spooler APIs forms the basis of the overall print job success as seen from the client. The other half of the equation, specifically the print server job submission to the targeted printer, requires the very same print ticket creation and eventual formation of IPP requests covered in Chapter 4, "The MS IPP Class Driver," for direct print. While a direct correlation between Windows Spooler APIs (called by the client) and IPP requests made to the printer is impossible to ascertain, a rough mapping might look like the following:

Windows Print API (on Print Server) called by Client	Purpose	Rough IPP Request Mapping	Information
OpenPrinterEx/DocumentProperties	Queries the printer, retrieves print job properties requested.	Validate-Job	
StartDocPrinter	Notifies the (server) print spooler that a document is to be spooled for printing.	Create-Job	Job Id Returned must be mapped to the WritePrinter API formation of Send-Document IPP Request
WritePrinter	IPP byte stream for document (in HTTP POST message) created	Send-Document	
GetJob	The GetJob function retrieves information about a specified print job.	Get-Job-Attributes	

Rough Mapping of Windows API to IPP Requests

You might be questioning where the printer gets the default printer job properties that are required for the formation of the print ticket used. The answer is essentially the same location as on the client: the Windows registry (on the print server). You will recall the default print ticket reflects the settings stored in the Windows Registry from when the printer was first installed (on the server) or last configured on that client. These registry values act as the basis for the initial print ticket used for the job [10]. In summary,

When a Windows 11 client tenders a document to a shared IPP printer via Point and Print:

- The details of the print job transport to the IPP printer are obfuscated from the client.
- The client communicates over RPC (DCERPC/SPOOLSS) to the server to leverage spooler APIs.
- The print server translates those Windows Print API calls into IPP requests (using the MS IPP Class Driver).

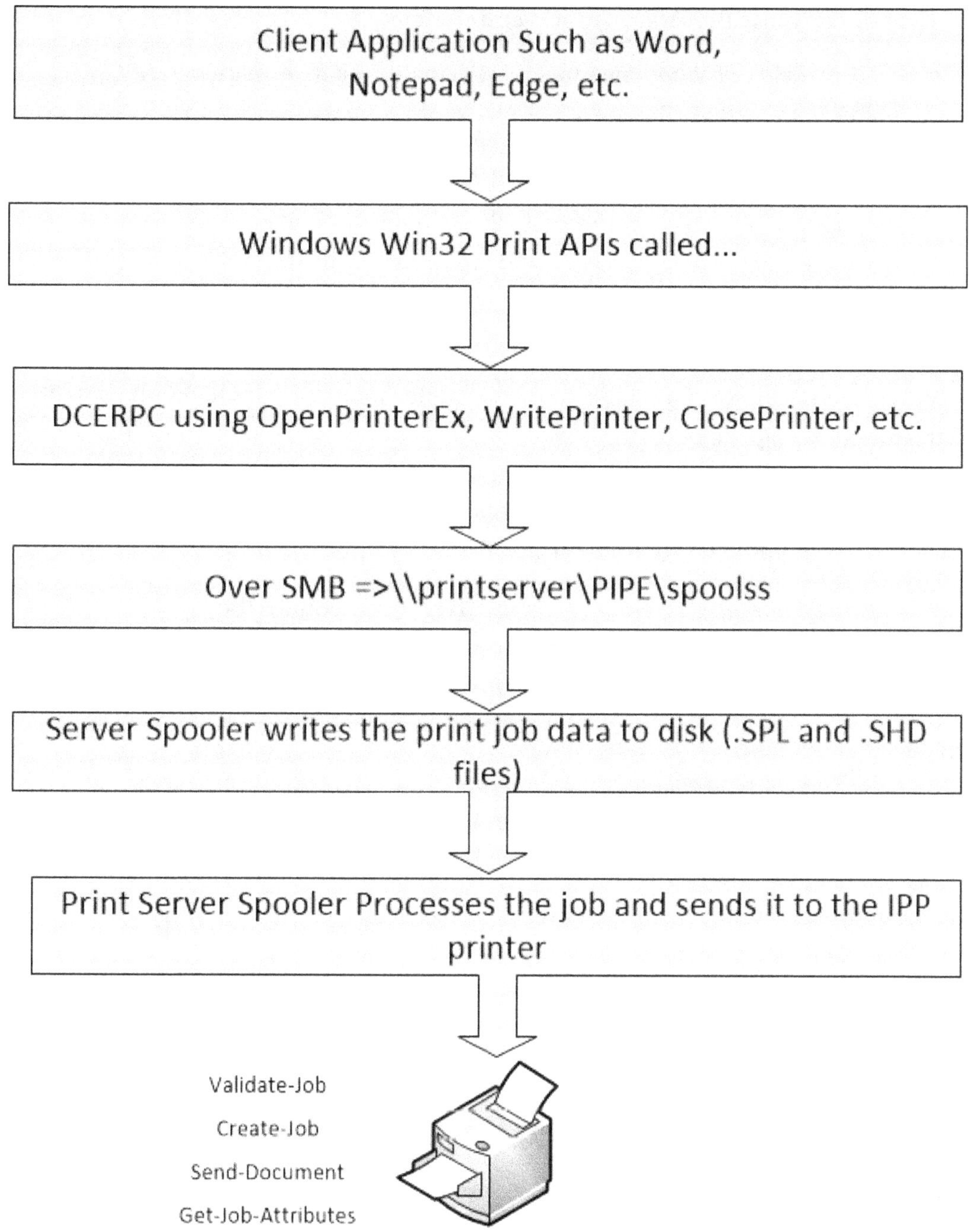

Print Job Flow from Client to Server to Printer

The MS IPP Class Driver on the server handles:

- Conversion of print data into an HTTP byte stream formatted to IPP RFC request specifications.
- Possible Chunking (Send-Document) byte streams (if necessary).
- Mapping IPP job-ids returned to the Windows Spooler service from Create-Job (and for subsequent IPP requests by the MS IPP Class Driver).

So now that the process of submitting a print job to an IPP printer shared from a server is understood, we can establish some troubleshooting basics to handle potential print issues that might arise.

On the submission end from the client to the server, we will not be looking for IPP request errors; they will not appear here. On the other hand, we should be on the lookout (via Wireshark) for issues such as

EndPoint Mapper Resolution Issues: The client requires the Endpoint Mapper (EPM) to provide the TCP port being used for spools on the server. If this fails, the spoolss service listening port cannot be determined, and the job submission will fail.

SPOOLSS Binding Failure: When the TCP port resolved via EPM is determined, the client DCERPC must bind to this port.

In both above scenarios, a firewall blocking the port or an unresponsive spoolss service on the server may impair the process. These failures can be found on a Wireshark trace.

OpenPrinterEx Issues: This API requires the submitting user to have rights on the target printer object and that the printer object be responsive. For instance, trying to submit a job to a printer that is powered off or is having network issues (DNS resolution?) might cause failure.

Any Other Print API Issues: At any point, a Win32 error incurred on the server side will cause the job to fail.

Key Troubleshooting Events

The key event to look for (on a Wireshark trace) to ascertain that the print job has been successfully copied to the listening Print Server's spooler is Server Message Block events. Server Message Block (SMB) enables file sharing, printer sharing, network browsing, and inter-process communication (through named pipes) over a computer network [7]. These key events (if using SMB 2 or 3 as on Windows 10/11) are

SMB2 Create a request opening a new file in the spool directory (of the server).

A series of **SMB2 Writes** conveying the job information from the client machine to the print server's new spool file.

The **SMB2 Close** operation indicates the job has been written in full and thus delivered.

Once the job has been successfully submitted to the print server, Wireshark traces taken from the print server to the printer would take the form of the requests covered in Chapters 5, "IPP Standards Print," and 6, "Additional Operations." Thus, if you are certain the job has been copied to the server, concentrate on potential errors arising from the job rendering (by the MS IPP Class Driver) to the IPP printer.

Potential Security Issue Addressed

Notice: While RPCs over named pipes continue to be the primary mechanism for Windows clients to facilitate job submission to print servers (i.e., print connections), Windows 11 version 22H2 initiated an important change. Starting with this version of Windows 11, the default communication method (the "highway") changed from SMB named pipes to direct TCP transport. This was done to give the calling client more direct control over the authentication process. Critically, Named Pipes will allow unrestrained delegation if the print server is configured in that way in Active Directory.

Functionally, most aspects of print job submission remain unchanged. However, the move away from named pipes disables a key component: the use of unconstrained delegation, which is implicitly enabled when named pipes are used by default. This has important security implications.

Unconstrained delegation can allow any authenticated caller (low-privilege attacker) to impersonate other users when communicating with services like the Domain Controller's spooler service. For example, a malicious client can issue the

RpcRemoteFindFirstPrinterChange-Notification call and instruct the server to send the response to a system configured with unconstrained delegation. In doing so, the print server creates and sends a Kerberos service ticket (TGS) that contains the server's computer account's ticket-granting ticket (TGT)—since Kerberos is involved and the client is trusted for delegation. This is a critical issue if the print server is also a Domain Controller (DC).

Example: an attacker wants to obtain the Kerberos TGT of a server (a DC if possible) and configure the spooler service to send an event callback from the RpcRemoteFindFirstPrinterChangeNotification to their system configured with unconstrained delegation. The server (or optimally a DC) authenticates the machine and provides a Kerberos service ticket that includes the server's TGT, enabling the attacker to impersonate the server (or DC). This results in the attacker obtaining a Kerberos TGT for the print server's computer account (i.e., running as SYSTEM), which can be used for malicious purposes [12].

Using Event Viewer for Print Issues

The last item in this chapter is not specifically linked to IPP/IPPS implementation in Windows but can help mitigate support issues that arise thereof. Assuming your IPP/IPPS rollout went well, you could potentially be tasked with identifying and fixing client print issues as they appear. This can sometimes be difficult to assess, particularly regarding issues where no output from the printer is the user's complaint. For these troubles, you might consider monitoring events as they happen using PrintService logging in Event Viewer. To do this, you will need to open Event Viewer and then click on the **Applications and Services** Logs category. Depending on the speed of your machine and the size of the existing log database, it may take anywhere from a few seconds to a few minutes to complete the enumeration of all the children of the Applications and Services Logs parent. Once complete, navigate to Microsoft ↗ Windows ↗ PrintService. If this is the first time you have used the Operational log, you will need to enable it, as by default it is disabled. Right-click on Operational and click Enable Log. Once complete, you are ready to receive print service events as they happen.

The Operational Event Log for PrintServices

A successful event sequence for job number 5, for instance, would resemble the entries below:

1. Spooling job 5
2. Printing Job 5
3. The print job 5 was sent through the print processor MS_XPS_PROC on printer HP LaserJet M608 [01D26A], driver Microsoft IPP Class Driver, in the isolation mode 0 (0 - loaded in the spooler, 1 - loaded in shared sandbox, 2 - loaded in isolated sandbox). The Win32 error code returned by the print processoris 0x0.
4. Rendering job 5
5. Document 5, Print Document owned by User57 on \\WinMachine54 was printed on HP M608 [01D345] through port **WSD-55780aa0-109a-56b0-345f-b55d99b4a10f**. Size in bytes: 84724. Pages printed: 1. No user action is required.
6. Deleting job 5

All print events will be logged with the corresponding date and time of incident. An unsuccessful event sequence might not contain all the steps above or would have Win32 error codes in step 3. While the log information at first is unimpressive, it does provide an indication of the following:

1. The print processor that handled the print event and the Win32 error code returned by the print processor (0x0 is successful). If there is an error returned, you can look up the error code using the command **Net HelpMsg <error_code>** in a console window.
2. Whether the job was rendered locally on the machine or not.
3. The port used to send the job to the named printer, the number of pages printed, and the size of the document printed.

Keep in mind that you can use the Event Viewer and connect to remote machines for troubleshooting purposes. You will need sufficient rights to connect to the remote machine and read the logs. Additionally, loading times will increase significantly, so be patient. Finally, if you will not be working on the client anymore, be sure to disable logging for Operational events as they consume resources on the host machine.

Chapter Summary

This chapter reviewed a variety of topics not covered in the first nine chapters. It started out by providing more information on Windows Protected Print, most specifically on backing up the existing Windows print environment prior to implementing WPP. The topic of printer firmware updates via the IPP Firmware Update Extension is then introduced. While this extension has not yet been formally adopted, it does specify method(s) of updating printer firmware in a vendor-neutral manner that is sorely lacking in the existing enterprise print management environment. If adopted, enterprises will finally have a way of maintaining firmware across entrenched fleets of printer hardware without having to resort to installing multiple vendor-specific tools to do so.

The next subject concerns how to create multiple instances of shared IPP printers on a server, albeit using different names. This ability is provided for Windows Server only. Multiple shared instances of the same IPP printer enable enterprises to configure distinct default settings such as paper tray source, duplexing, or print quality, for enhanced user convenience. Next, the chapter covers processing a PDF file from disk to eventual printout in code, provided an installed IPP/IPPS printer is known to Windows. The solution uses the PdfiumViewer, which makes the printing process a breeze and provides multiple options for the user.

The chapter then goes into detail examining how a Point and Print connection in Windows is implemented and how to troubleshoot the operation in the event of failure. While using a print connection may appear easy (and should be so for the user), this is a complex endeavor involving RPC operations. The existing security threat within named pipes is uncovered, and the changes Microsoft is recommending to secure your network are provided. Finally, we end by using the Windows Event Viewer to troubleshoot print job operations. This tool can be used to identify print issues within the operating system itself.

References

1. IPP Firmware Update Extensions v1.0, The Printer Working Group, October 10, 2024
2. MicroMvvm, NuGet, https://www.nuget.org/packages/MicroMVVM
3. Configuring Windows Protected Print, Windows OS Hub, https://woshub.com/enable-windows-protected-print-mode-wpp/
4. What is Windows Protected Print Mode and How to Enable it?, TheWindowsClub, https://www.thewindowsclub.com/windows-protected-print-mode
5. PdfiumViewer, Nuget, https://www.nuget.org/packages/PdfiumViewer/
6. DCE/RPC & [MS-RPCE], Scapy, https://scapy.readthedocs.io/en/latest/layers/dcerpc.htm
7. Server Message Block, WikiPedia, https://en.wikipedia.org/wiki/Server_Message_Block
8. Introduction to spooler components, Windows Learn, https://learn.microsoft.com/en-us/windows-hardware/drivers/print/introduction-to-spooler-components
9. Transport, Microsoft Learn, https://learn.microsoft.com/en-us/openspecs/windows_protocols/ms-rprn/fdf1138a-f6b9-4b00-ada6-1fbb6097d683
10. PrintTicket Class, Microsoft Learn, https://learn.microsoft.com/en-us/dotnet/api/system.printing.printticket?view=windowsdesktop-9.0
11. RPC connection updates for print in Windows 11, Windows Learn, https://learn.microsoft.com/en-us/troubleshoot/windows-client/printing/windows-11-rpc-connection-updates-for-print
12. Domain Controller Print Server + Unconstrained Kerberos Delegation = Pwned Active Directory Forest, Active Directory Security, https://adsecurity.org/?p=4056

Addendum 1: IppCheck

IppCheck is a compact utility that completes the development cycle from Chapters 5 and 6 by utilizing the C# library created. The purpose of this exercise is to display the potential uses of the library while providing a useful tool. The utility is called IppCheck as it can help test many scenarios that arise when converting from legacy print protocols to IPP on Windows. The solution houses a WPF utility leveraging Model-View-View Model (MVVM) techniques using the excellent MicroMvvm library [2] I found in NuGet years ago. I selected a GUI application as it would best convey to the user the state of any given printer. If you don't follow the MVVM design, don't sweat the details - the important point is to see how it calls the methods from the library created earlier in the book. Of course, we could also simply use the library for any command-line utility you require, so if a WPF GUI is not for you, a console-based design would work just as well. The overall intent is to indicate (to the user) if printer hardware is compatible with Microsoft's Modern Print platform. The code is available (in the Addendum code section of this book) for modification if you would like to improve or append it to the current code base.

When installed via the accompanying MSI, IppCheck should appear in the user start menu with other installed Apps. When selected, the utility will initialize for the first time in the default

J. Marion, *Adopting Internet Printing Protocol for Windows*, https://doi.org/10.1007/979-8-8688-2010-6

configuration – i.e., in single printer test mode (no printer list is specified by default). In this mode, a printer is specified in the **Printers to test** box, and the **Test** button is clicked to start the IPP conformance testing.

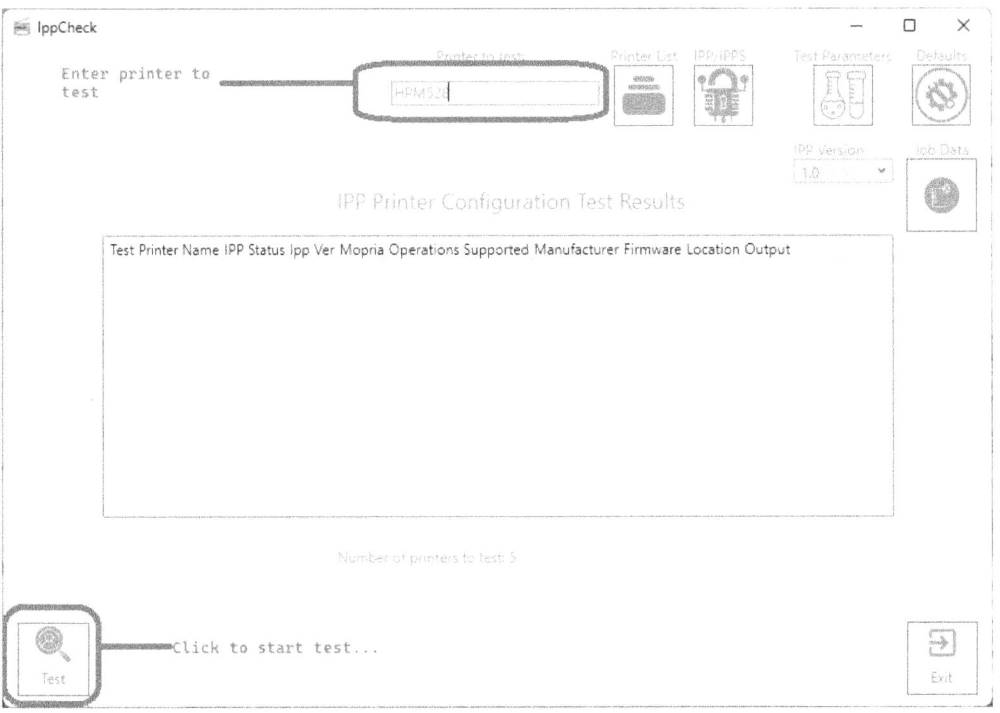

Default Test Setup

In this mode the utility queries the printer specified and presents the findings in the results Listview.

Operational Buttons

The Application Defaults Setup button allows the user to configure the application for the printers list (txt) file, the test parameters (xml) file, any potential csv file created file path, and finally the path of the job attributes file (txt). Setting the test parameter file is mandatory for the program to operate. A sample (TestParams.xml) is included in the IppCheck project files.

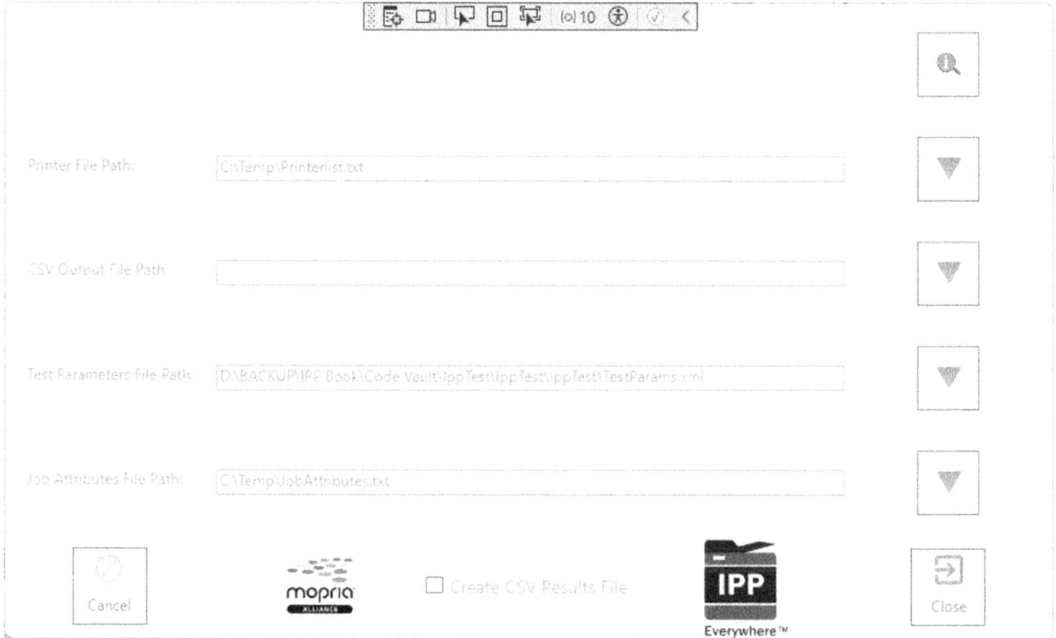

Default File Locations

As installed by the MSI, IppCheck provides a test parameters file and a job attributes file. These are referenced in HKCU\Software\IppCheck for the utility and physically located (by default) in the file path C:\Users\<user>\AppData\Roaming\IppCheck, although the user is free to change this.

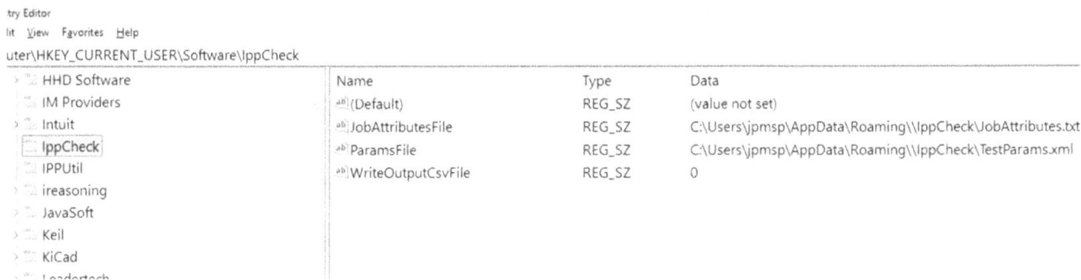

Default File Path for Configuration Files

Optionally, a user can also specify a text file containing printers to test (1 per line) for the utility. Create a list of printers (1 per line) and open the **Defaults** dialog. Specify the printer's file by entering the path (or using the file dialog to do so) in the **Printer File Path** textbox. Once specified, the utility will use this file as a source of printers to test unless a printer is entered in the **Printer to test** box. Note: once a printer's file is specified, restart the utility to load the change.

Printer File Path: C:\Temp\printers.txt

Specifying the File of Printers to Test

The printers list dialog can be viewed using the printers list button. While this will display the current list, you can modify this by adding or removing printers as necessary. In the graphic below, when a new printer is added, the "+" button appears. When clicked, this adds the new printer to the list. Right-clicking on a printer in the list and selecting "Remove Printer" will remove the printer from the list. When you are finished, click Close, and the entries will be saved. To modify a list or create a file, an existing printer list file must be specified in the default application setup dialog.

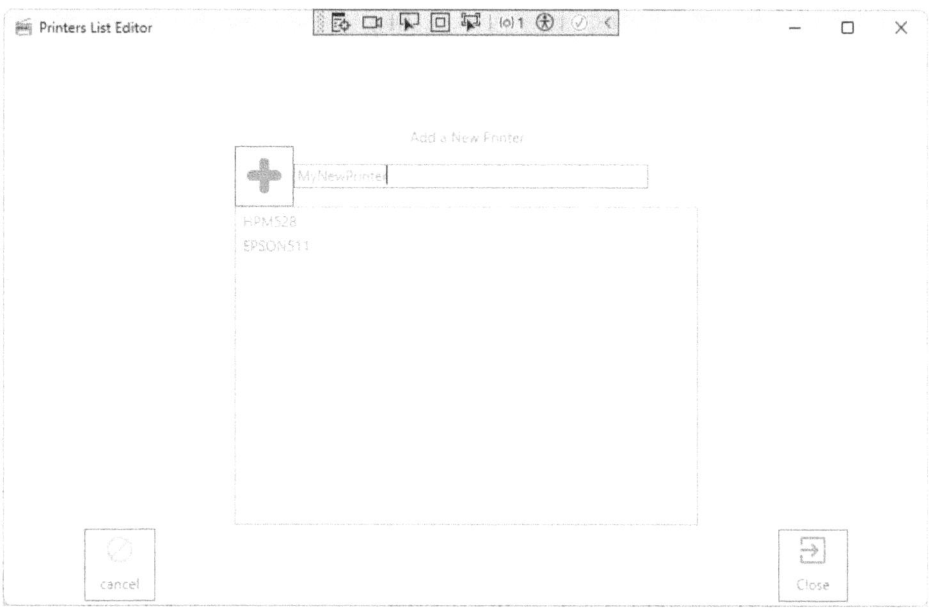

The IPP/IPPS button allows the user to test whether the printer will respond to unencrypted or encrypted transport that IPPS/IPP provides. If the button is out, port 631 IPP is used for all requests. If the button is depressed, IPPS is used for the requests. This allows the user to determine if IPP or IPPS is configured on the printer in question. Thus, a printer that fails requests for IPPS but successfully responds to IPP reveals issues with IPPS implementation (certificate issues and router port blocked), or IPPS is not enabled on the printer.

The IPP/IPPS version textbox allows the user to stipulate the version of IPP to be used for printer requests. This allows testing against a printer to see which version is supported.

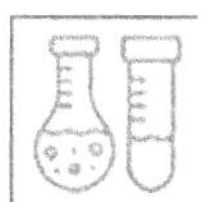

The Test Parameters Setup button is used to display the parameters that determine compliance. This is a read-only view of the xml file used by the utility and includes the IPP minimum version, minimum Mopria certification level, and all operations deemed essential. A sample xml file (which the read-only combo box loads) is shown below. This file itself may be altered to suit different environmental requirements as needed. Feel free to modify this to suit your needs. A sample (TestParams.xml) is included in the IppCheck project files. As a start, the utility checks for minimum IPP version and Mopria level. The utility also checks the IPP operations supported and returned from the printer against the list of operations in the test parameters file.

```
<?xml version="1.0" encoding="UTF-8"?>
<Printer>
  <IppAttributes>
    <IppVersionMax>2.2</IppVersionMax>
    <IppVersionMin>1.0</IppVersionMin>
    <MopriaCertification>1.0</MopriaCertification>
    <OperationsSupported>
        <Operation>get-printer-attributes</Operation>
        <Operation>cancel-job</Operation>
        <Operation>validate-job</Operation>
        <Operation>create-job</Operation>
        <Operation>print-job</Operation>
        <Operation>send-document</Operation>
        <Operation>identify-printer</Operation>
    </OperationsSupported>
  </IppAttributes>
</Printer>
```

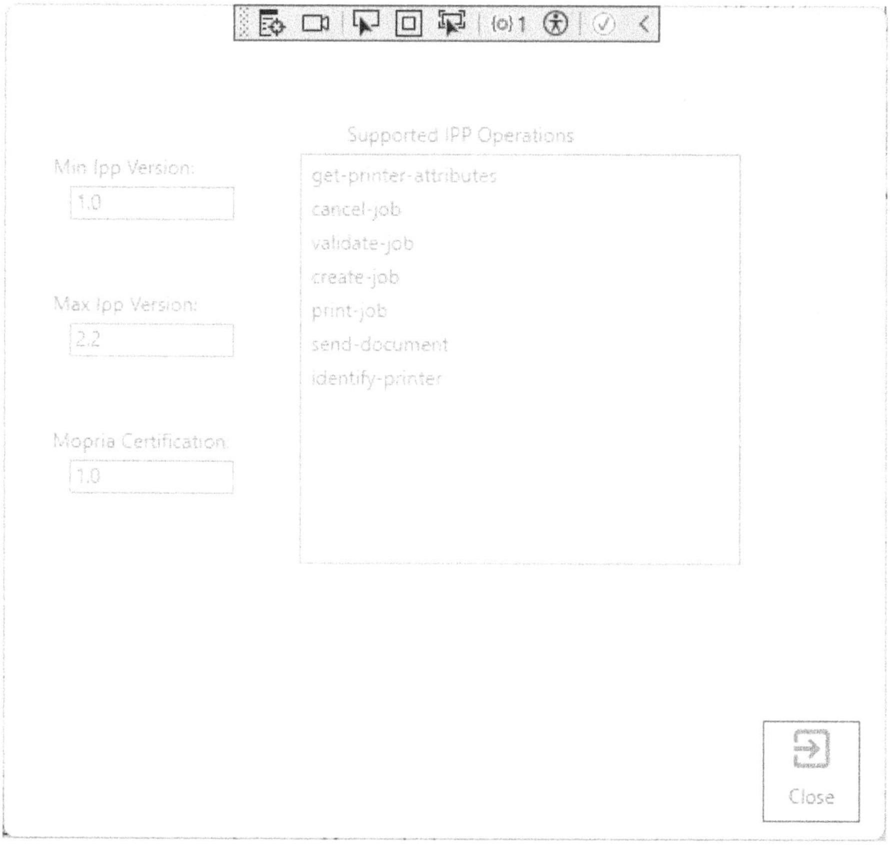

A Read-Only View of the Compliance Parameters

Start Testing

If there is a printer in the **Printer to Test** textbox at the top, or printers are found in the printers list, the **Test** button will appear as shown in the next graphic. The Printer to Test entry takes precedence over a list of printers; thus, you can instantly test any printer by entering its name in that box. If there is no entry in the Printer to Test textbox, but printers are found in the printer list, they will be tested when the Test button is clicked. The number of printers in the printer list available for testing will show if a printers list is found.

Once the test is started, the utility will query the printer(s) listed to obtain the results. The IPP status is displayed graphically for easy comprehension.

Results of Testing

View Printer Attributes

Once an IPP printer successfully returns the response, you can view the printer attributes collected. Right-click the printer of interest and choose View Printer Attributes for a more detailed look at results.

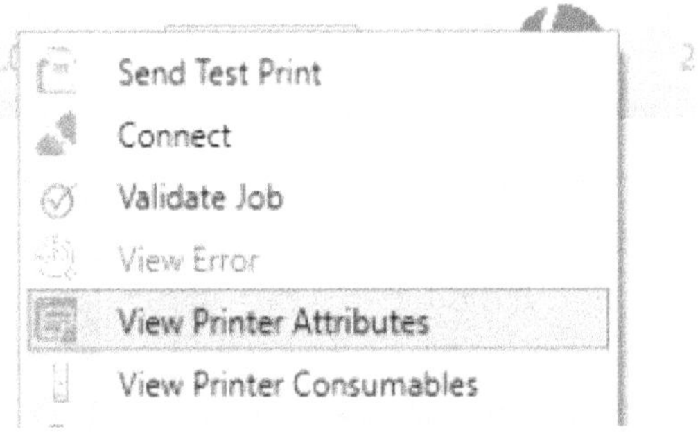

The printer attribute window displays the attributes associated with a printer. Once displayed, a graphic of the printer is made available on the left of the listbox. Users may search through the returned collection of attributes by name.

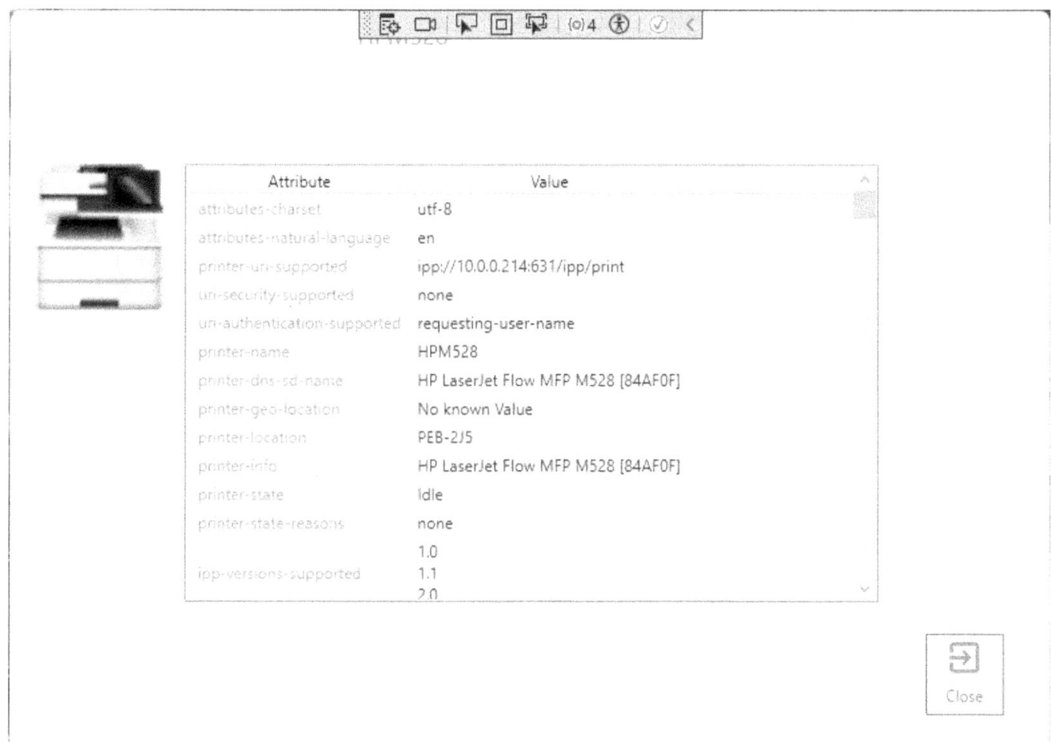

A View of Printer Attributes Returned

View Marker-Level Consumables

On any successful printer query, select marker levels (toner levels) can be viewed. The percentage of the current marker level relative to the total is displayed as a percentage.

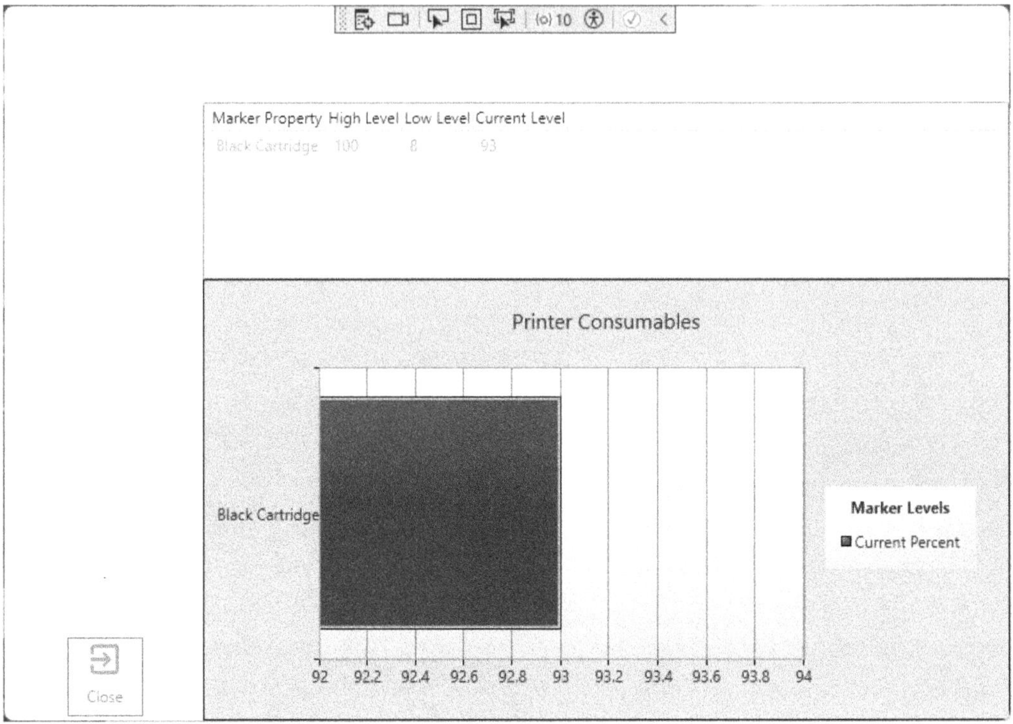

The Marker Levels of My HP528 Printer

Viewing Potential Job Attributes

The job attributes a printer can support are available as well. To view these, right-click on a returned printer and choose Job Creation Info from the menu.

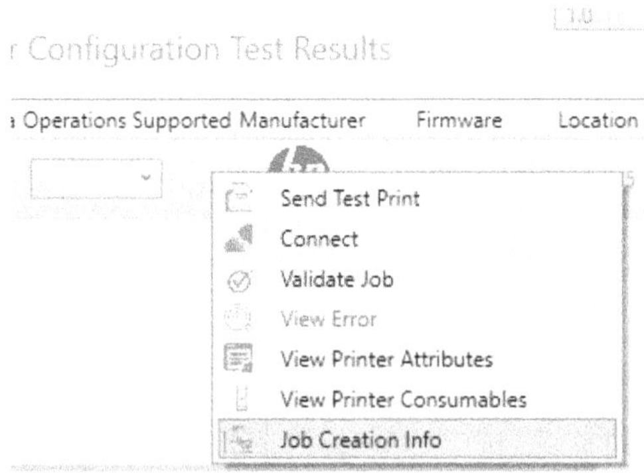

This will display the job attributes that the printer supports. If you click on one of the job attributes in the listview and choose "Default," the default setting for that job attribute will be displayed. You can use this to create a new job attributes file to test the Validate request. Given more time, I would link the context menu for this window to the job attributes file so a user would not have to type in new entries used for validation.

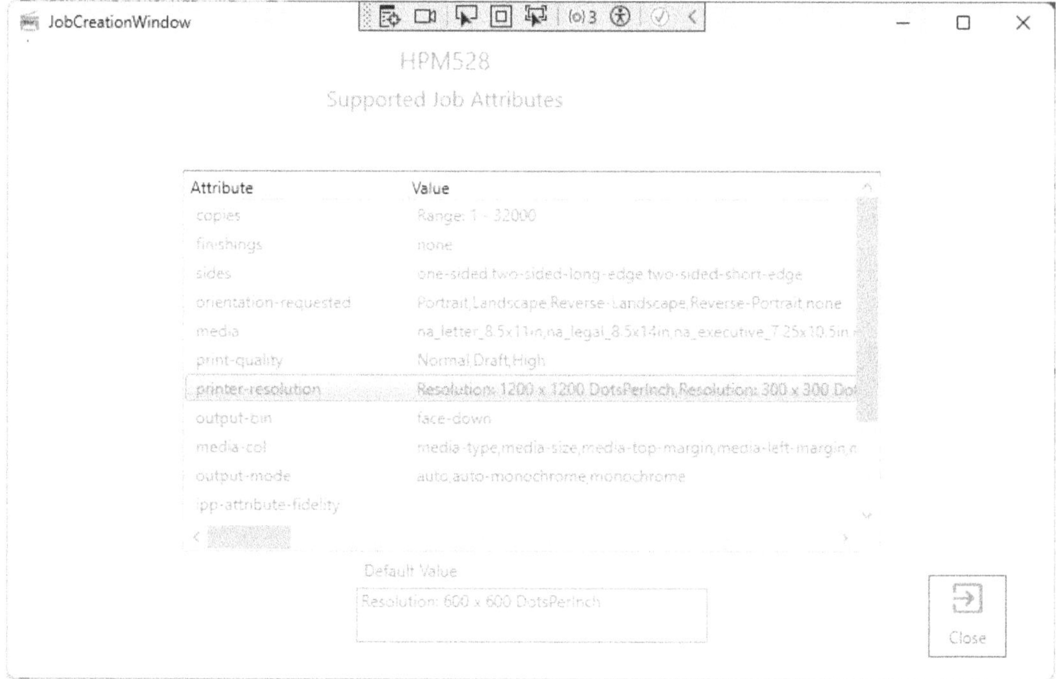

Job Attributes Supported and the Default Value(s)

As mentioned earlier, you can use any information gleaned in this window to create a job attributes file for print job validation tests.

Connect to Test Printer

You will be connected to the test printer (if it has an embedded web server) by right-clicking on a printer and then clicking on the Connect menu item.

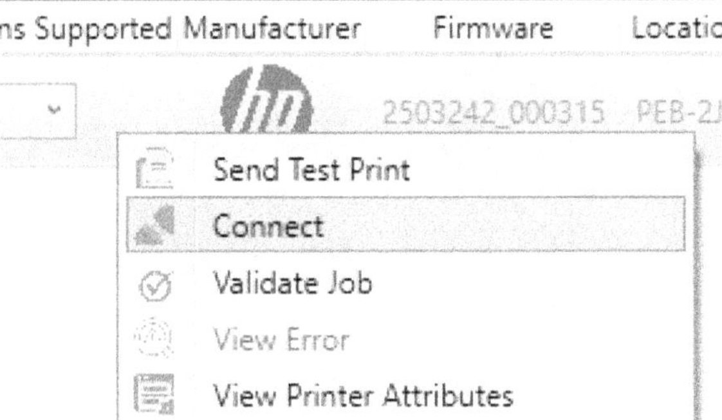

The Connect Menu Choice

This is a convenience that allows the user to connect to the test printer and make any (provided the user has the rights) changes or modifications necessary.

Testing IPP Print

You can send a test page to the IPP/IPPS printer to ensure it will print. The test page is a document with a few specifics about the printer, such as Mopria certification, IPP versions supported, etc. If the printer successfully prints out the page, your IPP/IPPS setup is successful.

Send a Test Page to the Printer

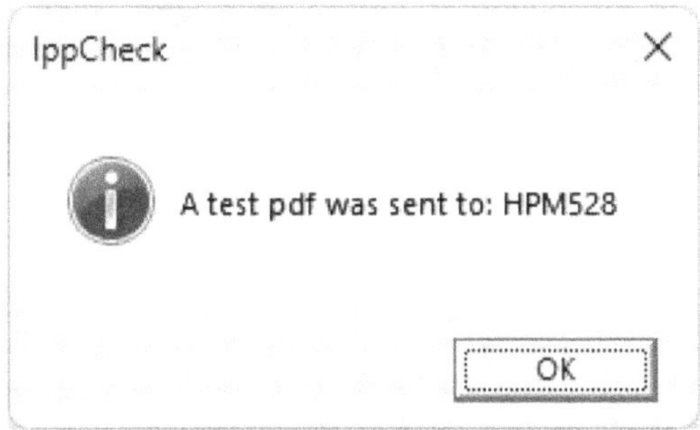

Result

Identify Printer

The Identify Printer request can be used to identify the physical location of a printer by a flashing screen or sound. To identify a printer, right-click the printer returned in the **IPP Printer Configuration Test Results** Listbox and select Identify Printer from the drop-down menu.

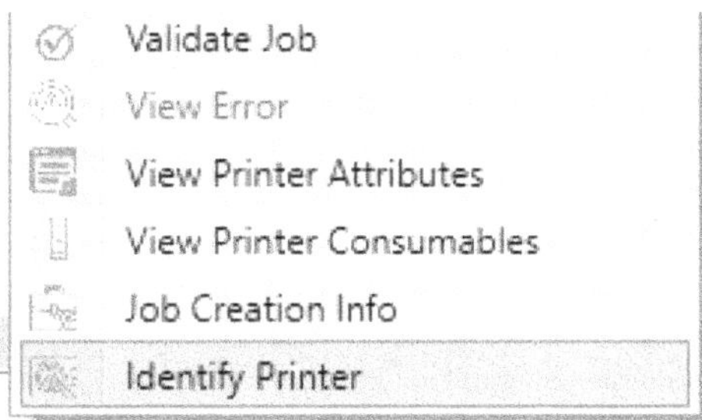

Identify the Printer Action

Application Design

IppCheck is a small application created to display the ability to test IPP/IPPS printers using an educational library. As such, it lacks the sophistication that would be required from larger applications intended for production. The main focus was to show how the library could be used, and thus some of the more professional MVVM design features are missing for clarity. For instance, a singleton class is used to pass parameters from the View to the ViewModel, which introduces tight coupling between components. Regardless, it should be a start for those interested in wanting to learn the basics of IPP and how it operates on a Windows platform.

As far as NuGet Packages used in the solution, there are three packages added:

> *DotNetProjects.WpfToolkit.DataVisualization (6.1.94)*: Used for the data visualization in the chart control when displaying marker levels in the consumables check.
>
> *Itext (9.1.0)*: Used for the creation of dynamic test page pdf.
>
> *itext.bouncy-castle-adapter (9.1.0)*: Used for the creation of pdf file requiring cryptographic operations.

While these are already added to the solution project IppCheck, you should know which ones were used in the event you want to create your own offshoot. Additionally, there are 2 Assemblies referenced by this solution for inclusion: MicroMvvm and CsIppRequestLib, both of which are included in the Libs folder of the project.

As for IO, the setup project (creatively named Setup) by default installs the default test parameters file (TestParams.xml) and the default job attributes file (JobAttributes.txt) both in the user profile AppData\Roaming path. It then creates the necessary user registry entries in the HKEY_CURRENT_USER\Software\IppCheck hive to link those files. This makes the initial run of the program go without complaints from the utility that critical files are missing. The user is free to change these settings after this first run or any time thereafter. A computer file list is not created, of course, as the network the utility runs on is not yet known.

The backbone of the program uses the same IPP methods created in chapters 5 and 6, most specifically GetPrinterAttributes. Stripping away much of the existing code, we find the ExecuteQueryCommandAsync method on MainWindowsViewModel calls either a method to get attributes from one printer (PrinterAttributeQuery.GetPrinterAttributesAsync) or to obtain attributes from multiple printers (PrinterAttributeQuery.GetAllPrinterAttributesAsync). Both of these methods call the GetPrinterAttributesRequestAsync method of the PrinterAttributeQuery file, which itself calls the GetIppAttributesRequest method used in Chapters 5 and 6 library we created. Viewed as a call diagram, it might appear as shown below:

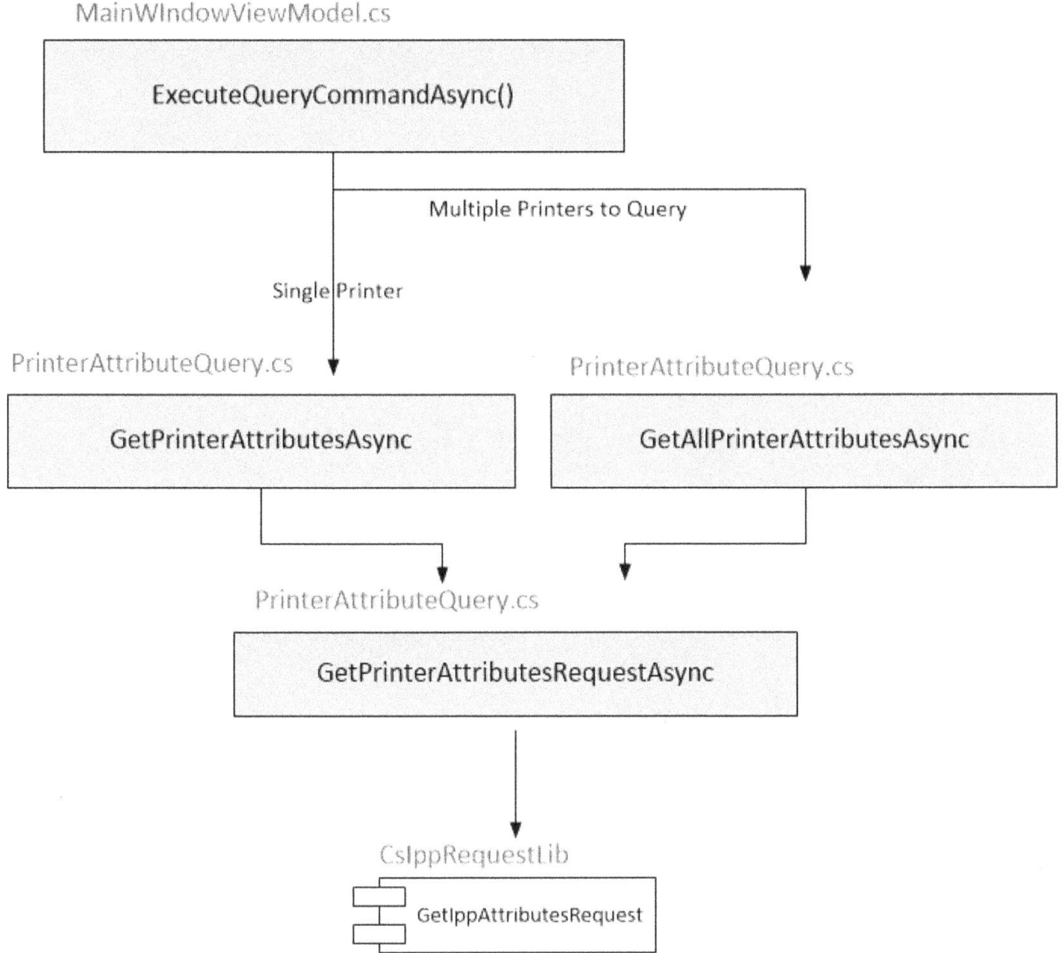

High-Level Call Diagram

The bulk of the program uses calls to the GetIppAttributesRequest library method to collect attributes from the printer and then search through the returned collection of attributes or a specific purpose, whether that be job attributes, marker attributes, or just general printer attributes and display the results to the user.

Printing a Test Page

The excellent iText extension was used to create a dynamic test page. The vendor (Apryse Software) describes this extension as a "library for PDF generation written entirely in C#." This extension made creating a custom pdf page a snap, and I would highly recommend it. The actual file is printed using the CsIppRequestLib's PrintJobRequest method. The code for this is in the PrinterAtributeQuery.cs file and is shown below.

Code to Print Test Page

```
public static async Task<int> PrintTestPageAsync(string printer, string
file, Dictionary<string, List<object>> jobAttributes)
 {
     int request = 1;
     try
     {
  PrintJobRequest pjr = new PrintJobRequest("1.1", printer, false, request,
  file, jobAttributes, true);
         CompletionStruct cs = await pjr.SendRequestAsync();
         if (cs.status < (int)Status.IPP_STATUS.IPP_STATUS_OK_EVENTS_
         COMPLETE)
         {
             return 0;
         }
         else
         {
             return -1;
         }
     }
     catch (Exception ex)
     {
         throw new Exception($"Error printing test page {ex.Message}");
     }
 }
```

Packaging and Installation

It is best to package this utility up in a setup file and install it as an MSI since that ensures the correct installation of all the supporting files. In addition, an MSI allows for easy subsequent removal (and reinstallation) necessary in a development or test environment. This utility relies on many support files and DLLs (located in the

(*\bin\x64\Release\net8.0-windows\ folder) in order to execute. To make changes to the MSI, you will need to download and install the MS Visual Studio Installer Project from Microsoft Marketplace. This is a VISX file that automatically installs the Setup Project into Visual Studio (in this case, 2022). An existing setup MSI project has been created and can be found in the Addendum Code folder under the name Setup. It will install the application and all the dependencies onto Windows 11 via an MSI setup file and create an icon in the start menu. If you make alterations to IppCheck, you must update the Setup project if you want those changes reflected in the MSI.

IppCheck in the Installed Apps Dialog

Addendum 2: Character Encoding

According to RFC 8011 (Section 5.14.18), all text strings in IPP are to be encoded (and thus decoded) in UTF-8. This has obvious significance to the way the character sequences are encoded (and decoded) in code. While the assumption is that most readers will know why UTF-8 is used, a bit of background detail on this subject matter will help those who do not. If we were just assuming all conversation would be in English, the standard ASCII table, where characters are represented in 0x7F characters, would certainly suffice. However, since this is not the case, a representation of all language characters needs to be provided, and 0x7F (127 decimal) characters is not enough to accomplish that.

UTF-8 provides a clever way to represent all the necessary characters required - using multiple bytes for character mapping (up to 4) based on the Most Significant Bits (MSB) of the first byte. As you can see from the table below, this allows the existing ASCII table to remain as it is (in the first 127 positions), provided the first bit is a 0.

UTF-8 Bytes Pattern

Number of Bytes	First Byte Pattern (in binary)	Range (Hex)	Unicode Range
1	0xxxxxxx	00–7F	U+0000 to U+007F
2	110xxxxx	C2–DF	U+0080 to U+07FF
3	1110xxxx	E0–EF	U+0800 to U+FFFF
4	11110xxx	F0–F4	U+10000 to U+10FFFF

How Conversion Works

For ASCII (0x00 - 0x7F), the byte value is the code point, making that conversion easy. However, for code points above 0x7F, a pattern of leading byte(s) and continuation byte(s) are required to find the Unicode code point.

J. Marion, *Adopting Internet Printing Protocol for Windows*, https://doi.org/10.1007/979-8-8688-2010-6

UTF-8 Multi-Byte Sequences

Bytes	First Byte Pattern	Continuation Byte(s)	Unicode Range
1	0xxxxxxx	—	U+0000–U+007F
2	110xxxxx	10xxxxxx	U+0080–U+07FF
3	1110xxxx	10xxxxxx 10xxxxxx	U+0800–U+FFFF
4	11110xxx	10xxxxxx 10xxxxxx 10xxxxxx	U+10000–U+10FFFF

An example decoding sequence for a 2-byte UTF-8 character might be in order. Suppose you have two bytes: 0xC3 and 0xA9. Thus, 0xC3 in binary is 11000011, and 0xA9 in binary is 10101001. To decode, remove the 110 prefix from the first byte (0xC3), leaving 00011. Remove the 10 prefix from the second byte (0xA9), leaving 101001. Concatenate the remaining bits:

```
00011 + 101001 = 00011101001
```

Convert 00011101001 to hexadecimal, which is 0xE9. This corresponds to Unicode code point U+00E9, which is the character é.

For .NET developers, there is no need to handle this level of complexity, as it is done for you in the System.Text.Encoding.UTF8 property. You might be asking how this works when Windows uses UTF-16 internally. However, when you decode a UTF-8 byte array using .NET Encoding.UTF8.GetString method, the resulting string is automatically stored as UTF-16. You will not need to perform any additional conversion for display or further processing in .NET.

Addendum 3: Encoding IPP Collection Job Attributes

Collection attributes exist to group or organize related information within a single attribute. For instance, you might want to group page or paper characteristics together rather than submit multiple individual attributes that detail essentially the same data. This makes it easier to replicate the same job attributes across multiple print jobs, so a consistent print output is achieved. While this does provide convenience to the user, it can represent a challenge for the developer. As a task, encoding collection print job attributes from a string representation such as

`media-col={media-size{x-dimension=21590}{y-dimension=27940},media-type=stationery}`

to a byte array conforming to RFC 8010 Section 3.1.6 layout is tedious since it requires careful handling of nested data structures. The biggest hurdle is ensuring your code exactly conforms to the Collection Attribute Encoding layout in the RFC. The human-readable format that displays a collection string with curly braces (as shown for media-col above) does not appear to be a specified standard; however, it is used in RFC8010 section A.7 (Create-Job Request with Collection Attributes). This human-readable format is also shown in the Wireshark IPP dissector when collection bytes are analyzed. So, for the purposes of discussion, we will use this format to specify a human-readable collection attribute.

As a side note, many of the older printer models support few collection attributes other than media-col. I expect this has primarily to do with the fact that Collection Attributes were not introduced until September 2002 in RFC 3382.

J. Marion, *Adopting Internet Printing Protocol for Windows*, https://doi.org/10.1007/979-8-8688-2010-6

Encoding a Collection Attribute

If you are interested in how to convert the human-readable collection attribute(s) to the required byte structure of RFC 8010, you can open the **Ipp** folder in the CsIppRequestLib project and look at the RequestHelper.cs file. Keep in mind that this code does not handle nested collections and is limited to single-level collections.

The object of the CreateCollectionByteArray function within the RequestHelper.cs file is to take the collection name string and collection description string provided as function arguments and return a properly formatted byte array that conforms to RFC 8010 Section 3.1.6 layout. To do this, the collection string is parsed from the input string representation (as provided in a job attributes file) to a collection of MemberAttribute objects – this is performed in the CollectionAttribute.cs file. Once this collection of MemberAttribute objects is created, it then becomes a matter of encoding the collection elements in proper order to a byte array. A truly elegant solution might be to accomplish this via recursion, but CreateCollectionByteArray is a rather blunt approach and thus achieves this iteratively. I would direct your attention to the EndCollectionByteArray and BeginCollectionByteArray byte arrays created within the first few lines of the function. These byte arrays have to precisely follow the RFC 8010 Section 3.1.6 layout, or the collection attribute will be rejected. The graphic below shows how RFC 8010 Section 3.1.6 stipulates the byte format that closes a collection.

1 Byte	End-value-tag (value is 0x37)
2 Bytes	End-name-length (value is 0x0000)
2 Bytes	End-value-length (value is 0x0000)

Closing a Collection

The EndCollectionByteArray constructs the array to match this:

```
byte[] EndCollectionByteArray = new byte[]{ byte)AttributeHelper.ValueTag.
EndCollection, 0x00, 0x00, 0x00, 0x00};
```

Member Attributes

RFC 8010 Section 3.1.7 also specifies how Member Attributes are to be handled. These Member Attributes can be nested in a collection or not. The important idea is to follow the Member Attribute Encoding schedule exactly as indicated. For instance, looking at Section 3.1.7 of RFC 8010, you can see how the member attributes are encoded.

Value-tag (value is 0x4a – MemberAttrName)	1 byte
Name-length (value is 0x0000)	2 bytes
Value-length (value is w)	2 bytes
Value (member- name)	w bytes
Member-value-tag	1 byte
Name-length (value is 0x0000)	2 bytes
Member-value-length (value is x)	2 bytes
Member-value	x bytes

RFC 8010 Section 3.1.7

By looking at Section 3.1.7 and then reading the code in the foreach loop, you can piece together how the byte array is constructed.

```
 var memberNameBytes = Encoding.UTF8.GetBytes(memberAttr.Name);
 CollByteArray.Add(new[] { (byte)AttributeHelper.ValueTag.
MemberAttrName });
 CollByteArray.Add(ToBigEndianBytes(0));
 CollByteArray.Add(ToBigEndianBytes((ushort)memberNameBytes.Length));
 CollByteArray.Add(memberNameBytes);
```

For instance, the Value-tag byte is encoded by the line:

```
CollByteArray.Add(new[] { (byte)AttributeHelper.ValueTag.MemberAttrName });
```

And the Name-length (specified as 2 bytes – 0x00, 0x00) is encoded by the next line:

```
CollByteArray.Add(ToBigEndianBytes(0));
```

The Value-length will be variable, and calculated by the next line:

```
CollByteArray.Add(ToBigEndianBytes((ushort)memberNameBytes.Length));
```

The actual value is captured by the next line of code:

```
CollByteArray.Add(memberNameBytes);
```

A Graphical Look at the Encoding Process

At this point, an illustration for the byte encoding might provide a better understanding of how RFC 8010 specifies this to work. At the top of each box is the task – numbered in order of execution. For subsequent lines in each box, the byte(s) encoded are shown on the left, and on the right is a comment on their textual representation. This illustration represents the encoding required for the human-readable collection:

media-col={media-size{x-dimension=21590}{y-dimension=27940},media-type=stationery}

```
1. Start Outer Collection (media-col)
34                                begCollection value-tag
00 09                             name-length = 9
6D 65 64 69 61 2D 63 6F 6C        "media-col"
00 00                             value-length = 0
```

```
2. Member name: media-size
4A                                memberAttrName value-tag
00 00                             name-length = 0 (must be 0
                                  in collections)
00 0A                             value-length = 10
6D 65 64 69 61 2D 73 69 7A 65     "media-size
```

```
3. Begin nested collection        (media-size)
34                                begCollection value-tag
00 00                             name-length = 0
00 00                             value-length = 0
```

```
4. Sub-member name: x-dimension
4A                                memberAttrName value-tag
00 00                             name-length = 0
00 0B                             value-length = 11
78 2D 64 69 6D 65 6E 73 69 6F 6E  "x-dimension"
```

```
5. Sub-member value: 21590
21                                integer value-tag
00 00                             name-length = 0
00 04                             value-length = 4
00 00 54 56                       integer (21590)
```

```
6. Sub-member name: y-dimension
4A                                memberAttrName value-tag
00 00                             name-length = 0
00 0B                             11 bytes
79 2D 64 69 6D 65 6E 73 69 6F 6E  "y-dimension"
```

7. Sub-member value: 27940

21	integer value-tag
00 00	name-length = 0
00 04	4 bytes
00 00 6D 24	integer (27940)

8. End nested collection (media-size)

37	endCollection value-tag
00 00	name-length = (0x0000)
00 00	value-length = (0x0000)

9. Member name: media-type

4A	memberAttrName value-tag
00 00	name-length = 0
00 0A	10 bytes
6D 65 64 69 61 2D 74 79 70 65	"media-type"

10. Member value: "stationery"

44	keyword value-tag
00 00	name-length = 0
00 0A	10 bytes
73 74 61 74 69 6F 6E 65 72 79	"stationery"

11. End outer collection (media-col)

37	endCollection value-tag
00 00	End-Name-Length (0x0000)
00 00	End-Value-Length (0x0000)

Note the collection name needs to be known in the GetJobAttributeByte function at the top of AttributeHelper.cs and should return a BegCollection (0x34) byte value. This allows the CreateJobAttributesByteArray function to route the job attribute to the CreateCollectionByteArray function, where it is ultimately encoded to a byte array that the list of bytes (lstbytes) can assemble.

If you find yourself in the unenviable position of having to write a collection attribute byte encoder, your effort will likely require Wireshark to view the resulting human-readable string that the dissector will try to create. Always follow the RFC layout, particularly ensuring that member attributes have a Name-length of 0x00, 0x00 and ensuring you close collections by setting the End-name-length and End-value-length to 0x00, 0x00 as well. I had quite a few rejected (malformed packets) Wireshark traces until I finally got this right.

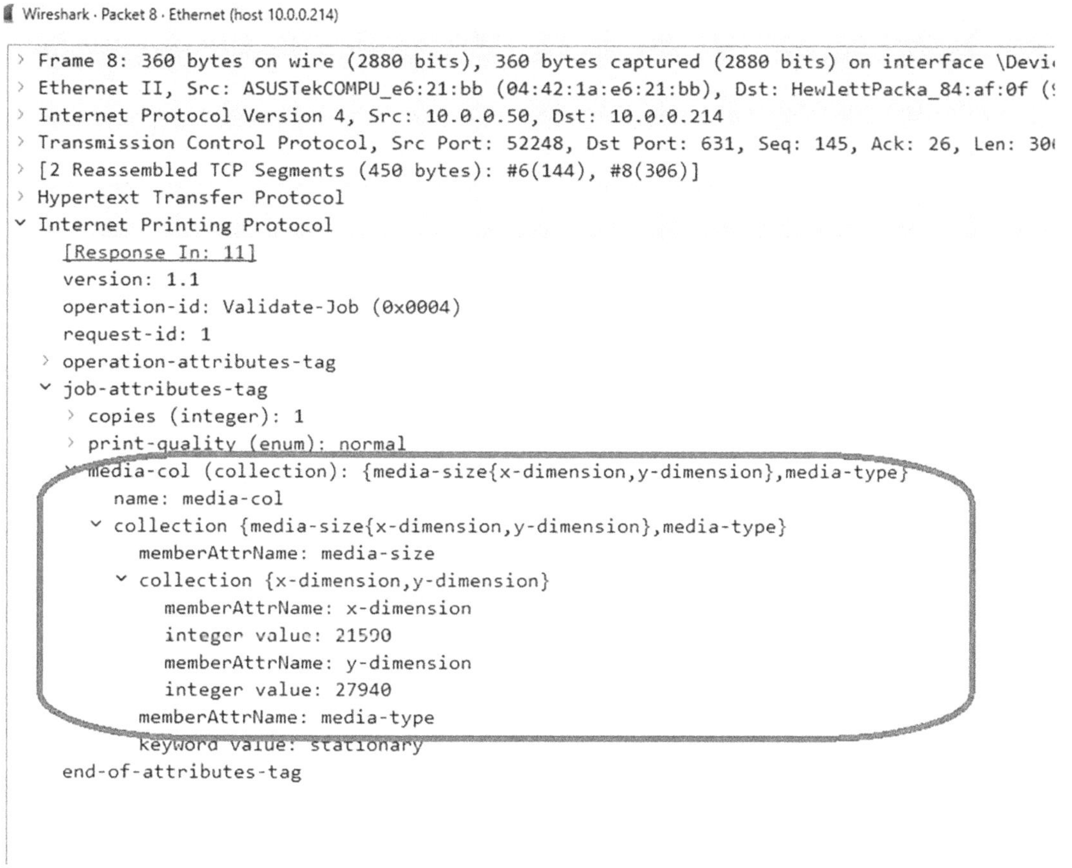

```
Wireshark · Packet 8 · Ethernet (host 10.0.0.214)

> Frame 8: 360 bytes on wire (2880 bits), 360 bytes captured (2880 bits) on interface \Devi
> Ethernet II, Src: ASUSTekCOMPU_e6:21:bb (04:42:1a:e6:21:bb), Dst: HewlettPacka_84:af:0f (
> Internet Protocol Version 4, Src: 10.0.0.50, Dst: 10.0.0.214
> Transmission Control Protocol, Src Port: 52248, Dst Port: 631, Seq: 145, Ack: 26, Len: 30
> [2 Reassembled TCP Segments (450 bytes): #6(144), #8(306)]
> Hypertext Transfer Protocol
v Internet Printing Protocol
    [Response In: 11]
    version: 1.1
    operation-id: Validate-Job (0x0004)
    request-id: 1
  > operation-attributes-tag
  v job-attributes-tag
    > copies (integer): 1
    > print-quality (enum): normal
    v media-col (collection): {media-size{x-dimension,y-dimension},media-type}
        name: media-col
      v collection {media-size{x-dimension,y-dimension},media-type}
          memberAttrName: media-size
        v collection {x-dimension,y-dimension}
            memberAttrName: x-dimension
            integer value: 21590
            memberAttrName: y-dimension
            integer value: 27940
          memberAttrName: media-type
          keyword value: stationary
    end-of-attributes-tag
```

Wireshark Trace of "media-col" Collection Attribute

Index

J. Marion, *Adopting Internet Printing Protocol for Windows*, https://doi.org/10.1007/979-8-8688-2010-6

D

E

J

K

L

M

N

O

R

X, Y, Z

GPSR Compliance
The European Union's (EU) General Product Safety Regulation (GPSR) is a set of rules that requires consumer products to be safe and our obligations to ensure this.

If you have any concerns about our products, you can contact us on

ProductSafety@springernature.com

In case Publisher is established outside the EU, the EU authorized representative is:

Springer Nature Customer Service Center GmbH
Europaplatz 3
69115 Heidelberg, Germany

www.ingramcontent.com/pod-product-compliance
Lightning Source LLC
LaVergne TN
LVHW081345060526
838201LV00050B/1714

* 9 7 9 8 8 6 8 8 2 0 0 9 0 *